Chevrolet Impala & Monte Carlo Automotive Repair Manual

by Mike Stubblefield and John H Haynes

Member of the Guild of Motoring Writers

Models covered:

All Chevrolet Impala models - 2006 through 2011
All Chevrolet Monte Carlo models - 2006 and 2007

(24047 - 4X7)

ABCDE
F

Haynes Publishing Group
Sparkford Nr Yeovil
Somerset BA22 7JJ England

Haynes North America, Inc
859 Lawrence Drive
Newbury Park
California 91320 USA
www.haynes.com

Acknowledgements

Technical writers who contributed to this project include Joe Hamilton, Tim Imhoff and John Wegmann. Wiring diagrams originated exclusively for Haynes North America, Inc. by Solution Builders.

© **Haynes North America, Inc. 2008, 2010, 2011**

With permission from J.H. Haynes & Co. Ltd.

A book in the Haynes Automotive Repair Manual Series

Printed in Malaysia

ISBN-13: 978-1-56392-967-0
ISBN-10: 1-56392-967-8

Library of Congress Control Number: 2011944101

While every attempt is made to ensure that the information in this man-ual is correct, no liability can be accepted by the authors or publishers for loss, damage or injury caused by any errors in, or omissions from, the information given.

Contents

Haynes author and photographer with a 2006 Chevrolet Impala SS

About this manual

Its purpose

The purpose of this manual is to help you get the best value from your vehicle. It can do so in several ways. It can help you decide what work must be done, even if you choose to have it done by a dealer service department or a repair shop; it provides information and procedures for routine maintenance and servicing; and it offers diagnostic and repair procedures to follow when trouble occurs.

We hope you use the manual to tackle the work yourself. For many simpler jobs, doing it yourself may be quicker than arranging an appointment to get the vehicle into a shop and making the trips to leave it and pick it up. More importantly, a lot of money can be saved by avoiding the expense the shop must pass on to you to cover its labor and overhead costs. An added benefit is the sense of satisfaction and accomplishment that you feel after doing the job yourself.

Using the manual

The manual is divided into Chapters. Each Chapter is divided into numbered Sections, which are headed in bold type between horizontal lines. Each Section consists of consecutively numbered paragraphs.

At the beginning of each numbered Section you will be referred to any illustrations which apply to the procedures in that Section. The reference numbers used in illustration captions pinpoint the pertinent Section and the Step within that Section. That is, illustration 3.2 means the illustration refers to Section 3 and Step (or paragraph) 2 within that Section.

Procedures, once described in the text, are not normally repeated. When it's necessary to refer to another Chapter, the reference will be given as Chapter and Section number. Cross references given without use of the word "Chapter" apply to Sections and/or paragraphs in the same Chapter. For example, "see Section 8" means in the same Chapter.

References to the left or right side of the vehicle assume you are sitting in the driver's seat, facing forward.

Even though we have prepared this manual with extreme care, neither the publisher nor the author can accept responsibility for any errors in, or omissions from, the information given.

NOTE

A **Note** provides information necessary to properly complete a procedure or information which will make the procedure easier to understand.

CAUTION

A **Caution** provides a special procedure or special steps which must be taken while completing the procedure where the Caution is found. Not heeding a Caution can result in damage to the assembly being worked on.

WARNING

A **Warning** provides a special procedure or special steps which must be taken while completing the procedure where the Warning is found. Not heeding a Warning can result in personal injury.

Introduction to the Chevrolet Impala and Monte Carlo

The models covered by this manual are available in four-door sedan (Impala) or two-door coupe (Monte Carlo) body styles. They feature transversely mounted 3.5L and 3.9L V6 engines, or a 5.3L V8 engine (SS models).

All models are equipped with an electronically controlled Sequential Fuel Injection (SFI) system.

The engine transmits power to the front wheels through a four-speed automatic transaxle via independent driveaxles.

The front suspension is a MacPherson strut design. The rear suspension utilizes strut/coil spring assemblies, trailing arms, and two tubular control arms per side. Stabilizer bars are used front and rear to reduce body roll during cornering.

The standard power-assisted rack-and-pinion steering unit is mounted behind the engine on the front suspension subframe.

All models are equipped with power assisted front and rear disc brakes, with an Anti-lock Brake System (ABS) available as an option.

Vehicle identification numbers

Modifications are a continuing and unpublicized process in vehicle manufacturing. Since spare parts manuals and lists are compiled on a numerical basis, the individual vehicle numbers are essential to correctly identify the component required.

Vehicle Identification Number (VIN)

This very important identification number is stamped on a plate attached to the dashboard inside the windshield on the driver's side of the vehicle (see illustration). It can also be found on the certification label located on the driver's side door post. The VIN also appears on the Vehicle Certificate of Title and Registration. It contains information such as where and when the vehicle was manufactured, the model year and the body style.

VIN engine and model year codes

Two particularly important pieces of information found in the VIN are the engine code and the model year code. Counting from the left, the engine code letter designation is the 8th digit and the model year code letter designation is the 10th digit.

On the models covered by this manual the engine codes are:

K .... 3.5L V6 (flex-fuel)
M .... 3.9L V6 (flex-fuel)
N .... 3.5L V6 (non flex-fuel)
1 .... 3.9L V6
3 .... 3.9L V6
8 .... 3.9L V6
R............. 3.9L V6
C............. 5.3L V8

On the models covered by this manual the model year codes are:

6 2006
7 2007
8 2008
9 2009
A............. 2010
B............. 2011

Certification label

The certification label is attached to the end of the driver's door (see illustration). The plate contains the name of the manufacturer, the month and year of production, the Gross Vehicle Weight Rating (GVWR), the Gross Axle Weight Rating (GAWR) and the certification statement.

Engine identification numbers

On 3.5L V6 engines, the engine serial number can be found stamped on the left side rear of the engine block, and on 3.9L V6 engines it can be found on the front and left side of the engine block. On the 5.3L V8 engine the number is stamped into a machined pad on the front side of the engine block, near the transaxle end of the engine.

The Vehicle Identification Number (VIN) is located on a plate on top of the dash (visible through the windshield)

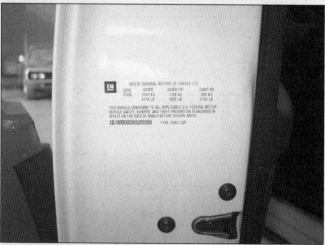

The vehicle certification label is located on the end of the driver's door

The engine identification number on the V8 engine is located on the front side of the block, near the transaxle

Recall information

Vehicle recalls are carried out by the manufacturer in the rare event of a possible safety-related defect. The vehicle's registered owner is contacted at the address on file at the Department of Motor Vehicles and given the details of the recall. Remedial work is carried out free of charge at a dealer service department.

If you are the new owner of a used vehicle which was subject to a recall and you want to be sure that the work has been carried out, it's best to contact a dealer service department and ask about your individual vehicle - you'll need to furnish them your Vehicle Identification Number (VIN).

The table below is based on information provided by the National Highway Traffic Safety Administration (NHTSA), the body which oversees vehicle recalls in the United States. The recall database is updated constantly. For the latest information on vehicle recalls, check the NHTSA website at www.nhtsa.gov, www.safercar.gov or call the NHTSA hotline at 1-888-327-4236.

Recall date	Recall campaign number	Model(s) affected	Concern
June 14, 2006	06V215000	2006 Impala	Certain vehicles equipped with a manual passenger seat adjuster fail to comply with the requirements of Federal Motor Vehicle Safety Standard no. 210, "seat belt assembly anchorages." The left floor mounting bracket may be mislocated. In a severe vehicle crash, the seat adjuster may separate from the mounting bracket, increasing the risk of occupant injury.
Oct 31, 2006	06V419000	2007 Impala	On certain vehicles, the fuel tank is missing the adhesive layer that bonds the barrier layer to the outer shell of the fuel tank. With this condition, fuel and/or fuel vapors could seep out between the layers, increasing the risk of a fire.
October 3, 2008	08V517000	2009 Impala	Some models have a passenger-side front airbag inflator that could fracture at an inflator tube during a deployment. During a passenger-side air bag deployment, pieces of the inflator tube could strike and injure vehicle occupants and the airbag cushion would not inflate fully, reducing the capability of the bag to protect the passenger.
October 13, 2010	10V480000	2009, 2010 Impala	Some models fail to comply with the requirements of Federal Motor Vehicle Safety Standard No. 210, "Seat belt assembly anchorages." The front safety belt webbing may not have been properly secured to the lap belt anchor pretensioner mounted to the side of the seat nearest the door. The safety belt may not restrain the occupant as intended during a crash, which could result in injury to the occupant.

Buying parts

Replacement parts are available from many sources, which generally fall into one of two categories - authorized dealer parts departments and independent retail auto parts stores. Our advice concerning these parts is as follows:

Retail auto parts stores: Good auto parts stores will stock frequently needed components which wear out relatively fast, such as clutch components, exhaust systems, brake parts, tune-up parts, etc. These stores often supply new or reconditioned parts on an exchange basis, which can save a considerable amount of money. Discount auto parts stores are often very good places to buy materials and parts needed for general vehicle maintenance such as oil, grease, filters, spark plugs, belts, touch-up paint, bulbs, etc. They also usually sell tools and general accessories, have convenient hours, charge lower prices and can often be found not far from home.

Authorized dealer parts department: This is the best source for parts which are unique to the vehicle and not generally available elsewhere (such as major engine parts, transmission parts, trim pieces, etc.).

Warranty information: If the vehicle is still covered under warranty, be sure that any replacement parts purchased - regardless of the source - do not invalidate the warranty!

To be sure of obtaining the correct parts, have engine and chassis numbers available and, if possible, take the old parts along for positive identification.

Maintenance techniques, tools and working facilities

Maintenance techniques

There are a number of techniques involved in maintenance and repair that will be referred to throughout this manual. Application of these techniques will enable the home mechanic to be more efficient, better organized and capable of performing the various tasks properly, which will ensure that the repair job is thorough and complete.

Fasteners

Fasteners are nuts, bolts, studs and screws used to hold two or more parts together. There are a few things to keep in mind when working with fasteners. Almost all of them use a locking device of some type, either a lockwasher, locknut, locking tab or thread adhesive. All threaded fasteners should be clean and straight, with undamaged threads and undamaged corners on the hex head where the wrench fits. Develop the habit of replacing all damaged nuts and bolts with new ones. Special locknuts with nylon or fiber inserts can only be used once. If they are removed, they lose their locking ability and must be replaced with new ones.

Rusted nuts and bolts should be treated with a penetrating fluid to ease removal and prevent breakage. Some mechanics use turpentine in a spout-type oil can, which works quite well. After applying the rust penetrant, let it work for a few minutes before trying to loosen the nut or bolt. Badly rusted fasteners may have to be chiseled or sawed off or removed with a special nut breaker, available at tool stores.

If a bolt or stud breaks off in an assembly, it can be drilled and removed with a special tool commonly available for this purpose. Most automotive machine shops can perform this task, as well as other repair procedures, such as the repair of threaded holes that have been stripped out.

Flat washers and lockwashers, when removed from an assembly, should always be replaced exactly as removed. Replace any damaged washers with new ones. Never use a lockwasher on any soft metal surface (such as aluminum), thin sheet metal or plastic.

Fastener sizes

For a number of reasons, automobile manufacturers are making wider and wider use of metric fasteners. Therefore, it is important to be able to tell the difference between standard (sometimes called U.S. or SAE) and metric hardware, since they cannot be interchanged.

All bolts, whether standard or metric, are sized according to diameter, thread pitch and length. For example, a standard 1/2 - 13 x 1 bolt is 1/2 inch in diameter, has 13 threads per inch and is 1 inch long. An M12 - 1.75 x 25 metric bolt is 12 mm in diameter, has a thread pitch of 1.75 mm (the distance between threads) and is 25 mm long. The two bolts are nearly identical, and easily confused, but they are not interchangeable.

In addition to the differences in diameter, thread pitch and length, metric and standard bolts can also be distinguished by examining the bolt heads. To begin with, the distance across the flats on a standard bolt head is measured in inches, while the same dimension on a metric bolt is sized in millimeters (the same is true for nuts). As a result, a standard wrench should not be used on a metric bolt and a metric wrench should not be used on a standard bolt. Also, most standard bolts have slashes radiating out from the center of the head to denote the grade or strength of the bolt, which is an indication of the amount of torque that can be applied to it. The greater the number of slashes, the greater the strength of the bolt. Grades 0 through 5 are commonly used on automobiles. Metric bolts have a property class (grade) number, rather than a slash, molded into their heads to indicate bolt strength. In this case, the higher the number, the stronger the bolt. Property class numbers 8.8, 9.8 and 10.9 are commonly used on automobiles.

Strength markings can also be used to distinguish standard hex nuts from metric hex nuts. Many standard nuts have dots stamped into one side, while metric nuts are marked with a number. The greater the number of

dots, or the higher the number, the greater the strength of the nut.

Metric studs are also marked on their ends according to property class (grade). Larger studs are numbered (the same as metric bolts), while smaller studs carry a geometric code to denote grade.

It should be noted that many fasteners, especially Grades 0 through 2, have no distinguishing marks on them. When such is the case, the only way to determine whether it is standard or metric is to measure the thread pitch or compare it to a known fastener of the same size.

Standard fasteners are often referred to as SAE, as opposed to metric. However, it should be noted that SAE technically refers to a non-metric fine thread fastener only. Coarse thread non-metric fasteners are referred to as USS sizes.

Since fasteners of the same size (both standard and metric) may have different

strength ratings, be sure to reinstall any bolts, studs or nuts removed from your vehicle in their original locations. Also, when replacing a fastener with a new one, make sure that the new one has a strength rating equal to or greater than the original.

Tightening sequences and procedures

Most threaded fasteners should be tightened to a specific torque value (torque is the twisting force applied to a threaded component such as a nut or bolt). Overtightening the fastener can weaken it and cause it to break, while undertightening can cause it to eventually come loose. Bolts, screws and studs, depending on the material they are made of and their thread diameters, have specific torque values, many of which are noted in the Specifications at the beginning of each Chapter. Be sure to follow the torque recommendations closely. For fasteners not assigned a

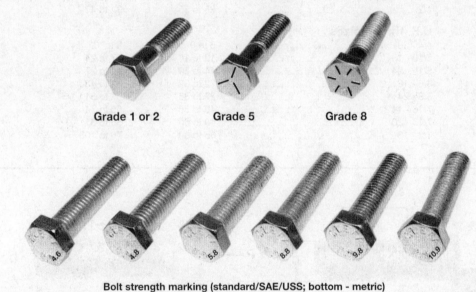

Grade 1 or 2   Grade 5   Grade 8

Bolt strength marking (standard/SAE/USS; bottom - metric)

Grade	Identification
Hex Nut Grade 5	3 Dots
Hex Nut Grade 8	6 Dots

Standard hex nut strength markings

Grade	Identification
Hex Nut Property Class 9	Arabic 9
Hex Nut Property Class 10	Arabic 10

Metric hex nut strength markings

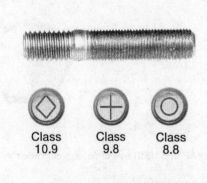

Class 10.9   Class 9.8   Class 8.8

Metric stud strength markings

specific torque, a general torque value chart is presented here as a guide. These torque values are for dry (unlubricated) fasteners threaded into steel or cast iron (not aluminum). As was previously mentioned, the size and grade of a fastener determine the amount of torque that can safely be applied to it. The figures listed here are approximate for Grade 2 and Grade 3 fasteners. Higher grades can tolerate higher torque values.

Fasteners laid out in a pattern, such as cylinder head bolts, oil pan bolts, differential cover bolts, etc., must be loosened or tightened in sequence to avoid warping the component. This sequence will normally be shown in the appropriate Chapter. If a specific pattern is not given, the following procedures can be used to prevent warping.

Initially, the bolts or nuts should be assembled finger-tight only. Next, they should be tightened one full turn each, in a criss-cross or diagonal pattern. After each one has been tightened one full turn, return to the first one and tighten them all one-half turn, following the same pattern. Finally, tighten each of them one-quarter turn at a time until each fastener has been tightened to the proper torque. To loosen and remove the fasteners, the procedure would be reversed.

Component disassembly

Component disassembly should be done with care and purpose to help ensure that

Metric thread sizes	Ft-lbs	Nm
M-6	6 to 9	9 to 12
M-8	14 to 21	19 to 28
M-10	28 to 40	38 to 54
M-12	50 to 71	68 to 96
M-14	80 to 140	109 to 154
Pipe thread sizes		
1/8	5 to 8	7 to 10
1/4	12 to 18	17 to 24
3/8	22 to 33	30 to 44
1/2	25 to 35	34 to 47
U.S. thread sizes		
1/4 - 20	6 to 9	9 to 12
5/16 - 18	12 to 18	17 to 24
5/16 - 24	14 to 20	19 to 27
3/8 - 16	22 to 32	30 to 43
3/8 - 24	27 to 38	37 to 51
7/16 - 14	40 to 55	55 to 74
7/16 - 20	40 to 60	55 to 81
1/2 - 13	55 to 80	75 to 108

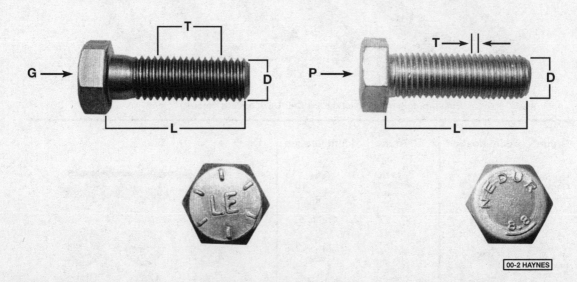

Standard (SAE and USS) bolt dimensions/grade marks   **Metric bolt dimensions/grade marks**

G	Grade marks (bolt strength)	P	Property class (bolt strength)
L	Length (in inches)	L	Length (in millimeters)
T	Thread pitch (number of threads per inch)	T	Thread pitch (distance between threads in millimeters)
D	Nominal diameter (in inches)	D	Diameter

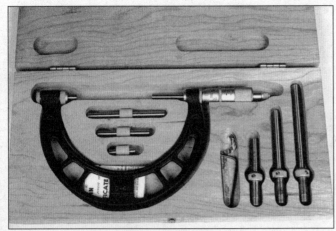

Micrometer set

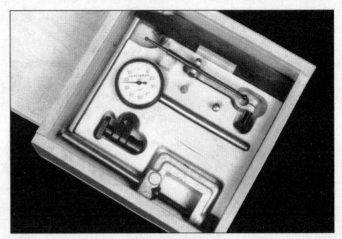

Dial indicator set

the parts go back together properly. Always keep track of the sequence in which parts are removed. Make note of special characteristics or marks on parts that can be installed more than one way, such as a grooved thrust washer on a shaft. It is a good idea to lay the disassembled parts out on a clean surface in the order that they were removed. It may also be helpful to make sketches or take instant photos of components before removal.

When removing fasteners from a component, keep track of their locations. Sometimes threading a bolt back in a part, or putting the washers and nut back on a stud, can prevent mix-ups later. If nuts and bolts cannot be returned to their original locations, they should be kept in a compartmented box or a series of small boxes. A cupcake or muffin tin is ideal for this purpose, since each cavity can hold the bolts and nuts from a particular area (i.e. oil pan bolts, valve cover bolts, engine mount bolts, etc.). A pan of this type is especially helpful when working on assemblies with very small parts, such as the carburetor, alternator, valve train or interior dash and trim pieces. The cavities can be marked with paint or tape to identify the contents.

Whenever wiring looms, harnesses or connectors are separated, it is a good idea to identify the two halves with numbered pieces of masking tape so they can be easily reconnected.

Gasket sealing surfaces

Throughout any vehicle, gaskets are used to seal the mating surfaces between two parts and keep lubricants, fluids, vacuum or pressure contained in an assembly.

Many times these gaskets are coated with a liquid or paste-type gasket sealing compound before assembly. Age, heat and pressure can sometimes cause the two parts to stick together so tightly that they are very difficult to separate. Often, the assembly can be loosened by striking it with a soft-face hammer near the mating surfaces. A regular hammer can be used if a block of wood is placed between the hammer and the part. Do

not hammer on cast parts or parts that could be easily damaged. With any particularly stubborn part, always recheck to make sure that every fastener has been removed.

Avoid using a screwdriver or bar to pry apart an assembly, as they can easily mar the gasket sealing surfaces of the parts, which must remain smooth. If prying is absolutely necessary, use an old broom handle, but keep in mind that extra clean up will be necessary if the wood splinters.

After the parts are separated, the old gasket must be carefully scraped off and the gasket surfaces cleaned. Stubborn gasket material can be soaked with rust penetrant or treated with a special chemical to soften it so it can be easily scraped off. **Caution:** *Never use gasket removal solutions or caustic chemicals on plastic or other composite components.* A scraper can be fashioned from a piece of copper tubing by flattening and sharpening one end. Copper is recommended because it is usually softer than the surfaces to be scraped, which reduces the chance of gouging the part. Some gaskets can be removed with a wire brush, but regardless of the method used, the mating surfaces must be left clean and smooth. If for some reason the gasket surface is gouged, then a gasket sealer thick enough to fill scratches will have to be used during reassembly of the components. For most applications, a non-drying (or semi-drying) gasket sealer should be used.

Hose removal tips

Warning: *If the vehicle is equipped with air conditioning, do not disconnect any of the A/C hoses without first having the system depressurized by a dealer service department or a service station.*

Hose removal precautions closely parallel gasket removal precautions. Avoid scratching or gouging the surface that the hose mates against or the connection may leak. This is especially true for radiator hoses. Because of various chemical reactions, the rubber in hoses can bond itself to the metal spigot that the hose fits over. To remove

a hose, first loosen the hose clamps that secure it to the spigot. Then, with slip-joint pliers, grab the hose at the clamp and rotate it around the spigot. Work it back and forth until it is completely free, then pull it off. Silicone or other lubricants will ease removal if they can be applied between the hose and the outside of the spigot. Apply the same lubricant to the inside of the hose and the outside of the spigot to simplify installation.

As a last resort (and if the hose is to be replaced with a new one anyway), the rubber can be slit with a knife and the hose peeled from the spigot. If this must be done, be careful that the metal connection is not damaged.

If a hose clamp is broken or damaged, do not reuse it. Wire-type clamps usually weaken with age, so it is a good idea to replace them with screw-type clamps whenever a hose is removed.

Tools

A selection of good tools is a basic requirement for anyone who plans to maintain and repair his or her own vehicle. For the owner who has few tools, the initial investment might seem high, but when compared to the spiraling costs of professional auto maintenance and repair, it is a wise one.

To help the owner decide which tools are needed to perform the tasks detailed in this manual, the following tool lists are offered: *Maintenance and minor repair, Repair/overhaul* and *Special.*

The newcomer to practical mechanics should start off with the *maintenance and minor repair* tool kit, which is adequate for the simpler jobs performed on a vehicle. Then, as confidence and experience grow, the owner can tackle more difficult tasks, buying additional tools as they are needed. Eventually the basic kit will be expanded into the *repair and overhaul* tool set. Over a period of time, the experienced do-it-yourselfer will assemble a tool set complete enough for most repair and overhaul procedures and will add tools from the special category when it is felt that the expense is justified by the frequency of use.

Dial caliper

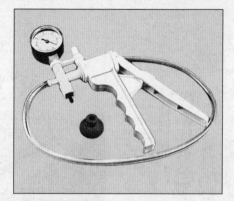

Hand-operated vacuum pump

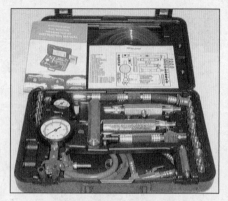

Fuel pressure gauge set

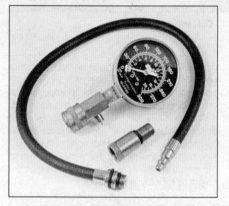

Compression gauge with spark plug
hole adapter

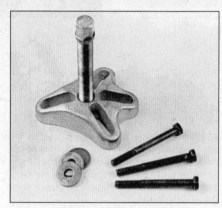

Damper/steering wheel puller

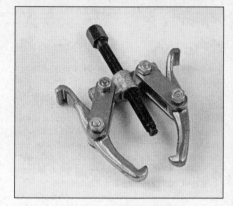

General purpose puller

Hydraulic lifter removal tool

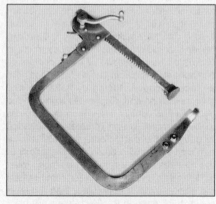

Valve spring compressor

Valve spring compressor

Ridge reamer

Piston ring groove cleaning tool

Ring removal/installation tool

Ring compressor

Cylinder hone

Brake hold-down spring tool

Torque angle gauge

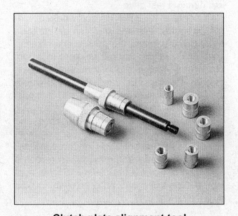

Clutch plate alignment tool

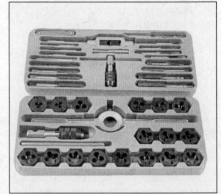

Tap and die set

Maintenance and minor repair tool kit

The tools in this list should be considered the minimum required for performance of routine maintenance, servicing and minor repair work. We recommend the purchase of combination wrenches (box-end and open-end combined in one wrench). While more expensive than open end wrenches, they offer the advantages of both types of wrench.

Combination wrench set (1/4-inch to 1 inch or 6 mm to 19 mm)
Adjustable wrench, 8 inch
Spark plug wrench with rubber insert
Spark plug gap adjusting tool
Feeler gauge set
Brake bleeder wrench
Standard screwdriver (5/16-inch x 6 inch)
Phillips screwdriver (No. 2 x 6 inch)
Combination pliers - 6 inch
Hacksaw and assortment of blades
Tire pressure gauge
Grease gun
Oil can
Fine emery cloth
Wire brush
Battery post and cable cleaning tool
Oil filter wrench
Funnel (medium size)
Safety goggles
Jackstands (2)
Drain pan

Note: *If basic tune-ups are going to be part of routine maintenance, it will be necessary to purchase a good quality stroboscopic timing light and combination tachometer/dwell meter. Although they are included in the list of special tools, it is mentioned here because they are absolutely necessary for tuning most vehicles properly.*

Repair and overhaul tool set

These tools are essential for anyone who plans to perform major repairs and are in addition to those in the maintenance and minor repair tool kit. Included is a comprehensive set of sockets which, though expensive, are invaluable because of their versatility, especially when various extensions and drives are available. We recommend the 1/2-inch drive over the 3/8-inch drive. Although the larger drive is bulky and more expensive, it has the capacity of accepting a very wide range of large sockets. Ideally, however, the mechanic should have a 3/8-inch drive set and a 1/2-inch drive set.

Socket set(s)
Reversible ratchet
Extension - 10 inch
Universal joint
Torque wrench (same size drive as sockets)
Ball peen hammer - 8 ounce
Soft-face hammer (plastic/rubber)
Standard screwdriver (1/4-inch x 6 inch)

Standard screwdriver (stubby - 5/16-inch)
Phillips screwdriver (No. 3 x 8 inch)
Phillips screwdriver (stubby - No. 2)
Pliers - vise grip
Pliers - lineman's
Pliers - needle nose
Pliers - snap-ring (internal and external)
Cold chisel - 1/2-inch
Scribe
Scraper (made from flattened copper tubing)
Centerpunch
Pin punches (1/16, 1/8, 3/16-inch)
Steel rule/straightedge - 12 inch
Allen wrench set (1/8 to 3/8-inch or 4 mm to 10 mm)
A selection of files
Wire brush (large)
Jackstands (second set)
Jack (scissor or hydraulic type)

Note: *Another tool which is often useful is an electric drill with a chuck capacity of 3/8-inch and a set of good quality drill bits.*

Special tools

The tools in this list include those which are not used regularly, are expensive to buy, or which need to be used in accordance with their manufacturer's instructions. Unless these tools will be used frequently, it is not very economical to purchase many of them. A consideration would be to split the cost and use between yourself and a friend or friends. In addition, most of these tools can be obtained from a tool rental shop on a temporary basis.

This list primarily contains only those tools and instruments widely available to the public, and not those special tools produced by the vehicle manufacturer for distribution to dealer service departments. Occasionally, references to the manufacturer's special tools are included in the text of this manual. Generally, an alternative method of doing the job without the special tool is offered. However, sometimes there is no alternative to their use. Where this is the case, and the tool cannot be purchased or borrowed, the work should be turned over to the dealer service department or an automotive repair shop.

Valve spring compressor
Piston ring groove cleaning tool
Piston ring compressor
Piston ring installation tool
Cylinder compression gauge
Cylinder ridge reamer
Cylinder surfacing hone
Cylinder bore gauge
Micrometers and/or dial calipers
Hydraulic lifter removal tool
Balljoint separator
Universal-type puller
Impact screwdriver
Dial indicator set
Stroboscopic timing light (inductive pick-up)
Hand operated vacuum/pressure pump
Tachometer/dwell meter
Universal electrical multimeter
Cable hoist
Brake spring removal and installation tools
Floor jack

Buying tools

For the do-it-yourselfer who is just starting to get involved in vehicle maintenance and repair, there are a number of options available when purchasing tools. If maintenance and minor repair is the extent of the work to be done, the purchase of individual tools is satisfactory. If, on the other hand, extensive work is planned, it would be a good idea to purchase a modest tool set from one of the large retail chain stores. A set can usually be bought at a substantial savings over the individual tool prices, and they often come with a tool box. As additional tools are needed, add-on sets, individual tools and a larger tool box can be purchased to expand the tool selection. Building a tool set gradually allows the cost of the tools to be spread over a longer period of time and gives the mechanic the freedom to choose only those tools that will actually be used.

Tool stores will often be the only source of some of the special tools that are needed,

but regardless of where tools are bought, try to avoid cheap ones, especially when buying screwdrivers and sockets, because they won't last very long. The expense involved in replacing cheap tools will eventually be greater than the initial cost of quality tools.

Care and maintenance of tools

Good tools are expensive, so it makes sense to treat them with respect. Keep them clean and in usable condition and store them properly when not in use. Always wipe off any dirt, grease or metal chips before putting them away. Never leave tools lying around in the work area. Upon completion of a job, always check closely under the hood for tools that may have been left there so they won't get lost during a test drive.

Some tools, such as screwdrivers, pliers, wrenches and sockets, can be hung on a panel mounted on the garage or workshop wall, while others should be kept in a tool box or tray. Measuring instruments, gauges, meters, etc. must be carefully stored where they cannot be damaged by weather or impact from other tools.

When tools are used with care and stored properly, they will last a very long time. Even with the best of care, though, tools will wear out if used frequently. When a tool is damaged or worn out, replace it. Subsequent jobs will be safer and more enjoyable if you do.

How to repair damaged threads

Sometimes, the internal threads of a nut or bolt hole can become stripped, usually from overtightening. Stripping threads is an all-too-common occurrence, especially when working with aluminum parts, because aluminum is so soft that it easily strips out.

Usually, external or internal threads are only partially stripped. After they've been cleaned up with a tap or die, they'll still work. Sometimes, however, threads are badly damaged. When this happens, you've got three choices:

1) *Drill and tap the hole to the next suitable oversize and install a larger diameter bolt, screw or stud.*

2) *Drill and tap the hole to accept a threaded plug, then drill and tap the plug to the original screw size. You can also buy a plug already threaded to the original size. Then you simply drill a hole to the specified size, then run the threaded plug into the hole with a bolt and jam nut. Once the plug is fully seated, remove the jam nut and bolt.*

3) *The third method uses a patented thread repair kit like Heli-Coil or Slimsert. These*

easy-to-use kits are designed to repair damaged threads in straight-through holes and blind holes. Both are available as kits which can handle a variety of sizes and thread patterns. Drill the hole, then tap it with the special included tap. Install the Heli-Coil and the hole is back to its original diameter and thread pitch.

Regardless of which method you use, be sure to proceed calmly and carefully. A little impatience or carelessness during one of these relatively simple procedures can ruin your whole day's work and cost you a bundle if you wreck an expensive part.

Working facilities

Not to be overlooked when discussing tools is the workshop. If anything more than routine maintenance is to be carried out, some sort of suitable work area is essential.

It is understood, and appreciated, that many home mechanics do not have a good workshop or garage available, and end up removing an engine or doing major repairs outside. It is recommended, however, that the overhaul or repair be completed under the cover of a roof.

A clean, flat workbench or table of comfortable working height is an absolute necessity. The workbench should be equipped with a vise that has a jaw opening of at least four inches.

As mentioned previously, some clean, dry storage space is also required for tools, as well as the lubricants, fluids, cleaning solvents, etc. which soon become necessary.

Sometimes waste oil and fluids, drained from the engine or cooling system during normal maintenance or repairs, present a disposal problem. To avoid pouring them on the ground or into a sewage system, pour the used fluids into large containers, seal them with caps and take them to an authorized disposal site or recycling center. Plastic jugs, such as old antifreeze containers, are ideal for this purpose.

Always keep a supply of old newspapers and clean rags available. Old towels are excellent for mopping up spills. Many mechanics use rolls of paper towels for most work because they are readily available and disposable. To help keep the area under the vehicle clean, a large cardboard box can be cut open and flattened to protect the garage or shop floor.

Whenever working over a painted surface, such as when leaning over a fender to service something under the hood, always cover it with an old blanket or bedspread to protect the finish. Vinyl covered pads, made especially for this purpose, are available at auto parts stores.

Jacking and towing

Jacking

The jack supplied with the vehicle should only be used for raising the vehicle for changing a tire or placing jackstands under the frame. **Warning:** *Never crawl under the vehicle or start the engine when the jack is being used as the only means of support.*

All models are supplied with a scissors-type jack. When jacking the vehicle, it should be engaged with the notch in the rocker panel flange **(see illustration)**.

The vehicle should be on level ground with the wheels blocked and the transmission in Park. Pry off the hub cap (if equipped) using the tapered end of the lug wrench. Loosen the lug nuts one-half turn and leave them in place until the wheel is raised off the ground.

Place the jack under the side of the vehicle in the indicated position. Use the supplied wrench to turn the jackscrew clockwise until the wheel is raised off the ground. Remove the lug nuts, pull off the wheel and install the spare.

With the beveled side in, install the lug nuts and tighten them until snug. Lower the vehicle by turning the jackscrew counterclockwise. Remove the jack and tighten the nuts in a diagonal pattern to the torque listed in the Chapter 1 Specifications. If a torque wrench is not available, have the torque checked by a service station as soon as possible. Install the hubcap by placing it in position and using the heel of your hand or a rubber mallet to seat it.

Towing

The vehicle must be towed with the front (drive) wheels off the ground or, preferably, on a flat bed car carrier. If the front wheels can't be raised or a carrier isn't available, place them on a dolly.

Traction control

On models equipped with Traction Control System, push in the traction control (TC) switch anytime the vehicle is on a "rolling road" tester such as a speedometer test machine or chassis dynamometer. The TRAC OFF indicator light should illuminate when the system is turned off.

The jack fits over the rocker panel flange (there are two jacking points on each side of the vehicle)

Booster battery (jump) starting

Observe the following precautions when using a booster battery to start a vehicle:

a) Before connecting the booster battery, make sure the ignition switch is in the Off position.
b) Turn off the lights, heater and other electrical loads.
c) Your eyes should be shielded. Safety goggles are a good idea.
d) Make sure the booster battery is the same voltage as the dead one in the vehicle.
e) The two vehicles MUST NOT TOUCH each other.
f) Make sure the transaxle is in Park.
g) If the booster battery is not a maintenance-free type, remove the vent caps and lay a cloth over the vent holes.

Connect the red jumper cable to the positive (+) terminals of each battery. **Note:** On these models there is a remote positive terminal under the fuse box cover. It's easier to attach the jumper cable to this terminal than the positive terminal at the battery.

Connect one end of the black cable to the negative (-) terminal of the booster battery. The other end of this cable should be connected to a good ground on the engine block **(see illustration)**. Make sure the cable will not come into contact with the fan, drivebelts or other moving parts of the engine.

Start the engine using the booster battery, then, with the engine running at idle speed, disconnect the jumper cables in the reverse order of connection.

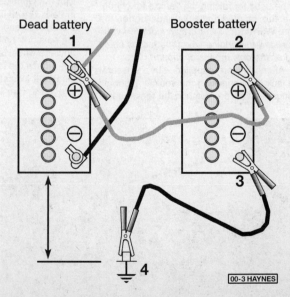

Make the booster battery cable connections in the numerical order shown (note that the negative cable of the booster battery is NOT attached to the negative terminal of the dead battery)

Automotive chemicals and lubricants

A number of automotive chemicals and lubricants are available for use during vehicle maintenance and repair. They include a wide variety of products ranging from cleaning solvents and degreasers to lubricants and protective sprays for rubber, plastic and vinyl.

Cleaners

Carburetor cleaner and choke cleaner is a strong solvent for gum, varnish and carbon. Most carburetor cleaners leave a dry-type lubricant film which will not harden or gum up. Because of this film it is not recommended for use on electrical components.

Brake system cleaner is used to remove brake dust, grease and brake fluid from the brake system, where clean surfaces are absolutely necessary. It leaves no residue and often eliminates brake squeal caused by contaminants.

Electrical cleaner removes oxidation, corrosion and carbon deposits from electrical contacts, restoring full current flow. It can also be used to clean spark plugs, carburetor jets, voltage regulators and other parts where an oil-free surface is desired.

Demoisturants remove water and moisture from electrical components such as alternators, voltage regulators, electrical connectors and fuse blocks. They are non-conductive and non-corrosive.

Degreasers are heavy-duty solvents used to remove grease from the outside of the engine and from chassis components. They can be sprayed or brushed on and, depending on the type, are rinsed off either with water or solvent.

Lubricants

Motor oil is the lubricant formulated for use in engines. It normally contains a wide variety of additives to prevent corrosion and reduce foaming and wear. Motor oil comes in various weights (viscosity ratings) from 0 to 50. The recommended weight of the oil depends on the season, temperature and the demands on the engine. Light oil is used in cold climates and under light load conditions. Heavy oil is used in hot climates and where high loads are encountered. Multi-viscosity oils are designed to have characteristics of both light and heavy oils and are available in a number of weights from 0W-20 to 20W-50.

Gear oil is designed to be used in differentials, manual transmissions and other areas where high-temperature lubrication is required.

Chassis and wheel bearing grease is a heavy grease used where increased loads and friction are encountered, such as for wheel bearings, balljoints, tie-rod ends and universal joints.

High-temperature wheel bearing grease is designed to withstand the extreme temper-atures encountered by wheel bearings in disc brake equipped vehicles. It usually contains molybdenum disulfide (moly), which is a dry-type lubricant.

White grease is a heavy grease for metal-to-metal applications where water is a problem. White grease stays soft under both low and high temperatures (usually from -100 to +190-degrees F), and will not wash off or dilute in the presence of water.

Assembly lube is a special extreme pressure lubricant, usually containing moly, used to lubricate high-load parts (such as main and rod bearings and cam lobes) for initial start-up of a new engine. The assembly lube lubricates the parts without being squeezed out or washed away until the engine oiling system begins to function.

Silicone lubricants are used to protect rubber, plastic, vinyl and nylon parts.

Graphite lubricants are used where oils cannot be used due to contamination problems, such as in locks. The dry graphite will lubricate metal parts while remaining uncontaminated by dirt, water, oil or acids. It is electrically conductive and will not foul electrical contacts in locks such as the ignition switch.

Moly penetrants loosen and lubricate frozen, rusted and corroded fasteners and prevent future rusting or freezing.

Heat-sink grease is a special electrically non-conductive grease that is used for mounting electronic ignition modules where it is essential that heat is transferred away from the module.

Sealants

RTV sealant is one of the most widely used gasket compounds. Made from silicone, RTV is air curing, it seals, bonds, waterproofs, fills surface irregularities, remains flexible, doesn't shrink, is relatively easy to remove, and is used as a supplementary sealer with almost all low and medium temperature gaskets.

Anaerobic sealant is much like RTV in that it can be used either to seal gaskets or to form gaskets by itself. It remains flexible, is solvent resistant and fills surface imperfections. The difference between an anaerobic sealant and an RTV-type sealant is in the curing. RTV cures when exposed to air, while an anaerobic sealant cures only in the absence of air. This means that an anaerobic sealant cures only after the assembly of parts, sealing them together.

Thread and pipe sealant is used for sealing hydraulic and pneumatic fittings and vacuum lines. It is usually made from a Teflon compound, and comes in a spray, a paint-on liquid and as a wrap-around tape.

Chemicals

Anti-seize compound prevents seiz-ing, galling, cold welding, rust and corrosion in fasteners. High-temperature ant-seize, usually made with copper and graphite lubricants, is used for exhaust system and exhaust manifold bolts.

Anaerobic locking compounds are used to keep fasteners from vibrating or working loose and cure only after installation, in the absence of air. Medium strength locking compound is used for small nuts, bolts and screws that may be removed later. High-strength locking compound is for large nuts, bolts and studs which aren't removed on a regular basis.

Oil additives range from viscosity index improvers to chemical treatments that claim to reduce internal engine friction. It should be noted that most oil manufacturers caution against using additives with their oils.

Gas additives perform several functions, depending on their chemical makeup. They usually contain solvents that help dissolve gum and varnish that build up on carburetor, fuel injection and intake parts. They also serve to break down carbon deposits that form on the inside surfaces of the combustion chambers. Some additives contain upper cylinder lubricants for valves and piston rings, and others contain chemicals to remove condensation from the gas tank.

Miscellaneous

Brake fluid is specially formulated hydraulic fluid that can withstand the heat and pressure encountered in brake systems. Care must be taken so this fluid does not come in contact with painted surfaces or plastics. An opened container should always be resealed to prevent contamination by water or dirt.

Weatherstrip adhesive is used to bond weatherstripping around doors, windows and trunk lids. It is sometimes used to attach trim pieces.

Undercoating is a petroleum-based, tar-like substance that is designed to protect metal surfaces on the underside of the vehicle from corrosion. It also acts as a sound-deadening agent by insulating the bottom of the vehicle.

Waxes and polishes are used to help protect painted and plated surfaces from the weather. Different types of paint may require the use of different types of wax and polish. Some polishes utilize a chemical or abrasive cleaner to help remove the top layer of oxidized (dull) paint on older vehicles. In recent years many non-wax polishes that contain a wide variety of chemicals such as polymers and silicones have been introduced. These non-wax polishes are usually easier to apply and last longer than conventional waxes and polishes.

Conversion factors

Length (distance)

Inches (in)	X	25.4	= Millimeters (mm)	X 0.0394	= Inches (in)
Feet (ft)	X	0.305	= Meters (m)	X 3.281	= Feet (ft)
Miles	X	1.609	= Kilometers (km)	X 0.621	= Miles

Volume (capacity)

Cubic inches (cu in; in³)	X	16.387	= Cubic centimeters (cc; cm³)	X 0.061	= Cubic inches (cu in; in³)
Imperial pints (Imp pt)	X	0.568	= Liters (l)	X 1.76	= Imperial pints (Imp pt)
Imperial quarts (Imp qt)	X	1.137	= Liters (l)	X 0.88	= Imperial quarts (Imp qt)
Imperial quarts (Imp qt)	X	1.201	= US quarts (US qt)	X 0.833	= Imperial quarts (Imp qt)
US quarts (US qt)	X	0.946	= Liters (l)	X 1.057	= US quarts (US qt)
Imperial gallons (Imp gal)	X	4.546	= Liters (l)	X 0.22	= Imperial gallons (Imp gal)
Imperial gallons (Imp gal)	X	1.201	= US gallons (US gal)	X 0.833	= Imperial gallons (Imp gal)
US gallons (US gal)	X	3.785	= Liters (l)	X 0.264	= US gallons (US gal)

Mass (weight)

Ounces (oz)	X	28.35	= Grams (g)	X 0.035	= Ounces (oz)
Pounds (lb)	X	0.454	= Kilograms (kg)	X 2.205	= Pounds (lb)

Force

Ounces-force (ozf; oz)	X	0.278	= Newtons (N)	X 3.6	= Ounces-force (ozf; oz)
Pounds-force (lbf; lb)	X	4.448	= Newtons (N)	X 0.225	= Pounds-force (lbf; lb)
Newtons (N)	X	0.1	= Kilograms-force (kgf; kg)	X 9.81	= Newtons (N)

Pressure

Pounds-force per square inch (psi; lbf/in²; lb/in²)	X	0.070	= Kilograms-force per square centimeter (kgf/cm²; kg/cm²)	X 14.223	= Pounds-force per square inch (psi; lbf/in²; lb/in²)
Pounds-force per square inch (psi; lbf/in²; lb/in²)	X	0.068	= Atmospheres (atm)	X 14.696	= Pounds-force per square inch (psi; lbf/in²; lb/in²)
Pounds-force per square inch (psi; lbf/in²; lb/in²)	X	0.069	= Bars	X 14.5	= Pounds-force per square inch (psi; lbf/in²; lb/in²)
Pounds-force per square inch (psi; lbf/in²; lb/in²)	X	6.895	= Kilopascals (kPa)	X 0.145	= Pounds-force per square inch (psi; lbf/in²; lb/in²)
Kilopascals (kPa)	X	0.01	= Kilograms-force per square centimeter (kgf/cm²; kg/cm²)	X 98.1	= Kilopascals (kPa)

Torque (moment of force)

Pounds-force inches (lbf in; lb in)	X	1.152	= Kilograms-force centimeter (kgf cm; kg cm)	X 0.868	= Pounds-force inches (lbf in; lb in)
Pounds-force inches (lbf in; lb in)	X	0.113	= Newton meters (Nm)	X 8.85	= Pounds-force inches (lbf in; lb in)
Pounds-force inches (lbf in; lb in)	X	0.083	= Pounds-force feet (lbf ft; lb ft)	X 12	= Pounds-force inches (lbf in; lb in)
Pounds-force feet (lbf ft; lb ft)	X	0.138	= Kilograms-force meters (kgf m; kg m)	X 7.233	= Pounds-force feet (lbf ft; lb ft)
Pounds-force feet (lbf ft; lb ft)	X	1.356	= Newton meters (Nm)	X 0.738	= Pounds-force feet (lbf ft; lb ft)
Newton meters (Nm)	X	0.102	= Kilograms-force meters (kgf m; kg m)	X 9.804	= Newton meters (Nm)

Vacuum

Inches mercury (in. Hg)	X	3.377	= Kilopascals (kPa)	X 0.2961	= Inches mercury
Inches mercury (in. Hg)	X	25.4	= Millimeters mercury (mm Hg)	X 0.0394	= Inches mercury

Power

Horsepower (hp)	X	745.7	= Watts (W)	X 0.0013	= Horsepower (hp)

Velocity (speed)

Miles per hour (miles/hr; mph)	X	1.609	= Kilometers per hour (km/hr; kph)	X 0.621	= Miles per hour (miles/hr; mph)

Fuel consumption*

Miles per gallon, Imperial (mpg)	X	0.354	= Kilometers per liter (km/l)	X 2.825	= Miles per gallon, Imperial (mpg)
Miles per gallon, US (mpg)	X	0.425	= Kilometers per liter (km/l)	X 2.352	= Miles per gallon, US (mpg)

Temperature

Degrees Fahrenheit = ($°C \times 1.8$) + 32

Degrees Celsius (Degrees Centigrade; °C) = ($°F - 32$) x 0.56

*It is common practice to convert from miles per gallon (mpg) to liters/100 kilometers (l/100km), where mpg (Imperial) x l/100 km = 282 and mpg (US) x l/100 km = 235

DECIMALS to MILLIMETERS

Decimal	mm	Decimal	mm
0.001	0.0254	0.500	12.7000
0.002	0.0508	0.510	12.9540
0.003	0.0762	0.520	13.2080
0.004	0.1016	0.530	13.4620
0.005	0.1270	0.540	13.7160
0.006	0.1524	0.550	13.9700
0.007	0.1778	0.560	14.2240
0.008	0.2032	0.570	14.4780
0.009	0.2286	0.580	14.7320
		0.590	14.9860
0.010	0.2540		
0.020	0.5080		
0.030	0.7620		
0.040	1.0160	0.600	15.2400
0.050	1.2700	0.610	15.4940
0.060	1.5240	0.620	15.7480
0.070	1.7780	0.630	16.0020
0.080	2.0320	0.640	16.2560
0.090	2.2860	0.650	16.5100
		0.660	16.7640
0.100	2.5400	0.670	17.0180
0.110	2.7940	0.680	17.2720
0.120	3.0480	0.690	17.5260
0.130	3.3020		
0.140	3.5560		
0.150	3.8100		
0.160	4.0640	0.700	17.7800
0.170	4.3180	0.710	18.0340
0.180	4.5720	0.720	18.2880
0.190	4.8260	0.730	18.5420
		0.740	18.7960
0.200	5.0800	0.750	19.0500
0.210	5.3340	0.760	19.3040
0.220	5.5880	0.770	19.5580
0.230	5.8420	0.780	19.8120
0.240	6.0960	0.790	20.0660
0.250	6.3500		
0.260	6.6040		
0.270	6.8580	0.800	20.3200
0.280	7.1120	0.810	20.5740
0.290	7.3660	0.820	21.8280
		0.830	21.0820
0.300	7.6200	0.840	21.3360
0.310	7.8740	0.850	21.5900
0.320	8.1280	0.860	21.8440
0.330	8.3820	0.870	22.0980
0.340	8.6360	0.880	22.3520
0.350	8.8900	0.890	22.6060
0.360	9.1440		
0.370	9.3980		
0.380	9.6520		
0.390	9.9060	0.900	22.8600
0.400	10.1600	0.910	23.1140
0.410	10.4140	0.920	23.3680
0.420	10.6680	0.930	23.6220
0.430	10.9220	0.940	23.8760
0.440	11.1760	0.950	24.1300
0.450	11.4300	0.960	24.3840
0.460	11.6840	0.970	24.6380
0.470	11.9380	0.980	24.8920
0.480	12.1920	0.990	25.1460
0.490	12.4460	1.000	25.4000

FRACTIONS to DECIMALS to MILLIMETERS

Fraction	Decimal	mm	Fraction	Decimal	mm
1/64	0.0156	0.3969	33/64	0.5156	13.0969
1/32	0.0312	0.7938	17/32	0.5312	13.4938
3/64	0.0469	1.1906	35/64	0.5469	13.8906
1/16	0.0625	1.5875	9/16	0.5625	14.2875
5/64	0.0781	1.9844	37/64	0.5781	14.6844
3/32	0.0938	2.3812	19/32	0.5938	15.0812
7/64	0.1094	2.7781	39/64	0.6094	15.4781
1/8	0.1250	3.1750	5/8	0.6250	15.8750
9/64	0.1406	3.5719	41/64	0.6406	16.2719
5/32	0.1562	3.9688	21/32	0.6562	16.6688
11/64	0.1719	4.3656	43/64	0.6719	17.0656
3/16	0.1875	4.7625	11/16	0.6875	17.4625
13/64	0.2031	5.1594	45/64	0.7031	17.8594
7/32	0.2188	5.5562	23/32	0.7188	18.2562
15/64	0.2344	5.9531	47/64	0.7344	18.6531
1/4	0.2500	6.3500	3/4	0.7500	19.0500
17/64	0.2656	6.7469	49/64	0.7656	19.4469
9/32	0.2812	7.1438	25/32	0.7812	19.8438
19/64	0.2969	7.5406	51/64	0.7969	20.2406
5/16	0.3125	7.9375	13/16	0.8125	20.6375
21/64	0.3281	8.3344	53/64	0.8281	21.0344
11/32	0.3438	8.7312	27/32	0.8438	21.4312
23/64	0.3594	9.1281	55/64	0.8594	21.8281
3/8	0.3750	9.5250	7/8	0.8750	22.2250
25/64	0.3906	9.9219	57/64	0.8906	22.6219
13/32	0.4062	10.3188	29/32	0.9062	23.0188
27/64	0.4219	10.7156	59/64	0.9219	23.4156
7/16	0.4375	11.1125	15/16	0.9375	23.8125
29/64	0.4531	11.5094	61/64	0.9531	24.2094
15/32	0.4688	11.9062	31/32	0.9688	24.6062
31/64	0.4844	12.3031	63/64	0.9844	25.0031
1/2	0.5000	12.7000	1	1.0000	25.4000

Safety first!

Regardless of how enthusiastic you may be about getting on with the job at hand, take the time to ensure that your safety is not jeopardized. A moment's lack of attention can result in an accident, as can failure to observe certain simple safety precautions. The possibility of an accident will always exist, and the following points should not be considered a comprehensive list of all dangers. Rather, they are intended to make you aware of the risks and to encourage a safety conscious approach to all work you carry out on your vehicle.

Essential DOs and DON'Ts

DON'T rely on a jack when working under the vehicle. Always use approved jackstands to support the weight of the vehicle and place them under the recommended lift or support points.

DON'T attempt to loosen extremely tight fasteners (i.e. wheel lug nuts) while the vehicle is on a jack - it may fall.

DON'T start the engine without first making sure that the transmission is in Neutral (or Park where applicable) and the parking brake is set.

DON'T remove the radiator cap from a hot cooling system - let it cool or cover it with a cloth and release the pressure gradually.

DON'T attempt to drain the engine oil until you are sure it has cooled to the point that it will not burn you.

DON'T touch any part of the engine or exhaust system until it has cooled sufficiently to avoid burns.

DON'T siphon toxic liquids such as gasoline, antifreeze and brake fluid by mouth, or allow them to remain on your skin.

DON'T inhale brake lining dust - it is potentially hazardous (see *Asbestos* below).

DON'T allow spilled oil or grease to remain on the floor - wipe it up before someone slips on it.

DON'T use loose fitting wrenches or other tools which may slip and cause injury.

DON'T push on wrenches when loosening or tightening nuts or bolts. Always try to pull the wrench toward you. If the situation calls for pushing the wrench away, push with an open hand to avoid scraped knuckles if the wrench should slip.

DON'T attempt to lift a heavy component alone - get someone to help you.

DON'T *rush or take unsafe shortcuts to finish a job.*

DON'T allow children or animals in or around the vehicle while you are working on it.

DO wear eye protection when using power tools such as a drill, sander, bench grinder, etc. and when working under a vehicle.

DO keep loose clothing and long hair well out of the way of moving parts.

DO make sure that any hoist used has a safe working load rating adequate for the job.

DO get someone to check on you periodically when working alone on a vehicle.

DO carry out work in a logical sequence and make sure that everything is correctly assembled and tightened.

DO keep chemicals and fluids tightly capped and out of the reach of children and pets.

DO remember that your vehicle's safety affects that of yourself and others. If in doubt on any point, get professional advice.

Steering, suspension and brakes

These systems are essential to driving safety, so make sure you have a qualified shop or individual check your work. Also, compressed suspension springs can cause injury if released suddenly - be sure to use a spring compressor.

Airbags

Airbags are explosive devices that can **CAUSE** injury if they deploy while you're working on the vehicle. Follow the manufacturer's instructions to disable the airbag whenever you're working in the vicinity of airbag components.

Asbestos

Certain friction, insulating, sealing, and other products - such as brake linings, brake bands, clutch linings, torque converters, gaskets, etc. - may contain asbestos or other hazardous friction material. Extreme care must be taken to avoid inhalation of dust from such products, since it is hazardous to health. If in doubt, assume that they do contain asbestos.

Fire

Remember at all times that gasoline is highly flammable. Never smoke or have any kind of open flame around when working on a vehicle. But the risk does not end there. A spark caused by an electrical short circuit, by two metal surfaces contacting each other, or even by static electricity built up in your body under certain conditions, can ignite gasoline vapors, which in a confined space are highly explosive. Do not, under any circumstances, use gasoline for cleaning parts. Use an approved safety solvent.

Always disconnect the battery ground (-) cable at the battery before working on any part of the fuel system or electrical system. Never risk spilling fuel on a hot engine or exhaust component. It is strongly recommended that a fire extinguisher suitable for use on fuel and electrical fires be kept handy in the garage or workshop at all times. Never try to extinguish a fuel or electrical fire with water.

Fumes

Certain fumes are highly toxic and can quickly cause unconsciousness and even death if inhaled to any extent. Gasoline vapor falls into this category, as do the vapors from some cleaning solvents. Any draining or pouring of such volatile fluids should be done in a well ventilated area.

When using cleaning fluids and solvents, read the instructions on the container carefully. Never use materials from unmarked containers.

Never run the engine in an enclosed space, such as a garage. Exhaust fumes contain carbon monoxide, which is extremely poisonous. If you need to run the engine, always do so in the open air, or at least have the rear of the vehicle outside the work area.

The battery

Never create a spark or allow a bare light bulb near a battery. They normally give off a certain amount of hydrogen gas, which is highly explosive.

Always disconnect the battery ground (-) cable at the battery before working on the fuel or electrical systems.

If possible, loosen the filler caps or cover when charging the battery from an external source (this does not apply to sealed or maintenance-free batteries). Do not charge at an excessive rate or the battery may burst.

Take care when adding water to a non maintenance-free battery and when carrying a battery. The electrolyte, even when diluted, is very corrosive and should not be allowed to contact clothing or skin.

Always wear eye protection when cleaning the battery to prevent the caustic deposits from entering your eyes.

Household current

When using an electric power tool, inspection light, etc., which operates on household current, always make sure that the tool is correctly connected to its plug and that, where necessary, it is properly grounded. Do not use such items in damp conditions and, again, do not create a spark or apply excessive heat in the vicinity of fuel or fuel vapor.

Secondary ignition system voltage

A severe electric shock can result from touching certain parts of the ignition system (such as the spark plug wires) when the engine is running or being cranked, particularly if components are damp or the insulation is defective. In the case of an electronic ignition system, the secondary system voltage is much higher and could prove fatal.

Hydrofluoric acid

This extremely corrosive acid is formed when certain types of synthetic rubber, found in some O-rings, oil seals, fuel hoses, etc. are exposed to temperatures above 750-degrees F (400-degrees C). The rubber changes into a charred or sticky substance containing the acid. *Once formed, the acid remains dangerous for years. If it gets onto the skin, it may be necessary to amputate the limb concerned.*

When dealing with a vehicle which has suffered a fire, or with components salvaged from such a vehicle, wear protective gloves and discard them after use.

Troubleshooting

Contents

This section provides an easy reference guide to the more common problems which may occur during the operation of your vehicle. Various symptoms and their possible causes are grouped under headings denoting components or systems, such as Engine, Cooling system, etc. They also refer to the Chapter and/or Section that deals with the problem.

Remember that successful troubleshooting isn't a mysterious art practiced only by professional mechanics. It's simply the result of knowledge combined with an intelligent, systematic approach to a problem. Always use a process of elimination, starting with the simplest solution and working through to the most complex - and never overlook the obvious. Anyone can run the gas tank dry or leave the lights on overnight, so don't assume that you're exempt from such oversights.

Finally, always establish a clear idea why a problem has occurred and take steps to ensure that it doesn't happen again. If the electrical system fails because of a poor connection, check all other connections in the system to make sure they don't fail as well. If a particular fuse continues to blow, find out why - don't just go on replacing fuses. Remember, failure of a small component can often be indicative of potential failure or incorrect functioning of a more important component or system.

Engine and performance

1 Engine will not rotate when attempting to start

1　Battery terminal connections loose or corroded (Chapter 1).
2　Battery discharged or faulty (Chapter 1).
3　Automatic transaxle not completely engaged in Park (Chapter 7).
4　Broken, loose or disconnected wiring in the starting circuit (Chapters 5 and 12).
5　Starter motor pinion jammed in flywheel ring gear (Chapter 5).
6　Starter solenoid faulty (Chapter 5).
7　Starter motor faulty (Chapter 5).
8　Ignition switch faulty (Chapter 12).
9　Transaxle range switch faulty (Chapter 6).
10　Starter pinion or driveplate teeth worn or broken (Chapter 5).

2 Engine rotates but will not start

1　Fuel tank empty.
2　Battery discharged (engine rotates slowly) (Chapter 5).
3　Battery terminal connections loose or corroded (Chapter 1).
4　Leaking fuel injector(s), fuel pump, pressure regulator, etc. (Chapter 4).
5　Fuel not reaching fuel injection system (Chapter 4).
6　Ignition components damp or damaged (Chapter 5).
7　Worn, faulty or incorrectly gapped spark plugs (Chapter 1).
8　Broken, loose or disconnected wires at the ignition coil(s) or faulty coil(s) (Chapter 5).
9　Vehicle theft deterrent system problem (Chapter 12).

3 Engine hard to start when cold

1　Battery discharged or low (Chapter 1).
2　Fuel system malfunctioning (Chapter 4).
3　Emissions or engine control system malfunctioning (Chapter 6).

4 Engine hard to start when hot

1　Air filter clogged (Chapter 1).
2　Fuel not reaching the fuel injection system (Chapter 4).
3　Corroded battery connections, especially ground (Chapter 1).
4　Emissions or engine control system malfunctioning (Chapter 6).

5 Starter motor noisy or excessively rough in engagement

1　Pinion or driveplate gear teeth worn or broken (Chapter 5).

2　Starter motor mounting bolts loose or missing (Chapter 5).

6 Engine starts but stops immediately

1　Loose or faulty electrical connections at coil pack or alternator (Chapter 5).
2　Insufficient fuel reaching the fuel injectors (Chapter 4).
3　Vacuum leak at the gasket between the intake manifold/plenum and throttle body (Chapters 1 and 4).
4　Restricted exhaust system (most likely the catalytic converter) (Chapters 4 and 6).
5　Vehicle theft deterrent system problem (Chapter 12).

7 Oil puddle under engine

1　Oil pan gasket and/or oil pan drain bolt seal leaking (Chapters 1 and 2).
2　Oil pressure sending unit leaking (Chapter 2).
3　Valve cover gaskets leaking (Chapter 2).
4　Engine oil seals leaking (Chapter 2).

8 Engine lopes while idling or idles erratically

1　Vacuum leakage (Chapter 4).
2　Leaking EGR valve or plugged PCV system (Chapter 6).
3　Air filter clogged (Chapter 1).
4　Fuel pump not delivering sufficient fuel to the fuel injection system (Chapter 4).
5　Leaking head gasket (Chapter 2).
6　Camshaft lobes worn (Chapter 2).

9 Engine misses at idle speed

1　Spark plugs worn or not gapped properly (Chapter 1).
2　Faulty spark plug wires (Chapter 1).
3　Vacuum leaks (Chapters 1 and 4).
4　Uneven or low compression (Chapter 2C).

10 Engine misses throughout driving speed range

1　Fuel filter clogged and/or impurities in the fuel system (Chapters 1 and 4).
2　Low fuel output at the injector (Chapter 4).
3　Faulty or incorrectly gapped spark plugs (Chapter 1).
4　Leaking spark plug wires (Chapter 1) or faulty ignition coil (see Chapter 5).
5　Faulty emission system components (Chapter 6).

6　Low or uneven cylinder compression pressures (Chapter 2).
7　Weak or faulty ignition system (Chapter 5).
8　Vacuum leak in fuel injection system, intake manifold or vacuum hoses (Chapter 4).

11 Engine stumbles on acceleration

1　Spark plugs fouled (Chapter 1).
2　Fuel injection system malfunctioning (Chapter 4).
3　Fuel filter clogged (Chapter 1).
4　Intake manifold air leak (Chapter 4).

12 Engine surges while holding accelerator steady

1　Intake air leak (Chapter 4).
2　Fuel pump faulty (Chapter 4).
3　Defective Throttle Position (TP) sensor (Chapter 6).
4　Defective ECM (Chapter 6).

13 Engine stalls

1　Idle speed incorrect (Chapters 1 and 4).
2　Fuel filter clogged and/or water and impurities in the fuel system (Chapters 1 and 4).
3　Ignition components damp or damaged (Chapter 5).
4　Faulty emissions system components (Chapter 6).
5　Faulty or incorrectly gapped spark plugs (Chapter 1).
6　Faulty spark plug wires (Chapter 1).
7　Vacuum leak in the intake manifold or vacuum hoses (Chapter 4).
8　Throttle body dirty.

14 Engine lacks power

1　Faulty or incorrectly gapped spark plugs (Chapter 1).
2　Restricted exhaust system (most likely the catalytic converter (Chapters 4 and 6).
3　Fuel injection system malfunctioning (Chapter 4).
4　Faulty coil(s) (Chapter 5).
5　Brakes binding (Chapter 9).
6　Automatic transaxle fluid level incorrect (Chapter 1).
7　Fuel filter clogged and/or impurities in the fuel system (Chapter 1).
8　Emission control system not functioning properly (Chapter 6).
9　Low or uneven cylinder compression pressures (Chapter 2).

15 Engine backfires

1　Emissions system not functioning properly (Chapter 6).

2 Fuel injection system malfunctioning (Chapter 4).
3 Vacuum leak at fuel injectors, intake manifold or vacuum hoses (Chapter 4).
4 Valves sticking (Chapter 2).

16 Pinging or knocking engine sounds during acceleration or uphill

1 Incorrect grade of fuel.
2 Fuel injection system malfunctioning (Chapter 4).
3 Improper or damaged spark plugs or wires (Chapter 1).
4 Worn or damaged ignition components (Chapter 5).
5 Faulty emissions system (Chapter 6).
6 Vacuum leak (Chapter 4).

17 Engine runs with oil pressure light on

1 Low oil level (Chapter 1).
2 Short in wiring circuit (Chapter 12).
3 Faulty oil pressure sender (Chapter 2).
4 Oil viscosity too low or oil diluted.
5 Worn engine bearings and/or oil pump (Chapter 2).

18 Engine diesels (continues to run) after switching off

1 Excessive engine operating temperature (Chapter 3).
2 Excessive carbon deposits on valves and pistons.

Engine electrical system

19 Battery will not hold a charge

1 Alternator drivebelt defective or not adjusted properly (Chapter 1).
2 Battery terminals loose or corroded (Chapter 1).
3 Alternator not charging properly (Chapter 5).
4 Loose, broken or faulty wiring in the charging circuit (Chapter 5).
5 Short in vehicle wiring (Chapters 5 and 12).
6 Internally defective battery (Chapters 1 and 5).

20 Voltage warning light fails to go out

1 Faulty alternator or charging circuit (Chapter 5).

2 Alternator drivebelt defective or out of adjustment (Chapter 1).
3 Alternator voltage regulator inoperative (Chapter 5).

21 Voltage warning light fails to come on when key is turned on

1 Warning light bulb defective (Chapter 12).
2 Fault in the printed circuit, dash wiring or bulb holder (Chapter 12).

Fuel system

22 Excessive fuel consumption

1 Dirty or clogged air filter element (Chapter 1).
2 Emissions system not functioning properly (Chapter 6).
3 Fuel injection system malfunctioning (Chapter 4).
4 Low tire pressure or incorrect tire size (Chapter 1).
5 Missing or incorrect thermostat.

23 Fuel leakage and/or fuel odor

1 Leak in a fuel feed or vent line (Chapter 4).
2 Tank overfilled.
3 Evaporative emissions control canister defective (Chapters 1 and 6).
4 Fuel injector seals faulty (Chapter 4).

Cooling system

24 Overheating

1 Insufficient coolant in system (Chapter 1).
2 Water pump drivebelt defective or out of adjustment (Chapter 1).
3 Expansion tank core blocked or grille restricted (Chapter 3).
4 Thermostat faulty (Chapter 3).
5 Electric cooling fan blades broken or cracked (Chapter 3).
6 Expansion tank cap not maintaining proper pressure.

25 Overcooling

Incorrect (opening temperature too low) or faulty thermostat (Chapter 3).

26 External coolant leakage

1 Deteriorated/damaged hoses or loose clamps (Chapters 1 and 3).

2 Water pump seal defective (Chapters 1 and 3).
3 Leakage from radiator core (Chapter 3).
4 Engine drain or water jacket core plugs leaking (Chapter 2).

27 Internal coolant leakage

1 Leaking cylinder head gasket (Chapter 2).
2 Cracked cylinder bore or cylinder head (Chapter 2).

28 Coolant loss

1 Too much coolant in system (Chapter 1).
2 Coolant boiling away because of overheating (Chapter 3).
3 Internal or external leakage (Chapter 3).
4 Faulty expansion tank cap.

29 Poor coolant circulation

1 Inoperative water pump (Chapter 3).
2 Restriction in cooling system (Chapters 1 and 3).
3 Water pump drivebelt defective or out of adjustment (Chapter 1).
4 Thermostat sticking (Chapter 3).

Automatic transaxle

Note: *Due to the complexity of the automatic transaxle, it's difficult for the home mechanic to properly diagnose and service this component. For problems other than the following, the vehicle should be taken to a dealer service department or a transmission shop.*

30 Fluid leakage

1 Automatic transmission fluid is a deep red color. Fluid leaks should not be confused with engine oil, which can easily be blown by airflow to the transaxle.
2 To pinpoint a leak, first remove all built-up dirt and grime from the transaxle housing with degreasing agents and/or steam cleaning. Drive the vehicle at low speeds so air flow will not blow the leak far from its source. Raise the vehicle and determine where the leak is coming from. Common areas of leakage are:

a) *Fluid pan*
b) *Fill plug (Chapter 1)*
c) *Fluid cooler lines (Chapter 7)*
d) *Vehicle Speed Sensor (Chapter 6)*

31 Transaxle fluid brown or has a burned smell

Transaxle overheated. Change fluid (Chapter 1).

32 General shift mechanism problems

1   Chapter 7 deals with checking and adjusting the shift cable on automatic transaxles. Common problems which may be attributed to a poorly adjusted cable are:

a) *Engine starting in gears other than Park or Neutral.*
b) *Indicator on shifter pointing to a gear other than the one actually being used.*
c) *Vehicle moves when in Park.*

2   Refer to Chapter 7 for the shift cable adjustment procedure.

33 Engine will start in gears other than Park or Neutral

Transmission range switch malfunctioning (Chapter 6).

34 Transaxle slips, shifts roughly, is noisy or has no drive in forward or reverse gears

There are many probable causes for the above problems, but the home mechanic should be concerned with only one possibility - fluid level. Before taking the vehicle to a repair shop, check the level and condition of the fluid as described in Chapter 1.

Correct the fluid level as necessary or change the fluid and filter if needed. If the problem persists, have a professional diagnose the probable cause.

Driveaxles

35 Clicking noise in turns

Worn or damaged outer CV joint. Check for cut or damaged boots (Chapter 1). Repair as necessary (Chapter 8).

36 Knock or clunk when accelerating after coasting

Worn or damaged CV joint. Check for cut or damaged boots (Chapter 1). Repair as necessary (Chapter 8).

37 Shudder or vibration during acceleration

1   Worn or damaged CV joints. Repair or replace as necessary (Chapter 8).
2   Sticking inner joint assembly. Correct or replace as necessary (Chapter 8).

Brakes

Note: *Before assuming that a brake problem exists, make sure . . .*

a) *The tires are in good condition and properly inflated (Chapter 1).*
b) *The front end alignment is correct (Chapter 10).*
c) *The vehicle isn't loaded with weight in an unequal manner.*

38 Vehicle pulls to one side during braking

1   Incorrect tire pressures (Chapter 1).
2   Front end out of alignment (have the front end aligned).
3   Unmatched tires on same axle.
4   Restricted brake lines or hoses (Chapter 9).
5   Sticking caliper piston (Chapter 9).
6   Loose suspension parts (Chapter 10).
7   Contaminated brake pad material (Chapter 9).

39 Noise (grinding or high-pitched squeal) when the brakes are applied

Disc brake pads worn out. Replace pads with new ones immediately (Chapter 9).

40 Brake roughness or chatter (pedal pulsates)

1   Excessive brake disc lateral runout (Chapter 9).
2   Parallelism of disc not within specifications (Chapter 9).
3   Uneven pad wear caused by caliper not sliding due to improper clearance or dirt (Chapter 9).
4   Defective brake disc (Chapter 9).

41 Excessive pedal effort required to stop vehicle

1   Malfunctioning power brake booster (Chapter 9).
2   Partial system failure (Chapter 9).
3   Excessively worn pads (Chapter 9).
4   One or more calipers seized or sticking (Chapter 9).
5   Brake pads contaminated with oil or grease (Chapter 9).
6   New pads installed and not yet seated. It will take a while for the new material to seat.

42 Excessive brake pedal travel

1   Partial brake system failure (Chapter 9).
2   Insufficient fluid in master cylinder (Chapters 1 and 9).

3   Air trapped in system (Chapter 9).
4   Faulty master cylinder (Chapter 9).

43 Dragging brakes

1   Master cylinder pistons not returning correctly (Chapter 9).
2   Restricted brake lines or hoses (Chapters 1 and 9).
3   Incorrect parking brake adjustment (Chapter 9).
4   Defective brake calipers (Chapter 9).

44 Grabbing or uneven braking action

1   Malfunction of proportioning valve (Chapter 9).
2   Malfunction of power brake booster unit (Chapter 9).
3   Binding brake pedal mechanism (Chapter 9).
4   Contaminated brake linings (Chapter 9).

45 Brake pedal feels spongy when depressed

1   Air in hydraulic lines (Chapter 9).
2   Master cylinder mounting bolts loose (Chapter 9).
3   Master cylinder defective (Chapter 9).

46 Brake pedal travels to the floor with little resistance

Little or no fluid in the master cylinder reservoir caused by leaking caliper, or loose, damaged or disconnected brake lines (Chapter 9).

47 Parking brake does not hold

Parking brake cables improperly adjusted (Chapter 9).

Suspension and steering systems

Note: *Before attempting to diagnose the suspension and steering systems, perform the following preliminary checks:*

a) *Check the tire pressures and look for uneven wear.*
b) *Check the steering universal joints or coupling from the column to the steering gear for loose fasteners and wear.*
c) *Check the front and rear suspension and the steering gear assembly for loose and damaged parts.*
d) *Look for out-of-round or out-of-balance tires, bent rims and loose and/or rough wheel bearings.*

48 Vehicle pulls to one side

1   Mismatched or uneven tires (Chapter 10).
2   Broken or sagging springs (Chapter 10).
3   Wheel alignment incorrect (Chapter 10).
4   Front brakes dragging (Chapter 9).

49 Abnormal or excessive tire wear

1   Wheel alignment incorrect (Chapter 10).
2   Sagging or broken springs (Chapter 10).
3   Tire out-of-balance (Chapter 10).
4   Worn strut/coil spring assembly (Chapter 10).
5   Overloaded vehicle.
6   Tires not rotated regularly.

50 Wheel makes a "thumping" noise

1   Blister or bump on tire (Chapter 1).
2   Improper strut action (Chapter 10).

51 Shimmy, shake or vibration

1   Tire or wheel out-of-balance or out-of-round (Chapter 10).
2   Loose or worn wheel bearings (Chapter 10).
3   Worn tie-rod ends (Chapter 10).
4   Worn balljoints (Chapter 10).
5   Excessive wheel runout (Chapter 10).
6   Blister or bump on tire (Chapter 1).

52 Hard steering

1   Lack of lubrication at balljoints, tie-rod ends and steering gear assembly (Chapter 10).
2   Front wheel alignment incorrect (Chapter 10).
3   Low tire pressure (Chapter 1).

53 Steering wheel does not return to center position correctly

1   Lack of lubrication at balljoints and tie-rod ends (Chapters 1 and 10).
2   Binding in steering column (Chapter 10).
3   Defective rack-and-pinion assembly (Chapter 10).
4   Front wheel alignment problem (Chapter 10).

54 Abnormal noise at the front end

1   Lack of lubrication at balljoints and tie-rod ends (Chapter 1).
2   Loose upper strut mount (Chapter 10).
3   Worn tie-rod ends (Chapter 10).
4   Loose stabilizer bar (Chapter 10).
5   Loose wheel lug nuts (Chapter 1).
6   Loose suspension bolts (Chapter 10).

55 Wander or poor steering stability

1   Mismatched or uneven tires (Chapter 10).
2   Lack of lubrication at balljoints or tie-rod ends (Chapters 1 and 10).
3   Worn struts or shock absorbers (Chapter 10).
4   Loose stabilizer bar (Chapter 10).
5   Broken or sagging springs (Chapter 10).
6   Wheel alignment incorrect.
7   Loose steering gear mounting fasteners (Chapter 10).

56 Erratic steering when braking

1   Wheel bearings worn (Chapter 10).
2   Broken or sagging springs (Chapter 10).
3   Leaking caliper (Chapter 9).
4   Warped brake discs (Chapter 9).
5   Worn steering gear clamp bushing (Chapter 10).
6   Wheel alignment incorrect.

57 Excessive pitching and/or rolling around corners or during braking

1   Loose stabilizer bar (Chapter 10).
2   Worn struts or mounts (Chapter 10).
3   Broken or sagging springs (Chapter 10).
4   Overloaded vehicle.

58 Suspension bottoms

1   Overloaded vehicle.
2   Worn struts (Chapter 10).
3   Incorrect, broken or sagging springs (Chapter 10).

59 Cupped tires

1   Wheel alignment incorrect (Chapter 10).
2   Worn struts (Chapter 10).

3   Wheel bearings worn (Chapter 10).
4   Excessive tire or wheel runout (Chapter 10).
5   Worn balljoints (Chapter 10).

60 Excessive tire wear on outside edge

1   Inflation pressures incorrect (Chapter 1).
2   Excessive speed in turns.
3   Wheel alignment incorrect (excessive toe-in or positive camber). Have professionally aligned.
4   Suspension arm bent or twisted (Chapter 10).

61 Excessive tire wear on inside edge

1   Inflation pressures incorrect (Chapter 1).
2   Wheel alignment incorrect (toe-out or excessive negative camber). Have professionally aligned.
3   Loose or damaged steering components (Chapter 10).

62 Tire tread worn in one place

1   Tires out-of-balance.
2   Damaged or buckled wheel. Inspect and replace if necessary.
3   Defective tire (Chapter 1).

63 Excessive play or looseness in steering system

1   Wheel bearings worn (Chapter 10).
2   Tie-rod end loose or worn (Chapter 10).
3   Steering gear loose (Chapter 10).

64 Rattling or clicking noise in steering gear

1   Steering gear mounting bolts loose (Chapter 10).
2   Steering gear defective (Chapter 10).

Notes

Chapter 1
Tune-up and routine maintenance

Contents

Specifications

Recommended lubricants and fluids

Note: *Listed here are manufacturer recommendations at the time this manual was written. Manufacturers occasionally upgrade their fluid and lubricant specifications, so check with your local auto parts store for current recommendations.*

Engine oil	
Type	API "certified for gasoline engines"
Viscosity	SAE 5W-30
Fuel	
3.5L and 3.9L V6 models	Unleaded gasoline, 87 octane minimum
5.3L V8 models	Unleaded gasoline, 91 or higher octane
Automatic transaxle fluid	DEXRON ® VI Automatic transmission fluid
Brake fluid	DOT 3 brake fluid
Engine coolant	50/50 mixture of DEX-COOL® and distilled water
Power steering system	GM power steering fluid

Capacities*

Engine oil (including filter)
3.5L and 3.9L V6 engines .... 4.0 quarts
5.3L V8 engine .... 6.0 quarts
Coolant
3.5L and 3.9L V6 engines
2006 models .... 12.2 quarts
2007 and later models .... 10.1 quarts
5.3L V8 engine
2006 models .... 12.8 quarts
2007 and later models .... 13.3 quarts
Automatic transaxle .... 7.4 quarts

Note: *This is an initial-fill specification for routine fluid replacement. Be sure to follow the fluid check procedure in Section 25, as additional fluid may be required.*

All capacities approximate. Add as necessary to bring up to appropriate level.

Ignition system

Spark plug type and gap
Type
V6 engine.. AC41-100 or equivalent
V8 engine.. AC41-985 or equivalent
Gap .... 0.040 inch
Engine firing order
V6 engine 1-2-3-4-5-6
V8 engine 1-8-7-2-6-5-4-3

Brakes

Disc brake pad lining thickness (minimum) .... 1/8 inch

Torque specifications

Ft-lbs (unless otherwise indicated)

Note: *One foot-pound (ft-lb) of torque is equivalent to 12 inch-pounds (in-lbs) of torque. Torque values below approximately 15 foot-pounds are expressed in inch-pounds, because most foot-pound torque wrenches are not accurate at these smaller values.*

Engine oil drain plug
V6 engine 19
V8 engine 18
Automatic transaxle fluid pan bolts.. 124 in-lbs
Spark plugs... 132 in-lbs
Wheel lug nuts.. 100

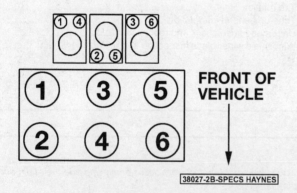

**Cylinder location and coil terminal identification
diagram - V6 engine**

Cylinder location diagram - V8 engine

Engine compartment layout (V8 engine)

1	Pressure cap	5	Automatic transaxle dipstick	9	Engine oil filler cap
2	Windshield washer fluid reservoir	6	Brake fluid reservoir	10	Engine oil dipstick
3	Underhood fuse/relay block	7	Coolant expansion tank	11	Battery
4	Power steering fluid reservoir	8	Air filter housing		

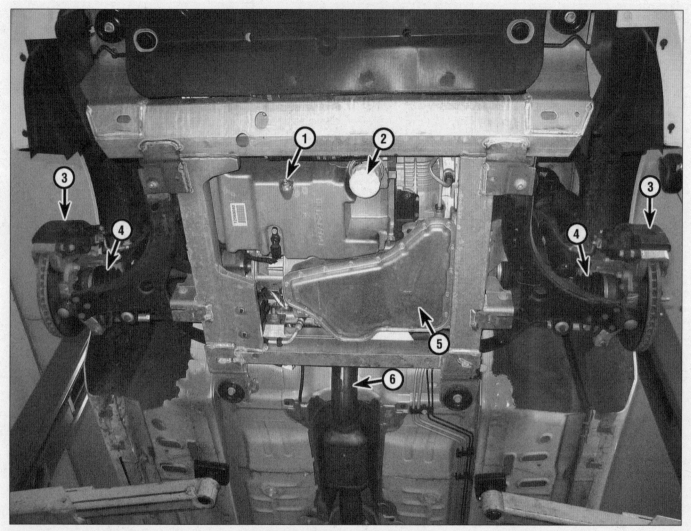

Typical engine underside components

1	Engine oil drain plug	3	Brake caliper	5	Transaxle fluid pan
2	Oil filter	4	Driveaxle boot	6	Exhaust pipe

Typical rear underside components

1	Muffler	3	Fuel tank
2	Rear shock absorber	4	Exhaust pipe

1 Maintenance schedule

The maintenance intervals in this manual are provided with the assumption that you, not the dealer, will be doing the work. These are the minimum maintenance intervals recommended by the factory for vehicles that are driven daily. If you wish to keep your vehicle in peak condition at all times, you may wish to perform some of these procedures even more often. Because frequent maintenance enhances the efficiency, performance and resale value of your car, we encourage you to do so. If you drive in dusty areas, tow a trailer, idle or drive at low speeds for extended periods or drive for short distances (less than four miles) in below freezing temperatures, shorter intervals are also recommended.

When your vehicle is new, it should be serviced by a factory authorized dealer service department to protect the factory warranty. In many cases, the initial maintenance check is done at no cost to the owner.

Every 250 miles or weekly, whichever comes first

Check the engine oil level (Section 4)
Check the engine coolant level (Section 4)
Check the brake fluid level (Section 4)
Check the windshield washer fluid level (Section 4)
Check the power steering fluid level (Section 4)
Check the tires and tire pressures (Section 5)

Every 3000 miles or 3 months, whichever comes first

All items listed above plus:
Change the engine oil and oil filter (Section 6)

Every 6000 miles or 6 months, whichever comes first

All items listed above plus:
Inspect (and replace, if necessary) the windshield wiper blades (Section 7)
Check and service the battery (Section 8)
Check the cooling system (Section 9)
Rotate the tires (Section 10)
Check the seat belts (Section 11)
Inspect the brake system (Section 12)
Check the automatic transaxle fluid level (Section 25)

Every 15,000 miles or 12 months, whichever comes first

All items listed above plus:
Check all underhood hoses (Section 13)
Inspect the suspension and steering components (Section 14)
Inspect the driveaxle boots (Section 15)
Check the exhaust system (Section 16)
Check the fuel system (Section 17)
Replace the interior ventilation filter (Section 18)
Check the engine drivebelt (Section 19)

Every 30,000 miles or 24 months, whichever comes first

All items listed above plus:
Check (and replace, if necessary) the air filter (Section 20)*
Change the brake fluid (Section 21)
Replace the spark plugs (non-platinum type spark plugs) (Section 22)
Inspect the spark plug wires (Section 23)

Every 100,000 miles

Replace the spark plugs (Platinum type spark plugs) (Section 22)
Service the cooling system (drain, flush and refill) (Section 24)
Replace the automatic transaxle fluid and filter (Section 25)**

*This item is affected by "severe" operating conditions as described below. If your vehicle is operated under "severe" conditions, perform all maintenance indicated with an asterisk (*) at 3000 mile/3 month intervals. Severe conditions are indicated if you mainly operate your vehicle under one or more of the following conditions:

Operating in dusty areas
Towing a trailer
Idling for extended periods and/or low speed operation

** If operated under one or more of the following conditions, change the automatic transaxle fluid lubricant every 50,000 miles:

In heavy city traffic where the outside temperature regularly reaches 90-degrees F (32-degrees C) or higher
In hilly or mountainous terrain
Frequent towing of a trailer

2   Introduction

This Chapter is designed to help the home mechanic maintain the Impala and Monte Carlo with the goals of maximum performance, economy, safety and reliability in mind.

Included is a master maintenance schedule, followed by procedures dealing specifically with each item on the schedule. Visual checks, adjustments, component replacement and other helpful items are included. Refer to the accompanying illustrations of the engine compartment and the underside of the vehicle for the locations of various components.

Servicing the vehicle, in accordance with the mileage/time maintenance schedule and the step-by-step procedures will result in a planned maintenance program that should produce a long and reliable service life. Keep in mind that it is a comprehensive plan, so maintaining some items but not others at the specified intervals will not produce the same results.

As you service the vehicle, you will discover that many of the procedures can - and should - be grouped together because of the nature of the particular procedure you're performing or because of the close proximity of two otherwise unrelated components to one another.

For example, if the vehicle is raised for chassis lubrication, you should inspect the exhaust, suspension, steering and fuel systems while you're under the vehicle. When you're rotating the tires, it makes good sense to check the brakes since the wheels are already removed. Finally, let's suppose you have to borrow or rent a torque wrench. Even if you only need it to tighten the spark plugs, you might as well check the torque of as many critical fasteners as time allows.

The first step in this maintenance program is to prepare yourself before the actual work begins. Read through all the procedures you're planning to do, then gather up all the parts and tools needed. If it looks like you might run into problems during a particular job, seek advice from a mechanic or an experienced do-it-yourselfer.

Owner's Manual and VECI label information

Your vehicle owner's manual was written for your year and model and contains very specific information on component locations, specifications, fuse ratings, part numbers, etc. The Owner's Manual is an important resource for the do-it-yourselfer to have; if one was not supplied with your vehicle, it can generally be ordered from a dealer parts department.

Among other important information, the Vehicle Emissions Control Information (VECI) label contains specifications and procedures for applicable tune-up adjustments and, in some instances, spark plugs (see Chapter 6 for more information on the VECI label). The information on this label is the exact maintenance data recommended by the manufac-

4.2 Engine oil dipstick location - V8 engines

turer. This data often varies by intended operating altitude, local emissions regulations, month of manufacture, etc.

This Chapter contains procedural details, safety information and more ambitious maintenance intervals than you might find in manufacturer's literature. However, you may also find procedures or specifications in your Owner's Manual or VECI label that differ with what's printed here. In these cases, the Owner's Manual or VECI label can be considered correct, since it is specific to your particular vehicle.

3   Tune-up general information

The term tune-up is used in this manual to represent a combination of individual operations rather than one specific procedure.

If, from the time the vehicle is new, the routine maintenance schedule is followed closely and frequent checks are made of fluid levels and high wear items, as suggested throughout this manual, the engine will be kept in relatively good running condition and the need for additional work will be minimized.

More likely than not, however, there will be times when the engine is running poorly due to lack of regular maintenance. This is even more likely if a used vehicle, which has not received regular and frequent maintenance checks, is purchased. In such cases, an engine tune-up will be needed outside of the regular routine maintenance intervals.

The first step in any tune-up or diagnostic procedure to help correct a poor running engine is a cylinder compression check. A compression check (see Chapter 2C) will help determine the condition of internal engine components and should be used as a guide for tune-up and repair procedures. If, for instance, a compression check indicates serious internal engine wear, a conventional tune-up will not improve the performance of the engine and would be a waste of time and money. Because of its importance, the compression check should be done by someone with the right equipment and the knowledge to use it properly.

The following procedures are those most often needed to bring a generally poor running engine back into a proper state of tune.

Minor tune-up

Check all engine related fluids (Section 4)
Clean, inspect and test the battery
  (Section 8)
Check the cooling system (Section 9)
Check all underhood hoses (Section 13)
Check the fuel system (Section 17)
Check the air filter (Section 20)

Major tune-up

All items listed under Minor tune-up, plus . . .
  Check the drivebelt (Section 19)
  Replace the air filter (Section 20)
  Replace the spark plugs (Section 22)

4   Fluid level checks (every 250 miles or weekly)

Note: *Refer to Section 25 for the automatic transaxle fluid level check.*
1   Fluids are an essential part of the lubrication, cooling, brake and windshield washer systems. Because the fluids gradually become depleted and/or contaminated during normal operation of the vehicle, they must be periodically replenished. See *Recommended lubricants and fluids* at the beginning of this Chapter before adding fluid to any of the following components. **Note:** *The vehicle must be on level ground when fluid levels are checked.*

Engine oil

Refer to illustrations 4.2, 4.4 and 4.6
2   The oil level is checked with a dipstick, which is attached to the engine block (**see illustration**). The dipstick extends through a metal tube down into the oil pan.
3   The oil level should be checked before the vehicle has been driven, or about 5 minutes after the engine has been shut off. If the oil is checked immediately after driving the vehicle, some of the oil will remain in the upper part of the engine, resulting in an inaccurate reading on the dipstick.

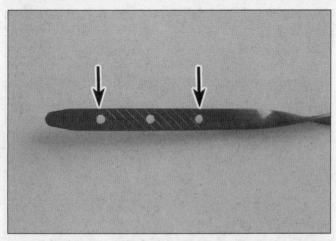

4.4 The oil level should be in the cross-hatched area - if it's below the lower hole, add enough oil to bring it up to or near the upper hole

4.6 The oil filler cap is located on the valve cover - always make sure the area around the opening is clean before unscrewing the cap to prevent dirt from contaminating the engine (V8 engine shown)

4   Pull the dipstick out of the tube and wipe all the oil from the end with a clean rag or paper towel. Insert the clean dipstick all the way back into the tube and pull it out again. Note the oil at the end of the dipstick. At its highest point, the level should be between the MIN and MAX marks or within the cross-hatched area on the dipstick **(see illustration).**

5   It takes one quart of oil to raise the level from the MIN mark to the MAX mark on the dipstick. Do not allow the level to drop below the MIN mark or oil starvation may cause engine damage. Conversely, overfilling the engine (adding oil above the MAX mark) may cause oil fouled spark plugs, oil leaks or oil seal failures. Maintaining the oil level above the MAX mark can cause excessive oil consumption.

6   To add oil, remove the filler cap from the valve cover **(see illustration).** After adding oil, wait a few minutes to allow the level to stabilize, then pull out the dipstick and check the level again. Add more oil if required. Install the filler cap and tighten it by hand only.

7   Checking the oil level is an important preventive maintenance step. A consistently low oil level indicates oil leakage through damaged seals, defective gaskets or past worn rings or valve guides. If the oil looks milky in color or has water droplets in it, the cylinder head gasket(s) may be blown or the head(s) or block may be cracked. The engine should be checked immediately. The condition of the oil should also be checked. Whenever you check the oil level, slide your thumb and index finger up the dipstick before wiping off the oil. If you see small dirt or metal particles clinging to the dipstick, the oil should be changed (see Section 6).

Engine coolant

Refer to illustrations 4.8 and 4.9

Warning: *Do not allow antifreeze to come in contact with your skin or painted surfaces of the vehicle. Flush contaminated areas immediately with plenty of water. Don't store new coolant or leave old coolant lying around where it's accessible to children or pets -*

they're attracted by its sweet smell. Ingestion of even a small amount of coolant can be fatal! Wipe up garage floor and drip pan spills immediately. Keep antifreeze containers covered and repair cooling system leaks as soon as they're noticed.

8   All vehicles covered by this manual are equipped with a pressurized coolant recovery system. A plastic expansion tank located at the rear of the engine compartment is connected by a hose to the radiator **(see illustration).** As the engine heats up during operation, the expanding coolant fills the tank.

9   The coolant level in the tank should be checked regularly. **Warning:** *Do not remove the expansion tank cap to check the coolant level when the engine is warm!* The level in the tank varies with the temperature of the engine. When the engine is cold, the coolant level should be at the COLD mark on the reservoir **(see illustration).** If it isn't, remove the cap from the tank and add a 50/50 mixture of ethylene glycol based antifreeze and water.

10   Drive the vehicle, let the engine cool completely then recheck the coolant level. Don't

4.8 The cooling system expansion tank is located at the rear of the engine compartment

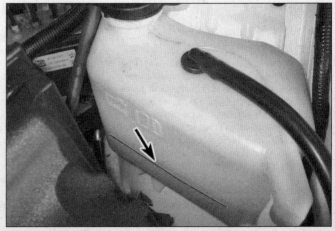

4.9 When the engine is cold, the engine coolant level should be at the COLD mark (expansion tank seam)

4.15 The brake fluid level should be kept between the MIN and MAX marks on the translucent plastic reservoir

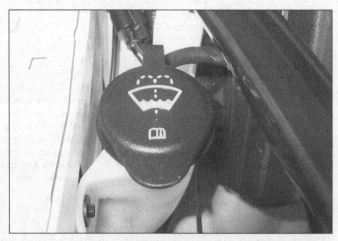

4.22 The windshield washer fluid reservoir is located in the right front corner of the engine compartment

use rust inhibitors or additives. If only a small amount of coolant is required to bring the system up to the proper level, water can be used. However, repeated additions of water will dilute the antifreeze and water solution. In order to maintain the proper ratio of antifreeze and water, always top up the coolant level with the correct mixture. An empty plastic milk jug or bleach bottle makes an excellent container for mixing coolant.

11 If the coolant level drops consistently, there may be a leak in the system. Inspect the radiator, hoses, filler cap, drain plugs and water pump (see Section 9). If no leaks are noted, have the pressure cap pressure tested by a service station.

12 If you have to remove the expansion tank cap wait until the engine has cooled completely, then wrap a thick cloth around the cap and unscrew it slowly, stopping if you hear a hissing noise. If coolant or steam escapes, let the engine cool down longer, then remove the cap.

13 Check the condition of the coolant as well. It should be relatively clear. If it's brown or rust colored, the system should be drained, flushed and refilled. Even if the coolant appears to be normal, the corrosion inhibitors wear out, so it must be replaced at the specified intervals.

Brake fluid

Refer to illustration 4.15

14 The brake master cylinder is mounted on the front of the power booster unit in the engine compartment.

15 To check the fluid level of brake system, simply look at the MAX and MIN marks on the brake fluid reservoir **(see illustration)**.

16 If the level is low, wipe the top of the reservoir cover with a clean rag to prevent contamination of the brake system before lifting the cover.

17 Add only the specified brake fluid to the reservoir (refer to *Recommended lubricants and fluids* at the front of this Chapter or to your owner's manual). Mixing different types of brake fluid can damage the system. Fill the

brake master cylinder reservoir only to the MAX line. **Warning:** *Use caution when filling the reservoir - brake fluid can harm your eyes and damage painted surfaces. Do not use brake fluid that is more than one year old or has been left open. Brake fluid absorbs moisture from the air. Excess moisture can cause a dangerous loss of braking.*

18 While the reservoir cap is removed, inspect the master cylinder reservoir for contamination. If deposits, dirt particles or water droplets are present, the system should be drained and refilled.

19 After filling the reservoir to the proper level, make sure the cap is properly seated to prevent fluid leakage.

20 The fluid in the brake master cylinder will drop slightly as the brake pads at each wheel wear down during normal operation. If the master cylinder requires repeated replenishing to keep it at the proper level, this is an indication of leakage in the brake system, which should be corrected immediately. If the brake system shows an indication of leakage check all brake lines and connections, along with the calipers and booster (see Section 12 for more information).

21 If, upon checking the brake master cylinder fluid level, you discover the reservoir empty or nearly empty, the system should be checked, repaired and bled (see Chapter 9).

Windshield washer fluid

Refer to illustration 4.22

22 Fluid for the windshield washer system is stored in a plastic reservoir located at the right front of the engine compartment **(see illustration)**.

23 In milder climates, plain water can be used in the reservoir, but it should be kept no more than 2/3 full to allow for expansion if the water freezes. In colder climates, use windshield washer system antifreeze, available at any auto parts store, to lower the freezing point of the fluid. Mix the antifreeze with water in accordance with the manufacturer's directions on the container. **Caution:** *Do not use cooling system antifreeze - it will damage the vehicle's paint.*

Power steering fluid

Refer to illustration 4.25

24 Check the power steering fluid level periodically to avoid steering system problems, such as damage to the pump. **Caution:** *DO NOT hold the steering wheel against either stop (extreme left or right turn) for more than five seconds. If you do, the power steering pump could be damaged.*

25 The fluid reservoir for the power steering system is mounted near the power steering pump **(see illustration)**.

4.25 Power steering fluid reservoir

26   The fluid level can be checked by removing the engine cool, the fluid level should be kept between the MIN and MAX marks on the dipstick.

27   Add small amounts of fluid until the level is correct. **Caution:** *Do not overfill the reservoir. If too much fluid is added, remove the excess with a clean syringe or suction pump.*

28   If the reservoir requires frequent fluid additions, all power steering hoses, hose connections, the power steering pump and the steering gear assembly should be carefully checked for leaks.

5   Tire and tire pressure checks (every 250 miles or weekly)

Refer to illustrations 5.2, 5.3, 5.4a, 5.4b and 5.8

1   Periodic inspection of the tires may spare you the inconvenience of being stranded with a flat tire. It can also provide you with vital information regarding possible problems in the steering and suspension systems before major damage occurs.

2   The original tires on this vehicle are equipped with 1/2-inch wide bands that will appear when tread depth reaches 1/16-inch, at which point they can be considered worn out. Tread wear can be monitored with a simple, inexpensive device known as a tread

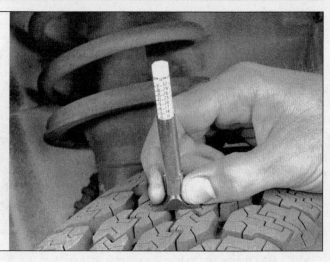

5.2 A tire tread depth indicator should be used to monitor tire wear - they are available at auto parts stores and service stations and cost very little

depth indicator **(see illustration)**.

3   Note any abnormal tread wear **(see illustration)**. Tread pattern irregularities such as cupping, flat spots and more wear on one side than the other are indications of front end alignment and/or balance problems. If any of these conditions are noted, take the vehicle to a tire shop or service station to correct the problem.

4   Look closely for cuts, punctures and embedded nails or tacks. Sometimes a tire will hold air pressure for a short time or leak down very slowly after a nail has embedded itself in the tread. If a slow leak persists, check the valve stem core to make sure it is tight **(see illustration)**. Examine the tread for an object that may have embedded itself in the tire or for a plug that may have begun to leak (radial tire punctures are repaired with a plug that is installed in a puncture). If a puncture is suspected, it can be easily verified by spraying a solution of soapy water onto the puncture area **(see illustration)**. The soapy solution will bubble if there is a leak. Unless

UNDERINFLATION

CUPPING

Cupping may be caused by:
• Underinflation and/or mechanical irregularities such as out-of-balance condition of wheel and/or tire, and bent or damaged wheel.
• Loose or worn steering tie-rod or steering idler arm.
• Loose, damaged or worn front suspension parts.

OVERINFLATION

INCORRECT TOE-IN OR EXTREME CAMBER

FEATHERING DUE TO MISALIGNMENT

5.3 This chart will help you determine the condition of your tires, the probable cause(s) of abnormal wear and the corrective action necessary

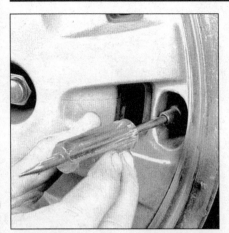

5.4a If a tire loses air on a steady basis, check the valve core first to make sure it's snug (special inexpensive wrenches are commonly available at auto parts stores)

5.4b If the valve core is tight, raise the corner of the vehicle with the low tire and spray a soapy water solution onto the tread as the tire is turned slowly - slow leaks will cause small bubbles to appear

5.8 To extend the life of your tires, check the air pressure at least once a week with an accurate gauge (don't forget the spare!)

the puncture is unusually large, a tire shop or service station can usually repair the tire.

5   Carefully inspect the inner sidewall of each tire for evidence of brake fluid leakage. If you see any, inspect the brakes immediately.

6   Correct air pressure adds miles to the life span of the tires, improves mileage and enhances overall ride quality. Tire pressure cannot be accurately estimated by looking at a tire, especially if it's a radial. A tire pressure gauge is essential. Keep an accurate gauge in the glove compartment. The pressure gauges attached to the nozzles of air hoses at gas stations are often inaccurate.

7   Always check tire pressure when the tires are cold. Cold, in this case, means the vehicle has not been driven over a mile in the three hours preceding a tire pressure check. A pressure rise of four to eight pounds is not uncommon once the tires are warm.

8   Unscrew the valve cap protruding from the wheel or hubcap and push the gauge firmly onto the valve stem **(see illustration)**. Note the reading on the gauge and compare the figure to the recommended tire pressure shown on the tire placard on the driver's side door. Be sure to reinstall the valve cap to keep dirt and moisture out of the valve stem mechanism. Check all four tires and, if necessary, add enough air to bring them up to the recommended pressure.

9   Don't forget to keep the spare tire inflated to the specified pressure (refer to the pressure molded into the tire sidewall).

6   Engine oil and filter change (every 3000 miles or 3 months)

Refer to illustrations 6.2, 6.7, 6.11, 6.14 and 6.19

Note: *These vehicles are equipped with an oil life indicator system that illuminates a light or message on the instrument panel when the system deems it necessary to change the oil. A number of factors are taken into consid-*

eration to determine when the oil should be considered "worn out." Generally, this system will allow the vehicle to accumulate more miles between oil changes than the traditional 3000 mile interval, but we believe that frequent oil changes are cheap insurance and will prolong engine life. If you do decide not to change your oil every 3000 miles and rely on the oil life indicator instead, make sure you don't exceed 10,000 miles before the oil is changed, regardless of what the oil life indicator shows.

1   Frequent oil changes are the most important preventive maintenance procedures that can be done by the home mechanic. As engine oil ages, it becomes diluted and contaminated, which leads to premature engine wear.

2   Make sure that you have all the necessary tools before you begin this procedure **(see illustration).** You should also have plenty of rags or newspapers handy for mopping up oil spills.

3   Access to the oil drain plug and filter will be improved if the vehicle can be lifted on a hoist, driven onto ramps or supported by jackstands. **Warning:** *Do not work under a vehicle supported only by a jack - always use jackstands!*

4   If you haven't changed the oil on this vehicle before, get under it and locate the oil drain plug and the oil filter. The exhaust components will be warm as you work, so note how they are routed to avoid touching them when you are under the vehicle.

5   Start the engine and allow it to reach normal operating temperature - oil and sludge will flow out more easily when warm. If new oil, a filter or tools are needed, use the vehicle to go get them and warm up the engine/oil at the same time. Park on a level surface and shut off the engine when it's warmed up. Remove the oil filler cap from the valve cover.

6   Raise the vehicle and support it on jackstands. Make sure it is safely supported!

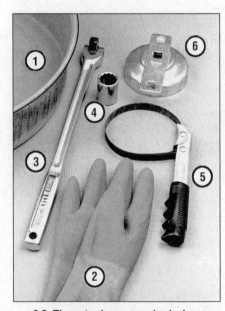

6.2 These tools are required when changing the engine oil and filter

1 Drain pan - It should be fairly shallow in depth, but wide in order to prevent spills

2 Rubber gloves - When removing the drain plug and filter, it is inevitable that you will get oil on your hands (the gloves will prevent burns)

3 Breaker bar - Sometimes the oil drain plug is pretty tight and a long breaker bar is needed to loosen it

4 Socket - To be used with the breaker bar or a ratchet (must be the correct size to fit the drain plug)

5 Filter wrench - This is a metal band-type wrench, which requires clearance around the filter to be effective

6 Filter wrench - This type fits on the bottom of the filter and can be turned with a ratchet or beaker bar (different size wrenches are available for different types of filters)

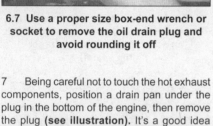

6.7 Use a proper size box-end wrench or socket to remove the oil drain plug and avoid rounding it off

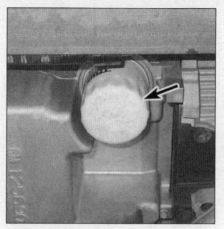

6.11 The oil filter is located at the front of the engine and is accessed from under the vehicle (V8 models)

6.14 Lubricate the oil filter gasket with clean engine oil before installing the filter on the engine

7   Being careful not to touch the hot exhaust components, position a drain pan under the plug in the bottom of the engine, then remove the plug **(see illustration)**. It's a good idea to wear a rubber glove while unscrewing the plug the final few turns to avoid being scalded by hot oil.

8   It may be necessary to move the drain pan slightly as oil flow slows to a trickle. Inspect the old oil for the presence of metal particles.

9   After all the oil has drained, wipe off the drain plug with a clean rag. Any small metal particles clinging to the plug would immediately contaminate the new oil.

10   Clean the area around the drain plug opening, reinstall the plug and tighten it securely, but don't strip the threads.

11   Move the drain pan into position under the oil filter. The filter is located at the front of the engine and is accessed from under the vehicle **(see illustration)**.

12   Loosen the oil filter by turning it counter-clockwise with the filter wrench. Any standard filter wrench should work. Once the filter is loose, use your hands to unscrew it from the

block. **Warning:** *The exhaust pipes may still be hot, so be careful.*

13   Use a clean rag to wipe off the mounting surface on the block. If a residue of old oil is allowed to remain, it will smoke when the block is heated up. It will also prevent the new filter from seating properly. Also make sure that the none of the old gasket remains stuck to the mounting surface. It can be removed with a scraper if necessary.

14   Compare the old filter with the new one to make sure they are the same type. Smear some engine oil on the rubber gasket of the new filter and screw it into place **(see illustration)**. Because over-tightening the filter will damage the gasket, do not use a filter wrench to tighten the filter. Tighten it by hand until the gasket contacts the seating surface. Then seat the filter by giving it an additional 3/4-turn.

15   Remove all tools and materials from under the vehicle, being careful not to spill the oil in the drain pan, then lower the vehicle.

16   Add new oil to the engine through the oil filler cap. Use a funnel to prevent oil from spilling onto the top of the engine. Pour four

quarts (V6 engines) or six quarts (V8 engine) of fresh oil into the engine. Wait a few minutes to allow the oil to drain into the pan, then check the level on the dipstick (see Section 4 if necessary). If the oil level is in the OK range, install the filler cap.

17   Start the engine and run it for about a minute. While the engine is running, look under the vehicle and check for leaks at the oil pan drain plug and around the oil filter. If either one is leaking, stop the engine and tighten the plug or filter slightly.

18   Wait a few minutes, then recheck the level on the dipstick. Add oil as necessary to bring the level into the OK range.

19   Be sure to reset the Change Engine Oil light. With the ignition key turned to the RUN position, display "Oil Life Reset" on the Driver's Information Center, then hold the set/reset button for more than five seconds **(see illustration)**. This should reset the system.

20   During the first few trips after an oil change, make it a point to check frequently for leaks and proper oil level.

21   The old oil drained from the engine can-

6.19 With "Oil Life Reset" displayed on the Driver's Information center, press and hold the set/reset button for at least five seconds

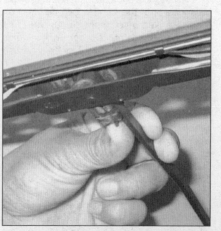

7.4a On early models, depress the release lever . . .

7.4b . . . and slide the wiper blade down the wiper arm and out of the hook in the end of the arm

7.4c On later models, pull up on the wiper cover until it is released at the base . . .

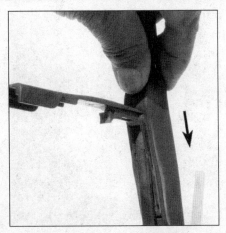

7.4d . . . slide the wiper blade down . . .

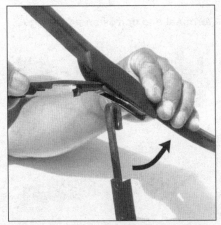

7.4e . . . and rotate the blade off the arm while holding the cover away from the arm

not be reused in its present state and should be disposed of. Check with your local auto parts store, disposal facility or environmental agency to see if they will accept the oil for recycling. After the oil has cooled it can be drained into a container (capped plastic jugs, topped bottles, milk cartons, etc.) for transport to one of these disposal sites. Don't dispose of the oil by pouring it on the ground or down a drain!

7   Windshield wiper blade inspection and replacement (every 6000 miles or 6 months)

Refer to illustrations 7.4a, 7.4b, 7.4c, 7.4d and 7.4e

1   The windshield wiper and blade assembly should be inspected periodically for damage, loose components and cracked or worn blade elements.

2   Road film can build up on the wiper blades and affect their efficiency, so they should be washed regularly with a mild detergent solution.
3   If the wiper blade elements are cracked, worn or warped, or no longer clean adequately, they should be replaced with new ones.
4   Lift the arm assembly away from the glass for clearance, then detach the blade from the arm **(see illustrations).**
5   Attach the new wiper to the arm. Connection can be confirmed by an audible click.

8   Battery check, maintenance and charging (every 6000 miles or 6 months)

Refer to illustrations 8.1, 8.5, 8.6a, 8.6b, 8.7a and 8.7b

Warning: *Certain precautions must be followed when checking and servicing the bat-*

tery. Hydrogen gas, which is highly flammable, is always present in the battery cells, so keep lighted tobacco and all other open flames and sparks away from the battery. The electrolyte inside the battery is actually dilute sulfuric acid, which will cause injury if splashed on your skin or in your eyes. It will also ruin clothes and painted surfaces. When removing the battery cables, always detach the negative cable first and hook it up last!
1   A routine preventive maintenance program for the battery in your vehicle is the only way to ensure quick and reliable starts. But before performing any battery maintenance, make sure that you have the proper equipment necessary to work safely around the battery **(see illustration).**
2   There are also several precautions that should be taken whenever battery maintenance is performed. Before servicing the battery, always turn the engine and all accessories off and disconnect the cable from the negative terminal of the battery.

8.1 Tools and materials required for battery maintenance

1   **Face shield/safety goggles** - *When removing corrosion with a brush, the acidic particles can easily fly up into your eyes*
2   **Baking soda** - *A solution of baking soda and water can be used to neutralize corrosion*
3   **Petroleum jelly** - *A layer of this on the battery posts will help prevent corrosion*
4   **Battery post/cable cleaner** - *This wire brush cleaning tool will remove all traces of corrosion from the battery posts and cable clamps*
5   *Treated felt washers* - *Placing one of these on each post, directly under the cable clamps, will help prevent corrosion*
6   **Puller** - *Sometimes the cable clamps are very difficult to pull off the posts, even after the nut/bolt has been completely loosened. This tool pulls the clamp straight up and off the post without damage*
7   **Battery post/cable cleaner** - *Here is another cleaning tool which is a slightly different version of number 4 above, but it does the same thing*
8   **Rubber gloves** - *Another safety item to consider when servicing the battery; remember that's acid inside the battery!*

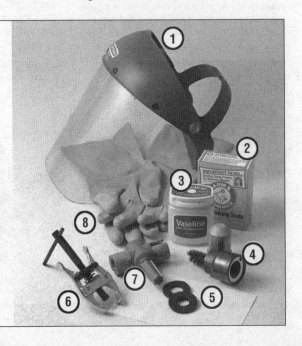

Terminal end corrosion or damage.

Insulation cracks.

Chafed insulation or exposed wires.

Burned or melted insulation.

8.5 Typical battery cable problems

3   The battery produces hydrogen gas, which is both flammable and explosive. Never create a spark, smoke or light a match around the battery. Always charge the battery in a ventilated area.

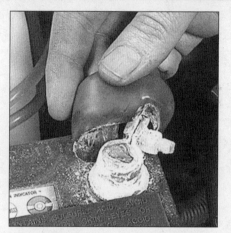

8.6a Battery terminal corrosion usually appears as light, fluffy powder

4   Electrolyte contains poisonous and corrosive sulfuric acid. Do not allow it to get in your eyes, on your skin or on your clothes. Never ingest it. Wear protective safety glasses when working near the battery. Keep children away from the battery.

5   Note the external condition of the battery. If the positive terminal and cable clamp on your vehicle's battery is equipped with a rubber protector, make sure that it's not torn or damaged. It should completely cover the terminal. Look for any corroded or loose connections, cracks in the case or cover or loose hold-down clamps. Also check the entire length of each cable for cracks and frayed conductors **(see illustration)**.

6   If corrosion, which looks like white, fluffy deposits is evident, particularly around the terminals, the battery should be removed for cleaning **(see illustration)**. Loosen the cable bolts with a wrench, being careful to remove the ground cable first, and slide them off the terminals **(see illustration)**. Then disconnect the hold-down clamp bolt and nut, remove the clamp and lift the battery from the engine compartment.

8.6b Removing a cable from the battery post with a wrench - sometimes a pair of special battery pliers are required for this procedure if corrosion has caused deterioration of the nut hex (always remove the ground (-) cable first and hook it up last!)

7   Clean the cable ends thoroughly with a battery brush or a terminal cleaner and a solution of warm water and baking soda. Wash the terminals and the side of the battery case with the same solution but make sure that the solution doesn't get into the battery. When cleaning the cables, terminals and battery case, wear safety goggles and rubber gloves to prevent any solution from coming in contact with your eyes or hands. Wear old clothes too - even diluted, sulfuric acid splashed onto clothes will burn holes in them. If the terminals have been corroded, clean them up with a terminal cleaner **(see illustrations)**. Thoroughly wash all cleaned areas with plain water.

8   Make sure that the battery tray is in good condition and the hold-down clamp bolts are tight. If the battery is removed from the tray, make sure no parts remain in the bottom of the tray when the battery is reinstalled. When reinstalling the hold-down clamp bolts, do not overtighten them.

8.7a When cleaning the cable clamps, all corrosion must be removed

8.7b Regardless of the type of tool used to clean the battery posts, a clean, shiny surface should be the result

9   Any metal parts of the vehicle damaged by corrosion should be covered with a zinc-based primer, then painted.

10   Information on removing and installing the battery can be found in Chapter 5. Information on jump starting can be found at the front of this manual. For more detailed battery checking procedures, refer to the *Haynes Automotive Electrical Manual.*

Charging

Warning: *When batteries are being charged, hydrogen gas, which is very explosive and flammable, is produced. Do not smoke or allow open flames near a charging or a recently charged battery. Wear eye protection when near the battery during charging. Also, make sure the charger is unplugged before connecting or disconnecting the battery from the charger.*

Note: *The manufacturer recommends the battery be removed from the vehicle for charging because the gas that escapes during this procedure can damage the paint. Fast charging with the battery cables connected can result in damage to the electrical system.*

11   Slow-rate charging is the best way to restore a battery that's discharged to the point where it will not start the engine. It's also a good way to maintain the battery charge in a vehicle that's only driven a few miles between starts. Maintaining the battery charge is particularly important in the winter when the battery must work harder to start the engine and electrical accessories that drain the battery are in greater use.

12   It's best to use a one or two-amp battery charger (sometimes called a trickle charger). They are the safest and put the least strain on the battery. They are also the least expensive. For a faster charge, you can use a higher amperage charger, but don't use one rated more than 1/10th the amp/hour rating of the battery. Rapid boost charges that claim to restore the power of the battery in one to two hours are hardest on the battery and can damage batteries not in good condition. This type of charging should only be used in emergency situations.

13   The average time necessary to charge a battery should be listed in the instructions that come with the charger. As a general rule, a trickle charger will charge a battery in 12 to 16 hours.

14   Remove all the cell caps (if equipped) and cover the holes with a clean cloth to prevent spattering electrolyte. Disconnect the negative battery cable and hook the battery charger cable clamps up to the battery posts (positive to positive, negative to negative), then plug in the charger. Make sure it is set at 12-volts if it has a selector switch.

15   If you're using a charger with a rate higher than two amps, check the battery regularly during charging to make sure it doesn't overheat. If you're using a trickle charger, you can safely let the battery charge overnight after you've checked it regularly for the first couple of hours.

16   If the battery has removable cell caps, measure the specific gravity with a hydrometer every hour during the last few hours of the charging cycle. Hydrometers are available inexpensively from auto parts stores - follow the instructions that come with the hydrometer. Consider the battery charged when there's no change in the specific gravity reading for two hours and the electrolyte in the cells is gassing (bubbling) freely. The specific gravity reading from each cell should be very close to the others. If not, the battery probably has a bad cell(s).

17   Some batteries with sealed tops have built-in hydrometers on the top that indicate the state of charge by the color displayed in the hydrometer window. Normally, a bright-colored hydrometer indicates a full charge and a dark hydrometer indicates the battery still needs charging.

18   If the battery has a sealed top and no built-in hydrometer, you can hook up a digital voltmeter across the battery terminals to check the charge. A fully charged battery should read 12.5 volts or higher.

19   Further information on the battery and jump-starting can be found in Chapter 5 and at the front of this manual.

9   Cooling system check (every 6000 miles or 6 months)

Refer to illustration 9.4

1   Many major engine failures can be caused by a faulty cooling system.

2   The engine must be cold for the cooling system check, so perform the following procedure before the vehicle is driven for the day or after it has been shut off for at least three hours.

3   Remove the pressure relief cap. Clean the cap thoroughly, inside and out, with clean water. The presence of rust or corrosion in the expansion tank means the coolant should be changed (see Section 24). The coolant inside the expansion tank should be relatively clean and transparent. If it's rust colored, drain the system and refill it with new coolant.

4   Carefully check the radiator hoses and the smaller diameter heater hoses (see illustrations in Chapter 3). Inspect each coolant hose along its entire length, replacing any hose which is cracked, swollen or deteriorated **(see illustration)**. Cracks will show up better if the hose is squeezed. Pay close attention to hose clamps that secure the hoses to cooling system components. Hose clamps can pinch and puncture hoses, resulting in coolant leaks.

5   Make sure that all hose connections are tight. A leak in the cooling system will usually show up as white or rust colored deposits on the area adjoining the leak. If wire-type clamps are used on the hoses, it may be a good idea to replace them with screw-type clamps.

6   Clean the front of the radiator and air conditioning condenser with compressed air, if available, or a soft brush. Remove all bugs,

Check for a chafed area that could fail prematurely.

Check for a soft area indicating the hose has deteriorated inside.

Overtightening the clamp on a hardened hose will damage the hose and cause a leak.

Check each hose for swelling and oil-soaked ends. Cracks and breaks can be located by squeezing the hose.

9.4 Hoses, like drivebelts, have a habit of failing at the worst possible time - to prevent the inconvenience of a blown radiator or heater hose, inspect them carefully as shown here

leaves, etc. embedded in the radiator fins. Be extremely careful not to damage the cooling fins or cut your fingers on them.

7   If the coolant level has been dropping consistently and no leaks are detectable, have the pressure cap and cooling system pressure checked at a service station.

10   Tire rotation (every 6000 miles or 6 months)

Refer to illustration 10.2

Note: *On vehicles with a Tire Pressure Monitoring system, after rotating the tires, the TPM system must re-learn the tire positions.*

1   The tires should be rotated at the specified intervals and whenever uneven wear is noticed. Since the vehicle will be raised and the tires removed anyway, check the brakes also (see Section 12).

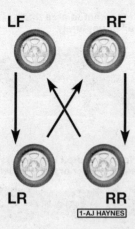

10.2 Four-tire rotation pattern

2   Radial tires must be rotated in a specific pattern **(see illustration)**. If your vehicle has a compact spare tire, don't include it in the rotation pattern.

3   Refer to the information in *Jacking and towing* at the front of this manual for the proper procedure to follow when raising the vehicle and changing a tire. If the brakes must be checked, don't apply the parking brake as stated.

4   The vehicle must be raised on a hoist or supported on jackstands to get all four wheels off the ground. Make sure the vehicle is safely supported!

5   After the rotation procedure is finished, check and adjust the tire pressures as necessary and be sure to check the lug nut tightness.

Tire pressure sensor position re-learn

Refer to illustration 10.7

6   Set the parking brake, then turn the ignition switch to the RUN position.

7   Using the Driver's Information Center, press the info button until it displays "Learn Tire Positions" **(see illustration)**.

8   Press the set/reset button until the TIRE LEARNING ACTIVE message displays, the horn will sound twice to indicate the system is ready **(see illustration 6.19)**.

9   Starting with the left front tire, remove the valve cap and using a valve stem core tool, decrease the tire's air pressure for five seconds **(see illustration 5.4a)**. A horn chirp will confirm the sensor has been matched to the tire position. **Note:** *The horn chirp may take up to 30 seconds to sound.*

10   Proceed to the right front tire, right rear tire and left rear tire, in that order, and perform the same procedure in Step 9. **Note:** *You only have two minutes per tire to match the tire sensor position, if it takes any longer, the matching process stops and you will need to start the process over.*

11   After the position re-learn procedure is finished, check and adjust the tire pressures.

11   Seat belt check (every 6000 miles or 6 months)

1   Check seat belts, buckles, latch plates and guide loops for obvious damage and signs of wear.

2   See if the seat belt reminder light comes on when the key is turned to the Run or Start position. A chime should also sound.

3   The seat belts are designed to lock up during a sudden stop or impact, yet allow free movement during normal driving. Make sure the retractors return the belt against your chest while driving and rewind the belt fully when the buckle is unlatched.

4   If any of the above checks reveal problems with the seat belt system, replace parts as necessary.

12   Brake check (every 6000 miles or 6 months)

Warning: *The dust created by the brake system is harmful to your health. Never blow it out with compressed air and don't inhale any of it. An approved filtering mask should be worn when working on the brakes. Do not, under any circumstances, use petroleum-based solvents to clean brake parts. Use brake system cleaner only!*
Note: *For detailed photographs of the brake system, refer to Chapter 9.*

1   In addition to the specified intervals, the brakes should be inspected every time the wheels are removed or whenever a defect is suspected.

2   Any of the following symptoms could indicate a potential brake system defect: The vehicle pulls to one side when the brake pedal is depressed; the brakes make squealing or dragging noises when applied; brake pedal travel is excessive; the pedal pulsates; or brake fluid leaks, usually onto the inside of the tire or wheel.

Disc brakes

Refer to illustration 12.6

3   Disc brakes can be visually checked without removing any parts except the wheels. Remove the hub caps (if applicable) and loosen the wheel lug nuts a quarter turn each.

4   Raise the vehicle and place it securely on jackstands. **Warning:** *Never work under a vehicle that is supported only by a jack!*

5   Remove the wheels. Now visible is the disc brake caliper which contains the pads. There is an outer brake pad and an inner pad. Both must be checked for wear.

6   Measure the thickness of the outer pad at each end of the caliper and the inner pad through the inspection hole in the caliper body **(see illustration)**. Compare the measure-

10.7 Press the info button (A) until it displays "Learn Tire Positions" (B)

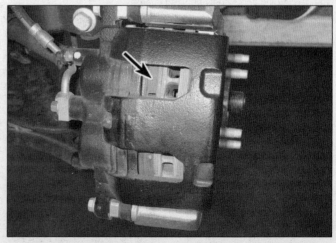

12.6 You will find an inspection hole like this in each caliper through which you can view the thickness of remaining friction material for the inner pad

ment with the limit given in this Chapter's Specifications; if any brake pad thickness is less than specified, then all brake pads must be replaced (see Chapter 9).

7   If you're in doubt as to the exact pad thickness or quality, remove them for measurement and further inspection (see Chapter 9).

8   Check the disc for score marks, wear and burned spots. If any of these conditions exist, the disc should be removed for servicing or replacement (see Chapter 9).

9   Before installing the wheels, check all the brake lines and hoses for damage, wear, deformation, cracks, corrosion, leakage, bends and twists, particularly in the vicinity of the rubber hoses and calipers.

10   Install the wheels, lower the vehicle and tighten the wheel lug nuts to the torque given in this Chapter's Specifications.

Brake booster check

11   Sit in the driver's seat and perform the following sequence of tests.

12   With the brake fully depressed, start the engine - the pedal should move down a little when the engine starts.

13   With the engine running, depress the brake pedal several times - the travel distance should not change.

14   Depress the brake, stop the engine and hold the pedal in for about 30 seconds - the pedal should neither sink nor rise.

15   Restart the engine, run it for about a minute and turn it off. Then, firmly depress the brake several times - the pedal travel should decrease with each application.

16   If your brakes do not operate as described, the brake booster has failed. Refer to Chapter 9 for the replacement procedure.

13   Underhood hose check and replacement (every 15,000 miles or 12 months)

Warning: *Replacement of air conditioning hoses must be left to a dealer service department or air conditioning shop that has the equipment to depressurize the system safely. Never remove air conditioning components or hoses until the system has been depressurized.*

General

1   High temperatures under the hood can cause deterioration of the rubber and plastic hoses used for engine, accessory and emission systems operation. Periodic inspection should be made for cracks, loose clamps, material hardening and leaks.

2   Information specific to the cooling system hoses can be found in Section 9.

3   Most (but not all) hoses are secured to the fittings with clamps. Where clamps are used, check to be sure they haven't lost their tension, allowing the hose to leak. If clamps aren't used, make sure the hose has not

expanded and/or hardened where it slips over the fitting, allowing it to leak.

PCV system hose

4   To reduce hydrocarbon emissions, crankcase blow-by gas is vented through the PCV valve in the rocker arm cover to the intake manifold via a rubber hose on most models. The blow-by gases mix with incoming air in the intake manifold before being burned in the combustion chambers.

5   Check the PCV hose for cracks, leaks and other damage. Disconnect it from the valve cover and the intake manifold and check the inside for obstructions. If it's clogged, clean it out with solvent.

Vacuum hoses

6   It's quite common for vacuum hoses, especially those in the emissions system, to be color coded or identified by colored stripes molded into them. Various systems require hoses with different wall thickness, collapse resistance and temperature resistance. When replacing hoses, be sure the new ones are made of the same material.

7   Often the only effective way to check a hose is to remove it completely from the vehicle. If more than one hose is removed, be sure to label the hoses and fittings to ensure correct installation.

8   When checking vacuum hoses, be sure to include any plastic T-fittings in the check. Inspect the fittings for cracks and check the hose, where it fits over each fitting, for distortion, which could cause leakage.

9   A small piece of vacuum hose (1/4-inch inside diameter) can be used as a stethoscope to detect vacuum leaks. Hold one end of the hose to your ear and probe around vacuum hoses and fittings, listening for the hissing sound characteristic of a vacuum leak. **Warning:** *When probing with the vacuum hose stethoscope, be careful not to come into contact with moving engine components such as drivebelts, the cooling fan, etc.*

Fuel hose

Warning: *Gasoline is flammable, so take extra precautions when you work on any part of the fuel system. Don't smoke or allow open flames or bare light bulbs near the work area, and don't work in a garage where a gas-type appliance (such as a water heater or clothes dryer) is present. Since fuel is carcinogenic, wear fuel-resistant gloves when there's a possibility of being exposed to fuel, and, if you spill any fuel on your skin, rinse it off immediately with soap and water. Mop up any spills immediately and do not store fuel-soaked rags where they could ignite. The fuel system is under constant pressure, so, if any fuel lines are to be disconnected, the fuel pressure in the system must be relieved first (see Chapter 4 for more information). When you perform any kind of work on the fuel system, wear safety glasses and have a Class B type fire extinguisher on hand.*

10   The fuel lines are usually under pressure,

so if any fuel lines are to be disconnected be prepared to catch spilled fuel. **Warning:** *Your vehicle is equipped with fuel injection and you must relieve the fuel system pressure before servicing the fuel lines. Refer to Chapter 4 for the fuel system pressure relief procedure.*

11   Check all flexible fuel lines for deterioration and chafing. Check especially for cracks in areas where the hose bends and just before fittings, such as where a hose attaches to the fuel pump, fuel filter and fuel injection unit.

12   When replacing a hose, use only hose that is specifically designed for your fuel injection system.

13   Spring-type clamps are sometimes used on fuel return or vapor lines. These clamps often lose their tension over a period of time, and can be sprung during removal. Replace all spring-type clamps with screw clamps whenever a hose is replaced. Some fuel lines use spring-lock type couplings, which require a special tool to disconnect. See Chapter 4 for more information on this type of coupling.

Metal lines

14   Sections of metal line are often used for fuel line between the fuel pump and the fuel injection unit. Check carefully to make sure the line isn't bent, crimped or cracked.

15   If a section of metal fuel line must be replaced, use seamless steel tubing only, since copper and aluminum tubing do not have the strength necessary to withstand vibration caused by the engine.

16   Check the metal brake lines where they enter the master cylinder and brake proportioning unit (if used) for cracks in the lines and loose fittings. Any sign of brake fluid leakage calls for an immediate thorough inspection of the brake system.

14   Steering and suspension check (every 15,000 miles or 12 months)

Note: *For detailed illustrations of the steering and suspension components, refer to Chapter 10.*

With the wheels on the ground

Refer to illustration 14.4

1   With the vehicle stopped and the front wheels pointed straight ahead, rock the steering wheel gently back and forth. If freeplay is excessive, a front wheel bearing, steering shaft universal joint or lower arm balljoint is worn or the steering gear is out of adjustment or broken. Refer to Chapter 10 for the appropriate repair procedure.

2   Other symptoms, such as excessive vehicle body movement over rough roads, swaying (leaning) around corners and binding as the steering wheel is turned, may indicate faulty steering and/or suspension components.

3   Check the shock absorbers by pushing down and releasing the vehicle several times at each corner. If the vehicle does not come back to a level position within one or two

14.4 Check the shocks for leakage at the indicated area

14.10 To check a balljoint for wear, try to pry the control arm up and down to make sure there is no play in the balljoint (if there is, replace it)

bounces, the shocks/struts are worn and must be replaced. When bouncing the vehicle up and down, listen for squeaks and noises from the suspension components.

4   Check the struts and shock absorbers for evidence of fluid leakage **(see illustration)**. A light film of fluid is no cause for concern. Make sure that any fluid noted is from the struts/shocks and not from some other source. If leakage is noted, replace the struts/shocks as a set.

5   Check the struts and shocks to be sure they are securely mounted and undamaged. Check the upper mounts for damage and wear. If damage or wear is noted, replace the shocks as a set (front and rear).

6   If the shocks must be replaced, refer to Chapter 10 for the procedure.

Under the vehicle

Refer to illustrations 14.10 and 14.11

7   Raise the vehicle with a floor jack and support it securely on jackstands. See *Jacking and towing* at the front of this book for the proper jacking points.

8   Check the tires for irregular wear patterns and proper inflation. See Section 5 in this Chapter for information regarding tire wear and Chapter 10 for information on wheel bearing replacement.

9   Inspect the universal joint between the steering shaft and the steering gear housing. Check the steering gear housing for lubricant leakage. Make sure that the dust seals and boots are not damaged and that the boot clamps are not loose. Check the steering linkage for looseness or damage. Check the tie-rod ends for excessive play. Look for loose bolts, broken or disconnected parts and deteriorated rubber bushings on all suspension and steering components. While an assistant turns the steering wheel from side to side, check the steering components for free movement, chafing and binding. If the steering components do not seem to be reacting with the movement of the steering wheel, try to determine where the slack is located.

10   Check the balljoints for wear by trying to move each control arm up and down with a prybar **(see illustration)** to ensure that

its balljoint has no play. If any balljoint does have play, replace it. See Chapter 10 for the balljoint replacement procedure.

11   Inspect the balljoint boots for damage and leaking grease **(see illustration)**. Replace the balljoints with new ones if they are damaged (see Chapter 10).

12   At the rear of the vehicle, inspect the suspension arm bushings for deterioration. Additional information on suspension components can be found in Chapter 10.

15   Driveaxle boot check (every 15,000 miles or 12 months)

Refer to illustration 15.2

Note: *For detailed illustrations of the driveaxles, refer to Chapter 8.*

1   The driveaxle boots are very important because they prevent dirt, water and foreign material from entering and damaging the constant velocity (CV) joints. Oil and grease can cause the boot material to deteriorate prematurely, so it's a good idea to wash the boots with soap and water. Because it constantly pivots back and forth following the steering action of the front hub, the outer CV boot wears out sooner and should be inspected.

2   Inspect the boots for tears and cracks as well as loose clamps **(see illustration)**. If there is any evidence of cracks or leaking lubricant, they must be replaced as described in Chapter 8.

16   Exhaust system check (every 15,000 miles or 12 months)

Refer to illustration 16.2

1   With the engine cold (at least three hours after the vehicle has been driven), check the complete exhaust system from the engine to

14.11 Check the balljoint boot for damage

15.2 Flex the driveaxle boots by hand to check for cracks and/or leaking grease

16.2 Be sure to check each exhaust system rubber hanger for damage

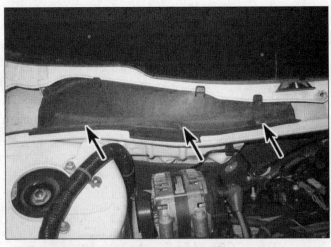

18.2 Remove the fasteners securing the filter cover and remove the cover

the end of the tailpipe. Ideally, the inspection should be done with the vehicle on a hoist to permit unrestricted access. If a hoist isn't available, raise the vehicle and support it securely on jackstands.

2   Check the exhaust pipes and connections for evidence of leaks, severe corrosion and damage. Make sure that all brackets and hangers are in good condition and tight **(see illustration).**

3   At the same time, inspect the underside of the body for holes, corrosion, open seams, etc. which may allow exhaust gases to enter the passenger compartment. Seal all body openings with silicone or body putty.

4   Rattles and other noises can often be traced to the exhaust system, especially the mounts and hangers. Try to move the pipes, muffler and catalytic converter. If the components can come in contact with the body or suspension parts, secure the exhaust system with new mounts.

5   Check the running condition of the engine by inspecting inside the end of the tailpipe. The exhaust deposits here are an indication of engine state-of-tune. If the pipe is black and sooty or coated with white deposits, the engine may need a tune-up, including a thorough fuel system inspection.

17 Fuel system check (every 15,000 miles or 12 months)

Warning: *Gasoline is flammable, so take extra precautions when you work on any part of the fuel system. Don't smoke or allow open flames or bare light bulbs near the work area, and don't work in a garage where a gas-type appliance (such as a water heater or clothes dryer) is present. Since fuel is carcinogenic, wear fuel-resistant gloves when there's a possibility of being exposed to fuel, and, if you spill any fuel on your skin, rinse it off immediately with soap and water. Mop up any spills immediately and do not store fuel-soaked*

rags where they could ignite. When you perform any kind of work on the fuel system, wear safety glasses and have a Class B type fire extinguisher on hand. The fuel system is under constant pressure, so, before any lines are disconnected, the fuel system pressure must be relieved (see Chapter 4).

1   If you smell gasoline while driving or after the vehicle has been sitting in the sun, inspect the fuel system immediately.

2   Remove the fuel filler cap and inspect if for damage and corrosion. The gasket should have an unbroken sealing imprint. If the gasket is damaged or corroded, install a new cap.

3   Inspect the fuel feed line for cracks. Make sure that the connections between the fuel lines and the fuel injection system and between the fuel lines and the in-line fuel filter are tight. **Warning:** *Your vehicle is fuel injected, so you must relieve the fuel system pressure before servicing fuel system components. The fuel system pressure relief procedure is outlined in Chapter 4.*

4   Since some components of the fuel system - the fuel tank and part of the fuel feed line, for example - are underneath the vehicle, they can be inspected more easily with the vehicle raised on a hoist. If that's not possible, raise the vehicle and support it on jackstands.

5   With the vehicle raised and safely supported, inspect the gas tank and filler neck for punctures, cracks and other damage. The connection between the filler neck and the tank is particularly critical. Sometimes a rubber filler neck will leak because of loose clamps or deteriorated rubber. Inspect all fuel tank mounting brackets and straps to be sure that the tank is securely attached to the vehicle. **Warning:** *Do not, under any circumstances, try to repair a fuel tank (except rubber components). A welding torch or any open flame can easily cause fuel vapors inside the tank to explode.*

6   Carefully check all rubber hoses and metal lines leading away from the fuel tank.

Check for loose connections, deteriorated hoses, crimped lines and other damage. Repair or replace damaged sections as necessary (see Chapter 4).

18 Interior ventilation filter replacement (every 15,000 miles or 12 months)

Refer to illustrations 18.2 and 18.3

1   Remove the cowl cover (see Chapter 11).

2   Remove the filter cover **(see illustration).**

3   Pull the filter out of the case **(see illustration).**

4   Installation is the reverse of removal.

19 Drivebelt check and replacement (every 15,000 miles or 12 months)

1   A single serpentine drivebelt is located at the front of the engine and plays an important

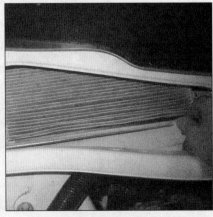

18.3 Pull the tab and lift the filter straight out

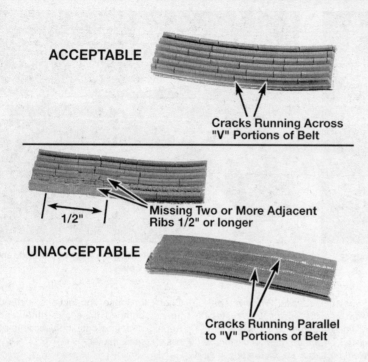

ACCEPTABLE

Cracks Running Across
"V" Portions of Belt

1/2"

Missing Two or More Adjacent
Ribs 1/2" or longer

UNACCEPTABLE

Cracks Running Parallel
to "V" Portions of Belt

19.3 Here are some of the more common problems associated with drivebelts (check the belts very carefully to prevent an untimely breakdown)

role in the overall operation of the engine and its components. Due to its function and material make up, the belt is prone to wear and should be periodically inspected. The serpentine belt drives the alternator and air conditioning compressor. Although the belt should be inspected at the recommended intervals, replacement may not be necessary for more than 100,000 miles.

Check

Refer to illustration 19.3

2   With the engine stopped, inspect the full length of the drivebelt for cracks and separa-

tion of the belt plies. It will be necessary to turn the engine (using a wrench or socket and bar on the crankshaft pulley bolt) in order to move the belt from the pulleys so that the belt can be inspected thoroughly. Twist the belt between the pulleys so that both sides can be viewed. Also check for fraying, and glazing which gives the belt a shiny appearance. Check the pulleys for nicks, cracks, distortion and corrosion.

3   Note that it is not unusual for a ribbed belt to exhibit small cracks in the edges of the belt ribs, and unless these are extensive or very deep, belt replacement is not essential **(see illustration).**

Replacement

Refer to illustrations 19.5a and 19.5b

Note: *If you're working on a V8 model, to perform this procedure, you will need a special tool (EN-47988) to release the drivebelt tension.*

4   Disconnect the cable from the negative terminal of the battery (see Chapter 5, Section 1).

5   On V6 models, remove the air filter housing (see Chapter 4), and the engine cover. If you're working on a V8 engine, remove the passenger side diagonal brace **(see illustration).** If necessary, unbolt the underhood fuse box and set it out of the way **(see illustration).**

6   If you're working on a V8 engine, insert special tool (EN-47988) into the tensioner hole and pull the handle clockwise to release the drivebelt tension.

7   On V6 models, insert a 3/8-inch drive ratchet or breaker bar into the tensioner hole and pull the handle clockwise to release the drivebelt tension. Note how the drivebelt is routed, then remove the belt from the pulleys.

8   Fit the new drivebelt onto the crankshaft, alternator, power steering pump, and air conditioning compressor pulleys, as applicable, then turn the release the tensioner and locate the drivebelt on the pulley. Make sure that the drivebelt is correctly seated in all of the pulley grooves, then release the tensioner.

9   Installation is the reverse of removal.

20   Air filter check and replacement (every 30,000 miles or 24 months)

Refer to illustrations 20.1a and 20.1b

1   The air filter is located inside a housing at the left (driver's) side of the engine compartment. To remove the air filter, loosen the clamp securing the inlet tube to the air filter cover, unlatch the clamps that secure the two halves of the air cleaner housing together, then separate the cover halves and remove the air filter element **(see illustrations).**

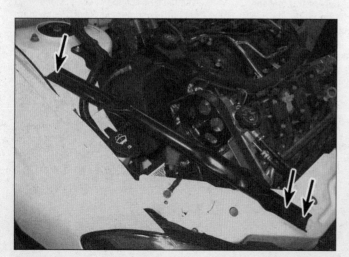

19.5a Remove the fasteners securing the diagonal brace

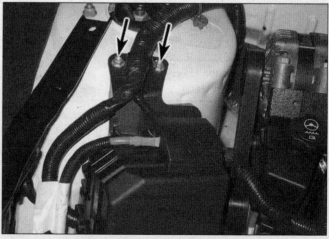

19.5b Remove the fasteners securing the underhood fuse box and move it out of the way

20.1a Loosen the intake hose clamp (A), disconnect the electrical connector (B), unlatch the clamps (C) . . .

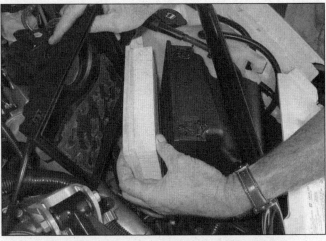

20.1b . . . pull the cover out of the way and lift the element out

2   Inspect the outer surface of the filter element. If it is dirty, replace it. If it is only moderately dusty, it can be reused by blowing it clean from the back to the front surface with compressed air. Because it is a pleated paper type filter, it cannot be washed or oiled. If it cannot be cleaned satisfactorily with compressed air, discard and replace it. While the cover is off, be careful not to drop anything down into the housing. **Caution:** *Never drive the vehicle with the air cleaner removed. Excessive engine wear could result and backfiring could even cause a fire under the hood.*

3   Wipe out the inside of the air cleaner housing.

4   Place the new filter into the air cleaner housing, making sure it seats properly.

5   Installation of the housing is the reverse of removal.

21   Brake fluid change (every 30,000 miles or 24 months)

Warning: *Brake fluid can harm your eyes and damage painted surfaces, so use extreme caution when handling or pouring it. Do not use brake fluid that has been standing open or is more than one year old. Brake fluid absorbs moisture from the air. Excess moisture can cause a dangerous loss of braking effectiveness.*

1   At the specified intervals, the brake fluid should be drained and replaced. Since the brake fluid may drip or splash when pouring it, place plenty of rags around the master cylinder to protect any surrounding painted surfaces.

2   Before beginning work, purchase the specified brake fluid (see *Recommended lubricants and fluids* at the beginning of this Chapter).

3   Remove the cap from the master cylinder reservoir.

4   Using a hand-held suction pump or simi-

lar device, withdraw the fluid from the master cylinder reservoir.

5   Add new fluid to the master cylinder until it rises to the base of the filler neck.

6   Bleed the brake system as described in Chapter 9 at all four brakes until new and uncontaminated fluid is expelled from the bleeder screw. Be sure to maintain the fluid level in the master cylinder as you perform the bleeding process. If you allow the master cylinder to run dry, air will enter the system.

7   Refill the master cylinder with fluid and check the operation of the brakes. The pedal should feel solid when depressed, with no sponginess. **Warning:** *Do not operate the vehicle if you are in doubt about the effectiveness of the brake system.*

22   Spark plug check and replacement (see Maintenance schedule for service intervals)

Refer to illustrations 22.2, 22.5a, 22.5b, 22.6, 22.7, 22.9 and 22.11

1   The spark plugs are located in the cylinder head(s).

2   In most cases, the tools necessary for spark plug replacement include a spark plug socket which fits onto a ratchet (spark plug sockets are padded inside to prevent damage to the porcelain insulators on the new plugs), various extensions and a gap gauge to check and adjust the gaps on the new plugs **(see illustration).** A torque wrench should be used to tighten the new plugs.

3   The best approach when replacing the spark plugs is to purchase the new ones in advance, adjust them to the proper gap and replace the plugs one at a time. When buying the new spark plugs, be sure to obtain the correct plug type for your particular engine. This information can be found in the Specifications Section at the beginning of this Chapter or in your owner's manual.

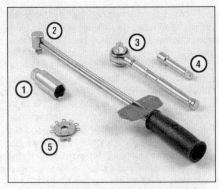

22.2 Tools required for changing spark plugs

1   *Spark plug socket - This will have special padding inside to protect the spark plug porcelain insulator*

2   *Torque wrench - Although not mandatory, use of this tool is the best way to ensure that the plugs are tightened properly*

3   *Ratchet - Standard hand tool to fit the plug socket*

4   *Extension - Depending on model and accessories, you may need special extensions and universal joints to reach one or more of the plugs*

5   *Spark plug gap gauge - This gauge for checking the gap comes in a variety of styles. Make sure the gap for your engine is included*

4   Allow the engine to cool completely before attempting to remove any of the plugs. These engines are equipped with aluminum cylinder heads, which can be damaged if the spark plugs are removed when the engine is hot. While you are waiting for the engine to cool, check the new plugs for defects and adjust the gaps.

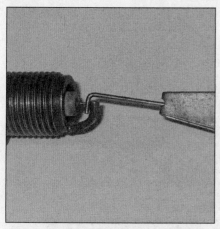

22.5a The manufacturer recommends using a wire-type thickness gauge when checking the gap - if the wire does not slide between the electrodes with a slight drag, adjustment is required

22.5b To change the gap, bend the side electrode only, and be very careful not to crack or chip the porcelain insulator surrounding the center electrode

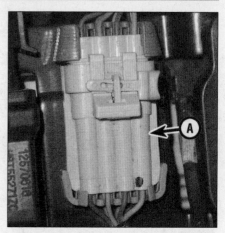

22.6 Disconnect the ignition coil main electrical connector (A), remove the spark plug wires from the coils, then remove the fasteners securing the ignition coil bracket and remove it from the valve cover

5   The gap is checked by inserting the proper-thickness gauge between the electrodes at the tip of the plug **(see illustration).** The gap between the electrodes should be the same as the one specified on the Vehicle Emissions Control Information label or in this Chapter's Specifications. The gauge should just slide between the electrodes with a slight amount of drag. If the gap is incorrect, use the adjuster on the gauge body to bend the curved side electrode slightly until the proper gap is obtained **(see illustration).** If the side electrode is not exactly over the center electrode, bend it with the adjuster until it is. Check for cracks in the porcelain insulator (if any are found, the plug should not be used). **Note:** *We recommend using a wire-type thickness gauge when checking platinum- or iridium-type spark plugs. Other types of gauges may scrape the thin coating from the electrodes, thus dramatically shortening the life of the plugs.*

6   Remove the engine cover. On V6 models remove the air intake duct (see Chapter 4). On V8 models, it may be necessary to remove the rear bank ignition coil mounting bracket **(see illustration),** for easier access to the rear spark plugs.

7   Remove the spark plug wire from one spark plug. Pull only on the boot at the end of the wire - do not pull on the wire. A plug wire removal tool should be used if available **(see illustration).**

8   If compressed air is available, use it to blow any dirt or foreign material away from the spark plug hole. The idea here is to eliminate the possibility of debris falling into the cylinder as the spark plug is removed.

9   Place the spark plug socket over the plug and remove it from the engine by turning it in a counterclockwise direction **(see illustration).**

10   Compare the spark plug to those shown in the photos located on the inside back cover

to get an indication of the general running condition of the engine.

11   Install one of the new plugs into the hole until you can no longer turn it with your fingers, then tighten it with a torque wrench (if available) or the ratchet. It is a good idea to slip a short length of rubber hose over the end of the plug to use as a tool to thread it into place **(see illustration).** The hose will grip the plug well enough to turn it, but will start to slip if the plug begins to cross-thread in the hole - this will prevent damaged threads and the accompanying repair costs.

12   Before pushing the spark plug wire onto the end of the plug, inspect it following the procedures outlined in Section 23.

13   Attach the plug wire to the new spark plug, again using a twisting motion on the boot until it's seated on the spark plug.

14   Repeat the procedure for the remaining spark plugs, replacing them one at a time to prevent mixing up the spark plug wires.

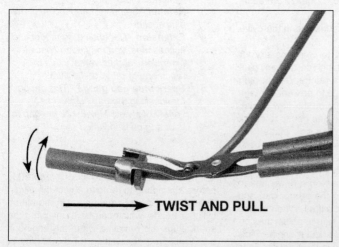

TWIST AND PULL

22.7 A tool like this one makes the job of removing the spark plug boot easier

22.9 Use a ratchet and extension to remove the spark plugs

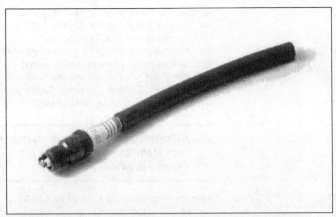

22.11 A length of snug-fitting rubber hose will save time and prevent damaged threads when installing the spark plugs

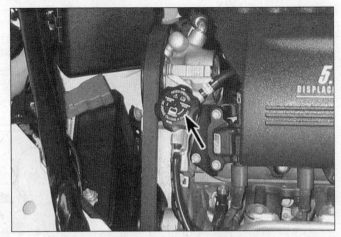

24.3 Cooling system pressure cap

23 Spark plug wire check and replacement (every 30,000 miles or 24 months)

1   The spark plug wires should be checked at the recommended intervals or whenever new spark plugs are installed.

2   Begin this procedure by making a visual check of the spark plug wires while the engine is running. In a darkened garage (make sure there is adequate ventilation) or at night, start the engine and observe each plug wire. Be careful not to come into contact with any moving engine parts. If possible, use an insulated or non-conductive object to wiggle each wire. If there is a break in the wire, you will see arcing or a small blue spark coming from the damaged area. Secondary ignition voltage increases with engine speed and sometimes a damaged wire will not produce an arc at idle speed. Have an assistant press the accelerator pedal to raise the engine speed to approximately 2000 rpm. Check the spark plug wires for arcing as stated previously. If arcing is noticed, replace all spark plug wires.

3   Disconnect the plug wire from one spark plug (with the engine Off). To do this, grab the rubber boot, twist slightly and pull the wire free. Do not pull on the wire itself, only on the rubber boot. A boot-pulling tool is helpful **(see illustration 22.7).**

4   Check inside the boot for corrosion, which will look like a white crusty powder. Push the wire and boot back onto the end of the spark plug. It should be a tight fit on the plug. If it isn't, remove the wire and use a pair of pliers to carefully crimp the metal connector inside the boot until it fits securely on the end of the spark plug.

5   Using a clean rag, wipe the entire length of the wire to remove any built-up dirt and grease. Once the wire is clean, check for holes, burned areas, cracks and other damage. Don't bend the wire excessively or the conductor inside might break.

6   Disconnect the wire from the ignition coil. Pull the wire straight out of the coil. Pull only on the rubber boot during removal. Check for corrosion and a tight fit in the same manner as the spark plug end. Reattach the wire to the individual coil.

7   Check the remaining spark plug wires one at a time, making sure they are securely fastened at both ends when the check is complete.

8   If new spark plug wires are required, purchase a new set for your specific engine model.

24 Cooling system servicing (draining, flushing and refilling) (every 100,000 miles)

Warning 1: *Wait until the engine is completely cool before beginning this procedure.*

Warning 2: *Do not allow antifreeze to come in contact with your skin or painted surfaces of the vehicle. Rinse off spills immediately with plenty of water. Antifreeze is highly toxic if ingested. Never leave antifreeze lying around in an open container or in puddles on the floor; children and pets are attracted by its sweet smell and may drink it. Check with local authorities on disposing of used antifreeze. Many communities have collection centers that will see that antifreeze is disposed of safely. Antifreeze is flammable under certain conditions - be sure to read the precautions on the container.*

Caution: *Never mix green-colored ethylene glycol antifreeze and orange-colored "DEX-COOL®" silicate-free coolant because doing so will destroy the efficiency of the "DEX-COOL®" coolant, which is designed to last for 100,000 miles or five years.*

Draining

Refer to illustration 24.3

1   Periodically, the cooling system should be drained, flushed and refilled to replenish the antifreeze mixture and prevent formation of rust and corrosion, which can impair the performance of the cooling system and cause engine damage. When the cooling system is serviced, all hoses and the radiator cap should be checked and replaced if necessary.

2   Apply the parking brake and block the wheels. **Warning:** *If the vehicle has just been driven, wait several hours to allow the engine to cool down before beginning this procedure.*

3   Move a large container under the radiator drain to catch the coolant. Open the drain valve - it's located on the lower right side of the radiator. Attach a drain hose to the drain fitting and direct it into the container, then open the drain fitting (a pair of pliers may be required to turn it). Remove the pressure cap **(see illustration).**

4   After coolant stops flowing out of the radiator, move the container under the engine block drain plugs - there's one on each side of the block. Remove the plugs and allow the coolant in the block to drain.

5   While the coolant is draining, check the condition of the radiator hoses, heater hoses and clamps (refer to Section 9 if necessary).

6   Replace any damaged clamps or hoses. Apply Teflon pipe sealant to the drain plugs, then reinstall the drain plugs and tighten them securely.

Flushing

Refer to illustration 24.9

7   Once the system is completely drained, remove the thermostat from the engine (see Chapter 3). Then reinstall the thermostat housing without the thermostat. This will allow the system to be thoroughly flushed.

8   Tighten the radiator drain plug. Turn your heating system controls to Hot, so that the heater core will be flushed at the same time as the rest of the cooling system.

9   Disconnect the upper radiator hose, then place a garden hose in the upper radiator inlet

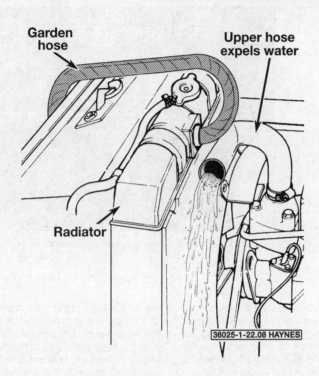

24.9 With the thermostat removed, disconnect the upper radiator hose and flush the radiator and engine block with a garden hose

and flush the system until the water runs clear at the upper radiator hose **(see illustration)**.

10   In severe cases of contamination or clogging of the radiator, remove the radiator (see Chapter 3) and have a radiator repair facility clean and repair it if necessary.

11   Many deposits can be removed by the chemical action of a cleaner available at auto parts stores. Follow the procedure outlined in the manufacturer's instructions. **Note:** *When the coolant is regularly drained and the system refilled with the correct antifreeze/water mixture, there should be no need to use chemical cleaners or descalers.*

Refilling

12   To refill the system, install the thermostat and reconnect any radiator hoses.

13   Place the heater temperature control(s) in the maximum heat position.

14   Be sure to use the proper coolant listed in this Chapter's Specifications. Slowly fill the radiator with the recommended mixture of antifreeze and water until the coolant level is up to 1/2-inch from the bottom of the filler neck. Add more coolant to the reservoir until it reaches the FULL COLD mark.

15   Run the engine until normal operating temperature is reached, then allow the engine

to cool. With the engine cool, add coolant as necessary to bring the level to the FULL COLD mark on the reservoir.

16   Keep a close watch on the coolant level and various cooling system hoses during the first few miles of driving and check for any coolant leaks. Tighten the hose clamps and add more coolant mixture as necessary.

25   Automatic transaxle fluid change (see Maintenance schedule for service intervals)

Refer to illustrations 25.5, 25.9a and 25.9b

1   At the specified time intervals, the transaxle fluid should be drained and replaced. Since the fluid will remain hot long after driving, perform this procedure only after everything has cooled down completely.

2   Before beginning work, purchase the specified transaxle fluid (see *Recommended lubricants and fluids* at the front of this Chapter) and a new filter.

3   Other tools necessary for this job include jackstands to support the vehicle in a raised position, a drain pan capable of holding several quarts, newspapers and clean rags.

4   Raise and support the vehicle on jackstands.

5   With a drain pan in place, loosen the bolts on the rear of the pan one turn **(see illustration)**.

6   Carefully pry the transaxle pan loose with a screwdriver, allowing the fluid to drain.

7   Remove the remaining bolts, pan and gasket. Carefully clean the gasket surface of the transaxle to remove all traces of the old gasket and sealant.

8   Drain the fluid from the transaxle pan, clean the pan with solvent and dry it with compressed air. Be careful not to lose the magnet.

9   Remove the filter and pry out the seal **(see illustrations)**.

10   Push a new filter seal fully into its bore, then install the new filter.

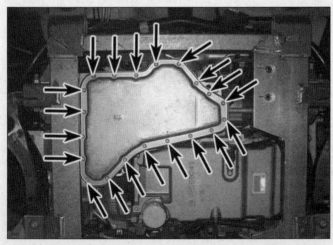

25.5 Automatic transaxle fluid pan mounting bolts

25.9a Pull the transaxle filter straight down and out of the transaxle - there are no fasteners

25.9b Pry out the old seal, being careful not to damage the aluminum housing

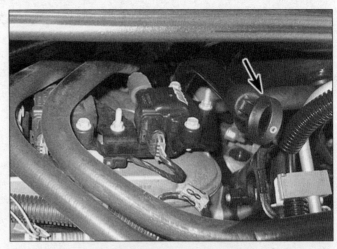

25.16 Transaxle fluid level dipstick

11   Make sure the gasket surface on the transaxle pan is clean, then install the new gasket. Put the pan in place against the transaxle and install the bolts. Working around the pan, tighten each bolt a little at a time until the final torque figure is reached.

12   Lower the vehicle and add the specified amount of automatic transmission fluid through the filler tube and check the fluid level (see below).

13   Check under the vehicle for leaks during the first few trips.

Fluid level check

Refer to illustration 25.16

14   The automatic transaxle fluid level should be carefully maintained. Low fluid level can lead to slipping or loss of drive, while overfill-

ing can cause foaming and loss of fluid.

15   With the parking brake set, start the engine, then move the shift lever through all the gear ranges, ending in Park. The fluid level must be checked with the vehicle level and the engine running at idle. **Note:** *Incorrect fluid level readings will result if the vehicle has just been driven at high speeds for an extended period, in hot weather in city traffic, or if it has been pulling a trailer. If any of these conditions apply, wait until the fluid has cooled (about 30 minutes).*

16   With the transaxle at normal operating temperature, remove the dipstick from the filler tube. The dipstick is located at the rear of the engine compartment on the driver's side **(see illustration).**

17   Wipe the fluid from the dipstick with a clean rag and push it back into the filler tube until the cap seats.

18   Pull the dipstick out again and note the fluid level.

19   If the fluid is hot, the level should be in the crosshatched area, near the MAX line. If additional fluid is required, add it directly into the tube using a funnel. It takes about one pint to raise the level from the bottom of the crosshatched area to the MAX line with a hot transaxle, so add the fluid a little at a time and keep checking the level until it's correct.

20   The condition of the fluid should also be checked along with the level. If the fluid at the end of the dipstick is a dark reddish-brown color, or if it smells burned, it should be changed. If you are in doubt about the condition of the fluid, purchase some new fluid and compare the two for color and smell.

Notes

Chapter 2 Part A
V6 engines

Contents

Specifications

General

Displacement
3.5L V6	214 cubic inches
3.9L V6	238 cubic inches

Bore and stroke
3.5L V6	
2004 through 2006	3.70 x 3.31 inches
2007 and later	3.90 x 2.99 inches
3.9L V6	3.90 x 3.31 inches

Cylinder numbers (drivebelt end-to-transaxle end)
Front bank (radiator side)	2-4-6
Rear bank	1-3-5
Firing order	1-2-3-4-5-6
Compression	See Chapter 2C
Oil pressure	See Chapter 2C

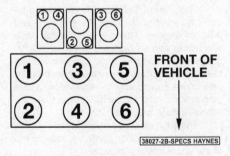

**Cylinder location and coil terminal
identification diagram**

FRONT OF VEHICLE

38027-2B-SPECS HAYNES

Camshaft

Bearing journal diameter	2.024 to 2.025 inches
Bearing oil clearance	0.003 to 0.005 inch
Lobe lift	0.273 inch

Torque specifications

Ft-lbs (unless otherwise indicated)

Note: *One foot-pound (ft-lb) of torque is equivalent to 12 inch-pounds (in-lbs) of torque. Torque values below approximately 15 foot-pounds are expressed in inch-pounds, because most foot-pound torque wrenches are not accurate at these smaller values.*

Camshaft sprocket/variable camshaft timing sprocket bolt(s)	144 in-lbs
Timing chain tensioner bolts	15
Catalytic converter-to-exhaust manifold flange nuts	23
Crankshaft balancer bolt	
Step 1	92
Step 2	Tighten an additional 130-degrees

Torque specifications (continued)

	Ft-lbs (unless otherwise indicated)
Cylinder head bolts (in sequence - **see illustration 8.16**)	
Step 1	44
Step 2	Rotate an additional 140-degrees
Coolant crossover pipe (3.9L and 2007 3.5L V6)	37
Driveplate-to-crankshaft bolts	52
Exhaust manifold retaining nuts/bolts	15
Exhaust heat shield bolts	89 in-lbs
Idler pulley (right and left side) bolts	22
Idler pulley (center) bolt	37
Intake manifold bolts (lower)	
Step 1	
Bolts 1 through 8	62 in-lbs
Step 2	
Bolts 1 through 4	115 in-lbs
Step 3	
Bolts 5 through 8	18
Intake manifold bolts (upper)	18
Oil pan bolts/nuts	
To block	18
Side bolts	37
Oil pump mounting bolt	30
Rocker arm bolts	25
Timing chain cover bolts	18
Timing chain tensioner plate bolts	15
Transaxle brace	37
Transaxle-to-oil pan brace bolts	
3.5L V6	37
3.9L V6	46
Valve cover-to-cylinder head bolts	89 in-lbs

1   General information

This Part of Chapter 2 is devoted to in-vehicle repair procedures for the 3.5L and 3.9L V6 engines. These engines utilize cast-iron blocks with six cylinders arranged in a "V" shape at a 60-degree angle between the two banks. The overhead valve aluminum cylinder heads are equipped with replaceable valve guides and seats. Hydraulic lifters actuate the valves through tubular pushrods.

The engines are easily identified by looking for the designations printed directly on top of the upper intake plenum.

Information concerning engine removal and installation and overhaul can be found in Part C of this Chapter. The following repair procedures are based on the assumption that the engine is installed in the vehicle. If the engine has been removed from the vehicle and mounted on a stand, many of the Steps outlined in this Part of Chapter 2 will not apply.

2   Repair operations possible with the engine in the vehicle

Many major repair operations can be accomplished without removing the engine from the vehicle.

Clean the engine compartment and the exterior of the engine with some type of degreaser before any work is done. It'll make the job easier and help keep dirt out of the internal areas of the engine.

Depending on the components involved, it may be helpful to remove the hood to improve access to the engine as repairs are performed (refer to Chapter 11 if necessary). Cover the fenders to prevent damage to the paint. Special pads are available, but an old bedspread or blanket will also work.

If vacuum, exhaust, oil or coolant leaks develop, indicating a need for gasket or seal replacement, the repairs can generally be done with the engine in the vehicle. The intake and exhaust manifold gaskets, timing chain cover gasket, oil pan gasket, crankshaft oil seals and cylinder head gaskets are all accessible with the engine in place.

Exterior engine components, such as the intake and exhaust manifolds, the oil pan (and the oil pump), the water pump, the starter motor, the alternator and the fuel system components can be removed for repair with the engine in place.

Since the cylinder heads can be removed without pulling the engine, valve component servicing can also be accomplished with the engine in the vehicle. Replacement of the timing chain and sprockets is also possible with the engine in the vehicle, although camshaft removal cannot be performed with the engine in the chassis (see Part C of this Chapter).

In extreme cases caused by a lack of necessary equipment, repair or replacement of piston rings, pistons, connecting rods and rod bearings is possible with the engine in the vehicle. However, this practice is not recommended because of the cleaning and preparation work that must be done to the components involved.

3   Top Dead Center (TDC) - locating

1   Top Dead Center (TDC) is the highest point in the cylinder that each piston reaches as it travels up-the cylinder bore. Each piston reaches TDC on the compression stroke and again on the exhaust stroke, but TDC generally refers to piston position on the compression stroke.

2   Positioning the piston(s) at TDC is an essential part of certain repair procedures discussed in this manual.

3   Before beginning this procedure, be sure to place the transmission in Park and apply the parking brake or block the rear wheels. Remove the spark plugs (see Chapter 1). Disable the ignition system by disconnecting the wiring harness connector from the ignition coil

pack (see Chapter 5). If in the next step you plan on using the starter motor to rotate the engine, disable the fuel pump by removing the fuel pump fuse (see Chapter 4, Section 2).

4   In order to bring any piston to TDC, the crankshaft must be turned using one of the methods outlined below. When looking at the front of the engine, normal crankshaft rotation is clockwise.

a) *The preferred method is to turn the crankshaft with a socket and ratchet attached to the bolt threaded into the front of the crankshaft. Turn the bolt in a clockwise direction only.*

b) *A remote starter switch, which may save some time, can also be used. Follow the instructions included with the switch. Once the piston is close to TDC, use a socket and ratchet as described in the previous paragraph.*

c) *If an assistant is available to turn the ignition switch to the Start position in short bursts, you can get the piston close to TDC without a remote starter switch. Make sure your assistant is out of the vehicle, away from the ignition switch, then use a socket and ratchet as described in Paragraph a) to complete the procedure.*

5   Install a compression gauge in the No. 1 spark plug hole. It should be a gauge with a screw-in type fitting and a hose at least six inches long.

6   Rotate the crankshaft using one of the methods described above while observing for pressure on the compression gauge. The moment the gauge shows pressure indicates that the No. 1 cylinder has begun the compression stroke.

7   Once the compression stroke has begun, TDC for the compression stroke is reached by bringing the piston to the top of the cylinder.

8   Continue turning the crankshaft until the TDC notch in the crankshaft damper is aligned with the TDC mark on the timing chain cover **(see illustration 9.9)**. At this point, the No. 1 cylinder is at TDC on the compression stroke. If the marks were aligned and there was no compression, the piston was on the exhaust stroke. Continue rotating the crankshaft 360 degrees (1-turn) and realign the marks. **Note:** *If a compression gauge is not available, you can simply place a blunt object over the spark plug hole and listen for compression as the engine is rotated. Once compression at the No. 1 spark plug hole is noted, the remainder of the Step is the same.*

9   After the No. 1 piston has been positioned at TDC on the compression stroke, TDC for any of the remaining pistons can be located by turning the crankshaft and following the firing order. Divide the crankshaft pulley into three equal sections with chalk marks at each point, each indicating 120 degrees of crankshaft rotation. Rotating the engine past TDC no. 1 to the next mark will place the engine at TDC for cylinder no. 2.

10   An even faster way to find TDC for any cylinder other than No. 1 is to make marks on

4.16 Loosen the valve cover mounting bolts (arrows indicate three) - the bolts will stay with the cover

the crankshaft damper in 120 degree intervals from the TDC mark on the damper. Install the compression gauge into the cylinder for which you want to find TDC, rotate the engine until compression begins to register on the compression gauge then continue turning the crankshaft until the next mark on the damper aligns with the mark on the timing chain cover.

---

4   Valve covers - removal and installation

Warning: *Wait until the engine is completely cool before beginning this procedure.*

Removal

1   Disconnect the cable from the negative terminal of the battery (see Chapter 5, Section 1)

Front valve cover

2   Drain about half of the coolant (see Chapter 1).

3   Pull the engine cover from its mounting studs.

4   On 3.5L engines, remove the dipstick and the dipstick tube.

5   Disconnect the spark plug wires from the front spark plugs. Unclip the spark plug wiring harness and set it out of the way.

6   Remove the PCV tube from the front valve cover.

7   Remove the interfering engine mount strut bracket.

8   Disconnect the heater hoses from the engine coolant tubes. Remove the coolant tube assembly from the engine.

Rear valve cover

9   Refer to Chapter 5 and remove the alternator.

10   Remove the PCV fresh air tube.

11   Disconnect the spark plug wiring from the spark plugs and the coil. Disconnect the spark plug wiring harness clips and remove it from the engine.

12   Disconnect the wiring from the MAP sen-

sor and the ignition coil.

13   Unclip the wiring harnesses from the ignition coil bracket.

14   Remove the ignition coil.

15   On 3.5L engines, remove the water crossover tube.

All models

Refer to illustration 4.16

16   Loosen the valve cover mounting bolts **(see illustration)**.

17   Detach the valve cover. **Note:** *If the cover sticks to the cylinder head, use a block of wood and a hammer to dislodge it. If the cover still won't come loose, pry on it carefully but don't distort the sealing flange.*

18   Trim the material from the intake manifold gasket at the cylinder head. The surface must be cleaned and prepared to prevent damage to the intake manifold gasket when the new valve cover and gasket are installed.

Installation

19   The mating surfaces of each cylinder head and valve cover must be perfectly clean when the covers are installed. Use a gasket scraper to remove all traces of sealant or old gasket material, then clean the mating surfaces with lacquer thinner or acetone (if there's sealant or oil on the mating surfaces when the cover is installed, oil leaks may develop). The valve covers are made of aluminum, so be extra careful not to nick or gouge the mating surfaces with the scraper.

20   Clean the mounting bolt threads with a die if necessary to remove any corrosion and restore damaged threads. Use a tap to clean the threaded holes in the heads.

21   Apply a dab of RTV sealant to the two joints where the intake manifold and cylinder head meet.

22   Place the valve cover and new gasket in position, then install the bolts. Tighten the bolts in several steps to the torque listed in this Chapter's Specifications.

23   Complete the installation by reversing the removal procedure. Start the engine and check carefully for oil leaks at the valve cover-to-head joints.

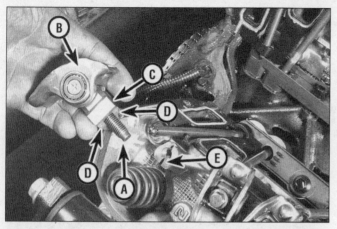

5.3 Rocker arm details - the rocker arms are kept as an assembly by a small sleeve between the bolt and the pedestal - note the projections on the pedestal; they fit into grooves in the head

A Rocker arm bolt	D Pedestal projections
B Rocker arm	E Grooves in the head
C Rocker arm pedestal	

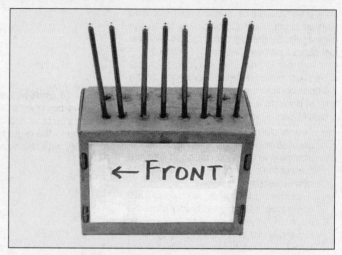

5.4 A perforated cardboard box can be used to store the pushrods to ensure they are reinstalled in their original locations - note the label indicating the front end of the engine

5   Rocker arms and pushrods - removal, inspection and installation

Removal

Refer to illustrations 5.3 and 5.4

1   Disconnect the cable from the negative terminal of the battery (see Chapter 5, Section 1).
2   Remove the valve cover(s) (see Section 4).
3   Beginning at the drivebelt end of one cylinder head, remove the rocker arm mounting bolts one at a time and detach the rocker arms, pivot balls and pedestals **(see illustration)**. Store each set of rocker arm components separately in a marked plastic bag to ensure they're reinstalled in their original locations. **Note:** *The rocker arms have the pedestal mount "captured" on the rocker arm bolt by a metal sleeve inside. The components can be separated if necessary by tapping the bolt out of the pedestal, but normally all components for a particular valve will stay as an assembly.*
4   Remove the pushrods and store them separately to make sure they don't get mixed up during installation **(see illustration)**. **Caution:** *Intake and exhaust pushrods are different lengths. Intake pushrods are approximately 5-3/4 inches long, while exhausts are 6.0 inches long. They may also have color codes to easily tell them apart.*

Inspection

5   Inspect each rocker arm for wear, cracks and other damage, especially where the pushrods and valve stems make contact.
6   Make sure the rollers operate freely as well.
7   Make sure the hole at the pushrod end of each rocker arm is open.
8   Inspect the pushrods for cracks and excessive wear at the ends. Roll each pushrod across a piece of plate glass to see if it's bent (if it wobbles, it's bent).

Installation

9   Lubricate the lower end of each pushrod with clean engine oil or moly-base grease and install them in their original locations. Make sure each pushrod seats completely in the lifter socket.
10   Apply moly-base grease to the ends of the valve stems and the upper ends of the pushrods.
11   Apply clean engine oil to the pivot balls and to the bearing surfaces of each rocker arm to prevent damage to the mating surfaces before engine oil pressure builds up. Install the rocker arms, pivot balls, pedestals and bolts and tighten them to the torque listed in this Chapter's Specifications. As the bolts are tightened, make sure the pushrods engage properly in the rocker arms and that the projections on the bottom of the pedestals fit into the grooves on the head before tightening the bolts **(see illustration 5.3)**.

12   Install the valve covers. Start and run the engine, then check for oil leaks and unusual sounds coming from the valve cover area.

6   Intake manifold - removal and installation

Warning: *The engine must be completely cool before starting this procedure.*
1   Relieve the fuel system pressure (see Chapter 4).
2   Disconnect the cable from the negative terminal of the battery (see Chapter 5, Section 1).
3   Drain the cooling system (see Chapter 1).

Upper intake manifold

Refer to illustration 6.4

4   Remove the engine cover **(see illustration)**.
5   Remove both PCV tubes.
6   Remove the brake booster vacuum hose.

6.4 Remove the oil filler cap, lift up on the upper left and right corners of the engine cover and separate the cover from the engine

6.28 Pry the manifold loose at a casting boss - don't pry between the gasket surfaces!

6.32 Install the intake gaskets against each cylinder head . . .

7   Disconnect and unbolt the heater hoses and tubes and then set them out of the way.

8   Disconnect the MAP sensor wiring and, on the 3.9L engine, the BARO sensor. Disconnect the throttle control wiring connector.

9   Disconnect the tube and wiring to the EVAP purge solenoid.

10   Remove the air inlet duct from the throttle body.

11   Disconnect and remove the front spark plug wiring.

12   Refer to Chapter 4 and remove the throttle body.

13   Remove the EVAP canister purge solenoid valve.

14   Remove the MAP sensor along with its bracket.

15   Unbolt the coil bracket from the intake manifold.

16   Remove the engine cover ball stud from the intake manifold stud.

17   Loosen the upper intake manifold bolts a little at a time, starting with the outer bolts and working towards the inner bolts, then remove the upper intake manifold with the throttle body attached.

18   Clean the mounting surfaces of the lower intake manifold and the upper intake manifold with brake system cleaner, removing all traces of the old gasket material or sealant.

19   Install the new gasket over the lower intake manifold. Install the upper intake manifold onto the lower intake manifold and tighten the bolts a little at a time, starting with the inner bolts and working towards the outer bolts, to the torque listed in this Chapter's Specifications. The remainder of the installation is the reverse of removal.

Lower intake manifold

Refer to illustrations 6.28, 6.32, 6.33 and 6.35

20   Remove the upper intake manifold (see Steps 1 through 17).

21   Remove both valve covers (see Section 4).

22   Disconnect the fuel supply tube.

23   Disconnect the fuel injector wiring harness connector.

24   Remove the injector harness bracket and disconnect the Engine Coolant Temperature (ECT) sensor wiring.

25   Disconnect the Camshaft Position (CMP) sensor wiring.

26   Remove the fuel rail (see Chapter 4).

27   Loosen the manifold mounting bolts/ nuts in 1/4-turn increments until they can be removed by hand.

28   The manifold will probably be stuck to the cylinder heads and force may be required to break the gasket seal **(see illustration)**. **Caution:** *Don't pry between the manifold and the heads or damage to the gasket sealing surfaces may occur, leading to vacuum leaks.*

29   Loosen the rocker arm bolts, rotate the rocker arms out of the way and remove the pushrods that go through the manifold gaskets (see Section 5).

30   Lift the old gaskets off. Use a gasket scraper to remove all traces of sealant and old gasket material, then clean the mating surfaces with lacquer thinner or acetone. **Note:** *The mating surfaces of the cylinder heads, block, coolant crossover housing and manifold must be perfectly clean when the mani-*

fold is installed. Gasket removal solvents are available at most auto parts stores and may be helpful when removing old gasket material that's stuck to the heads and manifold (since the manifold and the coolant crossover housing is made of aluminum, aggressive scraping can cause damage). Be sure to follow the directions printed on the container. If there's old sealant or oil on the mating surfaces when the manifold is installed, oil or vacuum leaks may develop. Use a vacuum cleaner to remove any gasket material that falls into the intake ports or the lifter valley.

31   Use a tap of the correct size to chase the threads in the bolt holes, if necessary, then use compressed air (if available) to remove the debris from the holes. **Warning:** *Wear safety glasses or a face shield to protect your eyes when using compressed air!*

32   Place the intake manifold gaskets in position on the heads **(see illustration)**. Then install the pushrods and rocker arms (see Section 4).

33   Apply a 3/16-inch (5 mm) bead of RTV sealant to the front and rear ridges of the engine block between the heads **(see illustration)**. Allow the RTV sealer to "set-up" (slightly harden) before installing the intake manifold.

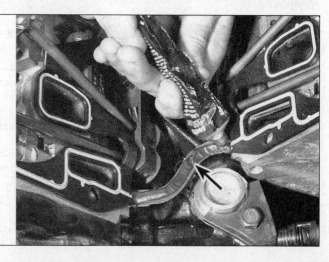

6.33 . . . then apply a bead of sealant to the end ridges between the cylinder heads

6.35 Intake manifold TIGHTENING sequence - make sure the bolts in the center (1 through 4) are completely tightened before tightening the end bolts (5 through 8)

7.4 Remove the six bolts (arrows indicate the upper three) from the exhaust manifold

34   Carefully lower the manifold into place and install the mounting bolts/nuts finger tight. **Note:** *Coat the bolt threads with pipe sealant before installing them.*

35   Tighten the four vertical bolts (1 through 4) at the center of the manifold in the recommended tightening sequence **(see illustration)** to the torque listed in this Chapter's Specifications.

36   Tighten the four angled bolts (5 through 8) at the ends of the manifold in the recommended tightening sequence to the torque listed in this Chapter's Specifications.

37   Install the coolant crossover housing and torque the bolts to the Specifications listed in this Chapter.

38   Install the remaining components in the reverse order of removal.

39   Change the oil and filter and refill the cooling system (see Chapter 1). Start the engine and check for leaks.

7   Exhaust manifolds - removal and installation

Removal

Front manifold

Refer to illustration 7.4

1   Disconnect the cable from the negative battery terminal (see Chapter 5, Section 1).

2   Remove the heat shields from the manifold and the crossover pipe.

3   Disconnect the crossover pipe from the front exhaust manifold.

4   Remove the front exhaust manifold **(see illustration)**.

Rear manifold

Refer to illustration 7.10

5   Remove the alternator (see Chapter 5).

6   Remove the rear manifold oxygen sensor (see Chapter 6).

7   Remove the manifold heat shield.

8   Remove the heat shield from the cross-over pipe.

9   Remove the exhaust crossover pipe.

10   Disconnect the exhaust pipe from the rear manifold **(see illustration)**.

11   Remove the manifold and the gasket.

Installation (front or rear)

12   Clean the mating surfaces to remove all traces of old gasket material, then inspect the manifold for distortion and cracks. Warpage can be checked with a precision straightedge held against the mating flange. If a feeler gauge thicker than 0.030-inch can be inserted between the straightedge and flange surface, take the manifold to an automotive machine shop for resurfacing.

13   Remove the exhaust manifold inner heat shield/gasket.

14   Using a new heat shield/gasket, place the manifold against the head and install the bolts.

15   Starting in the middle and working out toward the ends, tighten the mounting bolts a little at a time until all of them are at the torque listed in this Chapter's Specifications.

16   Install the remaining components in the reverse order of removal.

17   Start the engine and check for exhaust leaks between the manifold and cylinder head and between the manifold and exhaust pipe.

8   Cylinder heads - removal and installation

Refer to illustrations 8.3, 8.10, 8.13a, 8.13b and 8.15

Warning: *Wait until the engine is completely cool before beginning this procedure.*

Removal

1   Disconnect the cable from the negative battery terminal (see Chapter 5, Section 1). Drain the engine coolant (see Chapter 1).

2   Remove the lower intake manifold (see

Section 6). Remove the rocker arms and pushrods (see Section 5).

3   Remove the dipstick and the dipstick tube **(see illustration)**.

4   Remove the exhaust manifolds (see Section 7).

5   Remove the spark plug wires, the wire brackets and the spark plugs.

6   Remove the alternator (see Chapter 5).

7   Loosen each of the cylinder head bolts 1/4-turn at a time until they can be removed by hand - work from bolt-to-bolt in a pattern that's the reverse of the tightening sequence **(see illustrations 8.15)**. Discard the bolts - new ones must be used during installation, but note which ones are studs and their locations. **Caution:** *The engine must be completely cool before loosening the cylinder head bolts.*

8   Lift the head(s) off the engine. If resistance is felt, don't pry between the head and block, as damage to the mating surfaces will result. Recheck for head bolts that may have been overlooked, then use a hammer and block of wood to tap up on the head and break the gasket seal. Be careful because there are locating dowels in the block which

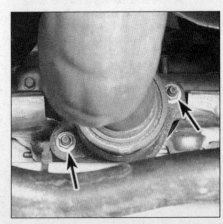

7.10 Remove the nuts holding the exhaust pipe to the rear manifold

8.3 Remove the bolt holding the oil dipstick tube to the front cylinder head

8.10 Remove the old gasket and carefully scrape off all old gasket material and sealant

position each head. As a last resort, pry each head up at the rear corner only and be careful not to damage anything. After removal, place the head on blocks of wood to prevent damage to the gasket surfaces.

Installation

9   The mating surfaces of each cylinder head and block must be perfectly clean when the head is installed.

10   Use a gasket scraper to remove all traces of carbon and old gasket material **(see illustration)**, then clean the mating surfaces with lacquer thinner or acetone. If there's oil on the mating surfaces when the head is installed, the gasket may not seal correctly and leaks may develop. When working on the block, it's a good idea to cover the lifter valley with shop rags to keep debris out of the engine. Use a shop rag or vacuum cleaner to remove any debris that falls into the cylinders.

11   Check the block and head mating surfaces for nicks, deep scratches and other damage. If damage is slight, it can be removed with a file; if it's excessive, machining may be the only alternative.

12   Use a tap of the correct size to chase

8.13a Position the new gasket over the dowel pins . . .

the threads in the head bolt holes. Dirt, corrosion, sealant and damaged threads will affect torque readings.

13   Position the new gasket over the dowel pins in the block. Some gaskets are marked TOP or THIS SIDE UP to ensure correct installation **(see illustrations)**.

14   Carefully position the head on the block without disturbing the gasket.

15   Install the **new** cylinder head bolts.

Tighten the bolts, using the recommended sequence **(see illustration)**, to the torque listed in this Chapter's Specifications. Then, using the same sequence, turn each bolt the amount of angle listed in this Chapter's Specifications.

16   The remaining installation steps are the reverse of removal.

17   Change the engine oil and filter, and refill the cooling system (see Chapter 1).

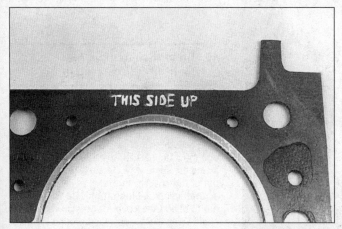

8.13b . . . with the correct side facing up

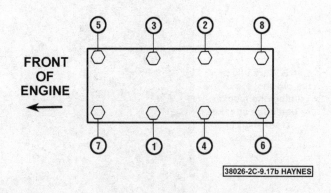

8.15 Cylinder head bolt TIGHTENING sequence

9.6 Remove the crankshaft bolt - it's very tight, so use a six-point socket and a breaker bar

9.9 The pulley keyway must be aligned with the Woodruff key in the crankshaft nose

9 Crankshaft pulley - removal and installation

Refer to illustrations 9.6 and 9.9

1   Disconnect the cable from the negative terminal of the battery (see Chapter 5, Section 1).

2   With the parking brake applied and the shift lever in Park, loosen the lug nuts from the right front wheel, then raise the front of the vehicle and support it securely on jackstands.

3   Remove the right inner fender splash shield (see Chapter 11), then remove the drivebelt (see Chapter 1).

4   Put a floor jack under the right side of the engine subframe. Support the left side of the frame with another floor jack.

5   Loosen the bolts on the left side of the engine frame. Remove the bolts from the right side. Carefully lower the right side of the frame with the jack just enough to get access to the crankshaft balancer.

6   Remove the bolt from the front of the crankshaft **(see illustration)**. The bolt is nor-

mally very tight, so use a large breaker bar and a six-point socket to remove it. Obtain a new bolt, but save the old one for the initial installation of the pulley. **Note:** *Remove the starter cover and the starter (see Chapter 5) and position a large screwdriver in the ring gear teeth to keep the crankshaft from turning while an assistant removes the crankshaft pulley bolt.*

7   Use a large three-arm puller to hook into the balancer in each of its three holes. These pullers can be rented at most rental yards. Tighten the puller screw to draw the balancer from the crankshaft. **Caution:** *On these engines, a rubber sleeve connects the inertia weight to the balancer hub. Be careful when working on the crankshaft pulley/balancer that you do not accidentally shift the inertia weight's position relative to the sleeve or balancer hub, as this will upset the tuning of the balancer. Additionally, a spacer, such as a deep socket that just fits into the hole in the pulley and bears on the nose of the crankshaft will be required to avoid damage to the crankshaft.*

8   Apply a small amount of RTV sealant onto the crankshaft keyway and allow the sealant to "set-up" (slightly harden).

9   Position the crankshaft pulley/balancer on the crankshaft and slide it on as far as it will go. Note that the slot (keyway) in the hub must be aligned with the Woodruff key in the end of the crankshaft **(see illustration)**.

10   Using a crankshaft balancer installation tool, available at most auto parts stores, press the crankshaft pulley/balancer onto the crankshaft. Note that the crankshaft bolt can also be used to press the crankshaft balancer into position, but when doing so, use a liberal amount of clean engine oil on the bolt threads and under the bolt head to prevent galling.

11   Install the old bolt and washer and tighten the bolt to the Step 1 torque listed in this Chapter's Specifications, then remove the bolt. Install the new bolt and washer, tightening it to the Step 1 torque listed in this Chapter's Specifications, followed by the Step 2 angle torque.

12   The remaining installation Steps are the reverse of removal. When tightening the subframe bolts, tighten them to the torque listed in the Chapter 10 Specifications.

10 Crankshaft front oil seal - removal and installation

Refer to illustrations 10.2, 10.3 and 10.4

1   Remove the crankshaft pulley (see Section 9).

2   Note how the seal is installed - the new one must be installed to the same depth and facing the same way. Carefully pry the oil seal out of the cover with a seal puller or a large screwdriver **(see illustration)**. Be very careful not to distort the cover or scratch the crankshaft! Wrap electrician's tape around the tip of

10.2 Carefully pry the old seal out of the timing chain cover - don't damage the crankshaft in the process

10.3 Drive the new seal into place with a seal driver or a large socket and hammer

10.4 If the sealing surface of the pulley hub has a wear groove from contact with the seal, repair sleeves are available at most auto parts stores

the screwdriver to avoid damage to the crankshaft.

3   Apply clean engine oil or multi-purpose grease to the outer edge of the new seal, then install it in the cover with the lip (spring side) facing IN. Drive the seal into place **(see illustration)** with a seal driver or a large socket and a hammer. Make sure the seal enters the bore squarely and stop when the front face is at the proper depth.

4   Check the surface on the pulley hub that the oil seal rides on. If the surface has been grooved from long-time contact with the seal, a press-on sleeve may be available to renew the sealing surface **(see illustration)**. This sleeve is pressed into place with a hammer and a block of wood and is commonly available at auto parts stores for various applications.

5   Lubricate the pulley hub with clean engine oil and reinstall the crankshaft pulley. Use a vibration damper installation tool to press the pulley onto the crankshaft.

6   Install the crankshaft pulley retaining bolt and tighten it to the torque listed in this Chapter's Specifications.

7   The remainder of installation is the reverse of the removal.

11   Timing chain and sprockets - removal, inspection and installation

Removal

Refer to illustrations 11.8a, 11.8b and 11.10

1   Disconnect the cable from the negative terminal of the battery (see Chapter 5, Section 1).

2   Refer to Chapter 1 and drain the coolant.

3   Remove the drivebelt and the tensioner.

4   Remove the engine oil pan (see Section 13).

5   Remove the crankshaft balancer pulley (see Section 9).

6   Remove the camshaft position actuator magnet and its O-ring.

7   Remove the thermostat and the water pump (see Chapter 3).

8   Remove the timing chain cover-to-engine block bolts **(see illustrations)**.

9   Separate the cover from the engine. If it's stuck, tap it with a soft-face hammer, but don't try to pry it off.

10   Temporarily install the crankshaft pulley bolt and turn the crankshaft with the bolt to align the timing marks on the crankshaft and camshaft sprockets. When aligned at TDC for number 1 piston, the crankshaft sprocket timing mark should align with the mark on the bottom of the chain tensioner plate, and the small hole in the camshaft sprocket should be at the 6 o'clock position, aligned with the

11.8a Timing chain cover bolt locations, upper . . .

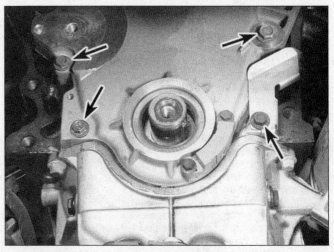

11.8b . . . and lower

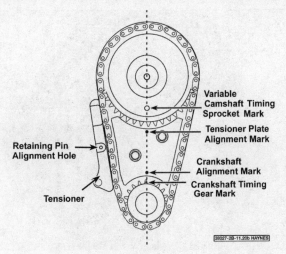

11.10 Timing mark locations and timing chain details

12.5 Remove the bolts (A) and pull up the roller lifter guides (B)

timing mark in the top of the tensioner **(see illustration).**

11   Remove the camshaft sprocket bolt(s). Do not turn the camshaft in the process (if you do, realign the timing marks before the bolt(s) are removed). **Caution:** *Some engines are equipped with TORX PLUS timing sprocket bolts. Use only a TORX PLUS socket on them. A regular TORX socket is NOT a substitute and may damage the bolts.*

12   Use two large screwdrivers to carefully pry the variable camshaft timing sprocket off the camshaft dowel pin. Slip the timing chain and camshaft sprocket off the engine.

Inspection

13   The timing chain should be replaced with a new one if the engine has high mileage, the chain has visible damage, or total freeplay midway between the sprockets exceeds one-inch. Failure to replace a worn timing chain may result in erratic engine performance, loss of power and decreased fuel mileage. Loose chains can "jump" timing. In the worst case, chain "jumping" or breakage will result in severe engine damage. Always replace the timing chain and sprockets in sets. If you intend to install a new timing chain, remove the crankshaft sprocket with a puller and install a new one.

14   Be sure to align the key in the crankshaft with the keyway in the sprocket during installation.

15   Inspect the timing chain tensioner and tensioner plate for wear, damage and correct operation. The tensioner plate must be reinstalled before installing the new timing chain. Also, use a special tool to retract the tensioner and install a pin into the alignment hole to lock the tensioner in this position.

16   Clean the timing chain and sprockets with solvent and dry them with compressed air (if available). **Warning:** *Wear eye protection when using compressed air.*

17   Inspect the components for wear and

damage. Look for teeth that are deformed, chipped, pitted and cracked.

Installation

18   Use a gasket scraper to remove all traces of old gasket material and sealant from the cover and engine block. The cover is made of aluminum, so be careful not to nick or gouge it. Clean the gasket sealing surfaces with lacquer thinner or acetone.

19   Install the tensioner plate, tightening the bolts to the torque listed in this Chapter's Specifications.

20   If the camshaft has turned at all since removal of the sprocket, turn the camshaft to position the dowel pin at 3 o'clock. Mesh the timing chain with the camshaft sprocket, then engage it with the crankshaft sprocket. The timing marks should be aligned as shown in **illustration 11.10**. **Note:** *If the crankshaft has been disturbed, turn it until the "O" stamped on the crankshaft sprocket is exactly at the top.*

21   Install the variable camshaft timing sprocket bolts (make sure the dowel hole in the sprocket is aligned with the dowel pin in the camshaft) and tighten to the torque listed in this Chapter's Specifications. **Note:** *Be sure to install a new camshaft sprocket filter when the sprocket has been removed from the camshaft.*

22   Lubricate the chain and sprocket with clean engine oil.

23   Remove the tensioner locking tool to release the tensioner.

24   Apply a thin layer of anaerobic sealant to both sides of the new gasket, then position the gasket on the engine block (the dowel pins should keep it in place). Apply sealant to the bottom of the gasket, where it meets the oil pan.

25   Attach the cover to the engine and install the bolts. Follow a criss-cross pattern when tightening the fasteners and work up to the torque listed in this Chapter's Specifications in three steps.

26   The remainder of installation is the reverse of removal.

27   Add oil and coolant, start the engine and check for leaks.

---

12   Valve lifters - removal, inspection and installation

---

1   A noisy valve lifter can be isolated when the engine is idling. Hold a mechanic's stethoscope or a length of hose near the location of each valve while listening at the other end. Another method is to remove the valve cover and, with the engine idling, touch each of the valve spring retainers, one at a time. If a valve lifter is defective, it'll be evident from the shock felt at the retainer each time the valve seats.

2   The most likely causes of noisy valve lifters are dirt trapped inside the lifter and lack of oil flow, viscosity or pressure. Before condemning the lifters, check the oil for fuel contamination, correct level, cleanliness and correct viscosity.

Removal

Refer to illustrations 12.5, 12.6a, 12.6b and 12.7

3   Remove the valve cover(s) and intake manifold as described in Sections 4 and 6.

4   Remove the rocker arms and pushrods (see Section 5).

5   Remove the bolts holding the roller lifter guide to the block, and remove the two roller lifter guides **(see illustration)**. Mark the guides as to which side they came from.

6   There are several ways to extract the lifters from the bores. A special tool designed to grip and remove lifters is manufactured by many tool companies and is widely available, but it may not be required in every case. On newer engines without a lot of varnish buildup, the lifters can often be removed with

12.6a A magnetic pick-up tool . . .

12.6b . . . or a scribe can be used to remove the lifters

a small magnet or even with your fingers. A machinist's scribe with a bent end can be used to pull the lifters out by positioning the point under the retainer ring in the top of each lifter **(see illustrations)**. **Caution:** *Don't use pliers to remove the lifters unless you intend to replace them with new ones (along with the camshaft). The pliers may damage the precision machined and hardened lifters, rendering them useless.*

7   Before removing the lifters, arrange to store them in a clearly labeled box to ensure they're reinstalled in their original locations. Remove the lifters and store them where they won't get dirty **(see illustration)**.

Inspection and installation

Refer to illustrations 12.10a and 12.10b

8   Parts for valve lifters are not available separately. The work required to remove them from the engine again if cleaning is unsuccessful outweighs any potential savings from repairing them.

9   Clean the lifters thoroughly with solvent and dry them thoroughly, without mixing them up.

12.7 Store the lifters in order to ensure installation in their original locations

10   Check each lifter wall and plunger seat for scuffing, score marks or uneven wear **(see illustration)**. Check the rollers carefully for wear or damage and make sure they turn freely without excessive play **(see illustration)**. If the lifters walls are worn (not very

likely), inspect the lifter bores in the block. If the pushrod seats are worn, inspect the pushrods also.

11   When reinstalling used lifters, make sure they're replaced in their original bores. Soak new lifters in oil to remove trapped air. Coat all lifters with moly-base grease or engine assembly lube prior to installation.

12   Install the pushrods and the rocker arms (see Section 5).

13   The remaining installation Steps are the reverse of removal.

14   Run the engine and check for oil leaks.

---

13   Oil pan - removal and installation

Removal

Refer to illustrations 13.12

1   Disconnect the cable from the negative terminal of the battery (see Chapter 5, Section 1).

2   Install an engine support fixture.

3   Remove the engine mount struts.

12.10a Check the pushrod seat in the top of each lifter for wear

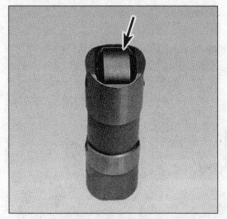

12.10b The roller on the roller lifters must turn freely - check for wear and excessive play as well

13.12 Disconnect the oil level sensor connector, if equipped

13.29 Apply a bead of RTV sealant on each side of the rear main cap, where the pan gasket will meet it

4   Remove the exhaust pipe with the cata-lytic converter (see Chapter 4).
5   Drain the engine oil (see Chapter 1).
6   Loosen the right front wheel lug nuts. Raise the vehicle and support it securely on jackstands, then remove the right front wheel.
7   Remove the inner fender splash shield (see Chapter 11).
8   Remove the drivebelt (see Chapter 1).
9   Remove the oil filter adapter.
10   Remove the starter (see Chapter 5).
11   Unbolt the air conditioning compressor and set it aside without disconnecting either of the refrigerant lines.
12   Disconnect the oil level sensor wiring and the wiring harness from the oil pan **(see illustration)**.
13   Remove the engine-to-transmission brace.
14   Remove the two nuts from the engine mount that is under the crankshaft pulley/bal-ancer.
15   Loosen the nuts at the bottom of the transmission mount.
16   Remove the transmission-to-oil pan brace.
17   Use the engine support fixture to raise the engine.
18   Remove the engine mount bracket from the front of the engine.

3.5L engines

19   Refer to Chapter 10 and remove the steering shaft pinch bolt at the steering gear.
20   Disconnect the tie-rod from the steering knuckle and the right control arm from the subframe (see Chapter 10).
21   Remove the right stabilizer link (see Chapter 10).
22   Place a floor jack under the right side of the subframe. Place another floor jack under the left side of the subframe.
23   Loosen the bolts on the left side of the subframe. Remove the bolts on the right side.
24   Use the floor jack to lower the right side of the subframe.
25   Raise the engine using the engine sup-port fixture.

All engines

26   Remove the side bolts (connecting the sides of the cast oil pan to the main cap sup-ports) on each side of the oil pan.
27   Remove the remaining oil pan-to-block bolts, then carefully separate the oil pan from the block. Don't pry between the block and the pan or damage to the sealing surfaces could occur and oil leaks may develop. Instead, tap the pan with a soft-face hammer to break the gasket seal.

Installation

Refer to illustration 13.29

28   Clean the pan with solvent and remove all old sealant and gasket material from the block and pan mating surfaces. Clean the mating surfaces with lacquer thinner or ace-tone and make sure the bolt holes in the block are clear.
29   Apply a bead of RTV sealant to the front of the gasket, where it contacts the front cover, and a short bead (9/32-inch wide) to either side of the rear main cap where it meets the block **(see illustration)**, then install the new one-piece oil pan gasket.
30   Place the oil pan in position on the block and install the nuts/bolts.
31   After the pan-to-block fasteners are installed, tighten them to the torque listed in this Chapter's Specifications. Starting at the center, follow a criss-cross pattern and work up to the final torque in three steps.
32   After all the pan-to-block bolts have been tightened, install the oil pan side bolts and tighten them to torque listed in this Chapter's Specifications.
33   The remaining steps are the reverse of the removal procedure. Tighten the subframe bolts to the torque listed in the Chapter 10 Specifications.
34   Refill the engine with oil, run it until nor-mal operating temperature is reached and check for leaks.

14   Oil pump - removal and installation

Refer to illustration 14.2

1   Remove the oil pan (see Section 13).
2   Unbolt the oil pump and lower it from the engine **(see illustration)**. **Note:** *The oil pump driveshaft will come out with the pump as you lower it. It's a rod with a flat-sided portion at each end.*
3   If the pump is defective, replace it with a new one - don't reuse the original or attempt to rebuild it. Inspect the ends of the oil pump

14.2 Oil pump mounting bolt location

15.2a Most driveplates have locating dowels - if the one you're working on doesn't have one, make some marks to ensure proper alignment on reassembly

15.2b A large screwdriver wedged in one of the holes in the driveplate can be used to keep the driveplate from turning as the mounting bolts are removed

driveshaft and the plastic collar that retains the driveshaft to the oil pump. If there are signs of wear on the shaft or if the plastic collar is cracked or missing, replace the shaft with a new one. **Note:** *The plastic collar centers the oil pump driveshaft over the oil pump shaft. If the collar is not used or is missing, damage to the oil pump driveshaft and the oil pump will occur. A new plastic collar is usually included with a new oil pump or driveshaft.*

4   Prime the pump by pouring clean engine oil into the pick-up screen while turning the pump driveshaft.

5   To install the pump, turn the flat on the driveshaft so it mates with the slot in the oil pump shaft. Make sure the plastic collar is fitted over the oil pump-to-oil pump driveshaft joint, then install the oil pump and driveshaft assembly into the block while engaging the upper end of the oil pump driveshaft into the oil pump drive.

6   Install the pump mounting bolt and tighten it to the torque listed in this Chapter's Specifications.

7   The remainder of assembly is the reverse of the removal procedure.

16.4 Carefully pry the old seal out

15   Driveplate - removal and installation

Removal

Refer to illustrations 15.2a and 15.2b

1   Raise the vehicle and support it securely on jackstands, then refer to Chapter 7 and remove the transaxle.

2   Remove the bolts that secure the driveplate to the crankshaft **(see illustration)**. If the crankshaft turns, wedge a screwdriver in the ring gear teeth to jam the driveplate **(see illustration)**. **Note:** *If there is a retaining ring between the bolts and the driveplate, note which side faces the driveplate when removing it.*

3   Remove the driveplate from the crankshaft. **Caution:** *When removing a driveplate, wear gloves to protect your fingers - the edges of the ring gear teeth may be sharp.*

4   Clean the driveplate to remove grease and oil. Inspect the surface for cracks, and check for cracked and broken ring gear teeth. Lay the driveplate on a flat surface to check for warpage.

5   Clean and inspect the mating surfaces of the driveplate and the crankshaft. If the crankshaft rear seal is leaking, replace it before reinstalling the driveplate (see Section 17).

Installation

6   Position the driveplate against the crankshaft. Be sure to align the marks made during removal. Note that some engines have an alignment dowel or staggered bolt holes to ensure correct installation. Before installing the bolts, apply thread locking compound to the threads and place the retaining ring in position on the driveplate.

7   Wedge a screwdriver through the ring gear teeth to keep the driveplate from turning as you tighten the bolts to the torque listed in this Chapter's Specifications. If the front pump seal/O-ring is leaking, now would be a very good time to replace it.

8   The remainder of installation is the reverse of the removal procedure.

16   Rear main oil seal - replacement

Refer to illustration 16.4

1   Remove the transaxle (see Chapter 7).

2   Remove the driveplate (see Section 15).

3   Inspect the oil seal, as well as the oil pan and engine block surface for signs of leakage. Sometimes an oil pan gasket leak can appear to be a rear oil seal leak.

4   Pry the oil seal from the block with a screwdriver **(see illustration)**. Be careful not to nick or scratch the crankshaft or the seal bore. Thoroughly clean the seal bore in the block with a shop towel. Remove all traces of oil and dirt.

5   Lubricate the lips of the new seal with engine oil or multi-purpose grease. Install the seal over the end of the crankshaft (make sure the lips of the seal point toward the engine) and carefully tap it into place. A special aftermarket tool may be available at your local auto parts store. The tool just fits the diameter

18.2 Remove the bolt and pull out the oil pump drive

18.4 Remove the retaining bolts and the camshaft thrust plate

of the seal and, used with a hammer, drives the seal in. **Note:** *Do not drive it in any farther than the original seal was installed.*

6   Install the driveplate (see Section 15).

7   Install the transaxle (see Chapter 7).

17 Powertrain mounts - check and replacement

Check

1   Engine mounts seldom require attention, but broken or deteriorated mounts should be replaced immediately or the added strain placed on the driveline components may cause damage or wear.

2   During the check, the engine must be raised slightly to remove the weight from the mounts.

3   Raise the vehicle and support it securely on jackstands, then position a jack under the engine oil pan. Place a large block of wood between the jack head and the oil pan, then carefully raise the engine just enough to take the weight off the mounts. **Warning:** *DO NOT place any part of your body under the engine when it's supported only by a jack!*

4   Check the mounts to see if the rubber is cracked, hardened or separated from the bushing in the center of the mount.

5   Check for relative movement between the mounts and the engine or frame (use a large screwdriver or pry bar to attempt to move the mounts).

6   If movement is noted, lower the engine and tighten the mount fasteners.

Replacement

7   Disconnect the cable from the negative terminal on the battery (see Chapter 5), then raise the vehicle and support it securely on jackstands.

8   Remove the right front wheel and the inner fender splash shield (see Chapter 11).

9   Place a large block of wood between the jack head and the oil pan, then carefully raise the engine just enough to take the weight off

the mounts. **Caution:** *Do not disconnect more than one mount at a time unless the engine will be removed from the vehicle.*

10   Remove the engine nuts and detach the mount from the chassis bracket.

11   Remove the nuts holding the mount to the engine bracket.

12   Installation is the reverse of removal. Use thread-locking compound on the mount bolts and be sure to tighten them securely.

13   Reconnect the battery (see Chapter 5, Section 1).

18 Camshaft - removal, inspection and installation

Removal

Refer to illustrations 18.2 and 18.4

1   Refer to Chapter 2C and remove the engine from the vehicle.

2   Remove the bolt and clamp holding the oil pump drive and pull the oil pump drive straight up and out of the block **(see illustration)**.

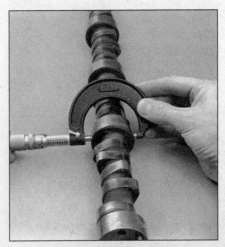

18.7a Measure the camshaft bearing journals with a micrometer

3   Refer to Sections 11 and 12 and remove the timing chain and sprockets and the valve lifters.

4   Remove the bolts holding the camshaft thrust plate to the block **(see illustration)** and remove the thrust plate.

5   Slide the camshaft straight out of the engine, using a long bolt (with the same thread as the camshaft sprocket bolt) screwed into the front of the camshaft as a handle. Support the shaft near the block and be careful not to scrape or nick the bearings.

Inspection

Refer to illustrations 18.7a and 18.7b

6   After the camshaft has been removed, clean it with solvent and dry it, then inspect the bearing journals for uneven wear, pitting and evidence of seizure. If the journals are damaged, the camshaft bearings are probably damaged as well. Both the shaft and bearings will have to be replaced.

7   Measure the bearing journals with a micrometer **(see illustration)** to determine whether they are excessively worn or out-of-

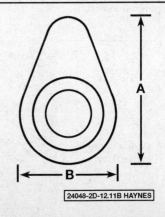

24048-2D-12.11B HAYNES

18.7b Measure the camshaft lobe maximum diameter (A) and the minimum diameter (B) - subtract B from A and the difference is the lobe lift

round. Measure the camshaft lobes also to check for wear. Measure the camshaft lobes at their highest point, then subtract the measurement of the lobe at its smallest diameter - the difference is the lobe lift **(see illustration)**. Refer to the Specifications listed in this Chapter.

8   Inspect the camshaft lobes for heat discoloration, score marks, chipped areas, pitting and uneven wear. If the lobes are in good condition and if the lobe lift measurements are as specified, you can reuse the camshaft.

9   Check the camshaft bearings in the block for wear and damage. Look for galling, pitting and discolored areas. Inspect the housing journals for damage and replace them if necessary.

10   The inside diameter of each bearing can be determined with a small hole gauge and outside micrometer or an inside micrometer. Subtract the camshaft bearing journal diameter(s) from the corresponding bearing inside diameter(s) to obtain the bearing oil clearance. If it's excessive, new bearings or housings will be required regardless of the condition of the originals. Refer to the Specifications listed in this Chapter.

11   Camshaft bearing replacement requires special tools and expertise that place it outside the scope of the home mechanic. Take the block to an automotive machine shop to ensure the job is done correctly.

Installation

12   Lubricate the camshaft bearing journals and cam lobes with a special camshaft installation lubricant.

13   Slide the camshaft into the engine, using a long bolt (the same thread as the camshaft sprocket bolt) screwed into the front of the camshaft as a handle. Support the cam near the block and be careful not to scrape or nick the bearings. Install the camshaft retainer plate and tighten the bolts to the torque listed in this Chapter's Specifications.

14   Dip the gear portion of the oil pump drive in engine oil and insert it into the block. It should be flush with its mounting boss before inserting the retaining bolt. **Note:** *Position a new O-ring on the oil pump driveshaft before installation.*

15   Complete the installation of the timing chain and sprockets by referring to Sections 11 and 12.

Notes

Chapter 2 Part B
V8 engine

Contents

Specifications

General

Displacement	(5.3L) 325 cubic inches
Bore and stroke	3.779 x 3.622 inches
Cylinder numbers (front-to-rear)	
Front cylinder bank	1-3-5-7
Rear cylinder bank	2-4-6-8
Firing order	1-8-7-2-6-5-4-3
Cylinder compression pressure	
Minimum	100 psi
Maximum variation between cylinders	25 percent from the highest reading

Camshaft

Displacement on Demand cylinders	1, 4, 6 and 7
Camshaft endplay	0.001 to 0.012 inch
Journal diameters	2.164 to 2.166 inches
Journal out-of-round	0.001 inch
Runout	0.002 inch
Lobe lift	
Cylinders 1, 4, 6, and 7	0.289 inch
Cylinders 2, 3, 5 and 8	0.283 inch

Front of vehicle

Cylinder numbering

Torque specifications*

Ft-lbs (unless otherwise indicated)

Note: *One foot-pound (ft-lb) of torque is equivalent to 12 inch-pounds (in-lbs) of torque. Torque values below approximately 15 foot-pounds are expressed in inch-pounds, because most foot-pound torque wrenches are not accurate at these smaller values.*

Camshaft sprocket bolts
    Three-bolt sprocket 18
    Single bolt sprocket
        Step 1 55
        Step 2 .... Tighten an additional 50-degrees
Camshaft retainer bolts
    Torx head .... 132 in-lbs
    Hex head.. 18
Crankshaft balancer bolt
    2008 and earlier models
        Step 1 (use old bolt)... 240
        Step 2 (use new bolt).. 37
        Step 3 (use new bolt).. Tighten an additional 140 degrees
    2009 and later models
        Step 1 (use old bolt)... 111
        Step 2 (use new bolt).. 37
        Step 3 .... Tighten an additional 230 degrees
Cylinder head bolts (in sequence - **see illustration 9.17**)**
    Step 1
        All 11 mm bolts (1 through 10).......................... 22
    Step 2
        All 11 mm bolts (1 through 10).......................... Tighten an additional 90 degrees
    Step 3
        All 11 mm bolts (1 through 10).......................... Tighten an additional 70 degrees
    Step 4
        All 8 mm bolts (11 through 15).......................... 22
Engine mount retaining bolts.. 37
Exhaust manifold bolts
    Step one .... 132 in-lbs
    Step two 15
Exhaust manifold heat shield bolt...................................... 80 in-lbs
Exhaust pipe flange nuts 18
Displacement-on-demand assembly bolts........................... 18
Driveplate bolts
    Step one 15
    Step two 37
    Step three.. 74
Intake manifold bolts
    Step one .... 44 in-lbs
    Step two .... 89 in-lbs
Lifter retainer bolts... 106 in-lbs
Oil pan baffle bolts... 106 in-lbs
Oil pan drain plug 18
Oil pan rear access plugs... 80 in-lbs
Oil pan bolts
    Step 1 (to engine and front cover) 18
    Step 2 (to rear cover) .... 106 in-lbs
    Step 3 (bellhousing, converter cover and transmission bolts)........... 37
Oil pump cover bolts.. 106 in-lbs
Oil pump mounting bolts... 18
Rocker arm bolts 22
Front timing chain cover bolts.. 18
Valve cover bolts .... 106 in-lbs
Vapor vent pipe bolts... 106 in-lbs
Water pump manifold bolts
    M10 bolts... 44
    M8 bolts... 22

***Note:** Refer to Part C for additional specifications.*

1 General information

This Part of Chapter 2 is devoted to in-vehicle repair procedures for the 5.3L V8 engine. This engine uses an aluminum block and heads with eight cylinders arranged in a "V" shape at a 90-degree angle between the two banks. The aluminum cylinder heads have an overhead valve arrangement with pressed-in valve guides and hardened valve seats. Hydraulic roller lifters actuate the valves through tubular pushrods and rocker arms. The oil pump is mounted at the front of the engine behind the timing chain cover and is driven by the crankshaft. The engine uses a Displacement on Demand system that allows it to operate on four cylinders when driveability conditions permit.

Information concerning engine removal and installation and engine overhaul can be found in Part C of this Chapter. The following repair procedures are based on the assumption that the engine is installed in the vehicle. If the engine has been removed from the vehicle and mounted on a stand, many of the steps outlined in this Part of Chapter 2 will not apply.

2 Repair operations possible with the engine in the vehicle

Many major repair operations can be accomplished without removing the engine from the vehicle.

Clean the engine compartment and the exterior of the engine with some type of pressure washer before any work is done. A clean engine will make the job easier and will help keep dirt out of the internal areas of the engine.

Depending on the components involved, it may be a good idea to remove the hood to improve access to the engine as repairs are performed (refer to Chapter 11 if necessary).

If oil or coolant leaks develop, indicating a need for gasket or seal replacement, the repairs can generally be made with the engine in the vehicle. The cylinder head gaskets, intake and exhaust manifold gaskets, and the crankshaft oil seals are all accessible with the engine in place.

Exterior engine components, such as the water pump, the starter motor, the alternator and the fuel injection components, as well as the intake and exhaust manifolds, can be removed for repair with the engine in place.

Since the cylinder heads can be removed without removing the engine, valve component servicing can also be accomplished with the engine in the vehicle.

Camshaft removal requires that the engine be removed from the vehicle. This procedure is traditionally included in this Chapter because engine removal is not necessary for replacing them in most vehicles. There are other procedures such as oil pan removal, timing chain replacement and driveplate removal that require the engine subframe to be removed.

3 Top Dead Center (TDC) for number one piston - locating

Refer to illustration 3.6

1 Top Dead Center (TDC) is the highest point in the cylinder that each piston reaches as it travels up the cylinder bore. Each piston reaches TDC on the compression stroke and again on the exhaust stroke, but TDC generally refers to piston position on the compression stroke.

2 Positioning the piston(s) at TDC is an essential part of certain procedures, such as timing chain/sprocket removal.

3 Before beginning this procedure, be sure to place the transmission in Park and apply the parking brake or block the front wheels. Also, disable the ignition system by disconnecting the primary electrical connectors at the ignition coil packs, then remove the spark plugs (see Chapter 1).

4 In order to bring any piston to TDC, the crankshaft must be turned using one of the methods outlined below. When looking at the front of the engine, normal crankshaft rotation is clockwise. **Warning:** *If method b) or c) is used, disable the fuel system (see Chapter 4, Section 2).*

a) *The preferred method is to turn the crankshaft with a socket and ratchet attached to the bolt threaded into the front of the crankshaft. Turn the bolt in a clockwise direction.*

b) *A remote starter switch, which may save some time, can also be used. Follow the instructions included with the switch. Once the piston is close to TDC, use a socket and ratchet as described in the previous paragraph.*

c) *If an assistant is available to turn the ignition switch to the Start position in short bursts, you can get the piston close to TDC without a remote starter switch. Make sure your assistant is out of the vehicle, away from the ignition switch, then use a socket and ratchet as described in Paragraph (a) to complete the procedure.*

5 Install a compression gauge in the No. 1 spark plug hole. It should be a gauge with a screw-in type fitting and a hose at least six inches long. Rotate the crankshaft using one of the methods described above while observing for pressure on the compression gauge. The moment the gauge shows pressure indicates that the No. 1 cylinder has begun the compression stroke.

6 To bring the piston to the top of the cylinder, insert a long screwdriver into the number one spark plug hole until it touches the top of the piston. **Note:** *Make sure to wrap the tip of the screwdriver with tape to avoid scratching the top of the piston and the cylinder walls.* Use the screwdriver (as a feeler gauge) to tell where the top of the piston is located in the cylinder while slowly rotating the crankshaft with a socket and breaker bar on the crankshaft pulley bolt **(see illustration)**. As the piston rises, the screwdriver will be pushed out. The point at which the screwdriver stops moving outward is TDC. **Note:** *Always hold the screwdriver upright while the engine is being rotated so that the screwdriver will not get wedged as the piston travels upward.*

7 If you go past TDC, rotate the crankshaft counterclockwise until the piston is approximately one inch below TDC, then slowly rotate the crankshaft clockwise again until TDC is reached.

8 After the number one piston has been positioned at TDC on the compression stroke, TDC for any of the remaining pistons can be located by turning the crankshaft 90-degrees (1/4 turn) at a time and following the firing order.

3.6 A long screwdriver inserted in the number one spark plug hole can be used to determine the highest point reached by that piston - make sure to wrap the tip of the screwdriver with tape to avoid scratching the top of the piston or the cylinder walls

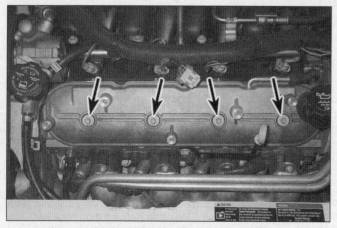

4.4 Valve cover mounting bolts (arrows)

4.7 Position the new gasket in the valve cover lip

4   Valve covers - removal and installation

Removal

Refer to illustration 4.4

1   Disconnect the cable from the negative terminal of the battery.

2   Pull the engine top cover from its mounting studs. Disconnect the wiring harness from the ignition coil assembly. Pull the harness out of the way.

3   Disconnect the spark plug wires from the ignition coils.

4   Remove the ignition coil bracket along with all of the coils mounted to it. Remove the interfering PCV tube. Remove the valve cover bolts **(see illustration)**, then detach the cover from the cylinder head. **Note:** *If the cover is stuck to the cylinder head, bump one end with a block of wood and a hammer to jar it loose. If that doesn't work, try to slip a flexible putty knife between the cylinder head and cover to break the gasket seal. Don't pry at the cover-to-head joint or damage to the sealing surfaces may occur (leading to oil leaks in the future).*

Installation

Refer to illustration 4.7

5   The mating surfaces of each cylinder head and valve cover must be perfectly clean when the covers are installed. Use a gasket scraper to remove all traces of sealant and old gasket material, then clean the mating surfaces with lacquer thinner or acetone. If there's sealant or oil on the mating surfaces when the cover is installed, oil leaks may develop.

6   Clean the mounting bolt threads with a die to remove any corrosion and restore damaged threads. Make sure the threaded holes in the cylinder head are clean - run a tap into them to remove corrosion and restore damaged threads.

7   The gaskets should be mated to the covers before the covers are installed. Position the gasket inside the cover lip **(see illustration)**. If the gasket will not stay in place in the cover lip, apply a thin coat of RTV sealant to the cover flange, then and allow the sealant to set up so the gasket adheres to the cover.

8   Inspect the valve cover bolt grommets for damage. If the grommets aren't damaged they can be reused. Carefully position the valve cover(s) on the cylinder head and install the

bolts and grommets. **Note:** *Do NOT remove the oil filler tube unless service is required. If the oil filler tube is removed, replace it with a new one.*

9   Tighten the bolts in three or four steps to the torque listed in this Chapter's Specifications.

10   The remaining installation steps are the reverse of removal.

11   Start the engine and check carefully for oil leaks as the engine warms up.

5   Rocker arms and pushrods - removal, inspection and installation

Removal

Refer to illustrations 5.2 and 5.3

1   Refer to Section 4 and detach the valve covers from the cylinder heads.

2   Loosen the rocker arm pivot bolts one at a time and detach the rocker arms and bolts, then detach the pivot support pedestal **(see illustration)**. Keep track of the rocker arm positions, since they must be returned to the

5.2 Remove the mounting bolts (A) and rocker arms, then remove the pivot support pedestal (B)

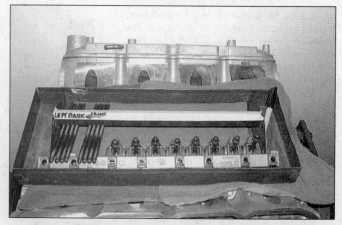

5.3 Store the pushrods and rocker arms in order to ensure they are reinstalled in their original locations - note the arrow indicating the front of the engine

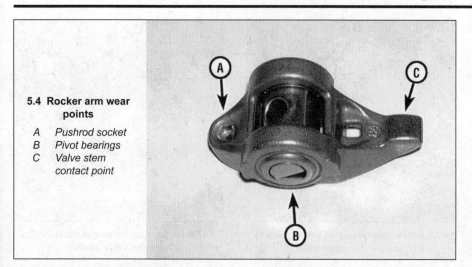

5.4 Rocker arm wear points

A   *Pushrod socket*
B   *Pivot bearings*
C   *Valve stem contact point*

ber 1, 3, 4, and 5 cylinders and the exhaust rocker arms for the Number 1, 2, 7, and 8 cylinders. Tighten each of the specified rocker arm bolts to the torque listed in this Chapter's Specifications.

11   Rotate the crankshaft 360 degrees. Tighten the intake valve rocker arms for the Number 2, 6, 7, and 8 cylinders and the exhaust rocker arms for the Number 3, 4, 5, and 6 cylinders. Tighten each of the rocker arm bolts to the torque listed in this Chapter's Specifications.

12   Refer to Section 4 and install the valve covers. Start the engine, listen for unusual valve train noses and check for oil leaks at the valve cover gaskets.

same locations. Store each set of rocker components separately in a marked plastic bag to ensure that they're reinstalled in their original locations.

3   Remove the pushrods and store them separately to make sure they don't get mixed up during installation **(see illustration)**.

Inspection

Refer to illustration 5.4

4   Check each rocker arm for wear, cracks and other damage, especially where the pushrods and valve stems contact the rocker arm **(see illustration)**.

5   Check the pivot bearings for binding and roughness. If the bearings are worn or damaged, replacement of the entire rocker arm will be necessary. **Note:** *Keep in mind that there is no valve adjustment on these engines, so excessive wear or damage in the valve train can easily result in excessive valve clearance, which in turn will cause valve noise when the engine is running.* Also check the rocker arm pivot support pedestal for cracks and other obvious damage.

6   Make sure the hole at the pushrod end of each rocker arm is open.

7   Inspect the pushrods for cracks and excessive wear at the ends, also check that the oil hole running through each pushrod is not clogged. Roll each pushrod across a piece of plate glass to see if it's bent (if it wobbles, it's bent).

Installation

Refer to illustration 5.9

8   Lubricate the lower end of each pushrod with clean engine oil or engine assembly lube and install them in their original locations. Make sure each pushrod seats completely in the lifter socket.

9   Apply engine assembly lube to the ends of the valve stems and to the upper ends of the pushrods to prevent damage to the mating surfaces on initial start-up **(see illustration)**. Also apply clean engine oil to the pivot shaft and bearing of each rocker arm and install the rocker arms loosely in their original locations. DO NOT tighten the bolts at this time!

10   Rotate the crankshaft until the number one piston is at TDC (see Section 3). With the number one piston is at TDC, tighten the intake valve rocker arms for the Num-

6   Valve springs, retainers and seals - replacement

Refer to illustrations 6.5, 6.8, 6.10, 6.15a, 6.15b and 6.19

Note: *Broken valve springs and defective valve stem seals can be replaced without removing the cylinder head. Two special tools and a compressed air source are normally required to perform this operation, so read through this Section carefully and rent or buy the tools before beginning the job.*

1   Remove the spark plugs (see Chapter 1).

2   Remove the valve covers (see Section 4).

3   Rotate the crankshaft until the number one piston is at top dead center on the compression stroke (see Section 3).

4   Remove the rocker arms for the number one piston.

5   Thread an adapter into the spark plug hole and connect an air hose from a compressed air source to it **(see illustration)**. Most auto parts stores can supply the air hose adapter. **Note:** *Many cylinder compression gauges utilize a screw-in fitting that may work with your air hose quick-disconnect fitting. If a cylinder compression gauge fitting is used*

5.9 Lubricate the pushrod ends and the valve stems with engine assembly lube before installing the rocker arms

6.5 This is what the air hose adapter that fits into the spark plug hole looks like - they're commonly available from auto parts stores

6.8 Once the spring is depressed, the keepers can be removed with a small magnet or needle-nose pliers (a magnet is preferred to prevent dropping the keepers)

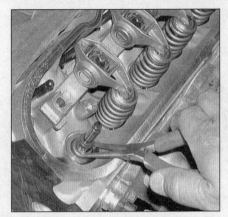

6.10 Use a pair of needle nose pliers to remove the valve seals

6.15a Be sure to install the seals on the correct valve stems

1   *Intake valve seal*
2   *Exhaust valve seal*

it will be necessary to remove the Schrader valve from the end of the fitting before using it in this procedure.

6   Apply compressed air to the cylinder. The valves should be held in place by the air pressure. **Warning:** *If the cylinder isn't exactly at TDC, air pressure may force the piston down, causing the engine to quickly rotate. DO NOT leave a wrench on the crankshaft balancer bolt or you may be injured by the tool.*

7   Stuff shop rags into the cylinder head holes around the valves to prevent parts and tools from falling into the engine.

8   Using a socket and a hammer gently tap on the top of each valve spring retainer several times (this will break the seal between the valve keeper and the spring retainer and allow the keeper to separate from the valve spring retainer as the valve spring is compressed), then use a valve spring compressor to compress the spring. Remove the keepers with small needle-nose pliers or a magnet **(see illustration)**. **Note:** *Several different types of tools are available for compressing the valve springs with the head in place. One type grips the lower spring coils and presses on the retainer as the knob is turned, while the lever-type shown here utilizes the rocker arm bolt for leverage. Both types work very well, although the lever type is usually less expensive.*

9   Remove the valve spring and retainer. **Note:** *If air pressure fails to retain the valve in the closed position during this operation, the valve face or seat may be damaged. If so, the cylinder head will have to be removed for repair.*

10   Remove the old valve stem seals, noting differences between the intake and exhaust seals **(see illustration)**.

11   Wrap a rubber band or tape around the top of the valve stem so the valve won't fall into the combustion chamber, then release the air pressure.

12   Inspect the valve stem for damage. Rotate the valve in the guide and check the end for eccentric movement, which would

indicate that the valve is bent.

13   Move the valve up-and-down in the guide and make sure it does not bind. If the valve stem binds, either the valve is bent or the guide is damaged. In either case, the head will have to be removed for repair.

14   Reapply air pressure to the cylinder to retain the valve in the closed position, then remove the tape or rubber band from the valve stem.

15   If you're working on an exhaust valve, install the new exhaust valve seal on the valve stem and press it down over the valve guide to the specified depth. Don't force the seal against the top of the guide **(see illustrations)**. **Note:** *Be sure to take this measurement from the steel spring seat to the top edge of the intake and exhaust valve seals, not from the aluminum seat on the head!*

16   If you're working on an intake valve, install a new intake valve stem seal over the valve stem and press it down over the valve guide to the specified depth. Don't force the intake valve seal against the top of the guide.

Caution: *Do not install an exhaust valve seal on an intake valve, as high oil consumption will result.*

17   Install the spring and retainer in position over the valve.

18   Compress the valve spring assembly only enough to install the keepers in the valve stem.

19   Position the keepers in the valve stem groove. Apply a small dab of grease to the inside of each keeper to hold it in place if necessary **(see illustration)**. Remove the pressure from the spring tool and make sure the keepers are seated.

20   Disconnect the air hose and remove the adapter from the spark plug hole.

21   Repeat the above procedure on the remaining cylinders, following the firing order sequence (see this Chapter's Specifications). Bring each piston to top dead center on the compression stroke before applying air pressure (see Section 3).

22   Reinstall the rocker arm assemblies and the valve covers (see Sections 4 and 5).

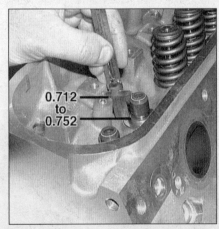

0.712 to 0.752

6.15b Install the intake and exhaust valve seals to the specified depth - measure from the spring seat to the top edge of the valve seal

6.19 Apply small dab of grease to each keeper as shown here before installation - it'll hold them in place on the valve stem as the spring is released

7.10a Displacement on Demand assembly mounting bolts

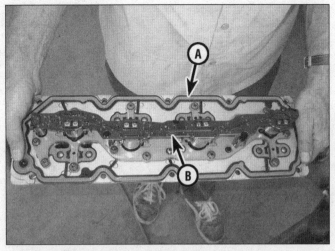

7.10b The Displacement on Demand assembly gasket (A) can be re-used if it's in good condition. Don't pick up the assembly by the electrical lead frame (B)

23   Start the engine, then check for oil leaks and unusual sounds coming from the valve cover area. Allow the engine to idle for at least five minutes before revving the engine.

7   Intake manifold - removal and installation

Warning: *Wait until the engine is completely cool before starting this procedure.*

Removal

Refer to illustrations 7.10a and 7.10b

1   Disconnect the cable from the negative terminal of the battery.
2   Remove the plastic engine cover by pulling it from its mounting studs.
3   Remove the vacuum line that attaches to the brake booster.
4   Remove both PCV air tubes. Disconnect the fuel supply line from the fuel rail (see Chapter 4).
5   Disconnect the EVAP tube from the purge solenoid and move it aside.
6   Label and disconnect all interfering wiring connectors. Free the large wiring harness from the plastic clips on the fuel rail.
7   Remove the MAP sensor from the top of the intake manifold. Pull the EVAP purge solenoid valve from its bracket, then remove the bracket.
8   Remove the intake manifold mounting bolts, in 1/4-turn increments, in the reverse order of the tightening sequence until they can be removed by hand **(see illustration 7.15)**.
9   Lift the manifold from the engine. The intake manifold can be removed with the throttle body, fuel rail and injectors all in place. **Caution:** *Do not pry between the manifold and the heads or damage to the gasket sealing surfaces may result and vacuum leaks could develop. Also, don't use too*

much force - the manifold is made of a plastic composite and could crack.
10   As the manifold is lifted from the engine, be sure to check for and disconnect anything still attached to the manifold. The Displacement on Demand assembly can be removed at this time **(see illustrations)**. This component de-energized cylinders when there is no demand for their power.

Installation

Refer to illustrations 7.13 and 7.15

Note: *The mating surfaces of the cylinder heads, block and manifold must be perfectly clean when the manifold is installed.*

11   Carefully remove all traces of old gasket material. Note that the intake manifold is made of a composite material and the cylinder heads on 5.3L engines are made of aluminum, therefore aggressive scraping is not suggested and will damage the sealing surfaces. After the gasket surfaces are cleaned and free of any gasket material wipe the

mating surfaces with a cloth saturated with safety solvent. If there is old sealant or oil on the mating surfaces when the manifold is installed, oil or vacuum leaks may develop. Use a vacuum cleaner to remove any gasket material that falls into the intake ports in the heads.
12   Use a tap of the correct size to chase the threads in the bolt holes, then use compressed air (if available) to remove the debris from the holes. **Warning:** *Wear safety glasses or a face shield to protect your eyes when using compressed air.*
13   Position the new gaskets on the intake manifold **(see illustration)**. Note that the gaskets are equipped with installation tabs that must snap into place on the intake manifold. The words "Manifold Side" may appear on the gasket, If so, this will ensure proper installation. Make sure the gaskets snap into place and all intake port openings align.
14   Carefully set the manifold in place.
15   Apply medium-strength thread locking compound to the threads of the bolts. Install

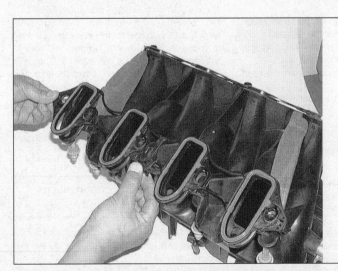

7.13 Align the tabs on the intake gaskets with the tabs on the manifold and snap the gasket into place

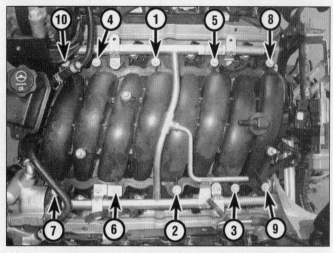

7.15 Intake manifold bolt tightening sequence

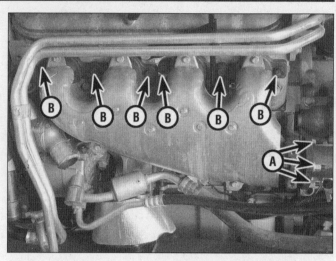

8.7 Exhaust crossover pipe nuts (A) and manifold mounting bolts (B) (front manifold shown, rear manifold similar)

the bolts and tighten them following the recommended sequence **(see illustration)** to the torque listed in this Chapter's Specifications. Do not overtighten the bolts or gasket leaks may develop.

16   The remaining installation steps are the reverse of removal. Check the coolant level, adding as necessary (see Chapter 1). Start the engine and check carefully for vacuum leaks at the intake manifold joints.

8   Exhaust manifolds - removal and installation

Removal

Refer to illustration 8.7

Warning: *Use caution when working around the exhaust manifolds - the sheetmetal heat shields can be sharp on the edges. Also, the engine should be cold when this procedure is followed.*

1   Disconnect the cable from the negative terminal of the battery.

Rear side

2   Raise the vehicle and support it securely on jackstands. Disconnect the exhaust pipe from the rear exhaust manifold. Support the weight of the exhaust system with wire.

3   Remove the ignition coils from the rear cylinder bank.

4   Remove the oxygen sensor (see Chapter 6).

Front side

5   Remove the dipstick tube.

Both manifolds

6   Remove the spark plugs.

7   Disconnect the exhaust crossover pipe from the manifold to be removed **(see illustration)**.

8   Remove the exhaust manifold heat shield if necessary for working room.

9   Remove the exhaust manifold mounting

bolts and separate the manifold from the cylinder head.

Installation

10   Check the manifold for cracks and make sure the bolt threads are clean and undamaged. The manifold and cylinder head mating surfaces must be clean before the manifolds are reinstalled - use a gasket scraper to remove all carbon deposits and gasket material. **Note:** *The cylinder heads are made of aluminum, therefore aggressive scraping is not suggested and will damage the sealing surfaces.*

11   Install the heat shields, then install the bolts and gaskets onto the manifold. Retaining tabs surrounding the gasket bolt holes should hold the assembly together as the manifold is installed.

12   Starting at the fourth thread, apply a 1/4-inch wide band of medium-strength threadlocking compound to the threads of the bolts. **Note:** *The manufacturer recommends not applying threadlocking compound on the first three threads.*

13   Place the manifold on the cylinder head and install the mounting bolts finger tight.

14   When tightening the mounting bolts, work from the center to the ends and be sure to use a torque wrench. Tighten the bolts in two steps to the torque listed in this Chapter's Specifications. If required, bend the exposed end of the exhaust manifold gasket back against the cylinder head.

15   The remaining installation steps are the reverse of removal.

16   Start the engine and check for exhaust leaks.

9   Cylinder heads - removal and installation

Note: *It will be necessary to purchase a new set of 11 mm head bolts before or during this procedure.*

Removal

Refer to illustration 9.12

1   Disconnect the cable from the negative terminal of the battery and drain the cooling system (see Chapter 1).

2   Remove the intake manifold (see Section 7) and the coolant air bleed pipe.

3   Detach both exhaust manifolds from the cylinder heads (see Section 8). It is not necessary to disconnect the manifolds from the exhaust pipes.

4   Remove the valve covers (see Section 4).

5   Remove the rocker arms and pushrods (see Section 5). **Caution:** *Again, as mentioned in Section 5, keep all the parts in order so they are reinstalled in the same location.*

Rear side

6   Remove the drivebelt (see Chapter 1) and the drivebelt idler pulley, then remove the alternator (see Chapter 5) and the alternator bracket. **Note:** *Rotate the drivebelt tensioner to access the lower alternator mounting bracket bolt.*

Front side

7   Remove the top engine mount strut.

8   Remove the drivebelt (see Chapter 1).

9   Using the correct power steering pulley removal tool, remove the pulley for access to the bolt behind its rim. (These removal tools can be rented at most auto supply stores if you don't already have one.) Alternatively, you can unbolt the power steering pump and pull it upward to get enough clearance for bolt removal.

10   Remove the three coolant manifold bolts that attach to the left end of the cylinder head.

Both sides

11   Loosen the head bolts in 1/4-turn increments in the reverse order of the tightening sequence **(see illustration 9.21)** until they

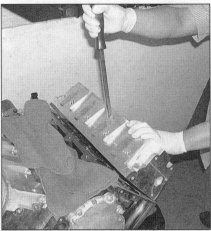

9.12 Using a prybar inserted into an intake port to break the head loose - do not use excessive force or damage to the head may result

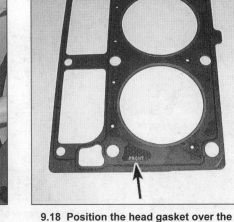

9.18 Position the head gasket over the dowels at each end of the cylinder head with the mark (arrow) facing the front of the vehicle

can be removed by hand. **Note:** *There will be different length and size head bolts for different locations. Make a note of the different sizes and lengths and where they go when removing the bolts to ensure correct installation of the new bolts.*

12   Lift the head(s) off the engine. If resistance is felt, do not pry between the head and block as damage to the mating surfaces will result. To dislodge the head, place a pry bar or long screwdriver into the intake port and carefully pry the head off the engine **(see illustration)**.

13   Store the heads on blocks of wood to prevent damage to the gasket sealing surfaces.

Installation

Refer to illustrations 9.18 and 9.21

14   The mating surfaces of the cylinder heads and block must be perfectly clean when the heads are installed. Gasket removal solvents are available at auto parts stores and may prove helpful.

15   Use a gasket scraper to remove all traces of carbon and old gasket material, then wipe the mating surfaces with a cloth saturated with lacquer thinner or acetone. **Note:** *The cylinder heads are made of aluminum, therefore aggressive scraping is not suggested and will damage the sealing surfaces.* If there is oil on the mating surfaces when the heads are installed, the gaskets may not seal correctly and leaks may develop. When working on the block, use a vacuum cleaner to remove any debris that falls into the cylinders.

16   Check the block and head mating surfaces for nicks, deep scratches and other damage. If damage is slight, it can be removed with emery cloth. If it is excessive, machining may be the only alternative.

17   Use a tap of the correct size to chase the threads in the head bolt holes in the block. If a tap is not available, spray a liberal amount of brake cleaner into each hole. Use compressed air (if available) to remove the debris from the holes. **Warning:** *Wear safety glasses or a face shield to protect your eyes when using compressed air.* All cylinder head bolts should

be replaced with **New** bolts.

18   Position the new gaskets over the dowels in the block **(see illustration)**.

19   Carefully position the heads on the block without disturbing the gaskets.

20   Before installing the 8mm head bolts, coat the threads with a medium-strength threadlocking compound. Then install the **New** 8mm head bolts (bolts 11 through 15).

21   Install **New** 11 mm head bolts (bolts 1 through 10) and tighten them finger tight. Following the recommended sequence **(see illustration)**, tighten the bolts in four steps to the torque listed in this Chapter's Specifications. **Warning:** *DO NOT reuse head bolts - always replace them with new ones.*

22   The remaining installation steps are the reverse of removal.

23   Add coolant and change the oil and filter (see Chapter 1). Start the engine and check for proper operation and coolant or oil leaks.

10   Crankshaft balancer - removal and installation

Refer to illustrations 10.17 and 10.20

Note: *This procedure requires a special balancer installation tool that is available through specialized tool manufacturers only and a new crankshaft balancer bolt. Read through the entire procedure and obtain the tool and materials before proceeding.*

1   Disconnect the cable from the negative terminal of the battery.

2   Raise the front of the vehicle and support it securely on jackstands. Then apply the parking brake.

3   Refer to Chapter 1 and remove the drivebelt.

4   Remove the upper part of the air filter housing (see Chapter 1).

5   Remove the top engine mounting strut.

6   Remove the inner plastic inner fender from the right side of the vehicle (see Chapter 11).

7   Disconnect the transmission cooler tubes from the transmission. Pull back the plastic covers and pry out the small wire retainers from each fitting with a screwdriver. Note that each clip engages in the fitting in a particular orientation.

8   Disconnect the stabilizer bar links at their lower points.

9   Pry up the plastic cover from the steering shaft and remove the pinch bolt (see Chapter 10). Push the steering shaft off of the lower shaft.

10   Refer to Chapter 11 and remove the lower air dam and its braces.

11   Remove the braces that attach the radiator to the lower engine frame.

12   Install an engine support fixture of the type that straddles the top of the engine onto the fender edges and attaches to the top of the engine to take its weight. These can be

9.21 Cylinder head bolt tightening sequence

10.17 The use of a three jaw puller will be necessary to remove the crankshaft balancer - always place the puller jaws around the hub, not the outer ring

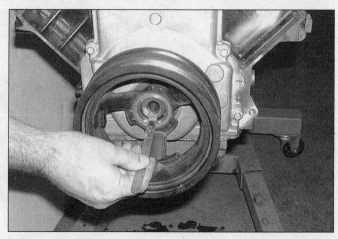

10.20 Before the new crankshaft bolt is installed and tightened, the balancer must be measured for proper installation - when properly installed, the balancer hub should extend 3/32 to 11/64-inch past the crankshaft snout (early-style balancer shown)

rented at most rental yards. Bolt it securely to the engine and tighten it to lift the weight of the engine off of its mounts.

13   Remove the subframe (see Chapter 10).

14   Remove the right front wheel.

15   Using the engine-support fixture, slowly and carefully lower the engine until there is enough clearance for removal of the crankshaft balancer/pulley.

16   Remove the bolt from the balancer. The easiest way to do this is with a heavy-duty impact gun. It can be done by hand, but it will be necessary to prevent the crankshaft from turning. Remove the starter motor (see Chapter 5). Have an assistant wedge a large screwdriver or prybar into the driveplate ring gear teeth, then loosen the crankshaft pulley center bolt.

17   Pull the balancer off the crankshaft with a puller **(see illustration)**. **Note:** *A spacer should be inserted into the crankshaft nose for the puller's tapered tip to push against to prevent damage to the crankshaft threads.*

18   Position the crankshaft pulley/balancer on the crankshaft and slide it on as far as it will go.

19   Using the specialized crankshaft balancer installation tool, press the crankshaft pulley/balancer onto the crankshaft.

20   Install the old crankshaft balancer bolt and tighten it to the Step 1 torque listed in this Chapter's Specifications. Remove the old bolt and measure the distance from the snout of the crankshaft to the balancer hub **(see illustration)**. When properly installed, the balancer hub should extend 3/32 to 11/64-inch past the crankshaft snout. If the measurement is incorrect, reinstall the balancer installation tool and press the balancer on the crankshaft until the measurement is correct.

21   Install a **New** crankshaft balancer bolt and tighten it in two steps to the torque and angle of rotation (steps 2 and 3) listed in this Chapter's Specifications.

22   The remaining installation steps are the reverse of removal.

11   Crankshaft front oil seal - removal and installation

Refer to illustrations 11.2, 11.4 and 11.5

1   Remove the crankshaft balancer (see Section 10).

2   Note how the seal is installed - the new one must be installed to the same depth and facing the same way. Carefully pry the oil seal out of the cover with a seal puller or a large screwdriver **(see illustration)**. Be very careful not to distort the cover or scratch the crankshaft! Wrap electrician's tape around the tip of the screwdriver to avoid damage to the crankshaft.

3   If the seal is being replaced with the timing chain cover removed, support the cover on top of two blocks of wood and drive the seal out from the backside with a hammer and punch. **Caution:** *Be careful not to scratch, gouge or distort the area that the seal fits into or a leak will develop.*

11.2 Carefully pry the old seal out of the timing chain cover - don't damage the crankshaft in the process

11.4 Drive the new seal into place with a large socket and hammer

11.5 If the sealing surface of the pulley hub has a wear groove from contact with the seal, repair sleeves are available at most auto parts stores

12.9 Detach the hoses, then remove the bolts and lift off the water pump manifold (engine removed for clarity)

12.13 Timing chain cover mounting bolts (arrows)

4   Apply clean engine oil or multi-purpose grease to the outer edge of the new seal, then install it in the cover with the lip (spring side) facing IN. Drive the seal into place **(see illustration)** with a large socket and a hammer (if a large socket isn't available, a piece of pipe will also work). Make sure the seal enters the bore squarely and stop when the front face is at the proper depth.

5   Check the surface on the balancer hub that the oil seal rides on. If the surface has been grooved from long-time contact with the seal, a press-on sleeve may be available to renew the sealing surface **(see illustration)**. This sleeve is pressed into place with a hammer and a block of wood and is commonly available at auto parts stores for various applications.

6   Lubricate the balancer hub with clean engine oil and reinstall the crankshaft balancer as described in Section 10.

7   The remainder of installation is the reverse of the removal.

12   Timing chain - removal, inspection and installation

Removal and inspection

Refer to illustrations 12.9, 12.13, 12.16 and 12.19

1   Disconnect the cable from the negative terminal of the battery.

2   Refer to Chapter 1 and drain the cooling system and engine oil.

3   Refer to Chapter 5 and remove the alternator.

4   Remove the power steering pump (see Chapter 10).

5   Refer to Chapter 3 and remove the water pump.

6   Remove the camshaft position sensor (see Chapter 6).

7   Disconnect the hoses from the coolant air bleed pipe.

8   Disconnect all of the hoses from the

coolant manifold and secure them out of the way using wire.

9   Using the correct power steering pulley removal tool, remove the pulley for access to the bolt behind its rim. (These removal tools can be rented at most auto supply stores if you don't already have one). Alternatively, you can unbolt the power steering pump and pull it upward to get enough clearance for bolt removal. Remove the water pump manifold **(see illustration)**.

10   Refer to Section 10 and remove the crankshaft balancer.

11   Remove one of the belt tensioner bolts and move the tensioner for access to the timing chain cover bolts.

12   Remove the bolts that attach the timing chain cover to the oil pan.

13   Remove the timing chain cover mounting bolts and separate the timing chain cover from the block **(see illustration)**. The cover may be stuck; if so, use a putty knife to break the gasket seal. Since the cover is made of aluminum it can easily be damaged, so DO NOT attempt to pry it off.

14   Remove the oil pump (see Section 15).

15   Measure the timing chain freeplay. If it is more than 5/8 inch, the chain and both sprockets should be replaced.

16   Loosen the camshaft sprocket bolts one

12.16 Timing chain alignment marks (arrows) - when properly aligned, the crankshaft gear should be in the 12 o'clock position, the camshaft gear should be in the 6 o'clock position and the number one piston should be at TDC

turn, then screw the crankshaft balancer bolt into the end of the crankshaft and rotate the crankshaft in the normal direction of rotation (clockwise) until the timing marks align **(see illustration)**. Verify that the number one piston is at TDC.

12.19 The sprocket on the crankshaft can be removed with a two or three-jaw puller

12.22 Slip the chain and camshaft sprocket in place over the crankshaft sprocket with the camshaft sprocket timing mark (arrow) at the bottom

17   Remove the three bolts from the end of the camshaft, then detach the camshaft sprocket and chain as an assembly. **Caution:** *Never rotate the crankshaft with the timing chain removed. The pistons may contact the valves and bend them.*

18   Inspect the camshaft and crankshaft sprockets for damage or wear.

19   If replacement of the timing chain is necessary, remove the sprocket on the crankshaft with a two-or three-jaw puller, but be careful not to damage the threads in the end of the crankshaft **(see illustration)**.

Installation

Refer to illustrations 12.22, 12.26 and 12.27

Note: *Timing chains must be replaced as a set with the camshaft and crankshaft sprockets. Never put a new chain on old sprockets.*

20   Use a gasket scraper to remove all traces of old gasket material and sealant from the cover and engine block.

21   Align the crankshaft sprocket with the Woodruff key and press the sprocket onto the crankshaft (if removed) with the vibration damper bolt, a large socket and some washers or tap it gently into place until it is completely seated. **Caution:** *If resistance is encountered, do not hammer the sprocket onto the crankshaft. It may eventually move onto the shaft, but it may be cracked in the process and fail later, causing extensive engine damage.*

22   Loop the new chain over the camshaft sprocket, then turn the sprocket until the timing mark is at the bottom **(see illustration)**. Mesh the chain with the crankshaft sprocket and position the camshaft sprocket on the end of the camshaft. If necessary, turn the camshaft so the dowel in the camshaft fits into the hole in the sprocket with the timing mark in the 6 o'clock position **(see illustration 12.16)**. When the chain is installed, the timing marks MUST align as shown.

23   Apply a thread locking compound to the camshaft sprocket bolt threads and tighten

the bolts to the torque listed in this Chapter's Specifications.

24   Lubricate the chain with clean engine oil.

25   Install the oil pump and the oil pick up tube onto the engine (see Section 15). Now would be a good time to replace the crankshaft front oil seal (see Section 11).

26   Install the timing chain cover on the engine loosely using a new gasket **(see illustration)**.

27   Align the timing chain cover as follows:

a) *Install the crankshaft balancer on the engine as described in Section 10. This Step will align the front oil seal with the balancer hub.*

b) *Place a straightedge on the engine block oil pan rail. Measure the distance on each side of the block from the oil pan rail to the timing chain cover with a feeler gauge **(see illustration)**. This Step measures the difference between the sealing surface of the oil pan and the sealing surface of the timing chain cover in relationship to each other.*

12.26 Install the timing chain cover with a new gasket onto the engine block LOOSELY - the cover must be aligned properly before final installation

12.27 With the crankshaft balancer in place and the front cover bolts installed LOOSELY, measure the distance between the oil pan rail and the front cover sealing surface on each side (arrows) - then adjust the cover so the measurements are even on both sides before tightening the cover bolts

13.3 Remove the bolts (arrows) and take off the camshaft retainer plate, noting which side faces the block

13.8a The roller lifters are held in place by retainers - remove the retainer bolts and remove the retainers and the lifters as an assembly - note that each retainer houses four individual lifters and they must be installed back in their original locations if they're going to be reused

c) *Tilt the timing chain cover as necessary to achieve an even measurement on each side. This Step properly aligns the front timing cover to oil pan sealing surfaces. Typically 0.000 to 0.020 inch is an acceptable tolerance.* **Note:** *Ideally the timing chain cover should be flush with the oil pan rail, but because of the differences in seal thickness, this may not always be obtainable. That is why there is a tolerance of 0.000 to 0.020 inch. Always let the front seal center itself around the crankshaft balancer hub and tilt the cover from side to side to even up the measurement at both oil pan rails. Never push downward on the front timing cover in an attempt to make the oil pan sealing surface flush, as this will distort the front oil seal and eventually lead to an oil leak!*

d) *With the timing chain cover properly aligned, tighten the cover bolts to the torque listed in this Chapter's Specifications.*

28 Apply a thin layer of RTV sealant to the areas where the timing chain cover and cylinder block meet, then install the oil pan as described in Section 14.

29 The remaining installation steps are the reverse of removal.

30 Add coolant and oil to the engine (see Chapter 1). Run the engine and check for oil and coolant leaks.

13 Camshaft and lifters - removal, inspection and installation

Warning: *Wait until the engine is completely cool before beginning this procedure.*
Caution: *If the camshaft is being replaced, always install new lifters as well. Do not use old lifters on a new camshaft.*

Removal

Refer to illustrations 13.8a, 13.8b and 13.10

1 Refer to Chapter 2C and remove the engine from the vehicle.
2 Remove the valve covers (see Section 4).
3 Remove the intake manifold (see Section 7).
4 Remove the rocker arms and pushrods (see Section 5).
5 Remove the timing chain and sprockets (see Section 12).
6 Remove the cylinder heads (see Section 9).
7 Before removing the lifters, arrange to

store them in a clearly labeled box to ensure that they're reinstalled in their original locations.
8 Remove the lifter retainers and lifters and store them where they won't get dirty **(see illustrations)**. DO NOT attempt to withdraw the camshaft with the lifters in place.
9 If the lifters are built up with gum and varnish they may not come out with the retainer. If so, there are several ways to extract the lifters from the bores. A special tool designed to grip and remove lifters is manufactured by many tool companies and is widely available, but it may not be required in every case. On engines without a lot of varnish buildup, the lifters can often be removed with a small magnet or even with your fingers. A machinist's scribe with a bent end can be used to pull the lifters out by positioning the point under the retainer ring in the top of each lifter. **Caution:** *Don't use pliers to remove the lifters unless you intend to replace them with new ones. The pliers will damage the precision machined and hardened lifters, rendering them useless.*
10 Remove the bolts and the camshaft retainer plate, noting which direction faces the block **(see illustration)**.

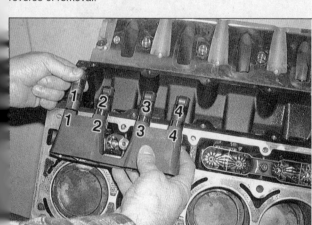

13.8b Once the lifters and retainers are removed from the block they can be marked (for location and installation purposes) and inspected

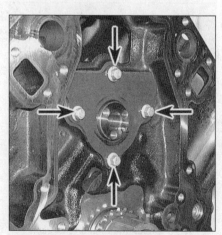

13.10 Remove the bolts and take off the camshaft retainer plate, noting which side faces the block

13.13a If the camshaft is removed from the engine, lobe lift can be obtained by measuring camshaft lobe height . . .

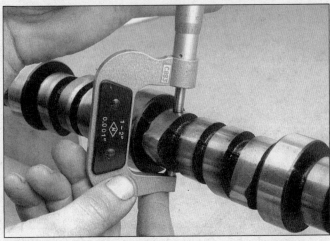

13.13b . . . and by measuring the camshaft base circle - the difference between the two measurements equals lobe lift

11   Thread a bolt into the camshaft sprocket bolt hole to use as a handle when removing the camshaft from the block.

12   Carefully and slowly pull the camshaft out. Support the cam near the block so the lobes don't nick or gouge the bearings as it's withdrawn.

Inspection

Camshaft lobe lift check

Refer to illustrations 13.13a and 13.13b

13   Measure the camshaft lobe height and the base circle **(see illustrations)**. The difference between the two measurements is the lobe lift (lobe height - base circle = lobe lift). Record this figure for future reference and repeat the check on the remaining camshaft lobes.

14   After the lobe lift check is complete, compare the results to the values listed in this Chapter's Specifications. If the lobe lift is 0.002 inch less than specified, cam lobe wear has occurred and a new camshaft should be installed.

Camshaft bearing journals, lobes and bearings

Refer to illustration 13.16

15   After the camshaft has been removed from the engine, cleaned with solvent and dried, inspect the bearing journals for uneven wear, pitting and evidence of seizure. If the journals are damaged, the bearing inserts in the block are probably damaged as well. Both the camshaft and bearings will have to be replaced. **Note:** *Camshaft bearing replacement requires special tools and expertise that place it beyond the scope of the average home mechanic. The tools for bearing removal and installation are available at stores that carry automotive tools, possibly even found at a tool rental business. It is advisable though, if the bearings are bad and the procedure is beyond your ability, take the engine to an automotive machine shop to ensure that the job is done correctly.*

16   Measure the bearing journals with a micrometer to determine if they are exces-

sively worn or out-of-round **(see illustration)**.

17   Check the camshaft lobes for heat discoloration, score marks, chipped areas, pitting and uneven wear. If the lobes are in good condition and if the lobe lift measurements recorded earlier are as specified, the camshaft can be reused.

Lifters

Refer to illustrations 13.18 and 13.19

18   Clean the lifters with solvent and dry them thoroughly without mixing them up. Check each lifter wall and pushrod seat and for score marks and uneven wear **(see illustration)**. If the lifter walls are damaged or worn (which is not very likely), inspect the lifter bores in the engine block as well. If the pushrod seats are worn, check the pushrod ends.

19   Check the rollers carefully for wear and damage and make sure they turn freely without excessive play **(see illustration)**.

20   Used roller lifters cannot be reinstalled with a new camshaft, but the original camshaft

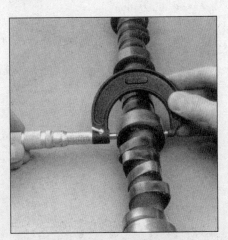

13.16 Check the diameter of each camshaft bearing journal to pinpoint excessive wear and out-of-round conditions

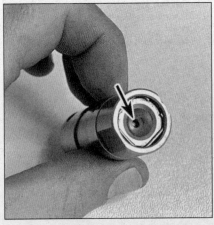

13.18 Check the pushrod seat in the top of each lifter for wear

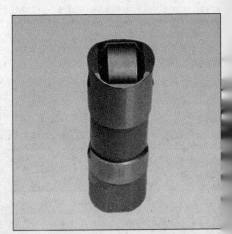

13.19 The roller on hydraulic roller lifters must turn freely - check for wear and excessive play as well

13.21 Be sure to apply camshaft assembly lube to the cam lobes and bearing journals before installing the camshaft

14.15 Subframe mounting bolts

can be used if new lifters are installed. Always use new lifters when installing a new camshaft.

Installation

Refer to illustration 13.21

21   Lubricate the camshaft bearing journals and cam lobes with camshaft and lifter assembly lube **(see illustration)**.

23   Slide the camshaft into the engine. Support the cam near the block and be careful not to scrape or nick the bearings.

24   Turn the camshaft until the dowel pin is in the 3 o'clock position, install the camshaft thrust plate and tighten the bolts to the torque listed in this Chapter's Specifications. Make sure the gasket surface on the camshaft thrust plate and the engine block are free from oil and dirt.

25   Install the timing chain and sprockets (see Section 12). Also install the camshaft position sensor using a new O-ring (see Chapter 6).

26   Lubricate the lifters with clean engine oil and install them in the lifter retainers. Be sure to align the flats on the lifters with the flats in the lifter retainers. Install the retainer and lifters into the engine block as an assembly. If the original lifters are being reinstalled, be sure to return them to their original locations. If a new camshaft is being installed, install new lifters as well. Tighten the lifter retainer bolts to the torque listed in this Chapter's Specifications.

27   The remainder of installation is the reverse of removal.

28   Before starting and running the engine, refill the cooling system, change the oil and install a new oil filter (see Chapter 1).

14 Oil pan - removal and installation

Removal

Refer to illustration 14.15

1   Disconnect the cable from the negative terminal of the battery.

2   Loosen the front wheel lug nuts. Raise the vehicle and support it securely on jackstands, then refer to Chapter 1 and drain the engine oil and remove the oil filter.

3   Install an engine support fixture. These can be rented at most rental yards. Bolt it securely to the engine and tighten it to lift the weight of the engine off of its mounts.

4   Remove the front wheels.

5   Refer to Chapter 11 and remove the lower air dam and its braces. Remove the engine drivebelt (see Chapter 1).

6   Move the battery cable harness clear of the subframe.

7   Disconnect the steering fluid cooler tube from the subframe.

8   Disconnect the stabilizer bar links and turn the stabilizer bar to provide access to the steering gear bolts.

9   Unbolt the power steering gear and tie it aside.

10   Unbolt the engine and transmission mounts from the frame.

11   Disconnect the front wheel speed sensor harnesses and release the harnesses from the control arms.

12   Disconnect the lower control arms from the subframe (see Chapter 10).

13   Support the subframe with two floor jacks - one placed on each side.

14   Remove the two subframe reinforcement plates.

15   Remove the four subframe bolts **(see illustration)**.

16   Carefully lower the subframe.

17   Remove the plastic cover from the torque converter.

18   Disconnect the wiring and wiring harness from the oil pan.

19   Remove the bolt from the lower drivebelt tensioner and push the tensioner aside for access to the oil pan bolt.

20   Remove the oil pan bolts and lower the oil pan. The pan will probably stick to the engine, so strike the pan with a rubber mallet until it breaks the gasket seal. **Caution:** *Before using force on the oil pan, be sure all*

the bolts have been removed. Carefully slide the oil pan down and out, to the rear.

Installation

Refer to illustrations 14.21 and 14.24

21   Drill out the rivets securing the oil pan gasket to the oil pan and remove the old gasket **(see illustration)**. Wash out the oil pan with solvent.

22   Thoroughly clean the mounting surfaces of the oil pan and engine block of old gasket material and sealer. Wipe the gasket surfaces clean with a rag soaked in lacquer thinner, acetone or brake system cleaner.

23   Apply a 3/16-inch wide, one inch long bead of RTV sealant to the corners of the block where the front cover and the rear cover meet the engine block. Then attach the new gasket to the pan, install the pan and tighten the bolts finger-tight. Be sure the oil gallery passages in the pan and the gasket are aligned properly. **Note:** *Oil pan gasket rivets do not need to be installed on assembly.*

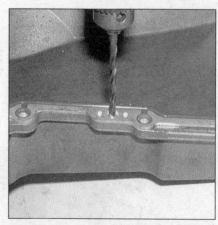

14.21 The manufacturer uses rivets to hold the gasket to the oil pan during assembly - carefully drill them out (it isn't necessary to rivet the new gasket to the oil pan)

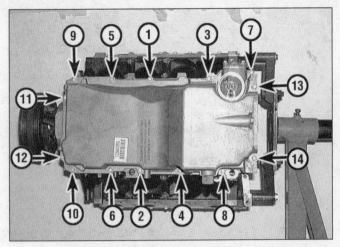

14.24 Oil pan TIGHTENING sequence - all V8 engines

15.4 Remove the bolt (arrow) securing the oil pick-up tube to the oil pump, then separate the tube from the pump

24   The alignment of the rear face of the aluminum pan to the rear of the block is important. Measure between the rear face of the pan and the front face of the transmission bellhousing with feeler gauges. Clearance should ideally be flush, but a gap of up to 0.010-inch is allowable. If the clearance is OK, tighten the pan bolts/studs in sequence to the torque listed in this Chapter's Specifications **(see illustration)**. If the clearance is not acceptable, install the two lower oil pan-to-bellhousing bolts and tighten them finger tight. This should draw the oil pan flush with the bellhousing. **Caution:** *The rear of the oil pan should never protrude rearward of the bellhousing plane of the block.*

25   The remainder of installation is the reverse of removal. Tighten the bolts to the torque listed in this Chapter's Specifications.

26   Add the proper type and quantity of oil (see Chapter 1), start the engine and check for leaks before placing the vehicle back in service.

15   Oil pump - removal, inspection and installation

Removal

Refer to illustrations 15.4 and 15.5

1   Refer to the Section 12 and remove the timing chain cover.

2   Raise the vehicle and support it securely on jackstands. Refer to Section 14 and disconnect or remove all of the components such as wiring harnesses that interfere with lowering of the oil pan.

3   Remove all of the oil pan bolts except the rear two; loosen them a few turns. This will allow the oil pan to drop at the front end, giving enough room to reach the oil pump pick-up bolt at the oil pump.

4   Remove the oil pump pick-up bolt, being careful to avoid dropping it into the pan **(see illustration)**. You can place a rag between the oil pan and the oil pump to avoid losing

the bolt or the O-ring.

5   Remove the oil pump bolts **(see illustration)** and slide the pump off of the crankshaft along with the pick-up tube O-ring.

Inspection

Refer to illustration 15.6

6   Remove the oil pump cover and withdraw the rotors from the pump body **(see illustration)**. Clean the components with solvent, dry them thoroughly and inspect for any obvious damage. Also check the bolt holes for damaged threads and the splined surfaces on the crankshaft sprocket for any apparent damage. If any of the components are scored, scratched or worn, replace the entire oil pump assembly. There are no serviceable parts currently available.

Installation

Refer to illustration 15.10

7   Prime the pump by pouring clean motor

15.5 Oil pump mounting bolts (arrows)

15.6 Oil pump cover-to-oil pump housing mounting bolts (arrows)

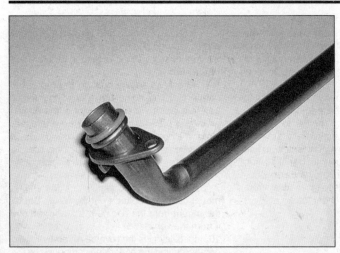

15.10 Always install a new O-ring on the oil pump pick up tube

17.3 Carefully pry the old seal out with a screwdriver at the notches provided in the rear cover

oil into the pick-up tube hole, while turning the pump by hand.

8   Position the oil pump over the end of the crankshaft and align the teeth on the crankshaft sprocket with the teeth on the oil pump drive gear. Making sure the pump is fully seated against the block.

9   Install the oil pump mounting bolts and tighten them to the torque listed in this Chapter's Specifications.

10   Install a new O-ring on the oil pump pick-up tube, then fasten it to the oil pump and the engine block main studs **(see illustration)**. **Caution:** *Be absolutely certain that the pick-up tube-to-oil pump bolts are properly tightened so that no air can be sucked into the oiling system at this connection.*

11   Install and align the timing chain cover, then install the oil pan. Refer to Sections 12 and 14 for the installation procedures.

12   The remainder of installation is the reverse of removal.

13   Add oil and coolant as necessary. Run the engine and check for oil and coolant leaks. Also check the oil pressure as described in Chapter 2C.

16   Driveplate - removal and installation

1   Refer to Chapter 7 and remove the transaxle.

2   Remove the driveplate and inspect it for wear and damage.

3   Before installing the bolts, apply locking compound to the bolt threads.

4   Set the driveplate in place and tighten the bolts to the torque values listed in this Chapter's Specifications. Make sure you tighten the bolts in three steps in a criss-cross pattern.

5   The remainder of the installation procedure is the reverse of removal.

17   Rear main oil seal - replacement

Refer to illustrations 17.3 and 17.4

Note: *If you're installing a new rear seal during a complete engine overhaul, refer to the procedure in Chapter 2C.*

1   Remove the transaxle (see Chapter 7).

2   Remove the driveplate (see Section 16).

3   Pry the oil seal from the rear cover with a screwdriver **(see illustration)**. Be careful not to nick or scratch the crankshaft or the seal bore. Be sure to note how far it's recessed into the housing bore before removal so the new seal can be installed to the same depth. Thoroughly clean the seal bore in the block with a shop towel. Remove all traces of oil and dirt.

4   Lubricate the outside diameter of the seal and install the seal over the end of the crankshaft. Make sure the lip of the seal points toward the engine. Preferably, a seal installation tool (available at most auto parts store) should be used to press the new seal back into place. If the proper seal installation tool is unavailable, use a large socket, section of pipe or a blunt tool and carefully drive the new seal squarely into the seal bore and flush

with the rear cover **(see illustration)**.

5   Install the flywheel/driveplate (see Section 16).

6   Install the transmission (see Chapter 7).

18   Engine mounts - check and replacement

1   Engine mounts seldom require attention, but broken or deteriorated mounts should be replaced immediately or the added strain placed on the driveline components may cause damage.

Check

2   During the check, the engine must be raised slightly to remove the weight from the mounts.

3   Raise the vehicle and support it securely on jackstands, then position the jack under the engine oil pan. Place a large block of wood between the jack head and the oil pan, then carefully raise the engine just enough to take the weight off the mounts. Do not use the jack to support the entire weight of the engine.

17.4 The rear oil seal can be pressed into place with a seal installation tool, a section of pipe or a blunt object shown here - in any case be sure the seal is installed squarely into the seal bore and flush with the rear cover

**18.7 Engine mount-to-subframe nuts
(right side shown)**

4   Check the mounts to see if the rubber is cracked, hardened or separated from the metal plates. Sometimes the rubber will split right down the center. Rubber preservative or WD-40 can be applied to the mounts to slow deterioration.

5   Check for relative movement between the mount plates and the engine or frame (use a large screwdriver or prybar to attempt to move the mounts). If movement is noted, check the tightness of the mount fasteners first before condemning the mounts. Usually when engine mounts are broken, they are very obvious as the engine will easily move away from the mount when pried or under load.

Replacement

Refer to illustration 18.7

6   Disconnect the cable from the negative terminal of the battery, then raise the vehicle and support it securely on jackstands.

7   Raise the vehicle and support it securely on jackstands. Remove the nuts that attach the mount studs to the engine subframe (see illustration).

8   Attach an engine hoist to the top of the engine for lifting; do not use a jack under the oil pan to support the entire weight of the engine or the oil pump pick-up could be damaged. **Note:** *If a hoist is not available, casting lugs on each side of the engine block can be used to support the entire weight of the engine while the engine mounts are being replaced.*

9   Raise the engine slightly until the engine mount can be unbolted from the block. Unbolt the mount from the engine block and remove it from the vehicle.

10   Installation is the reverse of removal. Use non-hardening thread-locking compound on the mount bolts and be sure to tighten them to the torque listed in this Chapter's Specifications.

Chapter 2 Part C
General engine overhaul procedures

Contents

Specifications

General

Displacement	
3.5L V6	214 cubic inches
3.9L V6	238 cubic inches
5.3L V8	325 cubic inches
Bore and stroke	
3.5L V6	3.90 x 2.99 inches
3.9L V6	3.90 x 3.31 inches
5.3L V8	3.78 x 3.62 inches
Cylinder compression pressure	
Minimum	100 psi
Maximum	25 percent from highest reading
Oil pressure (minimum, at operating temperature)	
1000 rpm	6 psi
2000 rpm	18 psi
4000 rpm	24 psi

Torque specifications

Ft-lbs (unless otherwise indicated)

Note: *One foot-pound (ft-lb) of torque is equivalent to 12 inch-pounds (in-lbs) of torque. Torque values below approximately 15 foot-pounds are expressed in inch-pounds, because most foot-pound torque wrenches are not accurate at these smaller values.*

Subframe/engine cradle mounting bolts (V8 models)	
Front	107
Rear	118
Driveplate-to-torque converter bolts	46
Connecting rod bearing cap bolts	
V6	
Step 1	18
Step 2	Tighten an additional 110-degrees
V8	
Step 1	15
Step 2	Tighten an additional 85-degrees
Main bearing cap bolts	
V6	
Step 1	37
Step 2	Tighten an additional 77-degrees
V8	
Bolts 1 through 10	
Step 1	15
Step 2	Tighten an additional 80-degrees
Bolts 11 through 20	
Step 1	15
Step 2	Tighten an additional 51-degrees
Bolts 21 through 30	18*
Transmission-to-engine bolts	55

*Must be replaced with new bolts

1.1 An engine block being bored. An engine rebuilder will use special machinery to recondition the cylinder bores

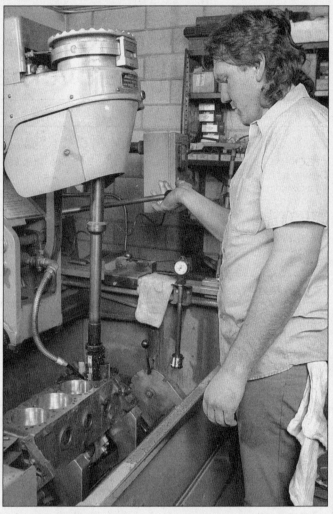

1.2 If the cylinders are bored, the machine shop will normally hone the engine on a machine like this

1   General information - engine overhaul

Refer to illustrations 1.1, 1.2, 1.3, 1.4, 1.5 and 1.6

Included in this portion of Chapter 2 are general information and diagnostic testing procedures for determining the overall mechanical condition of your engine.

The information ranges from advice concerning preparation for an overhaul and the purchase of replacement parts and/or components to detailed, step-by-step procedures covering removal and installation.

The following Sections have been written to help you determine whether your engine needs to be overhauled and how to remove and install it once you've determined it needs to be rebuilt. For information concerning in-vehicle engine repair, see Chapter 2A or 2B.

It's not always easy to determine when, or if, an engine should be completely over-hauled, because a number of factors must be considered.

High mileage is not necessarily an indication that an overhaul is needed, while low mileage doesn't preclude the need for an overhaul. Frequency of servicing is probably the most important consideration. An engine that's had regular and frequent oil and filter changes, as well as other required maintenance, will most likely give many thousands of miles of reliable service. Conversely, a neglected engine may require an overhaul very early in its service life.

Excessive oil consumption is an indication that piston rings, valve seals and/or valve guides are in need of attention. Make sure that oil leaks aren't responsible before deciding that the rings and/or guides are bad. Perform a cylinder compression check to determine the extent of the work required (see Section 3). Also check the vacuum readings under various conditions (see Section 4).

Check the oil pressure with a gauge installed in place of the oil pressure sending unit and compare it to this Chapter's Specifications (see Section 2). If it's extremely low, the bearings and/or oil pump are probably worn out.

Loss of power, rough running, knocking or metallic engine noises, excessive valve train noise and high fuel consumption rates may also point to the need for an overhaul, especially if they're all present at the same time. If a complete tune-up doesn't remedy the situation, major mechanical work is the only solution.

An engine overhaul involves restoring the internal parts to the specifications of a new engine. During an overhaul, the piston rings are replaced and the cylinder walls are reconditioned (rebored and/or honed) **(see illustrations 1.1 and 1.2)**. If a rebore is done by an automotive machine shop, new oversize pistons will also be installed. The main bearings, connecting rod bearings and camshaft bearings are generally replaced with new

1.3 A crankshaft having a main bearing journal ground

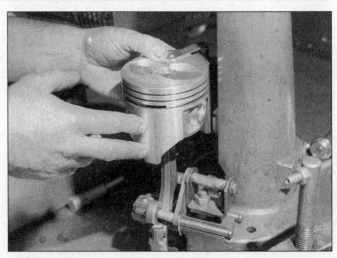

1.4 A machinist checks for a bent connecting rod, using specialized equipment

ones and, if necessary, the crankshaft may be reground to restore the journals **(see illustration 1.3)**. Generally, the valves are serviced as well, since they're usually in less-than-perfect condition at this point. While the engine is being overhauled, other components, such as the distributor, starter and alternator, can be rebuilt as well. The end result should be similar to a new engine that will give many trouble free miles. **Note:** *Critical cooling system components such as the hoses, drivebelts, thermostat and water pump should be replaced with new parts when an engine is overhauled. The radiator should be checked carefully to ensure that it isn't clogged or leaking (see Chapter 3). If you purchase a rebuilt engine or short block, some rebuilders will not warranty their engines unless the radiator has been professionally flushed. Also, we don't recommend overhauling the oil pump - always install a new one when an engine is rebuilt.*

Overhauling the internal components on today's engines is a difficult and time-consuming task which requires a significant amount of specialty tools and is best left to a professional engine rebuilder **(see illustrations 1.4, 1.5 and 1.6)**. A competent engine rebuilder will handle the inspection of your old parts and offer advice concerning the reconditioning or replacement of the original engine, never purchase parts or have machine work done on other components until the block has been thoroughly inspected by a professional machine shop. As a general rule, time is the primary cost of an overhaul, especially since the vehicle may be tied up for a minimum of two weeks or more. Be aware that some engine builders only have the capability to rebuild the engine you bring them while other rebuilders have a large inventory of rebuilt exchange engines in stock. Also be aware that many machine shops could take as much as two weeks time to completely rebuild your engine depending on shop work-

load. Sometimes it makes more sense to simply exchange your engine for another engine that's already rebuilt to save time.

2   Oil pressure check

Refer to illustrations 2.2a, 2.2b and 2.3

1   Low engine oil pressure can be a sign of an engine in need of rebuilding. A "low oil pressure" indicator (often called an "idiot light") is not a test of the oiling system. Such indicators only come on when the oil pressure is dangerously low. Even a factory oil pressure gauge in the instrument panel is only a relative indication, although much better for driver information than a warning light. A better test is with a mechanical (not electrical) oil pressure gauge.

2   Locate the engine oil pressure sending unit on the engine block:

1.5 A bore gauge being used to check the main bearing bore

1.6 Uneven piston wear like this indicates a bent connecting rod

2.2a On V8 engines the oil pressure sending unit is located at the left end (driver's side) of the engine, between the throttle body and intake manifold

2.2b Location of the oil pressure sending unit on V6 engines

a) *On V8 engines, the oil pressure sender is located at the end of the intake manifold near the throttle body. It screws into the displacement-on-demand valley cover* **(see illustration).**

b) *On V6 engines, the oil pressure sending unit is located near the oil filter housing on the front side of the engine* **(see illustration).** **Note:** *On some models a heat shield will have to be removed for access to the sending unit.*

3   Unscrew and remove the oil pressure sending unit and screw in the hose for your oil pressure gauge **(see illustration).** If necessary, install an adapter fitting. Use Teflon tape or thread sealant on the threads of the adapter and/or the fitting on the end of your gauge's hose.

4   Connect an accurate tachometer to the engine, according to the tachometer manufacturer's instructions.

5   Check the oil pressure with the engine running (normal operating temperature) at the specified engine speed, and compare it to this Chapter's Specifications. If it's extremely low, the bearings and/or oil pump are probably worn out.

3   Cylinder compression check

Refer to illustration 3.6

1   A compression check will tell you what mechanical condition the upper end of your engine (pistons, rings, valves, head gaskets) is in. Specifically, it can tell you if the compression is down due to leakage caused by worn piston rings, defective valves and seats or a blown head gasket. **Note:** *The engine must be at normal operating temperature and the battery must be fully charged for this check.*

2   Begin by cleaning the area around the spark plugs before you remove them (compressed air should be used, if available). The idea is to prevent dirt from getting into the cylinders as the compression check is being done.

3   Remove all of the spark plugs from the engine (see Chapter 1).

4   Remove the air intake duct (see Chapter 4) and block the throttle plate wide open.

5   On V6 models, disable the ignition system by disconnecting the primary (low voltage) wiring from the coil pack. On V8 engines, disconnect the large electrical connector for each ignition coil harness **(see illustration 13.7b in Chapter 4).** On all models, disable the fuel system by removing the fuel pump fuse (see Chapter 4, Section 2).

6   Install a compression gauge in the number one cylinder spark plug hole **(see illustration).**

7   Crank the engine over at least seven compression strokes and watch the gauge. The compression should build up quickly in a healthy engine. Low compression on the first

2.3 Remove the oil pressure sending unit and install an oil pressure gauge

3.6 Use a compression gauge with a threaded fitting for the spark plug hole, not the type that requires hand pressure to maintain the seal

stroke, followed by gradually increasing pressure on successive strokes, indicates worn piston rings. A low compression reading on the first stroke, which doesn't build up during successive strokes, indicates leaking valves or a blown head gasket (a cracked head could also be the cause). Deposits on the undersides of the valve heads can also cause low compression. Record the highest gauge reading obtained.

8   Repeat the procedure for the remaining cylinders and compare the results to this Chapter's Specifications.

9   Add some engine oil (about three squirts from a plunger-type oil can) to each cylinder, through the spark plug hole, and repeat the test.

10   If the compression increases after the oil is added, the piston rings are definitely worn. If the compression doesn't increase significantly, the leakage is occurring at the valves or head gasket. Leakage past the valves may be caused by burned valve seats and/or faces or warped, cracked or bent valves.

11   If two adjacent cylinders have equally low compression, there's a strong possibility that the head gasket between them is blown. The appearance of coolant in the combustion chambers or the crankcase would verify this condition.

12   If one cylinder is slightly lower than the others, and the engine has a slightly rough idle, a worn lobe on the camshaft could be the cause.

13   If the compression is unusually high, the combustion chambers are probably coated with carbon deposits. If that's the case, the cylinder head(s) should be removed and decarbonized.

14   If compression is way down or varies greatly between cylinders, it would be a good idea to have a leak-down test performed by an automotive repair shop. This test will pinpoint exactly where the leakage is occurring and how severe it is.

4   Vacuum gauge diagnostic checks

Refer to illustration 4.6

1   A vacuum gauge provides inexpensive but valuable information about what is going on in the engine. You can check for worn rings or cylinder walls, leaking head or intake manifold gaskets, incorrect carburetor adjustments, restricted exhaust, stuck or burned valves, weak valve springs, improper ignition or valve timing and ignition problems.

2   Unfortunately, vacuum gauge readings are easy to misinterpret, so they should be used in conjunction with other tests to confirm the diagnosis.

3   Both the absolute readings and the rate of needle movement are important for accurate interpretation. Most gauges measure vacuum in inches of mercury (in-Hg). The following references to vacuum assume the diagnosis is being performed at sea level. As elevation increases (or atmospheric pressure

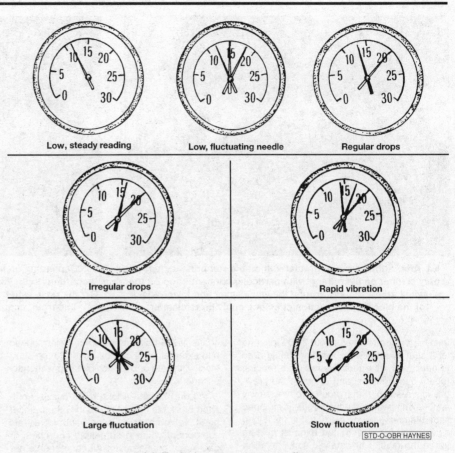

Low, steady reading   **Low, fluctuating needle**   **Regular drops**

Irregular drops   **Rapid vibration**

Large fluctuation   **Slow fluctuation**

STD-O-OBR HAYNES

4.6 Typical vacuum gauge readings

decreases), the reading will decrease. For every 1,000 foot increase in elevation above approximately 2,000 feet, the gauge readings will decrease about one inch of mercury.

4   Connect the vacuum gauge directly to the intake manifold vacuum, not to ported (throttle body) vacuum. Be sure no hoses are left disconnected during the test or false readings will result.

5   Before you begin the test, allow the engine to warm up completely. Block the wheels and set the parking brake. With the transaxle in Park, start the engine and allow it to run at normal idle speed. **Warning:** *Keep your hands and the vacuum gauge clear of the fans.*

6   Read the vacuum gauge; an average, healthy engine should normally produce about 17 to 22 in-Hg with a fairly steady needle **(see illustration)**. Refer to the following vacuum gauge readings and what they indicate about the engine's condition:

7   A low steady reading usually indicates a leaking gasket between the intake manifold and cylinder head(s) or throttle body, a leaky vacuum hose, late ignition timing or incorrect camshaft timing. Check ignition timing with a timing light and eliminate all other possible causes, utilizing the tests provided in this Chapter before you remove the timing chain cover to check the timing marks.

8   If the reading is three to eight inches

below normal and it fluctuates at that low reading, suspect an intake manifold gasket leak at an intake port or a faulty fuel injector.

9   If the needle has regular drops of about two-to-four inches at a steady rate, the valves are probably leaking. Perform a compression check or leak-down test to confirm this.

10   An irregular drop or down-flick of the needle can be caused by a sticking valve or an ignition misfire. Perform a compression check or leak-down test and read the spark plugs.

11   A rapid vibration of about four in-Hg vibration at idle combined with exhaust smoke indicates worn valve guides. Perform a leak-down test to confirm this. If the rapid vibration occurs with an increase in engine speed, check for a leaking intake manifold gasket or head gasket, weak valve springs, burned valves or ignition misfire.

12   A slight fluctuation, say one inch up and down, may mean ignition problems. Check all the usual tune-up items and, if necessary, run the engine on an ignition analyzer.

13   If there is a large fluctuation, perform a compression or leak-down test to look for a weak or dead cylinder or a blown head gasket.

14   If the needle moves slowly through a wide range, check for a clogged PCV system, incorrect idle fuel mixture, throttle body or intake manifold gasket leaks.

15   Check for a slow return after revving the engine by quickly snapping the throttle open

6.1 After tightly wrapping water-vulnerable components, use a spray cleaner on everything, with particular concentration on the greasiest areas, usually around the valve cover and lower edges of the block. If one section dries out, apply more cleaner

6.2 Depending on how dirty the engine is, let the cleaner soak in according to the directions and hose off the grime and cleaner. Get the rinse water down into every area you can get at; then dry important components with a hair dryer or paper towels

until the engine reaches about 2,500 rpm and let it shut. Normally the reading should drop to near zero, rise above normal idle reading (about 5 in-Hg over) and return to the previous idle reading. If the vacuum returns slowly and doesn't peak when the throttle is snapped shut, the rings may be worn. If there is a long delay, look for a restricted exhaust system (often the muffler or catalytic converter). An easy way to check this is to temporarily disconnect the exhaust ahead of the suspected part and redo the test.

5 Engine rebuilding alternatives

The do-it-yourselfer is faced with a number of options when purchasing a rebuilt engine. The major considerations are cost, warranty, parts availability and the time required for the rebuilder to complete the project. The decision to replace the engine block, piston/connecting rod assemblies and crankshaft depends on the final inspection results of your engine. Only then can you make a cost effective decision whether to have your engine overhauled or simply purchase an exchange engine for your vehicle.

Some of the rebuilding alternatives include:

Individual parts - If the inspection procedures reveal that the engine block and most engine components are in reusable condition, purchasing individual parts and having a rebuilder rebuild your engine may be the most economical alternative. The block, crankshaft and piston/connecting rod assemblies should all be inspected carefully by a machine shop first.

Short block - A short block consists of an engine block with a crankshaft and piston/connecting rod assemblies already installed. All new bearings are incorporated and all clearances will be correct. The existing cam-

shafts, valve train components, cylinder head and external parts can be bolted to the short block with little or no machine shop work necessary.

Long block - A long block consists of a short block plus an oil pump, oil pan, cylinder head, valve cover, camshaft and valve train components, timing sprockets and chain or gears and timing cover. All components are installed with new bearings, seals and gaskets incorporated throughout. The installation of manifolds and external parts is all that's necessary.

Low mileage used engines - Some companies now offer low mileage used engines which is a very cost effective way to get your vehicle up and running again. These engines often come from vehicles which have been in totaled in accidents or come from other countries which have a higher vehicle turn over rate. A low mileage used engine also usually has a similar warranty like the newly remanufactured engines.

Give careful thought to which alternative is best for you and discuss the situation with local automotive machine shops, auto parts dealers and experienced rebuilders before ordering or purchasing replacement parts.

6 Engine removal - methods and precautions

Refer to illustrations 6.1, 6.2, 6.3 and 6.4

If you've decided that an engine must be removed for overhaul or major repair work, several preliminary steps should be taken. Read all removal and installation procedures carefully prior to committing to this job.

Locating a suitable place to work is extremely important. Adequate work space, along with storage space for the vehicle, will be needed. If a shop or garage isn't available,

at the very least a flat, level, clean work surface made of concrete or asphalt is required.

Cleaning the engine compartment and engine before beginning the removal procedure will help keep tools clean and organized **(see illustrations 6.1 and 6.2)**.

An engine hoist will also be necessary. Make sure the hoist is rated in excess of the combined weight of the engine and transaxle. Safety is of primary importance, considering the potential hazards involved in removing the engine from the vehicle.

A vehicle hoist will be necessary for engine removal on V8 engines, since the engine and transaxle are removed as an assembly out the bottom of the vehicle. On V6 models, the engine is removed out the top.

If you're a novice at engine removal, get at least one helper. One person cannot easily do all the things you need to do to remove a big heavy engine and transaxle assembly from the engine compartment. Also helpful is to seek advice and assistance from someone who's experienced in engine removal.

Plan the operation ahead of time. Arrange for or obtain all of the tools and equipment you'll need prior to beginning the job **(see illustrations 6.3 and 6.4)**. Some of the equipment necessary to perform engine removal and installation safely and with relative ease are (in addition to a vehicle hoist and an engine hoist) a heavy duty floor jack (preferably fitted with a transaxle jack head adapter), complete sets of wrenches and sockets as described in the front of this manual, wooden blocks, plenty of rags and cleaning solvent for mopping up spilled oil, coolant and gasoline.

Plan for the vehicle to be out of use for quite a while. A machine shop can do the work that is beyond the scope of the home mechanic. Machine shops often have a busy schedule, so before removing the engine, consult the shop for an estimate of how long

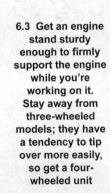

6.3 Get an engine stand sturdy enough to firmly support the engine while you're working on it. Stay away from three-wheeled models; they have a tendency to tip over more easily, so get a four-wheeled unit

6.4 Since many of the fasteners on these engines are tightened using the "angle torque" method, a torque angle gauge is essential for proper assembly

it will take to rebuild or repair the components that may need work.

7 Engine - removal and installation

Warning 1: *Gasoline is extremely flammable, so take extra precautions when you work on any part of the fuel system. Don't smoke or allow open flames or bare light bulbs near the work area, and don't work in a garage where a gas-type appliance (such as a water heater or clothes dryer) is present. Since gasoline is carcinogenic, wear fuel-resistant gloves when there's a possibility of being exposed to fuel, and, if you spill any fuel on your skin, rinse it off immediately with soap and water. Mop up any spills immediately and do not store fuel-soaked rags where they could ignite. The fuel system is under constant pressure, so, if any fuel lines are to be disconnected, the fuel pressure in the system must be relieved first (see Chapter 4 for more information). When you perform any kind of work on the fuel system, wear safety glasses and have a Class B type fire extinguisher on hand.*
Warning 2: *The engine must be completely cool before beginning this procedure.*

V6 models

Removal

Refer to illustrations 7.9 and 7.22
Note: *Keep in mind that during this procedure you'll have to adjust the height of the vehicle to perform certain operations.*

1   Relieve the fuel system pressure (see Chapter 4).
2   Disconnect the cable from the negative terminal of the battery (see Chapter 5, Section 1)
3   Refer to Chapter 11 and remove the hood.
4   Pull the engine cover off.
5   Remove the entire air cleaner assembly (see Chapter 4).
6   Remove the upper engine mount struts.
7   Remove the drivebelt (see Chapter 1).
8   Drain the coolant and the engine oil (see Chapter 1).
9   Disconnect the oil pressure sensor, the knock sensor, the starter wire harness, the air conditioning compressor wiring and the oil level sensor. Label each sensor and connector to simplify reconnection **(see illustration)**. Disconnect the wire harnesses from their clips.
10   Likewise, label and disconnect all the

wiring on top of the engine including the harness clips and the ground connections. Move the disconnected harnesses out of the way.
11   Remove the catalytic converter (see Chapter 4).
12   Unbolt the front engine mount from the subframe.
13   Remove the starter (see Chapter 5).
14   Remove the access cover and remove the torque converter-to-driveplate bolts.
15   Unbolt the air conditioning compressor and set it out of the way, but don't disconnect the refrigerant lines.
16   Remove the transmission brace.
17   Disconnect the lower radiator hose at the thermostat.
18   Disconnect the brake vacuum line, the fuel supply line (see Chapter 4) and the heater hoses.
19   Remove the exhaust crossover pipe (see Chapter 4).
20   Disconnect the EVAP purge tube and the radiator inlet hose.
21   Unbolt the power steering pump and set the pump aside without disconnecting the fluid hoses.
22   Attach an engine sling or a length of chain to the engine **(see illustration)**. There

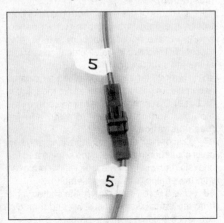

7.9 Label both ends of each wire and hose before disconnecting it

7.22 Support the engine from with an engine hoist securely attached by heavy-duty chains to the engine lifting brackets

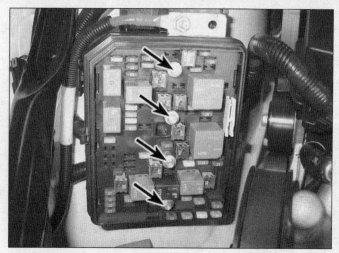

7.43 Remove the bolts from the fuse/relay block . . .

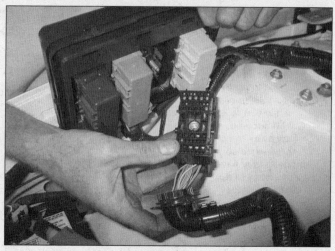

7.44 . . . then separate the fuse/relay block and detach the four large electrical connectors from the back

are lifting brackets in some of the engines but not all. If you can't find a lifting bracket, make sure to attach the chain to a secure point such as a cylinder head or the block. **Caution:** *DO NOT lift the engine by the intake manifold.*

23   Roll the engine hoist into position and connect the sling to it. Take up the slack in the chain, but don't lift the engine yet. **Warning:** *DO NOT place any part of your body under the engine when only a hoist or other lifting device supports it.*

24   Remove the transmission mounting bolts.

25   Check that there is nothing connecting the engine to the transmission or the vehicle.

26   Raise the engine slightly. Work it away from the transmission, being sure that the converter stays in the transmission (clamp vise-grips to the bellhousing to keep the converter from sliding out).

27   Carefully raise the engine from the engine compartment. Check as you go to make sure nothing is hanging up. Remove the driveplate and mount the engine on an engine stand.

7.46 Flip the locking levers back, then disconnect the electrical connectors from the PCM and TCM

Installation

28   Installation is the reverse of the removal procedure, noting the following points:

a) *Check the powertrain mounts. If they're worn or damaged, replace them.*

b) *When installing the subframe, tighten the subframe mounting bolts to the torque listed in the Chapter 10 Specifications.*

c) *Refill the cooling system with the proper mixture of antifreeze. Refill the crankcase with the recommended engine oil (see Chapter 1).*

d) *Reconnect the battery (see Chapter 5, Section 1).*

e) *Run the engine and check for proper operation and leaks. Shut off the engine and recheck fluid levels.*

V8 models

Refer to illustrations 7.43, 7.44, 7.46, 7.49, 7.51, 7.53, 7.63, 7.64 and 7.68

Note 1: *The engine is removed from the bottom of the engine compartment on V8 models. This procedure requires the use of a vehicle hoist. Only begin this procedure if all of the necessary equipment is at hand. With only a floor jack and jackstands, the vehicle can't safely be raised high enough for the engine/transmission to slide out from underneath.*

Note 2: *Read through the entire Section before beginning this procedure. The engine and transmission are removed as a unit from below and then separated once clear of the vehicle.*

29   Have the air conditioning refrigerant evacuated at an approved service facility.

30   Park the vehicle squarely on a frame-contact type hoist and adjust the hoist arms to correctly align with the jacking points of the vehicle. Point the wheels straight ahead. **Warning:** *Tie the front of the body down to the hoist so the car doesn't tilt back and fall off the hoist when the weight of the engine and transmission is removed.*

31   Remove the engine top cover. Relieve the fuel system pressure (see Chapter 4).

32   Disconnect the cable from the negative battery terminal (see Chapter 5, Section 1).

33   Loosen the front wheel lug nuts. Raise the vehicle and remove the front wheels.

34   Drain the engine oil and coolant (see Chapter 1).

35   Disconnect the radiator hoses at the engine.

36   Disconnect the air conditioning lines near the left side of the radiator.

37   Disconnect the power brake booster vacuum hose from the intake manifold.

38   Suction the fluid from the master cylinder, then remove the two brake lines.

39   Remove the master cylinder (see Chapter 9).

40   Disconnect the fuel supply tube from the intake manifold (see Chapter 4).

41   Remove the EVAP line from the purge solenoid.

42   Remove both fender braces.

43   Remove the cover from the electrical center, then unscrew the four captive bolts in the center of the fuse block **(see illustration)**.

44   Disconnect the four large harness connectors from the back of the fuse block **(see illustration)**.

45   Disconnect the wiring from the ABS controller, the camshaft position (CMP) sensor and the brake booster vacuum sensor. Also disconnect the two large electrical connectors at the left strut tower.

46   Remove the upper part of the air cleaner assembly, exposing the electronic modules in its base. Disconnect the harnesses from the modules and move them from the housing **(see illustration)**.

47   Disconnect the remaining wiring and harness clips running between the engine and the chassis (the wiring harnesses will be removed with the engine/transaxle assembly).

48   Use a screwdriver to pry the shifter cable from the transmission shift lever and then disconnect the cable from the bracket.

49   Working through the right-side wheel well, remove the heat shield from the vehicle

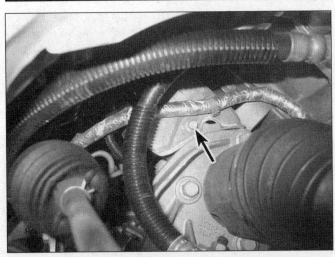

7.49 Remove the heat shield from over the vehicle speed sensor, then disconnect the electrical connector

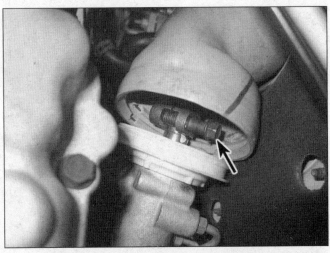

7.51 Remove the steering shaft pinch bolt

speed sensor and then disconnect the sensor **(see illustration)**.

50   Make sure all the wiring is disconnected and put the harnesses where they will not be damaged during engine removal.

51   Pull up the plastic cover from the steering shaft, then remove the shaft pinch bolt **(see illustration)**. Push the steering shaft off of the steering rack. **Note:** *The shaft might not come off all the way at this time; you may have to detach it as the vehicle is being raised from the engine/transaxle assembly.*

52   Disconnect the front wheel speed sensors at the hubs and release the wiring from the control arms.

53   Disconnect the heater hoses **(see illustration)**.

54   Disconnect the stabilizer bar links, the outer tie-rod ends and the lower ball joints (see Chapter 10).

55   Disconnect the power steering hoses as required.

56   Remove both driveaxles (see Chapter 8).

57   Disconnect the cooler lines from the transmission.

58   Disconnect the starter wiring and the grounds in the vicinity of the starter (see Chapter 5). Also disconnect the harnesses from the subframe.

59   Remove the catalytic converter (see Chapter 4).

60   Remove the torque converter bolt access cover, then remove the torque converter bolts.

61   Remove the lower air dam from beneath the front bumper (see Chapter 11).

62   Place four jackstands under the subframe and lower the vehicle slightly to put some weight on the jackstands.

63   Remove the four subframe bolts **(see illustration)**. Verify that there are no harnesses, hoses, etc. that will interfere with raising the vehicle off of the engine/transmission module.

64   Slowly raise the vehicle while checking for obstructions **(see illustration)**. Make sure that the engine and transmission are secure.

7.53 Squeeze the clamps and slide them back on the hoses, then disconnect the heater hoses from the pipes

65   Attach an engine hoist to the engine and raise it just enough to take weight off of the engine mounts.

7.63 Locations of the subframe mounting bolts

7.64 Once it has been confirmed that nothing is still attached between the engine/transaxle/subframe and the rest of the chassis, the vehicle can be raised on the hoist

7.68 Attach an engine hoist to the engine, remove the transaxle-to-engine bolts, then carefully lift the engine up and away from the transaxle

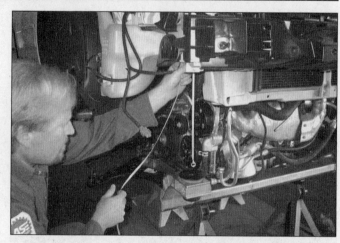

7.70 Use a plumb-bob to get the engine/transaxle/subframe lined-up with the bolt holes in the body

66   Disconnect both engine mounts from the subframe.

67   Remove the transaxle bolts.

68   Slowly and carefully lift the engine away from the transaxle and off of the subframe **(see illustration)**.

69   Remove the driveplate and mount the engine on an engine stand.

Installation

Refer to illustration 7.70

70   Installation is the reverse of the removal process, noting the following points:

a)   *Check the engine and transmission mounts. If they're worn, replace them.*

b)   *When positioning the subframe beneath the vehicle, make a plumb-bob from a piece of string and a nut. Hold the string at each subframe bolt hole on the body and verify that its corresponding subframe bolt hole is directly below it. This will eliminate trying to adjust the subframe as the vehicle is lowered over it* **(see illustration)**.

c)   *Tighten the subframe mounting bolts to the torque listed in this Chapter's Specifications.*

d)   *Tighten the torque converter bolts to the torque listed in this Chapter's Specifications.*

e)   *Refill the cooling system with the proper mixture of coolant and refill the engine with the recommended oil (see Chapter 1).*

f)   *Check the transmission fluid level and add fluid as necessary.*

g)   *Have the air conditioning system recharged by the shop that discharged it.*

8   Engine overhaul - disassembly sequence

1   It's much easier to remove the external components if the engine is mounted on a portable engine stand. A stand can often be rented quite cheaply from an equipment rental yard. Before the engine is mounted on a stand, the driveplate should be removed from the engine.

2   If a stand isn't available, it's possible to remove the external engine components with it blocked up on the floor. Be extra careful not to tip or drop the engine when working without a stand.

3   If you're going to obtain a rebuilt engine, all external components must come off first, to be transferred to the replacement engine. These components include:

> *Driveplate*
> *Ignition system components*
> *Emissions-related components*
> *Engine mounts and mount brackets*
> *Engine rear cover (spacer plate between driveplate and engine block), if equipped*
> *Intake/exhaust manifolds*
> *Fuel injection components*
> *Oil filter*
> *Spark plugs and ignition coil pack (and spark plug wires) or coil-over plug assemblies*
> *Thermostat and housing assembly*
> *Water pump*

Note: *When removing the external components from the engine, pay close attention to details that may be helpful or important during installation. Note the installed position of gaskets, seals, spacers, pins, brackets, washers, bolts and other small items.*

4   If you're going to obtain a short block (assembled engine block, crankshaft, pistons and connecting rods), then remove the timing chain or belt, cylinder head(s), oil pan, oil pump pick-up tube, oil pump and water pump from your engine so that you can turn in your old short block to the rebuilder as a core. See *Engine rebuilding alternatives* for additional information regarding the different possibilities to be considered.

9   Pistons and connecting rods - removal and installation

Removal

Refer to illustrations 9.1, 9.3 and 9.4

Note: *Prior to removing the piston/connecting rod assemblies, remove the cylinder head and oil pan (see Chapter 2A).*

1   Use your fingernail to feel if a ridge has formed at the upper limit of ring travel (about 1/4-inch down from the top of each cylinder). If carbon deposits or cylinder wear have produced ridges, they must be completely removed with a special tool **(see illustration)**. Follow the manufacturer's instructions provided with the tool. Failure to remove the ridges before attempting to remove the piston/connecting rod assemblies may result in piston breakage.

2   After the cylinder ridges have been removed, turn the engine so the crankshaft is facing up.

3   Before the main bearing cap assembly

9.1 Before you try to remove the pistons, use a ridge reamer to remove the raised material (ridge) from the top of the cylinders

9.3 Checking the connecting rod endplay (side clearance)

9.4 If the connecting rods and caps are not marked, use paint to mark the caps to the rods by cylinder number (for example, this would be the No. 4 connecting rod)

and connecting rods are removed, check the connecting rod endplay with feeler gauges. Slide them between the first connecting rod and the crankshaft throw until the play is removed **(see illustration)**. Repeat this procedure for each connecting rod. The endplay is equal to the thickness of the feeler gauge(s). Check with an automotive machine shop for the endplay service limit (a typical endplay limit should measure between 0.005 to 0.015 inch [0.127 to 0.396 mm]). If the play exceeds the service limit, new connecting rods will be required. If new rods (or a new crankshaft) are installed, the endplay may fall under the minimum allowable. If it does, the rods will have to be machined to restore it. If necessary, consult an automotive machine shop for advice.

4   Check the connecting rods and caps for identification marks. If they aren't plainly marked, use paint or marker to clearly identify each rod and cap (1, 2, 3, etc., depending on the cylinder they're associated with) **(see illustration)**.

5   Remove the connecting rod cap bolts.

6   Remove the number one connecting rod cap and bearing insert. Don't drop the bearing insert out of the cap.

7   Remove the bearing insert and push the connecting rod/piston assembly out through the top of the engine. Use a wooden or plastic hammer handle to push on the upper bearing surface in the connecting rod. If resistance is felt, double-check to make sure that all of the ridge was removed from the cylinder.

8   Repeat the procedure for the remaining cylinders.

9   After removal, reassemble the connecting rod caps and bearing inserts in their respective connecting rods and install the cap bolts finger tight. Leaving the old bearing inserts in place until reassembly will help prevent the connecting rod bearing surfaces from being accidentally nicked or gouged.

10   The pistons and connecting rods are now ready for inspection and overhaul at an automotive machine shop.

Piston ring installation

Refer to illustrations 9.13, 9.14, 9.15, 9.19a, 9.19b and 9.22

11   Before installing the new piston rings, the ring end gaps must be checked. It's assumed that the piston ring side clearance has been checked and verified correct. **Note:** *V6 engines are equipped with two different*

brand pistons. The correct piston rings must match the piston. To identify the piston brand, turn the piston over and look between the pin bores for an FM mark (Federal Mogul) or a no mark (Mahle) brand type. Use only the correct type of piston rings that match the piston manufacturer.

12   Lay out the piston/connecting rod assemblies and the new ring sets so the ring sets will be matched with the same piston and cylinder during the end gap measurement and engine assembly.

13   Insert the top (number one) ring into the first cylinder and square it up with the cylinder walls by pushing it in with the top of the piston **(see illustration)**. The ring should be near the bottom of the cylinder, at the lower limit of ring travel.

14   To measure the end gap, slip feeler gauges between the ends of the ring until a gauge equal to the gap width is found **(see illustration)**. The feeler gauge should slide between the ring ends with a slight amount of drag. A typical ring gap should fall between 0.010 and 0.020 inch [0.25 to 0.50 mm] for compression rings and up to 0.030 inch [0.76

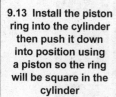

9.13 Install the piston ring into the cylinder then push it down into position using a piston so the ring will be square in the cylinder

9.14 With the ring square in the cylinder, measure the ring end gap with a feeler gauge

ENGINE BEARING ANALYSIS

Debris

Babbitt bearing embedded with debris from machinings

Microscopic detail of debris

Microscopic detail of gouges

Overplated copper alloy bearing gouged by cast iron debris

Aluminum bearing embedded with glass beads

Microscopic detail of glass beads

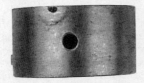

Damaged lining caused by dirt left on the bearing back

Misassembly

Result of a lower half assembled as an upper - blocking the oil flow

Excessive oil clearance is indicated by a short contact arc

Polished and oil-stained backs are a result of a poor fit in the housing bore

Result of a wrong, reversed, or shifted cap

Overloading

Damage from excessive idling which resulted in an oil film unable to support the load imposed

Damaged upper connecting rod bearings caused by engine lugging; the lower main bearings (not shown) were similarly affected

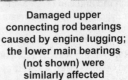

The damage shown in these upper and lower connecting rod bearings was caused by engine operation at a higher-than-rated speed under load

Misalignment

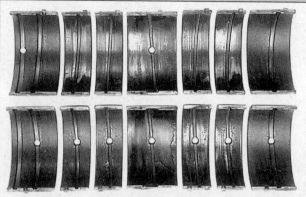

A warped crankshaft caused this pattern of severe wear in the center, diminishing toward the ends

A poorly finished crankshaft caused the equally spaced scoring shown

A tapered housing bore caused the damage along one edge of this pair

A bent connecting rod led to the damage in the "V" pattern

Lubrication

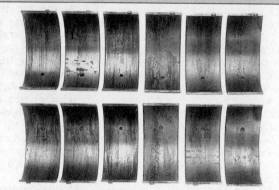

Result of dry start: The bearings on the left, farthest from the oil pump, show more damage

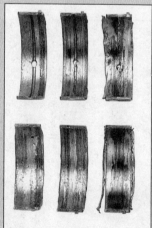

Result of a low oil supply or oil starvation

Severe wear as a result of inadequate oil clearance

Corrosion

Microscopic detail of corrosion

Corrosion is an acid attack on the bearing lining generally caused by inadequate maintenance, extremely hot or cold operation, or inferior oils or fuels

Microscopic detail of cavitation

Example of cavitation - a surface erosion caused by pressure changes in the oil film

Damage from excessive thrust or insufficient axial clearance

Bearing affected by oil dilution caused by excessive blow-by or a rich mixture

9.15 If the ring end gap is too small, clamp a file in a vise as shown and file the piston ring ends - be sure to remove all raised material

9.19a Installing the spacer/expander in the oil ring groove

mm] for the oil ring steel rails. If the gap is larger or smaller than specified, double-check to make sure you have the correct rings before proceeding.

15 If the gap is too small, it must be enlarged or the ring ends may come in contact with each other during engine operation, which can cause serious damage to the engine. If necessary, increase the end gaps by filing the ring ends very carefully with a fine file. Mount the file in a vise equipped with soft jaws, slip the ring over the file with the ends contacting the file face and slowly move the ring to remove material from the ends. When performing this operation, file only by pushing the ring from the outside end of the file towards the vise **(see illustration)**.

16 Excess end gap isn't critical unless it's greater than 0.040 inch (1.01 mm). Again, double-check to make sure you have the correct ring type.

17 Repeat the procedure for each ring that will be installed in the first cylinder and for each ring in the remaining cylinders. Remember to keep rings, pistons and cylinders matched up.

18 Once the ring end gaps have been checked/corrected, the rings can be installed on the pistons.

19 The oil control ring (lowest one on the piston) is usually installed first. It's composed of three separate components. Slip the spacer/expander into the groove **(see illustration)**. If an anti-rotation tang is used, make sure it's inserted into the drilled hole in the ring groove. Next, install the upper side rail in the same manner **(see illustration)**. Don't use a piston ring installation tool on the oil ring side rails, as they may be damaged. Instead, place one end of the side rail into the groove between the spacer/expander and the ring land, hold it firmly in place and slide a finger around the piston while pushing the rail into the groove. Finally, install the lower side rail.

20 After the three oil ring components have been installed, check to make sure that both the upper and lower side rails can be rotated smoothly inside the ring grooves.

21 The number two (middle) ring is installed next. It's usually stamped with a mark which must face up, toward the top of the piston. Do not mix up the top and middle rings, as they have different cross-sections. **Note 1:** *Always follow the instructions printed on the ring package or box - different manufacturers may require different approaches.* **Note 2:** *On V6 engines, original equipment compression rings are marked as follows: The top compression ring has a green stripe on the top side of the ring, 180-degrees from the gap. The second compression ring has a green stripe 90-degrees from the gap.*

22 Use a piston ring installation tool and make sure the identification mark is facing the top of the piston, then slip the ring into the middle groove on the piston **(see illustra-**

9.19b DO NOT use a piston ring installation tool when installing the oil control side rails

9.22 Use a piston ring installation tool to install the number 2 and the number 1 (top) rings - be sure the directional mark on the piston ring(s) is facing toward the top of the piston

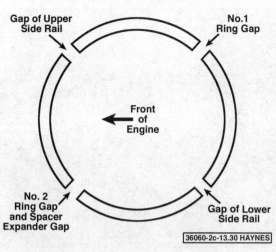

9.30 Piston ring end gap positions

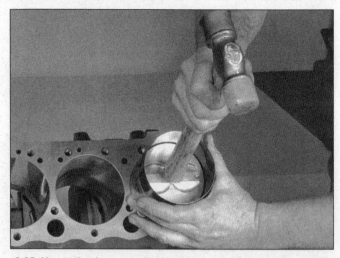

9.35 Use a plastic or wooden hammer handle to push the piston into the cylinder

tion). Don't expand the ring any more than necessary to slide it over the piston.

23 Install the number one (top) ring in the same manner. Make sure the mark is facing up. Be careful not to confuse the number one and number two rings.

24 Repeat the procedure for the remaining pistons and rings.

Installation

25 Before installing the piston/connecting rod assemblies, the cylinder walls must be perfectly clean, the top edge of each cylinder bore must be chamfered, and the crankshaft must be in place.

26 Remove the cap from the end of the number one connecting rod (refer to the marks made during removal). Remove the original bearing inserts and wipe the bearing surfaces of the connecting rod and cap with a clean, lint-free cloth. They must be kept spotlessly clean.

Connecting rod bearing oil clearance check

Refer to illustrations 9.30, 9.35, 9.37 and 9.41

27 Clean the back side of the new upper bearing insert, then lay it in place in the connecting rod.

28 Make sure the tab on the bearing fits into the recess in the rod. Don't hammer the bearing insert into place and be very careful not to nick or gouge the bearing face. Don't lubricate the bearing at this time.

29 Clean the back side of the other bearing insert and install it in the rod cap. Again, make sure the tab on the bearing fits into the recess in the cap, and don't apply any lubricant. It's critically important that the mating surfaces of the bearing and connecting rod are perfectly clean and oil free when they're assembled.

30 Position the piston ring gaps at the specified intervals around the piston as shown **(see illustration)**.

31 Lubricate the piston and rings with clean engine oil and attach a piston ring compressor to the piston. Leave the skirt protruding about 1/4-inch to guide the piston into the cylinder. The rings must be compressed until they're flush with the piston.

32 Rotate the crankshaft until the number one connecting rod journal is at BDC (bottom dead center) and apply a liberal coat of engine oil to the cylinder walls.

33 With the arrow on top of the piston facing the front (timing chain) of the engine, gently insert the piston/connecting rod assembly into the number one cylinder bore and rest the bottom edge of the ring compressor on the engine block.

34 Tap the top edge of the ring compressor to make sure it's contacting the block around its entire circumference.

35 Gently tap on the top of the piston with the end of a wooden or plastic hammer handle **(see illustration)** while guiding the end of the connecting rod into place on the crankshaft journal. The piston rings may try to pop out of the ring compressor just before entering the cylinder bore, so keep some downward pressure on the ring compressor. Work slowly, and if any resistance is felt as the piston enters the cylinder, stop immediately. Find out what's hanging up and fix it before proceeding. Do not, for any reason, force the piston into the cylinder - you might break a ring and/or the piston.

36 Once the piston/connecting rod assembly is installed, the connecting rod bearing oil clearance must be checked before the rod cap is permanently installed.

37 Cut a piece of the appropriate size Plastigage slightly shorter than the width of the connecting rod bearing and lay it in place on the number one connecting rod journal, parallel with the journal axis **(see illustration)**.

38 Clean the connecting rod cap bearing face and install the rod cap. Make sure the mating mark on the cap is on the same side as the mark on the connecting rod **(see illustration 9.4)**.

39 Install the rod bolts, and tighten them to the torque listed in this Chapter's Specifications. **Note:** *Use a thin-wall socket to avoid erroneous torque readings that can result if the socket is wedged between the rod cap and the bolt. If the socket tends to wedge itself between the fastener and the cap, lift up on it slightly until it no longer contacts the cap. DO NOT rotate the crankshaft at any time during this operation.*

9.37 Place Plastigage on each connecting rod bearing journal parallel to the crankshaft centerline

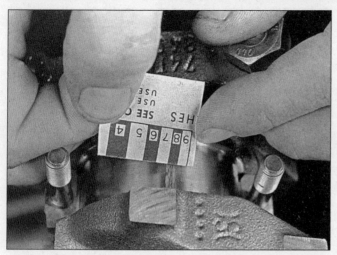

9.41 Use the scale on the Plastigage package to determine the bearing oil clearance - be sure to measure the widest part of the Plastigage and use the correct scale; it comes with both standard and metric scales

10.1 Checking crankshaft endplay with a dial indicator

40   Remove the fasteners and detach the rod cap, being very careful not to disturb the Plastigage.

41   Compare the width of the crushed Plastigage to the scale printed on the Plastigage envelope to obtain the oil clearance **(see illustration)**. The connecting rod oil clearance is usually about 0.001 to 0.002 inch. Consult an automotive machine shop for the clearance specified for the rod bearings on your engine.

42   If the clearance is not as specified, the bearing inserts may be the wrong size (which means different ones will be required). Before deciding that different inserts are needed, make sure that no dirt or oil was between the bearing inserts and the connecting rod or cap when the clearance was measured. Also, recheck the journal diameter. If the Plastigage was wider at one end than the other, the journal may be tapered. If the clearance still exceeds the limit specified, the bearing will have to be replaced with an undersize bearing. **Caution:** *When installing a new crankshaft always use a standard size bearing.*

Final installation

43   Carefully scrape all traces of the Plastigage material off the rod journal and/or bearing face. Be very careful not to scratch the bearing - use your fingernail or the edge of a plastic card.

44   Make sure the bearing faces are perfectly clean, then apply a uniform layer of clean moly-base grease or engine assembly lube to both of them. You'll have to push the piston into the cylinder to expose the face of the bearing insert in the connecting rod.

45   Slide the connecting rod back into place on the journal, install the rod cap, install the bolts and tighten them to the torque listed in this Chapter's Specifications.

46   Repeat the entire procedure for the remaining pistons/connecting rods.

47   The important points to remember are:

a) *Keep the back sides of the bearing inserts and the insides of the connecting rods and caps perfectly clean when assembling them.*

b) *Make sure you have the correct piston/rod assembly for each cylinder.*

c) *The arrow on the piston must face the front (timing chain) of the engine.*

d) *Lubricate the cylinder walls liberally with clean oil.*

e) *Lubricate the bearing faces when installing the rod caps after the oil clearance has been checked.*

48   After all the piston/connecting rod assemblies have been correctly installed, rotate the crankshaft a number of times by hand to check for any obvious binding.

49   As a final step, check the connecting rod endplay as described in Step 3. If it was correct before disassembly and the original crankshaft and rods were reinstalled, it should still be correct. If new rods or a new crankshaft were installed, the endplay may be inadequate. If so, the rods will have to be removed and taken to an automotive machine shop for resizing.

10 Crankshaft - removal and installation

Removal

Refer to illustrations 10.1 and 10.3

Note: *The crankshaft can be removed only after the engine has been removed from the vehicle. It's assumed that the driveplate, crankshaft pulley, timing chain, oil pan, oil pump body, oil filter and piston/connecting rod assemblies have already been removed. The rear main oil seal retainer must be unbolted and separated from the block before proceeding with crankshaft removal.*

1   Before the crankshaft is removed, measure the endplay. Mount a dial indicator with the indicator in line with the crankshaft and just touching the end of the crankshaft as shown **(see illustration)**.

2   Pry the crankshaft all the way to the rear and zero the dial indicator. Next, pry the crankshaft to the front as far as possible and check the reading on the dial indicator. The distance traveled is the endplay. A typical crankshaft endplay will fall between 0.003 to 0.010 inch (0.076 to 0.254 mm). If it is greater than that, check the crankshaft thrust surfaces for wear after it's removed. If no wear is evident, new main bearings should correct the endplay.

3   If a dial indicator isn't available, feeler gauges can be used. Gently pry the crankshaft all the way to the front of the engine. Slip feeler gauges between the crankshaft and the front face of the thrust bearing or washer to determine the clearance **(see illustration)**.

4   Loosen the main bearing cap bolts 1/4-turn at a time each, until they can be removed by hand.

10.3 Checking the crankshaft endplay with feeler gauges at the thrust bearing journal

10.17 Place the Plastigage onto the crankshaft bearing journal as shown

10.21 Use the scale on the Plastigage package to determine the bearing oil clearance - be sure to measure the widest part of the Plastigage and use the correct scale; it comes with both standard and metric scales

5   Remove the main bearing caps. Pull the main bearing cap straight up and off the cylinder block. Removing the caps from a V8 engine may require a special slide-hammer removal tool that threads into the caps. Gently tap the main bearing cap with a soft-face hammer, if necessary.

6   Carefully lift the crankshaft out of the engine. It may be a good idea to have an assistant available, since the crankshaft is quite heavy and awkward to handle. With the bearing inserts in place inside the engine block and main bearing caps, reinstall the main bearing caps onto the engine block and tighten the bolts finger tight. Make sure the caps are in the exact order they were removed with the arrow pointing toward the front (timing chain and front cover) of the engine.

Installation

7   Crankshaft installation is the first step in engine reassembly. It's assumed at this point that the engine block and crankshaft have been cleaned, inspected and repaired or reconditioned.

8   Position the engine block with the bottom facing up.

9   Remove the bolts and lift off the main bearing caps.

10   If they're still in place, remove the original bearing inserts from the block and from the main bearing caps. Wipe the bearing surfaces of the block and main bearing cap assembly with a clean, lint-free cloth. They must be kept spotlessly clean. This is critical for determining the correct bearing oil clearance.

Main bearing oil clearance check

Refer to illustrations 10.17 and 10.21

11   Without mixing them up, clean the back sides of the new upper main bearing inserts (with grooves and oil holes) and lay one in each main bearing saddle in the engine

block. Each upper bearing (engine block) has an oil groove and oil hole in it. **Caution:** *The oil holes in the block must line up with the oil holes in the engine block inserts.* The thrust washer or thrust bearing insert must be installed in the correct location. **Note:** *The thrust bearing is located on the 3rd journal in the main bearing cap journals (counting from the front).* Clean the back sides of the lower main bearing inserts and lay them in the corresponding location in the main bearing caps. Make sure the tab on the bearing insert fits into the recess in the block or main bearing caps. **Caution:** *Do not hammer the bearing insert into place and don't nick or gouge the bearing faces. DO NOT apply any lubrication at this time.*

12   Clean the faces of the bearing inserts in the block and the crankshaft main bearing journals with a clean, lint-free cloth.

13   Check or clean the oil holes in the crankshaft, as any dirt here can go only one way - straight through the new bearings.

14   Once you're certain the crankshaft is clean, carefully lay it in position in the cylinder block.

15   Before the crankshaft can be permanently installed, the main bearing oil clearance must be checked.

16   Cut several strips of the appropriate size of Plastigage. They must be slightly shorter than the width of the main bearing journal.

17   Place one piece on each crankshaft main bearing journal, parallel with the journal axis as shown **(see illustration)**.

18   Clean the faces of the bearing inserts in the main bearing caps or lower crankcase. Install the caps without disturbing the Plastigage.

19   Apply clean engine oil to all bolt threads prior to installation, install all bolts finger-tight, then tighten them to the torque listed in this Chapter's Specifications. DO NOT rotate the crankshaft at any time during this operation. **Note:** *On V8 engines, follow the correct*

torque sequence **(see illustration 10.30)**, *but note that it isn't necessary to install the side bolts at this time (just bolts 1 through 20).*

20   Remove the bolts and carefully lift the main bearing caps straight up and off the block. Do not disturb the Plastigage or rotate the crankshaft.

21   Compare the width of the crushed Plastigage on each journal to the scale printed on the Plastigage envelope to determine the main bearing oil clearance **(see illustration)**. Check with an automotive machine shop for the crankshaft bearing oil clearance for your engine.

22   If the clearance is not as specified, the bearing inserts may be the wrong size (which means different ones will be required). Before deciding if different inserts are needed, make sure that no dirt or oil was between the bearing inserts and the caps or block when the clearance was measured. If the Plastigage was wider at one end than the other, the crankshaft journal may be tapered. If the clearance still exceeds the limit specified, the bearing insert(s) will have to be replaced with an undersize bearing insert(s). **Caution:** *When installing a new crankshaft always install a standard bearing insert set.*

23   Carefully scrape all traces of the Plastigage material off the main bearing journals and/or the bearing insert faces. Be sure to remove all residue from the oil holes. Use your fingernail or the edge of a plastic card - don't nick or scratch the bearing faces.

Final installation

Refer to illustration 10.30

24   Carefully lift the crankshaft out of the cylinder block.

25   Clean the bearing insert faces in the cylinder block, then apply a thin, uniform layer of moly-base grease or engine assembly lube to each of the bearing surfaces. Be sure to coat the thrust faces as well as the journal face of the thrust bearing.

26   Make sure the crankshaft journals are clean, then lay the crankshaft back in place in the cylinder block.

27   Clean the bearing insert faces and apply the same lubricant to them. Clean the engine block and the bearing cap mating surfaces thoroughly. The surfaces must be free of oil residue.

28   Prior to installation, apply clean engine oil to all bolt threads wiping off any excess, then install all bolts finger-tight.

29   Tighten the main bearing cap bolts to the torque listed in this Chapter's Specifications.

30   On V8 engines, tighten bolts one through ten to the torque listed in Step 1 of this Chapter's Specifications. Be sure to follow the correct sequence **(see illustration)**. Tap the crankshaft to the rear and then to the front to align the thrust bearing on V8 engines. The last tap must be in the forward direction.

31   Proceed with the rest of the fastener tightening steps listed in this Chapter's Specifications for the V8 engine, ending with the tightening of the NEW side bolts.

32   Recheck the crankshaft endplay with a feeler gauge or a dial indicator. The endplay should be correct if the crankshaft thrust faces aren't worn or damaged and if new bearings have been installed.

33   Rotate the crankshaft a number of times by hand to check for any obvious binding. It should rotate with a running torque of 50 in-lbs or less. If the running torque is too high, correct the problem at this time.

34   Install the new rear main oil seal (see Chapter 2A or 2B).

11   Engine overhaul - reassembly sequence

1   Before beginning engine reassembly, make sure you have all the necessary new parts, gaskets and seals as well as the following items on hand:

> *Common hand tools*
> *A 1/2-inch drive torque wrench*
> *New engine oil*
> *Gasket sealant*
> *Thread locking compound*

2   If you obtained a short block it will be necessary to install the cylinder head, the oil pump and pick-up tube, the oil pan, the water pump, the timing belt and timing cover, and

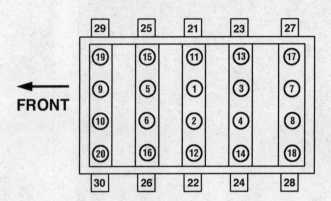

10.30 Main bearing cap tightening sequence - V8 engine

the valve cover (see Chapter 2A or 2B). In order to save time and avoid problems, the external components must be installed in the following general order:

> *Thermostat and housing cover*
> *Water pump*
> *Intake and exhaust manifolds*
> *Fuel injection components*
> *Emission control components*
> *Spark plugs*
> *Ignition coils or coil pack and spark plug wires*
> *Oil filter*
> *Engine mounts and mount brackets*
> *Driveplate*

12   Initial start-up and break-in after overhaul

Warning: *Have a fire extinguisher handy when starting the engine for the first time.*

1   Once the engine has been installed in the vehicle, double-check the engine oil and coolant levels.

2   With the spark plugs out of the engine and the ignition system and fuel pump disabled, crank the engine until oil pressure registers on the gauge or the light goes out.

3   Install the spark plugs, hook up the plug wires and restore the ignition system and fuel pump functions.

4   Start the engine. It may take a few moments for the fuel system to build up pressure, but the engine should start without a great deal of effort.

5   After the engine starts, it should be allowed to warm up to normal operating temperature. While the engine is warming up, make a thorough check for fuel, oil and coolant leaks.

6   Shut the engine off and recheck the engine oil and coolant levels.

7   Drive the vehicle to an area with minimum traffic, accelerate from 30 to 50 mph, then allow the vehicle to slow to 30 mph with the throttle closed. Repeat the procedure 10 or 12 times. This will load the piston rings and cause them to seat properly against the cylinder walls. Check again for oil and coolant leaks.

8   Drive the vehicle gently for the first 500 miles (no sustained high speeds) and keep a constant check on the oil level. It is not unusual for an engine to use oil during the break-in period.

9   At approximately 500 to 600 miles, change the oil and filter.

10   For the next few hundred miles, drive the vehicle normally. Do not pamper it or abuse it.

11   After 2,000 miles, change the oil and filter again and consider the engine broken in.

COMMON ENGINE OVERHAUL TERMS

B

Backlash - The amount of play between two parts. Usually refers to how much one gear can be moved back and forth without moving the gear with which it's meshed.

Bearing Caps - The caps held in place by nuts or bolts which, in turn, hold the bearing surface. This space is for lubricating oil to enter.

Bearing clearance - The amount of space left between shaft and bearing surface. This space is for lubricating oil to enter.

Bearing crush - The additional height which is purposely manufactured into each bearing half to ensure complete contact of the bearing back with the housing bore when the engine is assembled.

Bearing knock - The noise created by movement of a part in a loose or worn bearing.

Blueprinting - Dismantling an engine and reassembling it to EXACT specifications.

Bore - An engine cylinder, or any cylindrical hole; also used to describe the process of enlarging or accurately refinishing a hole with a cutting tool, as to bore an engine cylinder. The bore size is the diameter of the hole.

Boring - Renewing the cylinders by cutting them out to a specified size. A boring bar is used to make the cut.

Bottom end - A term which refers collectively to the engine block, crankshaft, main bearings and the big ends of the connecting rods.

Break-in - The period of operation between installation of new or rebuilt parts and time in which parts are worn to the correct fit. Driving at reduced and varying speed for a specified mileage to permit parts to wear to the correct fit.

Bushing - A one-piece sleeve placed in a bore to serve as a bearing surface for shaft, piston pin, etc. Usually replaceable.

C

Camshaft - The shaft in the engine, on which a series of lobes are located for operating the valve mechanisms. The camshaft is driven by gears or sprockets and a timing chain. Usually referred to simply as the cam.

Carbon - Hard, or soft, black deposits found in combustion chamber, on plugs, under rings, on and under valve heads.

Cast iron - An alloy of iron and more than two percent carbon, used for engine blocks and heads because it's relatively inexpensive and easy to mold into complex shapes.

Chamfer - To bevel across (or a bevel on) the sharp edge of an object.

Chase - To repair damaged threads with a tap or die.

Combustion chamber - The space between the piston and the cylinder head, with the piston at top dead center, in which air-fuel mixture is burned.

Compression ratio - The relationship between cylinder volume (clearance volume) when the piston is at top dead center and cylinder volume when the piston is at bottom dead center.

Connecting rod - The rod that connects the crank on the crankshaft with the piston. Sometimes called a con rod.

Connecting rod cap - The part of the connecting rod assembly that attaches the rod to the crankpin.

Core plug - Soft metal plug used to plug the casting holes for the coolant passages in the block.

Crankcase - The lower part of the engine in which the crankshaft rotates; includes the lower section of the cylinder block and the oil pan.

Crank kit - A reground or reconditioned crankshaft and new main and connecting rod bearings.

Crankpin - The part of a crankshaft to which a connecting rod is attached.

Crankshaft - The main rotating member, or shaft, running the length of the crankcase, with offset throws to which the connecting rods are attached; changes the reciprocating motion of the pistons into rotating motion.

Cylinder sleeve - A replaceable sleeve, or liner, pressed into the cylinder block to form the cylinder bore.

D

Deburring - Removing the burrs (rough edges or areas) from a bearing.

Deglazer - A tool, rotated by an electric motor, used to remove glaze from cylinder walls so a new set of rings will seat.

E

Endplay - The amount of lengthwise movement between two parts. As applied to a crankshaft, the distance that the crankshaft can move forward and back in the cylinder block.

F

Face - A machinist's term that refers to removing metal from the end of a shaft or the face of a larger part, such as a flywheel.

Fatigue - A breakdown of material through a large number of loading and unloading cycles. The first signs are cracks followed shortly by breaks.

Feeler gauge - A thin strip of hardened steel, ground to an exact thickness, used to check clearances between parts.

Free height - The unloaded length or height of a spring.

Freeplay - The looseness in a linkage, or an assembly of parts, between the initial application of force and actual movement. Usually perceived as slop or slight delay.

Freeze plug - See Core plug.

G

Gallery - A large passage in the block that forms a reservoir for engine oil pressure.

Glaze - The very smooth, glassy finish that develops on cylinder walls while an engine is in service.

H

Heli-Coil - A rethreading device used when threads are worn or damaged. The device is installed in a retapped hole to reduce the thread size to the original size.

I

Installed height - The spring's measured length or height, as installed on the cylinder head. Installed height is measured from the spring seat to the underside of the spring retainer.

J

Journal - The surface of a rotating shaft which turns in a bearing.

K

Keeper - The split lock that holds the valve spring retainer in position on the valve stem.

Key - A small piece of metal inserted into matching grooves machined into two parts fitted together - such as a gear pressed onto a shaft - which prevents slippage between the two parts.

Knock - The heavy metallic engine sound, produced in the combustion chamber as a result of abnormal combustion - usually detonation. Knock is usually caused by a loose or worn bearing. Also referred to as detonation, pinging and spark knock. Connecting rod or main bearing knocks are created by too much oil clearance or insufficient lubrication.

L

Lands - The portions of metal between the piston ring grooves.

Lapping the valves - Grinding a valve face and its seat together with lapping compound.

Lash - The amount of free motion in a gear train, between gears, or in a mechanical assembly, that occurs before movement can begin. Usually refers to the lash in a valve train.

Lifter - The part that rides against the cam to transfer motion to the rest of the valve train.

M

Machining - The process of using a machine to remove metal from a metal part.

Main bearings - The plain, or babbit, bearings that support the crankshaft.

Main bearing caps - The cast iron caps, bolted to the bottom of the block, that support the main bearings.

O

O.D. - Outside diameter.

Oil gallery - A pipe or drilled passageway in the engine used to carry engine oil from one area to another.

Oil ring - The lower ring, or rings, of a piston; designed to prevent excessive amounts of oil from working up the cylinder walls and into the combustion chamber. Also called an oil-control ring.

Oil seal - A seal which keeps oil from leaking out of a compartment. Usually refers to a dynamic seal around a rotating shaft or other moving part.

O-ring - A type of sealing ring made of a special rubber-like material; in use, the O-ring is compressed into a groove to provide the sealing action.

Overhaul - To completely disassemble a unit, clean and inspect all parts, reassemble it with the original or new parts and make all adjustments necessary for proper operation.

P

Pilot bearing - A small bearing installed in the center of the flywheel (or the rear end of the crankshaft) to support the front end of the input shaft of the transmission.

Pip mark - A little dot or indentation which indicates the top side of a compression ring.

Piston - The cylindrical part, attached to the connecting rod, that moves up and down in the cylinder as the crankshaft rotates. When the fuel charge is fired, the piston transfers the force of the explosion to the connecting rod, then to the crankshaft.

Piston pin (or wrist pin) - The cylindrical and usually hollow steel pin that passes through the piston. The piston pin fastens the piston to the upper end of the connecting rod.

Piston ring - The split ring fitted to the groove in a piston. The ring contacts the sides of the ring groove and also rubs against the cylinder wall, thus sealing space between piston and wall. There are two types of rings: Compression rings seal the compression pressure in the combustion chamber; oil rings scrape excessive oil off the cylinder wall.

Piston ring groove - The slots or grooves cut in piston heads to hold piston rings in position.

Piston skirt - The portion of the piston below the rings and the piston pin hole.

Plastigage - A thin strip of plastic thread, available in different sizes, used for measuring clearances. For example, a strip of plastigage is laid across a bearing journal and mashed as parts are assembled. Then parts are disassembled and the width of the strip is measured to determine clearance between journal and bearing. Commonly used to measure crankshaft main-bearing and connecting rod bearing clearances.

Press-fit - A tight fit between two parts that requires pressure to force the parts together. Also referred to as drive, or force, fit.

Prussian blue - A blue pigment; in solution, useful in determining the area of contact between two surfaces. Prussian blue is commonly used to determine the width and location of the contact area between the valve face and the valve seat.

R

Race (bearing) - The inner or outer ring that provides a contact surface for balls or rollers in bearing.

Ream - To size, enlarge or smooth a hole by using a round cutting tool with fluted edges.

Ring job - The process of reconditioning the cylinders and installing new rings.

Runout - Wobble. The amount a shaft rotates out-of-true.

S

Saddle - The upper main bearing seat.

Scored - Scratched or grooved, as a cylinder wall may be scored by abrasive particles moved up and down by the piston rings.

Scuffing - A type of wear in which there's a transfer of material between parts moving against each other; shows up as pits or grooves in the mating surfaces.

Seat - The surface upon which another part rests or seats. For example, the valve seat is the matched surface upon which the valve face rests. Also used to refer to wearing into a good fit; for example, piston rings seat after a few miles of driving.

Short block - An engine block complete with crankshaft and piston and, usually, camshaft assemblies.

Static balance - The balance of an object while it's stationary.

Step - The wear on the lower portion of a ring land caused by excessive side and back-clearance. The height of the step indicates the ring's extra side clearance and the length of the step projecting from the back wall of the groove represents the ring's back clearance.

Stroke - The distance the piston moves when traveling from top dead center to bottom dead center, or from bottom dead center to top dead center.

Stud - A metal rod with threads on both ends.

T

Tang - A lip on the end of a plain bearing used to align the bearing during assembly.

Tap - To cut threads in a hole. Also refers to the fluted tool used to cut threads.

Taper - A gradual reduction in the width of a shaft or hole; in an engine cylinder, taper usually takes the form of uneven wear, more pronounced at the top than at the bottom.

Throws - The offset portions of the crankshaft to which the connecting rods are affixed.

Thrust bearing - The main bearing that has thrust faces to prevent excessive endplay, or forward and backward movement of the crankshaft.

Thrust washer - A bronze or hardened steel washer placed between two moving parts. The washer prevents longitudinal movement and provides a bearing surface for thrust surfaces of parts.

Tolerance - The amount of variation permitted from an exact size of measurement. Actual amount from smallest acceptable dimension to largest acceptable dimension.

U

Umbrella - An oil deflector placed near the valve tip to throw oil from the valve stem area.

Undercut - A machined groove below the normal surface.

Undersize bearings - Smaller diameter bearings used with re-ground crankshaft journals.

V

Valve grinding - Refacing a valve in a valve-refacing machine.

Valve train - The valve-operating mechanism of an engine; includes all components from the camshaft to the valve.

Vibration damper - A cylindrical weight attached to the front of the crankshaft to minimize torsional vibration (the twist-untwist actions of the crankshaft caused by the cylinder firing impulses). Also called a harmonic balancer.

W

Water jacket - The spaces around the cylinders, between the inner and outer shells of the cylinder block or head, through which coolant circulates.

Web - A supporting structure across a cavity.

Woodruff key - A key with a radiused backside (viewed from the side).

Chapter 3
Cooling, heating and air conditioning systems

Contents

Specifications

General

Cooling system cap pressure rating	Refer to top of cap
Thermostat rating (opening temperature range).....................................	195 degrees F
Cooling system capacity..	See Chapter 1
HVAC refrigerant type...	R-134a
Refrigerant capacity..	Refer to HVAC specification tag

Torque specifications

Ft-lbs (unless otherwise indicated)

Note: One foot-pound (ft-lb) of torque is equivalent to 12 inch-pounds (in-lbs) of torque. Torque values below approximately 15 ft-lbs are expressed in inch-pounds, since most foot-pound torque wrenches are not accurate at these smaller values.

Compressor mounting bolts/nuts...	37
Compressor refrigerant line fitting nut	150 in-lbs
Compressor refrigerant line fitting stud..	89 in-lbs
Condenser hold-down bracket...	53 in-lbs
Condenser refrigerant line fitting nut	150 in-lbs
Fan motor mounting fasteners (replacement)	53 in-lbs
Thermostat housing cover bolts	
V6 engines	
2006 and 2007..	18
2008 and later..	89 in-lbs
V8 engines	132 in-lbs
Water pump mounting bolts...	89 in-lbs
Water pump pulley mounting bolts (V6 engines only)	18

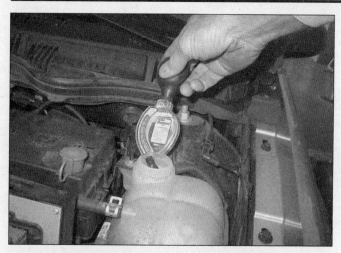

2.5 Use a hydrometer (available at auto parts stores) to test the condition of your coolant (typical shown)

3.10 The thermostat is located just below the exhaust manifold (V8 engine model shown - others are similar)

1   General information

Engine cooling system

All vehicles covered by this manual employ a pressurized engine cooling system with thermostatically controlled coolant circulation. An impeller-type water pump mounted on the engine block pumps coolant through the engine and radiator. The coolant flows around each cylinder and back to the radiator. Cast-in coolant passages direct coolant around the intake and exhaust ports, near the spark plug areas and the exhaust valve guides.

A wax-pellet type thermostat is located in a housing connected a radiator hose. During warm up the closed thermostat prevents coolant from circulating through the radiator. As the engine nears normal operating temperature, the thermostat opens and allows hot coolant to travel through the radiator, where it's cooled before returning to the engine.

A pressure cap, located at the top of the engine, seals the cooling system. The cap raises the boiling point of the coolant and increases the cooling efficiency of the radiator. If the system pressure exceeds the cap pressure relief value, the excess pressure in the system forces the spring-loaded valve inside the cap off its seat and allows the coolant to escape through a hose into a coolant reservoir. When the system cools, the excess coolant is automatically drawn from the reservoir back into the system.

The coolant reservoir serves as both the point at which fresh coolant is added to the cooling system to maintain the proper level and as a holding tank for expelled coolant.

This type of cooling system is known as a closed design because coolant that escapes past the pressure cap is saved and reused.

Transaxle cooling systems

All models are equipped with a transaxle cooler, located inside the radiator, which cools the transaxle fluid. The transaxle is connected to the cooler by a pair of hoses: one delivers hot transaxle fluid to the radiator and the other brings the cooled fluid back to the transaxle.

For more information on transaxle oil coolers, refer to Chapter 7.

Heating system

The heating system consists of the heater controls, the heater core, the heater blower assembly (which houses the blower motor and the blower motor resistor), and the hoses connecting the heater core to the engine cooling system. Hot engine coolant is circulated through the heater core. When the heater mode is activated, a flap door opens to expose the heater box to the passenger compartment. A fan switch on the heater controls activates the blower motor, which forces air through the core, heating the air.

Air conditioning system

The air conditioning system consists of the condenser with an integral receiver-drier, which is mounted in front of the radiator, the evaporator/heater case assembly under the dash, a compressor mounted on the engine, and the plumbing connecting all of the above components.

A blower fan forces the warmer air of the passenger compartment through the evaporator core (sort of a radiator-in-reverse), transferring the heat from the air to the refrigerant. The liquid refrigerant boils off into low pressure vapor, taking the heat with it when it leaves the evaporator.

2   Antifreeze - general information

Refer to illustration 2.5

Warning: *Do not allow antifreeze to come in contact with your skin or painted surfaces of the vehicle. Rinse off spills immediately with plenty of water. Antifreeze is highly toxic if ingested. Never leave antifreeze lying around in an open container or in puddles on the floor; children and pets are attracted by its sweet smell and may drink it. Check with local authorities about disposing of used antifreeze. Many communities have collection centers that will see that antifreeze is disposed of safely. Never dump used antifreeze on the ground or pour it into drains.*
Note: *Non-toxic antifreeze is now manufactured and available at local auto parts stores, but even this type must be disposed of properly.*

The cooling system should be filled with a water/ethylene glycol based antifreeze solution, which will prevent freezing down to at least -20-degrees F (even lower in cold climates). It also provides protection against corrosion and increases the coolant boiling point. The engines in these vehicles have aluminum heads. Depending on the engine and model year, the specified coolant may vary (see the Chapter 1 Specifications). The manufacturer recommends that the correct type of coolant be used and strongly urges that coolant types not be mixed.

Drain, flush and refill the cooling system at least every other year (see Chapter 1). The use of antifreeze solutions for periods of longer than two years is likely to cause damage and encourage the formation of rust and scale in the system.

Before adding antifreeze to the system, inspect all hose connections. Antifreeze can leak through very minute openings.

The exact mixture of antifreeze to water, which you should use, depends on the relative weather conditions. The mixture should contain at least 50-percent antifreeze, but should never contain more than 70-percent antifreeze. Consult the mixture ratio chart on the container before adding coolant.

Hydrometers are available at most auto parts stores to test the coolant (**see illustration**). Use antifreeze that meets the manufacturer's specifications for engines with alu-

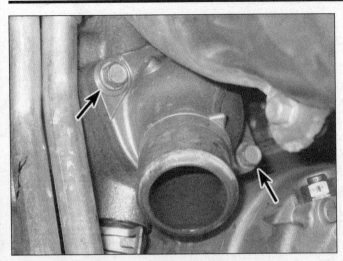

**3.14 Thermostat housing cover mounting bolts
(V8 engine shown, V6 similar)**

3.17 Place a new rubber seal on the thermostat

minum heads. **Warning:** *Do not remove the pressure cap, drain the coolant or replace the thermostat until the engine has cooled completely.*

3   Thermostat - check and replacement

Check

1   Before assuming the thermostat is to blame for a cooling system problem, check the coolant level, drivebelt tension (see Chapter 1) and temperature gauge operation.
2   If the engine seems to be taking a long time to warm up, based on heater output or temperature gauge operation, the thermostat is probably stuck open. Replace the thermostat with a new one.
3   If the engine runs hot, use your hand to check the temperature of the lower radiator hose. If the hose isn't hot, but the engine is, the thermostat is probably stuck closed, preventing the coolant inside the engine from circulating through the radiator. Replace the thermostat. **Caution:** *Don't drive the vehicle without a thermostat; the computer may stay in open loop and emissions and fuel economy will suffer.*
4   If the lower radiator hose is hot, it means that the coolant is flowing and the thermostat is open. Consult the *Troubleshooting* Section at the front of this manual for cooling system diagnosis.

Replacement

Warning: *The engine must be completely cool before beginning this procedure.*
5   Disconnect the cable from the negative terminal of the battery (see Chapter 5, Section 1).
6   Drain the cooling system (see Chapter 1). If the coolant is relatively new and still in good condition, save it and reuse it.

V6 engine models

7   Remove the air filter housing duct leading to the throttle body (see Chapter 4).
8   Follow the lower radiator hose to locate the thermostat housing.
9   Proceed to Step 12.

V8 engine models

Refer to illustration 3.10

10   The thermostat housing is located above the air conditioning compressor and near the right end (passenger's side) of the exhaust manifold **(see illustration)**. **Note:** *The manufacturer states to remove the thermostat from beneath the vehicle, but we believe that it is much easier to remove it from above the vehicle, by first removing the exhaust manifold.*
11   Remove the exhaust manifold (see Chapter 2B).

All models

Refer to illustrations 3.14 and 3.17

12   Loosen the radiator hose clamp, then detach the hose from the thermostat housing cover. If it's stuck, grasp it near the end with a pair of adjustable pliers and twist it to break the seal, then pull it off. If the hose is old or if it has deteriorated, cut it off and install a new one.
13   If the outer surface of the outlet (where it mates with the hose) is corroded, pitted, or otherwise deteriorated, removing the hose may damage it to the point where it must be replaced. Replace the thermostat housing cover if necessary.
14   Remove the two thermostat housing cover fasteners, then remove the cover **(see illustration)**. **Note:** *If the cover is stuck, tap it with a soft-face hammer to jar it loose. Be prepared for some coolant to spill as the seal is broken.*
15   Before removing the thermostat, note all of the details on how it's installed.
16   Remove all traces of the old seal from the housing and cover.

17   Install a new rubber seal on the replacement thermostat **(see illustration)**. Place the thermostat into the housing, spring end first.
18   Install the thermostat housing cover and mounting bolts, then tighten the bolts to the torque listed in this Chapter's Specifications.
19   Reattach the radiator hose to the outlet pipe on the thermostat housing cover. Make sure that the hose clamp is secure. If it isn't, replace it.
20   The remainder of the installation is the reverse of the removal.
21   Refill the cooling system (see Chapter 1).
22   Reconnect the battery (see Chapter 5, Section 1).
23   Start the engine and allow it to reach normal operating temperature. Check for leaks and proper thermostat operation (as described in Steps 3 and 4).

4   Engine cooling fans - check and replacement

Warning: *To avoid possible injury or damage, DO NOT operate the engine with a damaged fan. Do not attempt to repair fan blades - replace a damaged fan with a new one.*

Check

Refer to illustrations 4.2 and 4.3

1   These models are equipped with two cooling fans mounted side-by-side behind the radiator. The PCM (Powertrain Control Module - engine computer) and three relays are used to operate the fans at Low or High speeds depending on engine needs and other conditions. The fans are protected by fuses inside the engine compartment's fuse/relay box.
2   If the engine is overheating and neither of the cooling fans operate, locate the fuses in the engine compartment fuse/relay box **(see**

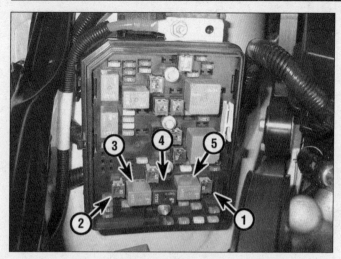

4.2 The engine compartment fuse/relay box with fan relay and fuse details (V8 engine model shown, V6 similar):

1	Fan fuse 1	3	Fan relay 3	5 Fan relay 1
2	Fan fuse 2	4	Fan relay 2	

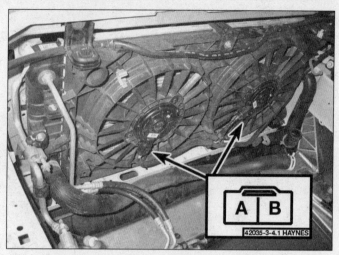

4.3 To test either fan motor, disconnect the electrical connector and use jumper wires to connect the fan directly to the battery (A) and ground (B) - if the fan still doesn't work, replace the motor (V8 engine model shown - others are similar)

illustration). Remove the fuse(s) and check for continuity (see Chapter 12). If a fuse is blown, replace it and see if it blows again. If it does, trace and repair the source of the short circuit.

3   If the fuses are okay, check each fan by unplugging the fan motor electrical connector and applying battery power directly to the motor terminals with fused jumper wires **(see illustration)**. When done correctly, the fan should come on. If a fan motor doesn't work, replace the motor.

4   If the fan motors are okay but are still not coming on when the engine gets hot, the fan relays might be defective. Locate the relays in the engine compartment's fuse/relay box **(see illustration 4.2)**. You can pull each relay out and test it individually (see Chapter 12). **Note:** *Relays are used to control a circuit by turning it on and off in response to a signal from the PCM. The control circuits themselves are fairly complex and checking them should be left to a dealer service department. It's also likely that a failure in one of these circuits will*

result in a warning light in the instrument display.

5   If no obvious problems are found, have the cooling fan system diagnosed by a dealer service department or other qualified repair shop.

Replacement

Refer to illustrations 4.12 and 4.13

Warning: *The engine must be completely cool before beginning this procedure.*

Note: *The manufacturer states to install a new fan blade when a fan motor is removed.*

6   Disconnect the cable from the negative terminal of the battery (see Chapter 5, Section 1).

7   Drain the cooling system (see Chapter 1).

8   Remove the air filter housing (see Chapter 4).

9   Remove the engine mount strut(s) from the top of the engine (See Chapter 2).

10   Disconnect the fan motor harness electrical connectors **(see illustration 4.3)**. Remove any hoses or wiring harnesses that may be attached to the fan shroud assembly.

11   Disconnect the upper transaxle cooler line from the left side (driver's side) of the radiator (see Chapter 7).

12   Remove the radiator hose from the right side (passenger's side) of the radiator **(see illustration)**.

13   Remove the radiator and condenser mounting brackets **(see illustration)**.

14   Remove the fan shroud assembly mounting bolts, then remove the assembly by lifting it up and out of the engine compartment.

15   Remove the fastener (drive plate) holding the fan blade to the motor shaft by turning it in the opposite direction of the arrow on the fan blade. Hold the fan blade firmly while loosening the fastener. Remove the fan blade and discard it.

16   Put tape over any openings on good motors when either one of them is removed to protect them from debris.

17   Accurately center-punch the rivets that secure the fan motor to the fan shroud from the rear of the assembly **(see illustration 4.12)**.

18   Drill out the ends of the rivets on the motor being removed with a 1/4-inch (6.35 mm) drill bit. Using a punch, carefully tap the rivets out and remove the motor.

19   After thoroughly cleaning all debris from the shroud, remove the protective tape from the motor(s).

20   For motor installation, replacement fasteners will be needed to replace the rivets. Obtain three bolts, six washers and three locking-type nuts, of the appropriate size, for each motor removed. **Caution:** *Do not use lock washers.*

21   Install the replacement mounting bolts from the front of the motor (fan blade side) and the locknuts to the rear of the motor (electrical connector side). Tighten the nuts to the torque listed in this Chapter's Specifications.

22   Prepare the new fan blade by heating the center portion (the hub) of the fan with hot tap water. Hold the hub under hot running water for at least one minute and make certain that the water is at least 120-degrees F. **Caution:** *Failure to do this could result in the fan cracking.*

23   Immediately place the fan onto the motor shaft and install the drive plate. Hold the fan blade securely while turning the drive plate in the same direction as the arrow on the fan blade until the fastener is fully seated into the three slots on the fan blade hub.

24   Turn the fan blade and confirm that it is correctly installed.

25   The remaining installation is the reverse of the removal. Tighten all fasteners securely.

26   Refill the cooling system and check the transaxle fluid level (see Chapter 1).

4.12 Right side radiator hose location

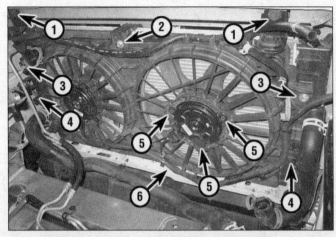

4.13 Fan shroud and motor assembly details:

1   Radiator mounting brackets
2   Condenser hold-down bracket
3   Fan shroud assembly mounting bolts
4   Fan shroud assembly mounting tabs
5   Fan motor mounting rivets
6   Fan motor wiring harness

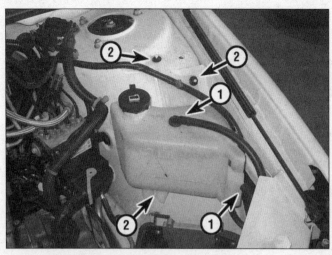

5.3 Reservoir tank details (V8 engine shown, V6 similar):

1   Hose fittings
2   Mounting points and fasteners

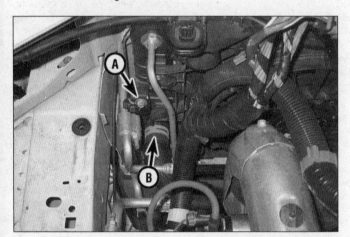

6.4 Detach the refrigerant line bracket (A) and radiator hose (B)

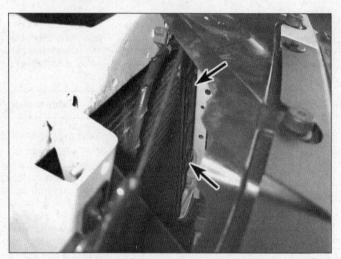

6.6 The air conditioning condenser mounting tab retainers on the left side of the radiator (the right side is similar)

5   Coolant reservoir tank - removal and installation

Refer to illustration 5.3

Warning: *Wait until the engine is completely cool before beginning this procedure.*

1   Drain the cooling system (see Chapter 1). If the coolant is relatively new and still in good condition, it can be saved and reused. *Be careful to clean up any spilled coolant as stated in the* **Warning** *at the beginning of Section 2.*

2   On V8 engine models, remove the diagonal brace above the reservoir.

3   Carefully detach all hoses **(see illustration)**.

4   Remove the reservoir tank mounting fasteners **(see illustration 5.3)**.

5   Clean out the tank with soapy water and a brush to remove any deposits inside. Inspect the reservoir carefully for cracks. If you find a

crack, replace the reservoir.

6   Installation is the reverse of removal. Refill the cooling system with the proper concentration and type of antifreeze (see Chapter 1).

6   Radiator - removal and installation

Warning: *Wait until the engine is completely cool before beginning this procedure.*

Removal

Refer to illustrations 6.4, 6.6 and 6.10

1   Disconnect the cable from the negative battery terminal (see Chapter 5, Section 1).

2   Drain the cooling system (see Chapter 1). If the coolant is relatively new or in good condition, save it and reuse it. Read the **Warning** in Section 2.

3   Remove the engine cooling fans (see Section 4).

4   Detach the refrigerant line bracket and radiator hose from the left side of the radiator **(see illustration)**.

5   Disconnect the lower transaxle cooler line from the left side (driver's side) of the radiator (see Chapter 7).

6   Tilt the radiator and air conditioning condenser back towards the firewall slightly, then disengage the condenser from the four mounting tab retainers on the radiator (two on each side) **(see illustration)**. Do this by raising the condenser up while holding the radiator down. Place the condenser back into its position, letting it rest loosely towards the front grill.

7   Carefully lift out the radiator. Don't spill coolant on the vehicle or scratch the paint.

8   Inspect the radiator for leaks and damage. If it needs repair, have a radiator shop or dealer service department perform the work, as special tools and techniques are required.

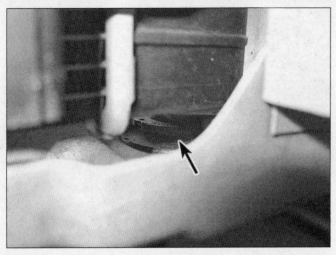

6.10 Rubber radiator mounts are located on the bottom of each side of the radiator

7.3 Look for leaks around the water pump shaft seal (A) and from below the water pump housing (B) (V8 engine shown, removed for clarity - others are similar)

9   Bugs and dirt can be removed from the radiator by spraying it with a garden hose nozzle from the back side. The radiator should be flushed out with a garden hose before reinstallation.

10   Check the radiator mounts for deterioration and replace them if necessary **(see illustration)**.

Installation

11   Installation is the reverse of the removal procedure. Carefully install the radiator while engaging the mounting tabs for the air conditioning condenser. Guide the radiator (and air conditioning condenser) into the bottom mounts until they seat properly **(see illustration 6.10)**.

12   Tighten the radiator bracket bolts securely.

13   After installation, fill the cooling system with the proper mixture of antifreeze and water (see Chapter 1).

14   Reconnect the battery (see Chapter 5, Section 1).

15   Start the engine and check for leaks. Allow the engine to reach normal operating temperature. Recheck the coolant level and add more if necessary.

16   Check the transaxle fluid level and add some, if necessary (see Chapter 1).

7   Water pump - check

Refer to illustration 7.3

1   A failure in the water pump can cause serious engine damage due to overheating.

2   If a failure occurs in the shaft seal on the water pump, a coolant leak can usually be seen coming from that area.

3   Most water pumps are equipped with small weep or vent holes. Although it might seem difficult, it is possible to check these holes for leaks using a flashlight and a mirror. In most cases, the leak can be detected from coolant streams or drips near the bottom of the water pump housing **(see illustration)**.

4   If the water pump shaft bearings fail, there may be a howling sound near the water pump while it's running. With the engine off, shaft wear can be felt if the water pump pulley is rocked up-and-down. Don't mistake drivebelt slippage, which causes a squealing sound, for water pump bearing failure.

5   A quick water pump performance check is to turn the heater on. If the pump is failing, it might not be able to efficiently circulate hot water all the way to the heater core as it should.

8   Water pump - replacement

Warning: *The engine must be completely cool before beginning this procedure.*

Note: *A special drivebelt tensioner wrench is required for drivebelt removal on V8 models. Before starting this procedure, make sure you have the tool (see Chapter 1).*

1   Drain the cooling system (see Chapter 1). If the coolant is relatively new and still in good condition, it can be saved and reused.

Note: *Be careful to clean up any spilled coolant as stated in the* **Warning** *at the beginning of Section 2.*

V6 engines

Refer to illustrations 8.2 and 8.5

2   Loosen, but do not remove, the water pump pulley bolts **(see illustration)**.

3   Remove the drivebelt (see Chapter 1).

4   Remove the pulley mounting bolts and the pulley from the water pump flange.

5   Remove the water pump mounting bolts **(see illustration)**.

V8 engines

Refer to illustration 8.8

6   Remove the battery and battery tray for access (see Chapter 5).

7   Remove the drivebelt (see Chapter 1).

8   Align the holes in the water pump pulley over the pump mounting bolts, then remove the bolts **(see illustration)**.

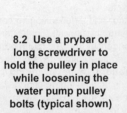

8.2 Use a prybar or long screwdriver to hold the pulley in place while loosening the water pump pulley bolts (typical shown)

8.5 Water pump mounting bolts - V6 engines   **8.8 Water pump mounting bolts - V8 engine**

All engines

9   Carefully remove the pump from the engine. If the water pump is stuck, gently tap it with a soft-faced hammer to break the seal.
10   Remove all traces of the old gasket seal from the mounting surface on the engine. Do the same on the water pump if the same pump is going to be re-installed.
11   Clean the mounting bolt threads and threaded holes on the mounting surface to remove corrosion and sealant, if necessary.
12   Compare the replacement pump with the old one to make sure that they're identical.
13   Place the gasket and water pump into position. Install the mounting bolts until they are all finger tight.
14   With everything correctly in place, tighten the water pump mounting bolts to the torque listed in this Chapter's Specifications.
15   The remaining installation is the reverse of the removal. On V6 engine models, tighten the water pump pulley bolts to the torque listed in this Chapter's Specifications. Refill the cooling system with the proper concentration of antifreeze (see Chapter 1). Start the engine and allow it to reach normal operating temperature while inspecting the system for leaks.

9   Coolant temperature sending unit - check

Warning: *Wait until the engine is completely cool before beginning this procedure.*
1   The coolant temperature indicator system consists of a temperature gauge, a warning light on the dash and a sensor mounted on the engine. The Engine Coolant Temperature (ECT) sensor (see Chapter 6), provides a signal to the Powertrain Control Module (PCM) and Body Control Module (BCM) which operate the temperature gauge.
2   If an overheating condition has occurred, first check the coolant level in the system (see Chapter 1) and that the coolant mixture is correct (see Section 2). Also, refer to the *Trouble-*

shooting Section at the beginning of this book before assuming that the temperature indicator is faulty.
3   If the temperature gauge does not move from the C position, check the wiring harness connections going to the instrument cluster.
4   If there is a problem with the ECT sensor, it is very likely that the *Check Engine* light will come on and the sensor will need replacing or the circuit will need repair (see Chapter 6).

10   Blower motor module and blower motor - replacement

Warning: *The models covered by this manual are equipped with Supplemental Restraint systems (SRS), more commonly known as airbags. Always disarm the airbag system before working in the vicinity of any airbag system component to avoid the possibility of accidental deployment of the airbag, which could cause personal injury (see Chapter 12). Do not use a memory saving device to preserve the PCM's memory when working on or near airbag system components.*
1   Disconnect the cable from the negative

battery terminal (see Chapter 5, Section 1).
2   Remove the insulating panel from below the dash and under the glove box in the passenger compartment.

Blower motor control module

Refer to illustration 10.3
3   Disconnect the electrical connector at the blower motor control module **(see illustration)**.
4   Using a very small chisel or screwdriver with a thin sharp blade, carefully remove the plastic heat stakes that secure the module, then pull it out of the evaporator/heater core housing.
5   Installation is the reverse of removal. Use two small screws to secure the module to the housing. Install the screws into the holes next to (not on) the old heat stakes. **Note:** *Specific screws are available at a dealership parts department.*

Blower motor

6   Disconnect the blower motor electrical connector.
7   Remove the mounting fasteners and lower the motor assembly out of the housing.
8   Installation is the reverse of removal.

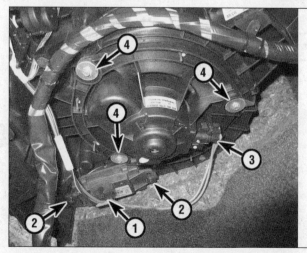

10.3 Blower motor and control module mounting details:

1   *Blower motor control module electrical connector.*
2   *Using a sharp thin chisel or screwdriver, remove the plastic heat stakes that secure the module*
3   *Blower motor electrical connector*
4   *Blower motor assembly mounting fasteners*

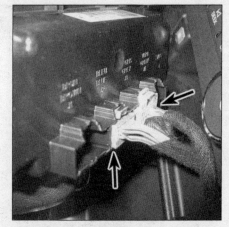

11.3 Remove the heater/air conditioner control assembly mounting screws

11.4 Disconnect the electrical connectors from the rear of the control assembly

11   Heater/air conditioner control assembly - removal and installation

Refer to illustrations 11.3 and 11.4

Warning: *The models covered by this manual are equipped with Supplemental Restraint systems (SRS), more commonly known as airbags. Always disarm the airbag system before working in the vicinity of any airbag system component to avoid the possibility of accidental deployment of the airbag, which could cause personal injury (see Chapter 12). Do not use a memory saving device to preserve the PCM's memory when working on or near airbag system components.*

Note: *If the heater/air conditioner control assembly is replaced, a special scan tool is required to program the replacement unit.*

1   Disconnect the cable from the negative battery terminal (see Chapter 5, Section 1).

2   Remove the center trim bezel (see Chapter 11).

3   Remove the heater/air conditioner control assembly retaining screws **(see illustration)** and pull the unit out.

4   Disconnect the electrical connectors on the back of the control assembly **(see illustration).**

5   Installation is the reverse of removal.

6   Reconnect the battery (see Chapter 5, Section 1).

12   Heater core - replacement

Refer to illustrations 12.3, 12.8a, 12.8b, 12.9a, 12.9b, 12.10, 12.11a and 12.11b

Warning: *The models covered by this manual are equipped with Supplemental Restraint systems (SRS), more commonly known as airbags. Always disarm the airbag system before working in the vicinity of any airbag system component to avoid the possibility of accidental deployment of the airbag, which could cause personal injury (see Chapter 12). Do not use a memory saving device to preserve the PCM's memory when working on or near airbag system components.*

1   Disconnect the cable from the negative battery terminal (see Chapter 5, Section 1). **Note:** *Make sure that the power seat(s) are in a position where the mounting fasteners are accessible before disconnecting the battery (see Chapter 11).*

2   Drain the cooling system (see Chapter 1). If the coolant is relatively new and still in good condition, it can be saved and reused. *Be careful to clean up any spilled coolant as stated in the* **Warning** *at the beginning of Section 2.*

3   Disconnect the heater hoses from the heater core fittings at the firewall **(see illustration).**

4   Remove the insulating panels mounted below each side of the dash (see Chapter 11).

5   Remove the front seats, the kick plate trim panels, and the center console (see Chapter 11).

6   Detach the front carpet fastener on each side of the door opening near the pinch-weld. Carefully peel the carpet back to gain access to the air duct beneath the center console.

7   Separate the floor air duct (that leads to the rear) from the outer heater core cover and set it aside.

8   Remove the screws and heat stakes that hold the outer cover in place **(see illustrations).** Use a small chisel or screwdriver with a thin sharp blade to remove the plastic heat

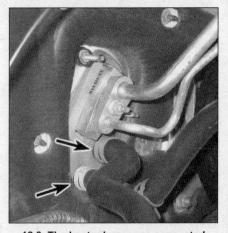

12.3 The heater hoses are connected to the heater core pipes next to the brake booster

stakes. **Caution:** *The bottom mounting tabs on each side of the cover use a heat stake and screw on each tab. Avoid breaking a tab by confirming that the screw and heat stake on each tab are removed before attempting to detach the cover.*

9   Use the same method to remove the inner heater core cover **(see illustrations).**

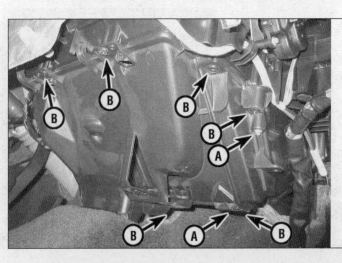

12.8a Screw (A) and heat stake (B) locations viewed from the right

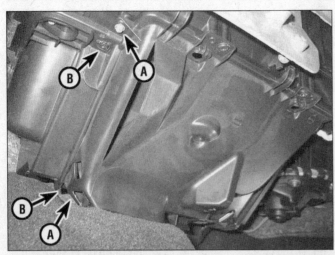

12.8b Screw (A) and heat stake (B) locations viewed from the left

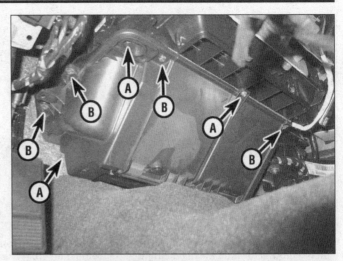

12.9a Screw (A) and heat stake (B) locations viewed from the left with the outer cover removed

12.9b Remove the two bottom screws for the inner cover

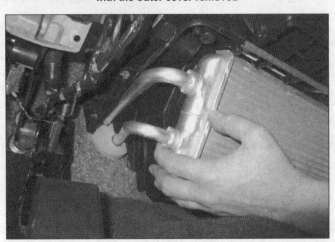

12.10 Carefully remove the heater core from the housing while withdrawing the pipes from the firewall and seal

10   Remove the heater core from the heater core housing **(see illustration)**. Place rags under the heater core pipes to catch any coolant that may spill.

11   Installation is the reverse of removal. Don't forget to reconnect the heater hoses at the firewall. **Note:** *The heater core covers are designed to be reinstalled onto the housing with mounting screws. You will need to get these screws from an authorized dealership parts department. Mounting holes will need to be drilled on the covers, but they are clearly marked* **(see illustrations)**.

12   Refill the cooling system when you're done (see Chapter 1).

13   Reconnect the battery (see Chapter 5, Section 1).

12.11a The inner cover mounting hole drill locations

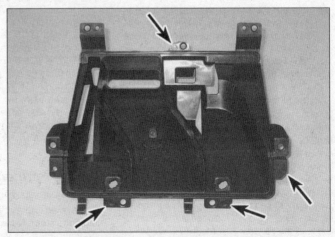

12.11b The outer cover mounting hole drill locations

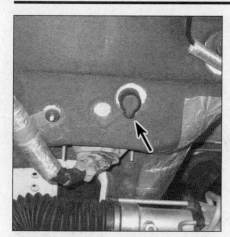

13.1 Look for the evaporator drain hose on the firewall towards the middle-right (passenger's) side

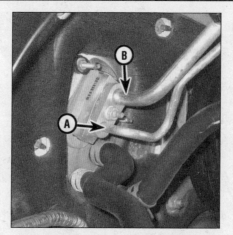

13.7 If the air conditioning system refrigerant charge is adequate, the small diameter line (A) should feel warm and the large diameter line (B) should feel cool

13.9 A basic R-134a charging kit is available at most auto parts stores - it must say R-134a (not R-12) on the kit and the can of refrigerant

13   Air conditioning and heating system - check and maintenance

Refer to illustration 13.1

Warning: *The air conditioning system is under high pressure. Do not loosen any hose fittings or remove any components until after the system has been discharged by an air conditioning technician. Always wear eye protection when disconnecting air conditioning system fittings.*

1   The following maintenance checks should be performed on a regular basis to ensure the air conditioner continues to operate at peak efficiency.

a) *Check the compressor drivebelt. If it's worn or deteriorated, replace it (see Chapter 1).*

b) *Check the drivebelt tension and, if necessary, adjust it (see Chapter 1).*

c) *Check the system hoses. Look for cracks, bubbles, hard spots and deterioration. Inspect the hoses and all fittings for oil bubbles and seepage. If there's any evidence of wear, damage or leaks, replace the hose(s).*

d) *Inspect the condenser fins for leaves, bugs and other debris. Use a "fin comb" or compressed air to clean the condenser.*

e) *Make sure the system has the correct refrigerant charge.*

f) *Check the evaporator housing drain tube* **(see illustration)** *for blockage.*

2   It's a good idea to operate the system for about 10 minutes at least once a month, particularly during the winter. Long term non-use can cause hardening, and subsequent failure, of the seals.

3   Because of the complexity of the air conditioning system and the special equipment necessary to service it, in-depth troubleshooting and repairs are not included in this manual (refer to the *Haynes Automotive Heating and Air Conditioning* Repair Manual). However,

simple checks and component replacement procedures are provided in this Chapter.

4   The most common cause of poor cooling is simply a low system refrigerant charge. If a noticeable drop in cool air output occurs, the following quick check will help you determine if the refrigerant level is low.

Checking the refrigerant charge

Refer to illustration 13.7

5   Warm the engine up to normal operating temperature.

6   Place the air conditioning temperature selector at the coldest setting and the blower at the highest setting. Open the vehicle doors (to make sure the air conditioning system doesn't cycle off as soon as it cools the passenger compartment).

7   Feel the refrigerant lines where they connect to the thermal expansion valve at the firewall **(see illustration)**. If the liquid line (small diameter) feels warm and the outlet pipe (large diameter) feels cool, the system is probably adequately charged.

8   Place a thermometer in the dashboard vent nearest the evaporator and operate the system until the indicated temperature is around 40 to 45-degrees F. If the ambient (outside) air temperature is very high, say 110-degrees F, the duct air temperature may be as high as 60-degrees F, but generally the air conditioning is 30 to 40-degrees F cooler than the ambient air. **Note:** *Humidity of the ambient air also affects the cooling capacity of the system. Higher ambient humidity lowers the effectiveness of the air conditioning system.*

Adding refrigerant

Refer to illustrations 13.9, 13.12 and 13.15

9   Buy an automotive charging kit at an auto parts store. A charging kit includes a can of refrigerant, a tap valve and a short section of hose that can be attached between the tap

valve and the system low side service valve **(see illustration)**. **Note:** *Leak detection kits with refrigerant dye, a UV light and special glasses are also available at most automotive supply stores. This kit can help you pinpoint leaks in your air conditioning system.* **Caution:** *There are two types of refrigerant used in automotive systems; R-12 - which has been widely used on earlier models - and the more environmentally-friendly R-134a used in all models covered by this manual. These two refrigerants (and their appropriate refrigerant oils) are not compatible and must never be mixed or components will be damaged. Use only R-134a refrigerant in the models covered by this manual.*

10   Hook up the charging kit by following the manufacturer's instructions. **Warning:** *DO NOT attempt to hook the charging kit hose to the system high side! The fittings on the charging kit are designed to fit only on the low side of the system.*

11   Back off the valve handle on the charging kit and screw the kit onto the refrigerant

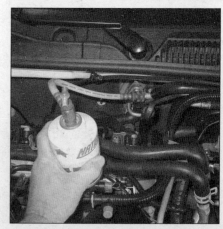

13.12 R-134A refrigerant (available at auto parts stores) can be added to the low side of the air conditioning system with a simple recharging kit

13.15 Insert a thermometer in the center vent, turn on the air conditioning system and wait for it to cool down; depending on the humidity, the output air should be 30 to 40-degrees F cooler than the ambient air temperature

13.23 Insert the disinfectant can's nozzle just inside the air intake duct at this location

can, making sure first that the O-ring or rubber seal inside the threaded portion of the kit is in place. **Warning:** *Wear protective eyewear when dealing with pressurized refrigerant cans.*

12   Remove the dust cap from the low-side charging connection and attach the quick-connect fitting on the kit hose **(see illustration)**.

13   Warm up the engine and turn on the air conditioner. Keep the charging kit hose away from the fan and other moving parts. **Note:** *The compressor needs to be running in order to charge the system. However, if your system is very low on refrigerant, the compressor may turn off or not come on at all. If this happens, disconnect the A/C pressure switch electrical connector and use a jumper wire between the two terminals in the harness connector* **(see illustration 16.2)**. *This will keep the compressor running.*

14   Turn the valve handle on the kit until the stem pierces the can, then back the handle out to release the refrigerant. You should be able to hear the rush of gas. Add refrigerant to the low side of the system until the compressor discharge line feels warm and the compressor inlet pipe feels cool. Allow stabilization time between each addition.

15   If you have an accurate thermometer, place it in the center air conditioning vent **(see illustration)** and then note the temperature of the air coming out of the vent. A fully-charged system which is working correctly should cool down to about 40-degrees F. Generally, an air conditioning system will put out air that is 30 to 40-degrees F cooler than the ambient air. For example, if the ambient (outside) air temperature is very high (over 100 degrees F), the temperature of the air coming out of the registers should be 60 to 70 degrees F.

16   When the can is empty, turn the valve handle to the closed position and release the connection from the low-side port. Replace the dust cap. **Caution:** *Never add more than one can of refrigerant to the system. If more*

refrigerant than that is required, the system should be evacuated and leak tested.

17   Remove the charging kit from the can and store the kit for future use with the piercing valve in the UP position, to prevent inadvertently piercing the can on the next use.

Heating systems

18   If the carpet under the heater core is damp, or if antifreeze vapor or steam is coming through the vents, the heater core is leaking. Remove it (see Section 12) and install a new unit (most radiator shops will not repair a leaking heater core).

19   If the air coming out of the heater vents isn't hot, the problem could stem from any of the following causes:

a)   *The thermostat is stuck open, preventing the engine coolant from warming up enough to carry heat to the heater core. Replace the thermostat (see Section 3).*

b)   *There is a blockage in the system, preventing the flow of coolant through the heater core. Feel both heater hoses at the firewall. They should be hot. If one of them is cold, there is an obstruction in one of the hoses or in the heater core, or the heater control valve is shut. Detach the hoses and back flush the heater core with a water hose. If the heater core is clear but circulation is impeded, remove the two hoses and flush them out with a water hose.*

c)   *If flushing fails to remove the blockage from the heater core, the core must be replaced (see Section 12).*

Eliminating air conditioning odors

Refer to illustration 13.23

20   Unpleasant odors that often develop in air conditioning systems are caused by the growth of a fungus, usually on the surface of the evaporator core. The warm, humid envi-

ronment there is a perfect breeding ground for mildew to develop.

21   The evaporator core on most vehicles is difficult to access, and factory dealerships have a lengthy, expensive process for eliminating the fungus by opening up the evaporator case and using a powerful disinfectant and rinse on the core until the fungus is gone. You can service your own system at home, but it takes something much stronger than basic household germ-killers or deodorizers.

22   Aerosol disinfectants for automotive air conditioning systems are available in most auto parts stores, but remember when shopping for them that the most effective treatments are also the most expensive. Make sure that the disinfectant can comes with a long spray hose. The basic procedure for using these sprays is to start by running the system in the RECIRC mode for ten minutes with the blower on its highest speed. Use the highest heat mode to dry out the system and keep the compressor from engaging by disconnecting the wiring connector at the compressor (see Section 14).

23   Change the blower motor setting to low and the temperature to the middle setting. Pivot the glove box door down (see Chapter 11) and guide the nozzle through the interior intake duct allowing it to protrude just inside the blower motor (and evaporator) housing **(see illustration)**, then spray according to the manufacturer's recommendations. Follow the manufacturer's recommendations for the length of spray and waiting time between applications. **Caution:** *Be careful not to place the hose too far into the housing because it could get caught in the blower motor fan that is just below the opening.*

24   Once the evaporator has been cleaned, the best way to prevent the mildew from coming back again is to make sure your evaporator housing drain tube is clear **(see illustration 13.1)**.

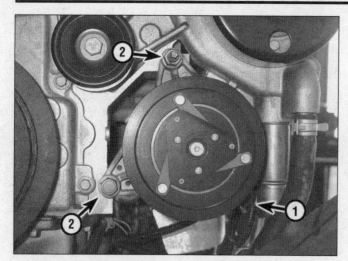

14.5 Air conditioning compressor mounting details - side view (V8 engine shown, V6 engines similar):

1   *Clutch field coil electrical connector*
2   *Mounting fasteners*

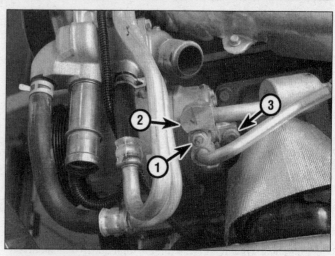

14.6 Air conditioning compressor mounting details - front view (V8 engine shown, V6 engines similar):

1   *Refrigerant line fitting mounting nut and stud*
2   *Refrigerant line fitting*
3   *Mounting fastener*

14   Air conditioning compressor - removal and installation

Warning: *The air conditioning system is under high pressure. DO NOT loosen any fittings or remove any components until after the system has been discharged. Air conditioning refrigerant must be properly discharged into an EPA-approved container at a dealer service department or an automotive air conditioning repair facility. Always wear eye protection when disconnecting air conditioning system fittings.*
Caution: *If you are replacing the compressor due to major internal damage, you must also replace the small screen refrigerant filter (see Section 17).*

Removal

Refer to illustrations 14.5 and 14.6

1   Have the air conditioning system discharged by a dealer service department or by an automotive air conditioning shop before proceeding (see **Warning** above).
2   Remove the drivebelt (see Chapter 1).
3   Raise the front of the vehicle and secure it on jackstands. Remove the right front wheel.
4   Remove the right front fender splash shield (see Chapter 11). On V8 engine models, remove the lower engine splash shield beneath the radiator (see Chapter 2).
5   Disconnect the electrical connector from the compressor clutch field coil **(see illustration)**.
6   Disconnect the compressor refrigerant line fitting from the compressor. On V8 engine models, remove the stud for the refrigerant line fitting as well. Discard the sealing O-rings **(see illustration)**.
7   Remove the compressor mounting fasteners and remove the compressor **(see illustrations 14.5 and 14.6)**.

Installation

8   If a new compressor is being installed, follow the directions with the compressor regarding the draining of excess oil prior to installation.
9   In the unlikely event that the replacement compressor is not equipped with a clutch, have the clutch from the original compressor transferred to the new one by a shop that specializes in air conditioning service.
10   Before connecting the refrigerant line fitting to the compressor, replace all O-rings. Be sure to lubricate the O-rings with R-134a compatible refrigerant oil.
11   The remainder of installation is the reverse of removal. Tighten the line fitting fastener(s) and compressor mounting fasteners to the torque listed in this Chapter's Specifications.
12   Have the system evacuated, recharged and leak tested by the shop that discharged it.

15   Air conditioning condenser - removal and installation

Refer to illustration 15.4

Warning: *The air conditioning system is under high pressure. DO NOT loosen any fittings or remove any components until after the system has been discharged. Air conditioning refrigerant must be properly discharged into an EPA-approved container at a dealer service department or an automotive air conditioning repair facility. Always wear eye protection when disconnecting air conditioning system fittings.*
Note: *The air conditioning condenser has an integral desiccant bag mounted inside of a housing on the left side of the condenser. These two components cannot be separated*

and are serviced as an assembly.

1   Have the air conditioning system discharged by a dealer service department or by an automotive air conditioning shop before proceeding (see **Warning** above).
2   Remove the air filter housing (see Chapter 4).
3   Remove the radiator (see Section 6).
4   Disconnect the two refrigerant lines for the condenser. Disconnect the top line fitting by removing the nut securing the two fittings together **(see illustration)**. **Note:** *Hold the fittings with a wrench to support them when loosening or tightening the nut or the lines and fittings may become damaged.* Disconnect the bottom line by following the procedure for replacing the air conditioning refrigerant filter in Section 17. Plug all open lines and fittings to prevent contamination of the air conditioning system.
5   Carefully guide the condenser out of the engine compartment.
6   Remove all of the sealing washers from the fittings and tubes and discard them.

15.4 The top refrigerant line fitting nut

16.2 The location of the air conditioning pressure sensor

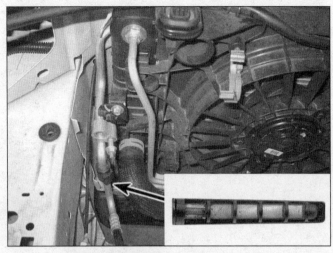

17.3a The filter is inside the lower refrigerant line that's located beneath the air cleaner

7   If you're going to install a new condenser, pour one ounce of refrigerant oil of the correct type into it prior to installation.

8   Before reconnecting the refrigerant lines for the condenser, be sure to use new sealing washers. Tighten the condenser line fitting nut to the torque listed in this Chapter's Specifications.

9   Installation is otherwise the reverse of removal.

10 Have the system evacuated, recharged and leak tested by the shop that discharged it.

16   Air conditioning pressure sensor - replacement

Refer to illustration 16.2

Note 1: *The air conditioning pressure sensor is threaded onto a Schrader valve. Therefore, it is not necessary to discharge the air conditioning system to replace it.*

Note 2: *The air conditioning pressure sensor is used to monitor excessively high and low system pressures and will prevent the system from operating if either condition occurs.*

1   Remove the air filter housing (see Chapter 4).

2   Unplug the electrical connector from the sensor **(see illustration).**

3   Unscrew the sensor from the Schrader valve. Use a back-up wrench on the fitting for the sensor to prevent damaging the refrigerant line.

4   Lubricate the switch O-ring with clean refrigerant oil of the correct type.

5   Screw the new sensor onto the threads until hand tight, then tighten it securely.

6   Reconnect the electrical connector.

17   Air conditioning refrigerant filter - replacement

Refer to illustrations 17.3a and 17.3b

Warning: *The air conditioning system is under high pressure. DO NOT loosen any fittings or remove any components until after the system has been discharged. Air conditioning refrigerant must be properly discharged into an EPA-approved container at a dealer service department or an automotive air conditioning repair facility. Always wear eye protection when disconnecting air conditioning system fittings.*

Note: *When major air conditioning components are replaced, this filter should be inspected or replaced also.*

1   Have the air conditioning system discharged by a dealer service department or by an automotive air conditioning shop before proceeding (see **Warning** above).

2   Remove the air filter housing (see Chapter 4).

3   Locate and remove the locking coupler securing the refrigerant line joint together **(see illustrations)**. Plug all open lines and fittings to prevent contamination of the air conditioning system.

4   Discard the sealing washers on the refrigerant line.

5   The refrigerant filter is located inside the refrigerant line coming from the condenser **(see illustration 17.3a)**. Care must taken when removing it, as it can easily be broken off inside the line. You can use a pair of needle-nose pliers to remove it. If it's really stuck, special extractor tools are available at most auto parts stores.

6   Install a new filter into the line.

7   Install new sealing washers on the refrigerant line and then fit the lines together.

8   Install the locking coupler over the line joint.

9   Reinstall the air filter housing.

10 Have the system evacuated, recharged and leak tested by the shop that discharged it.

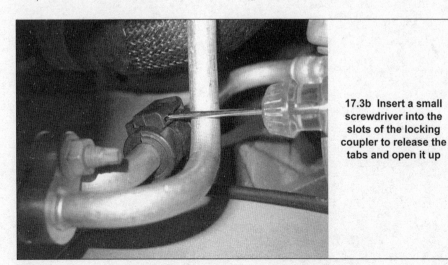

17.3b Insert a small screwdriver into the slots of the locking coupler to release the tabs and open it up

Notes

Chapter 4
Fuel and exhaust systems

Contents

Specifications

Fuel pressure (ignition key turned to ON, engine not running)
  2007 and earlier models
    V6 engines .... 50 to 60 psi
    V8 engines .... 55 to 62 psi
  2008 and later models .... 56 to 62 psi
Fuel pressure leakdown
  One minute after turning key to OFF .... No more than 5 psi drop
  Five minutes after relieving fuel pressure to 10 psi .... No more than 2 psi drop
Fuel injector coil resistance .... 11 to 14 ohms

Torque specifications

Note: *One foot-pound (ft-lb) of torque is equivalent to 12 inch-pounds (in-lbs) of torque. Torque values below approximately 15 ft-lbs are expressed in inch-pounds, since most foot-pound torque wrenches are not accurate at these smaller values.*

Throttle body mounting bolts/nuts (all engines, all years) .... 89 in-lbs

1   General information and precautions

This Chapter covers the removal and installation procedures for the important parts of the air intake, fuel and exhaust systems. Because emission-control systems are integral parts of the engine management system, there are many cross-references to Chapter 6. Information on the engine management system, information sensors and output actuators is in Chapter 6.

The air intake system consists of the air filter housing, the air intake duct, the throttle body and the intake manifold. Incoming air passes through the air filter element, the Mass Air Flow (MAF) sensor, the air intake duct, the throttle body, the intake manifold plenum and the intake manifold runners before being mixed with fuel sprayed into the intake ports by the fuel injectors.

The Sequential Fuel Injection (SFI) system consists of the fuel tank, an electric fuel pump/fuel level sending unit module mounted inside the tank, the fuel rail, the fuel injectors, the fuel pressure regulator and the metal and flexible fuel lines that connect the various components of the SFI system.

The exhaust system consists of the exhaust manifold(s), the catalytic converter(s), the resonator, the muffler and the exhaust pipes connecting these components. The system is suspended from the vehicle pan by rubber hangers. You'll find the removal and installation procedures for the exhaust manifold(s) in Chapter 2, and for the rest of the exhaust system in this Chapter. There is more information about - and the replacement procedures for - the catalytic converter(s) in Chapter 6.

2.3 The fuel pump fuse (A) is located on the fuse and relay panel, which is located on the right side of the engine compartment. The fuel pump relay (B) is located right below the fuel pump fuse

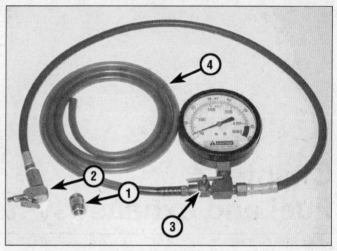

3.3 A typical fuel pressure gauge set up

1 *Screw-on adapter for the Schrader valve on the fuel rail*
2 *Hose with fitting to connect to the adapter*
3 *Bleeder valve (optional)*
4 *Bleeder hose (optional)*

2   Fuel pressure relief procedure

Refer to illustration 2.3

Warning: *Gasoline is extremely flammable, so take extra precautions when you work on any part of the fuel system. Don't smoke or allow open flames or bare light bulbs near the work area, and don't work in a garage where a gas-type appliance (such as a water heater or a clothes dryer) is present. Since gasoline is carcinogenic, wear fuel-resistant gloves when there's a possibility of being exposed to fuel, and, if you spill any fuel on your skin, rinse it off immediately with soap and water. Mop up any spills immediately and do not store fuel-soaked rags where they could ignite. The fuel system is under constant pressure, so, if any fuel lines are to be disconnected, the fuel pressure in the system must be relieved first. When you perform any kind of work on the fuel system, wear safety glasses and have a Class B type fire extinguisher on hand.*

Caution: *After the fuel pressure has been relieved, it's a good idea to lay a shop towel over any fuel connection to be disassembled, to absorb the residual fuel that may leak out when servicing the fuel system.*

1   The fuel system referred to in this Chapter is defined as the fuel tank and tank-mounted fuel pump/fuel gauge sender unit, the fuel filter, the fuel injectors and the metal pipes and flexible hoses of the fuel lines between these components. All these components contain fuel, which is pressurized as soon as the ignition key is turned to ON, and remains pressurized while the engine is running (and even after the ignition is switched off). And because the pressure remains for some time after the ignition has been switched off, it must be relieved before any fuel lines are disconnected.

2   Remove the fuel filler cap to relieve any pressure built-up in the fuel tank.

3   Open the fuse and relay panel inside the engine compartment and locate the fuel pump fuse **(see illustration)**. Pull the fuel pump fuse, start the engine and allow it to run until it stalls (it might not even start). Once it has stalled (or has failed to start), crank the starter for three more seconds, then turn off the ignition key.

4   The fuel pressure is now relieved. Be sure to disconnect the cable from the negative terminal of the battery before working on any fuel system component (see Chapter 5, Section 1). You may now open up the fuel system to service any component. **Warning:** *This procedure merely relieves the pressure that the engine needs to run. But remember that fuel is still present in the system components, and take precautions accordingly before disconnecting any of them.*

3   Fuel pump/fuel pressure - check

Warning: *Gasoline is extremely flammable, so take extra precautions when you work on any part of the fuel system. See the* **Warning** *in Section 2.*

Fuel pump operation check

1   The fuel pump is located inside the fuel tank, which muffles its sound when the engine is running. But you can actually hear the fuel pump. Sit inside the vehicle with the windows closed, turn the ignition key to ON (not START) and listen carefully for the soft whirring sound made by the fuel pump as it's briefly turned on by the PCM to pressurize the fuel system prior to starting the engine. You will only hear a soft whirring sound for a second or two, but that sound tells you that the pump is working. If

you can't hear the pump, remove the fuel filler cap, then have an assistant turn the ignition switch to ON while you listen for the sound of the pump operating for a couple of seconds. **Note:** *If the fuel system is already pressurized, the pump won't come on.*

2   If the pump does not come on when the ignition key is turned to ON, check the fuel pump fuse and relay **(see illustration 2.3)**. If the fuse and relay are okay, check the wiring back to the fuel pump. If the fuse, relay and wiring are okay, the fuel pump is probably defective. If the pump runs continuously with the ignition key in its ON position, the Powertrain Control Module (PCM) is probably defective. Have the PCM checked by a dealer service department or other qualified repair shop.

Fuel pressure check

Refer to illustrations 3.3, 3.5a and 3.5b

3   To measure the fuel pressure you'll need a fuel pressure gauge compatible with high-pressure fuel injection systems, and a hose and fitting suitable for connecting the gauge to the Schrader valve-type test port on the fuel feed line **(see illustration)**.

4   Relieve the fuel pressure (see Section 2).

5   Locate the fuel pressure test port **(see illustrations)**, unscrew the cap and connect a fuel pressure gauge.

6   Start the engine and allow it to idle. Note the gauge reading as soon as the pressure stabilizes, and compare it with the pressure listed in this Chapter's Specifications.

a) *If the pressure is lower than specified, check for a restriction in the fuel system. Two likely suspects are the fuel inlet strainer at the base of the fuel pump module in the left fuel tank, or a faulty*

3.5a The fuel pressure test port on V6 models is located on the right end of the fuel rail

3.5b The fuel pressure test port on V8 models is located at the left end of the rear fuel rail

fuel pressure regulator. **Note:** *Neither of these components can be inspected or replaced separately. It's also possible that there is a restriction in the fuel line (a blockage or a kink).*

b) *If the fuel pressure is higher than specified, replace the fuel pressure regulator, which is part of the left fuel pump module (see Section 7).*

7   Turn off the engine. Verify that the fuel pressure loses no more than 8 psi for five minutes after the engine is turned off.

8   Relieve the fuel pressure (see Section 2), then disconnect the fuel pressure gauge and screw on the test port cap. Clean up any spilled gasoline.

9   Start the engine and verify that there are no fuel leaks.

4   Fuel lines and fittings - general information

Warning 1: *Gasoline is extremely flammable, so take extra precautions when you work on any part of the fuel system. See the* **Warning** *in Section 2.*

Warning 2: *Before disconnecting any fuel line fittings, relieve the fuel system pressure (see Section 2) and equalize tank pressure by removing the fuel filler cap. This procedure will merely relieve the increased pressure necessary for the engine to run - remember that fuel will still be present in the system components, so you should be ready to mop up fuel spills when disconnecting fuel line fittings.*

1   Always relieve the fuel pressure (see Section 2) before servicing fuel lines or fittings, then disconnect the cable from the negative battery terminal (see Chapter 5, Section 1) before proceeding.

2   Whenever you're working under the vehicle, be sure to inspect all fuel and evaporative emission lines for leaks, kinks, dents and other damage. Always replace a damaged fuel or EVAP line immediately. Leaking fuel and EVAP lines will result in loss of fuel and excessive air pollution (the leaking raw fuel emits unburned hydrocarbon vapors into the atmosphere).

3   If you find signs of dirt in the lines during disassembly, disconnect all lines and blow them out with compressed air. Inspect the fuel strainer on the fuel pump pick-up unit (see Section 7) for damage and deterioration. (There is also a fuel filter inside the fuel pump/fuel level sending unit but you cannot replace it without replacing the pump module, so consider this option only if, after cleaning the strainer and all the fuel lines, the fuel system is still clogged.)

4   The fuel supply line connects the fuel pump in the fuel tank to the fuel rail on the engine. The Evaporative Emission (EVAP) system vapor lines connect the fuel tank to the EVAP canister and the canister to the intake manifold. The fuel and EVAP lines are secured to the underbody with plastic clips.

Steel tubing

5   Because fuel lines used on fuel-injected vehicles are under fairly high pressure, it is critical that they be replaced with lines of equivalent specification. Never use copper or aluminum tubing to replace steel tubing. These materials cannot withstand normal vehicle vibration.

6   Some steel fuel lines have threaded fittings. When loosening these fittings to service or replace components:

a) *Hold the stationary fitting with one wrench while loosening or tightening the tubing nut with another.*

b) *If you're going to replace one of these fittings, use original equipment parts or parts that meet original equipment standards.*

Plastic tubing

7   Most of the fuel (and EVAP) lines on the vehicles covered in this manual are plastic. If you ever have to replace a plastic line, use only plastic tubing meeting original equipment standards. **Caution:** *When removing or installing plastic fuel line tubing, be careful not to bend or twist it too much, which can damage it. And damaged fuel lines MUST be replaced! Also, be aware that the plastic fuel tubing is NOT heat resistant, so keep it away from excessive heat. Nor is it acid-proof, so don't wipe it off with a shop rag that has been used to wipe off battery electrolyte. If you accidentally spill or wipe electrolyte on plastic fuel tubing, replace the tubing.*

Flexible hoses

Warning: *Use only original equipment replacement hoses or their equivalent. Unapproved hoses might fail when subjected to the high operating pressures of the fuel system.*

8   Don't route fuel hoses within four inches of exhaust system components or within ten inches of a catalytic converter. Make sure that no rubber hoses are installed directly against the vehicle, particularly in places where there is any vibration. If allowed to touch some vibrating part of the vehicle, a hose can easily become chafed and it might start leaking. A good rule of thumb is to maintain a minimum of 1/4-inch clearance around a hose (or metal line) to prevent contact with the vehicle underbody.

Fuel line and EVAP line fittings

9   The vehicles covered in this manual use two kinds of fuel line quick-connect fittings (metal or plastic) for most connections at the fuel pump, the fuel tank, under the vehicle and in the engine compartment. (A third type of plastic quick-connect fitting is used only at the EVAP canister and on the vent hose connection at the fuel tank for the EVAP canister vent solenoid.)

10   The procedure for releasing each type of fuel line fitting is different. But a few rules of thumb apply to all fittings:

a) *Inspect the fitting for dirt. If the fitting is dirty, clean it off before disassembling*

4.12 Pull the end of the retainer off the fuel line, then disengage the other end from the female side of the fitting

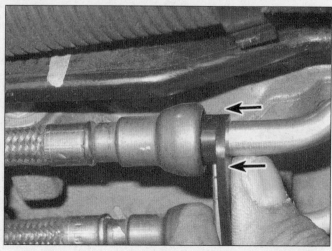

4.13a Insert the fuel line separator tool into the female side of the fitting, push it into the fitting until it releases the locking tabs inside the fitting . . .

it. The seals in the fitting will stick to the fuel line as they age. Twist the fitting on the line, then push and pull the fitting until it moves freely.

b) Always disconnect all fuel line fittings from a fuel system component before removing the component.

c) When disconnecting a quick-connect fitting, inspect the condition of the retainer before reconnecting the fitting. The best strategy with respect to retainers is to simply replace the retainer every time that you disconnect the fitting.

d) When you disconnect a fitting with an O-ring inside, inspect the O-ring before reconnecting the fitting. Fuel line fittings are under the same pressure as the rest of the fuel system, so to avoid leaks (and fires!) make VERY SURE that the O-ring is good condition. Even better, simply replace it.

e) In most cases, the fitting itself is a non-removable part of the fuel line, so you might have to replace an entire fuel line if a fitting is damaged or defective.

Metal collar quick-connect fittings

Disconnection

Refer to illustrations 4.12, 4.13a and 4.13b

Note 1: *You'll find these fittings at the connections between the fuel supply and return lines in the engine compartment.*

Note 2: *You'll need a special tool set (available at most auto parts stores) to disconnect these fittings.*

11   Relieve the fuel system pressure (see Section 2).

12   Pull off the clip end of the retainer, then remove it from the fitting **(see illustration)**.

13   Using a fuel line separator tool of the proper size (available at most auto parts stores), insert the tool into the female side of the fitting, then push it into the fitting to release the locking tabs and pull the fitting apart **(see illustrations)**.

Reconnection

Refer to illustrations 4.14 and 4.17

14   Inspect the O-ring **(see illustration)**. If it's dried out, cracked, torn or otherwise deteriorated, replace it.

15   Apply a few drops of clean engine oil to the male pipe end.

16   Push both sides of the fitting together until the retaining tabs snap into place. Pull on both sides of the fitting to verify that it's securely connected.

17   Install the retainer, making sure it clips into place **(see illustration)**.

18   Start the engine and check for fuel leaks.

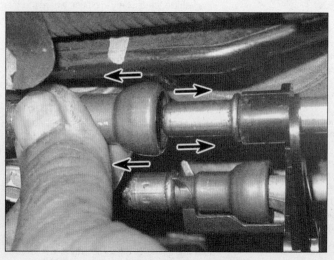

4.13b . . . then pull the two halves of the fitting apart

4.14 Inspect the old O-ring inside the female side of the fitting; if it's cracked, torn or deteriorated, replace it

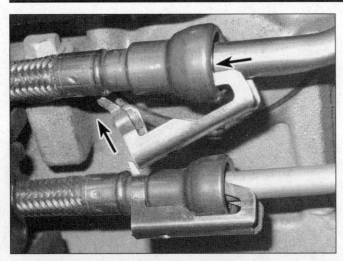

4.17 To install a retainer, insert the hooked end into the female side of the fitting, then push the clip end onto the fuel line until it snaps into place

4.19a To release a Bartholomew-type plastic quick-connect fitting, depress the tabs on the connector housing with a small screwdriver, then continue pressing on them . . .

Plastic collar quick-connect fittings

Bartholomew-type

Disconnection

Refer to illustrations 4.19a and 4.19b

19   To release a Bartholomew-type quick-connect fitting, depress the tabs of the retainer **(see illustration)**. Once the retainer is released, continue pressing on the tabs while pulling the two fuel lines apart **(see illustration)**.
20   Remove and discard the old retainer from the male side of the fitting.
21   Remove and discard the indicator ring from the male side of the fitting.

Reconnection

Refer to illustrations 4.22 and 4.23

22   Inspect the old O-ring inside the female side of the fitting **(see illustration)**. If it's dried

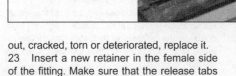

4.19b . . . until the two fuel lines are disconnected, then remove and discard the old retainer (1) and the indicator ring (2) (the indicator ring is used only during factory assembly; there is no need to reinstall it)

out, cracked, torn or deteriorated, replace it.
23   Insert a new retainer in the female side of the fitting. Make sure that the release tabs

are aligned with the windows of the connector **(see illustration)**.
24   Apply a few drops of engine oil to the tip

4.22 Inspect the old O-ring inside the female side of the fitting; if it's cracked, torn or deteriorated, replace it

4.23 Install a new retainer in the female side of the fitting; make sure that the release tabs are aligned with the windows in the connector

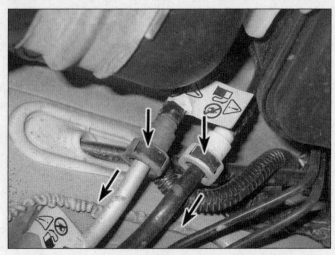

4.29 To disconnect a Push Down TI type plastic collar quick-connect fitting, depress the button on the side of the collar and pull the pipe out of the collar. To reconnect, simply push the pipe into the collar until it clicks into place

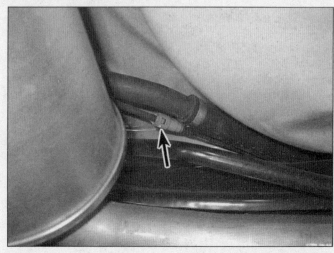

5.5 Disconnect the EVAP vent line quick-connect fitting above the left rear part of the suspension crossmember (see Section 4 for the disconnection technique, if necessary)

of the male fuel line.

25   Push both sides of the fitting together until the retainer release tabs snap into place.

26   Pull on both sides of the fitting to verify that it's securely connected.

27   Start the engine and check for fuel leaks.

Push Down TI type

Refer to illustration 4.29

28   Push Down TI type fittings are typically used as chassis fuel and EVAP line connections. They're frequently used to connect the fuel and EVAP lines that are coming from components in, on or near the fuel tank to the fuel/EVAP lines going forward to the engine compartment.

29   To disconnect a Push Down TI type fitting, simply depress the button on the female, or collar, side of the fitting **(see illustration)** and pull the fuel or EVAP pipe out of the collar.

30   Be sure to wipe off the end of the pipe with a clean cloth before reconnecting it to a Push Down TI fitting, then simply push it into the collar until it clicks into place.

5   Fuel tank - removal and installation

Refer to illustrations 5.5, 5.6, 5.8, 5.9a, 5.9b and 5.11

Warning 1: *Gasoline is extremely flammable, so take extra precautions when you work on any part of the fuel system. See the* **Warning** *in Section 2.*

Warning 2: *Before disconnecting or opening any part of the fuel system, relieve the fuel system pressure (see Section 2), and equalize the pressure inside the fuel tank by removing the fuel filler cap.*

1   Relieve the fuel system pressure (see Section 2).

2   Disconnect the cable from the negative battery terminal (see Chapter 5, Section 1).

3   Raise the vehicle and place it securely on jackstands.

4   You might want to remove the part of the exhaust system that's underneath the fuel tank (see Section 14). **Note:** *It's possible to lower the tank by simply removing the rubber exhaust hangers and supporting the exhaust system so that it's out of the way, but you'll have more room to maneuver if you simply remove the rear part of the exhaust system (everything behind the rear mounting flange of the catalytic converter).*

5   Locate the EVAP system vent line for the fuel filler neck hose right above the left rear part of the rear suspension crossmember **(see illustration)**. Disconnect the EVAP vent line quick-connect fitting at that location. If you're unfamiliar with quick-connect fittings, refer to Section 4.

6   Locate the fuel tank filler neck hose clamp between the backside of the fuel tank and the rear suspension crossmember. Using a long screwdriver, loosen the hose clamp that secures the fuel filler neck hose to the

fuel tank pipe **(see illustration)** and disconnect the filler neck hose from the tank pipe.

7   It's easier to remove the fuel tank when it's nearly empty. But there is no fuel tank drain plug, so if there's still a lot of fuel in the tank, siphon or hand-pump the remaining fuel from the tank through the tank filler neck pipe. **Warning:** *Don't start the siphoning action by mouth! Use a siphoning kit (available at most auto parts stores).*

8   Locate the fuel supply line and EVAP purge line quick-connect fittings at the left front corner of the fuel tank **(see illustration)** and disconnect the two quick-connect fittings. Be sure to plug both lines to prevent contamination from entering the fuel or EVAP systems.

9   Remove the fuel tank shield **(see illustrations)**.

10   Support the fuel tank.

11   The fuel tank is supported by two longitudinal straps that are hinged at their front ends so that they can swing down to lower the fuel tank. The rear end of each fuel tank strap is secured to the vehicle by a bolt. These bolts are located directly above the rear suspen-

5.6 To disconnect the fuel filler neck hose from the fuel tank pipe, use a long screwdriver to loosen the hose clamp screw, then pull off the hose

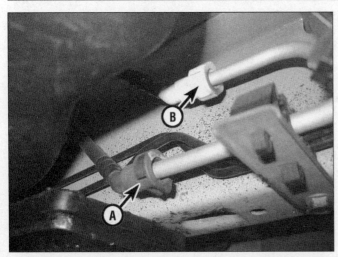

5.8 Disconnect the quick-connect fittings for the fuel (A) and EVAP (B) lines. If you're unfamiliar with quick-connect fittings, refer to Section 4

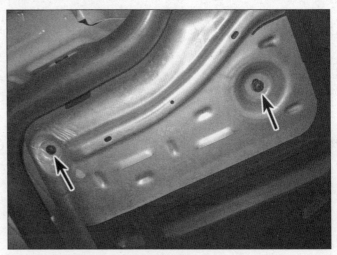

5.9a To detach the heat shield, remove these two push fasteners . . .

sion crossmember. To remove the fuel tank strap bolts, use a socket with a universal joint adapter and a long extension **(see illustration)**.

12 Carefully lower the tank just far enough to access the fuel pump/fuel level sensor module and the EVAP canister, then disconnect the fuel line quick-connect fitting and the electrical connector from the pump module, and disconnect the electrical connector and EVAP lines from the EVAP canister.

13 Lower the tank the rest of the way.

14 Installation is the reverse of removal.

6 Fuel tank cleaning and repair - general information

Warning: *Gasoline is extremely flammable, so take extra precautions when you work on*

any part of the fuel system. See the **Warning** *in Section 2.*

1 The fuel tank is plastic and cannot be repaired. No reliable repair procedures are available to correct leaks or damage. Fuel tank replacement is the only approved service.

2 To remove sediment from the bottom of the tank, have the fuel tank steam-cleaned. Remove the fuel pump/level sensor module (see Section 7) and all EVAP system components prior to cleaning. Allow plenty of time for the tank to air-dry before returning it to service.

7 Fuel pump/fuel level sensor module - removal and installation

Refer to illustrations 7.6, 7.7 and 7.8

Warning: *Gasoline is extremely flammable,*

so take extra precautions when you work on any part of the fuel system. See the **Warning** *in Section 2.*

1 Relieve the system fuel pressure (see Section 2), and equalize tank pressure by removing the fuel filler cap.

2 Disconnect the cable from the negative battery terminal (see Chapter 5, Section 1).

3 Remove the fuel tank (see Section 5).

4 Disconnect the fuel supply line from the fuel pump/fuel level sending unit module. Use a shop rag to soak up any spilled fuel.

5 Mark the orientation of the fuel pump in relation to the fuel tank to ensure that the fuel pump is correctly realigned when you install it again. (If you're going to install a new pump, note the location of your alignment mark on the old pump and make a mark at the same spot on the new unit.)

6 Using a pair of large water pump pliers, unscrew the fuel pump/fuel level sending unit

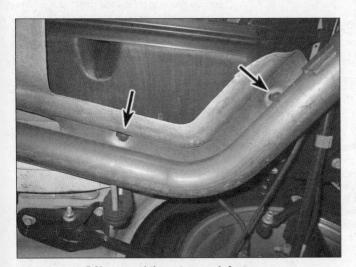

5.9b . . . and these two push fasteners

5.11 There are two fuel tank strap bolts (this is the left one); to remove the bolts, use a socket and universal joint adapter on a long extension inserted through the holes in the rear suspension crossmember

7.6 Use a large pair of water pump pliers to loosen and unscrew the fuel pump locknut; if the locknut is too tight to loosen this way, carefully tap it loose with a hammer and a brass punch

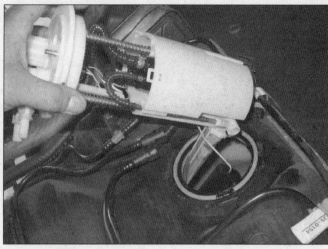

7.7 Carefully remove the fuel pump/fuel level sensor module from the fuel tank; once the module has cleared the mounting hole in the tank, angle it as shown to work the fuel pump inlet strainer and the fuel level sensor float and float arm through the hole without damaging anything

module locknut by turning it counterclockwise **(see illustration)**. If the locknut is tight, use a hammer and a *brass* punch to loosen it (don't use a steel punch, which could produce sparks when struck by the hammer).

7   Raise the fuel pump/fuel level sensor module high enough to disconnect the quick-connect fitting for the ventilation harness, then remove the pump assembly **(see illustration)**, taking care not to damage the fuel inlet strainer or the fuel level sensor float arm and float.

8   Before installing the pump, inspect the O-ring **(see illustration)** for cracks, tears and deterioration. If it's worn or damaged, replace it. Also inspect the fuel pump inlet strainer. Make sure that it's clean and free of debris and dirt. If it's dirty, try washing it with carburetor cleaner spray. If this filter is seriously damaged, you'll have to replace the fuel pump/fuel level sending unit module. The filter is not available separately.

9   Insert the fuel pump/fuel level sensor module into the fuel tank and connect the ventilation hose to the fuel pump assembly before locking the pump into place. Align the fuel pump/fuel level sending unit module with its hole in the tank and carefully insert it into the tank. Make sure that you don't damage the fuel inlet strainer, the float arm or the float during installation. If the float arm is bent, the fuel level that is indicated on the fuel level gauge on the instrument cluster will be incorrect.

10   Installation is otherwise the reverse of removal.

8   Fuel pump/fuel level sensor - component replacement

Refer to illustration 8.5

Note: *You can purchase the complete fuel pump/fuel level sensor module, or you can purchase either the fuel pump or the fuel level*

sensor separately. If only one component fails, use this procedure to separate the two components, then reassemble the good component and the new replacement component.

1   Remove the fuel pump/fuel level sensor module (see Section 7).

2   Place the fuel pump/fuel level sensor module on a clean workbench surface.

3   Disengage the fuel level sensor wiring harness from the molded-in harness guide.

4   Disconnect the fuel level sensor electrical connector from the pump module cover.

5   To remove the fuel level sensor unit, depress the locking tab **(see illustration)** and slide off the sensor.

6   No further disassembly of the fuel pump/fuel level sensor assembly is possible.

7   To install the fuel level sensor on the fuel pump module, slide the sensor unit into place until you hear a click, then gently pull on the sensor unit to verify that it's locked into place.

8   Installation is otherwise the reverse of removal.

7.8 Remove and inspect the O-ring seal for the fuel pump mounting flange; if it's cracked, torn or deteriorated, replace it

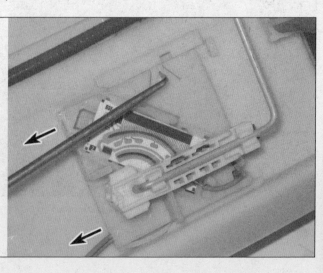

8.5 To detach the fuel level sensor from the fuel pump module, disengage the locking tab with a pick or a small screwdriver, then slide the sensor unit off the retaining rails

9.1 To remove the air intake duct, disconnect the PCV fresh air inlet hose (1), then loosen the hose clamp screws (2) and pull off the duct. If you're also removing the air filter housing, disconnect the electrical connector (3) from the Mass Air Flow (MAF) sensor (V8 model shown, V6 models similar)

9.7 To remove the left front diagonal brace, remove these three bolts

9 Air filter housing - removal and installation

Air intake duct

Refer to illustration 9.1

1 Disconnect the PCV fresh air inlet hose from the air intake duct **(see illustration)**.
2 Loosen the hose clamp screw at the air filter housing **(see illustration 9.1)** and pull back the clamp.
3 Loosen the hose clamp screw at the throttle body **(see illustration 9.1)**, pull back the clamp and remove the duct.
4 Installation is the reverse of removal.

Air filter housing

Refer to illustrations 9.7, 9.9a, 9.9b, 9.10 and 9.12

5 Disconnect the cable from the negative terminal of the battery (see Chapter 5, Section 1).

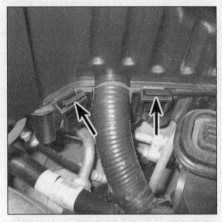

9.9a To remove the upper part of the air filter housing from the lower part, depress these two release latches on the front side of the filter housing . . .

9.9b . . . depress these two latches on the backside of the filter housing, and lift off the upper part of the housing

6 Remove the air intake duct (see Steps 1 through 3). Disconnect the electrical connec-

tor from the Mass Air Flow (MAF) sensor **(see illustration 9.1)**.
7 Remove the left front diagonal brace **(see illustration)**.
8 Remove the air filter element (see Chapter 1).
9 Remove the upper part of the air filter housing **(see illustrations)**.
10 Disconnect the electrical connectors from the Transmission Control Module (TCM) and the Powertrain Control Module (PCM) and remove the TCM and PCM from the air filter housing (see Chapter 6), then remove the TCM/PCM harness from the lower part of the housing **(see illustration)**.
11 The lower part of the air filter housing is secured by a pair of locator pins pushed into rubber mounting grommets. To remove the lower part of the air filter housing, grasp it firmly and simply lift it straight up.
12 While the air filter housing is out, inspect the rubber mounting grommets **(see illustra-**

9.10 After disconnecting the electrical connectors for the TCM and PCM and removing the TCM and PCM (see Chapter 6) from the lower part of the air filter housing, carefully lift the harness out of the semi-circular cutaway in the front side of the lower part of the filter housing

9.12 Inspect the condition of the rubber mounting grommets for the filter housing locator pins, replacing them if necessary

tion). If a grommet is cracked, torn or otherwise damaged, replace it.

13   Installation is the reverse of removal.

10   Sequential Fuel Injection (SFI) system - general information

These models are equipped with a Sequential Fuel Injection (SFI) system. The SFI system consists of three basic sub-systems: the air induction system, the fuel system and the electronic control system. **Note:** *Refer to Chapter 6 for more information on the components of the electronic control system.*

Air induction system

The air induction system consists of the air filter housing, the Mass Air Flow (MAF) sensor, the Intake Air Temperature (IAT) sensor (an integral part of the MAF sensor), the air intake duct, the throttle body, the Throttle Position (TP) sensor, the air intake plenum and the intake manifold. The MAF/IAT sensor is an information sensor for the Powertrain Control Module (PCM). The MAF sensor uses a heated wire system to send the PCM an analog (constantly variable) voltage signal corresponding to the volume of air passing into the engine. The IAT sensor measures the temperature of the intake air. The PCM uses these signals to calculate the mass (density) of air entering the engine. **Note:** *For more information about the MAF/IAT sensor, refer to Chapter 6. The TP sensor is an integral component of the throttle body and cannot be serviced separately.*

All models are equipped with an electronic throttle body. The electronic throttle control system consists of the Accelerator Pedal Position (APP) sensor, the Powertrain Control Module (PCM) and the solenoid motor inside the throttle body that controls the angle of the throttle plate. The APP sensor, which is an integral component of the accelerator pedal assembly, is a potentiometer (similar to a fuel level sensor or a throttle position sensor) that monitors the position (or angle) of the accel-

erator pedal. As you depress the accelerator pedal, the APP sensor outputs a variable voltage signal to the PCM, which sends a command to the throttle body's solenoid motor, which opens the throttle plate in proportion to the position (angle) of the accelerator pedal. As the throttle plate opens or closes, the amount of air that can pass through the system increases or decreases accordingly. As the throttle plate opens or closes, the Throttle Position (TP) sensor, which is located on the end of the throttle plate shaft, opens or closes with it. And as more or less air enters the engine, the MAF/IAT sensor signal to the PCM also changes. In response to these two signals from the TP and MAF/IAT sensors, the PCM opens each injector for a longer or shorter duration to increase the amount of fuel delivered to the inlet ports. The interval during which an injector is open is known as *pulse width.*

Fuel system

An electric fuel pump located inside the fuel tank supplies fuel under pressure to the fuel rail, which distributes fuel evenly to all injectors. A filter between the fuel pump and the fuel rail protects the components of the system. From the fuel rail, fuel is injected into the intake ports, just above the intake valves, by a fuel injector.

The amount of fuel supplied by the injectors is precisely controlled by injector drivers inside the PCM. The injector drivers, which are turned on and off by the PCM, control the ground side of each injector circuit. When the ground path is closed, the injectors are on; when the ground path is open, the injectors are off. The PCM uses signals from the Crankshaft Position (CKP) sensor and the Camshaft Position (CMP) sensor to determine when to trigger each injector in cylinder firing order (hence the term "sequential injection"). This precise control of injector timing produces more power, better fuel economy and lower exhaust emissions.

To prevent fuel starvation, the fuel pump delivers more fuel to the fuel rail than the injectors can use under most circumstances. When the pressure exceeds a certain threshold, the excess fuel is returned to the fuel tank by the fuel pressure regulator, which is an integral component of the fuel pump/fuel level sensor module. If the fuel pressure regulator fails, you must replace the fuel pump module.

Electronic control system

The PCM controls the SFI system and the engine management system. It receives signals from an array of information sensors that monitor such variables as intake air mass and temperature, coolant temperature, engine speed, crankshaft position, acceleration/deceleration, and exhaust gas oxygen content. These signals help the PCM determine the injection duration necessary for the optimal air/fuel ratio. These sensors and various PCM-controlled output actuators (relays, solenoids, etc.) are located throughout the

engine compartment. For further information regarding the PCM, the engine management system, the information sensors and the output actuators, see Chapter 6.

11   Sequential Fuel Injection (SFI) system - general check

Refer to illustrations 11.7 and 11.9

Warning: *Gasoline is extremely flammable, so take extra precautions when you work on any part of the fuel system. See the* **Warning** *in Section 2.*

1   Inspect the SFI system electrical connectors. Verify that all ground wire connections are tight. Loose connectors and poor grounds can cause many problems that resemble more serious malfunctions.

2   Verify that the battery is fully charged (see Chapters 1 and 5 for help with the battery). The PCM, information sensors and output actuators depend on a steady and adequate voltage to function correctly.

3   Inspect the air filter element (see Chapter 1). A dirty or partially blocked filter will severely impede performance and economy.

4   Inspect any fuses for the circuit you're checking. If you find a blown fuse, replace it and note whether it blows again. If it does, look for a short in the circuit.

5   Inspect the air intake duct, the throttle body and the intake manifold for leaks, which will cause an excessively lean mixture. Also inspect all vacuum hoses connected to the intake manifold and to the throttle body.

6   Remove the air intake duct (see Section 9) and inspect the throttle body for dirt, carbon, varnish or other residue inside the bore of the throttle body, particularly around the throttle plate. If it's dirty, clean it with carburetor cleaner spray and a shop towel.

7   With the engine running, place an automotive stethoscope against each injector **(see illustration)**, one at a time, and listen for a

11.7 Use an automotive stethoscope to listen to each injector. If an injector sounds different from the other injectors, or isn't making any sound at all, disconnect it and note whether there is any difference in the way the engine runs

11.9 If an injector is apparently not working, use a digital multimeter to measure the resistance across the two terminals of the injector, then compare your measurement with the resistance listed in this Chapter's Specifications

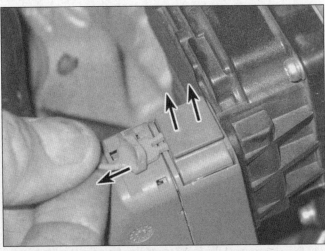

12.5a To disconnect the throttle body electrical connector on V6 models, pull out the lock, then carefully pry up the release tab with a small screwdriver and pull off the connector

clicking sound that indicates operation. If you don't have a stethoscope, you can place the tip of a long screwdriver against the injector and listen through the handle. If you can hear all of the injectors operating, but there is a misfire condition present, the electrical circuits are functioning, but the injectors might be dirty or fouled from carbon deposits. Commercial cleaning products might help. If not, then you might have to replace the injectors (see Section 13).

8   If you *can't* hear an injector operating, disconnect its electrical connector and note whether it makes any difference in the way the engine runs (engine rpm should drop if the injector is working). Unplugging a non-operational injector shouldn't make any difference in engine rpm. If the engine rpm *does* drop, or if the engine stalls, when you disconnect an injector, then the injector is probably still operating when it's connected (though it might be so dirty that it's not operating well).

9   If the rpm *doesn't* drop when you disconnect an injector, the injector is probably defective (provided that the cylinder has compression and spark is present). Disconnect the electrical connector and measure the resistance of the injector coil with an ohmmeter **(see illustration)**, then compare your measurement with the injector resistance listed in this Chapter's Specifications. **Note:** *On V6 models you will have to remove the upper intake manifold (see Chapter 2A) to access some of the injectors.* If the indicated injector resistance is out of the specified range of resistance, replace the injector.

10   If the injector coil resistance is okay, but the injector is not operating, the circuit between the PCM and the injector might be open somewhere. It might also indicate that the driver inside the PCM is defective. The signal to the injector can be tested with a "noid" light, available at most auto parts stores. If the light doesn't flash when connected to the

12.5b Disconnect the electrical connector from the throttle body (V8 engine)

injector harness connector and the engine is cranked, have the circuit between the PCM and the injectors tested by a dealer service department or other repair shop.

12 Throttle body - inspection, removal and installation

Inspection

1   Verify that the throttle linkage operates smoothly.

2   Remove the air intake duct from the throttle body, open the throttle plate and inspect the throttle body bore for carbon and residue build-up. If it's dirty, clean it with solvent or carburetor cleaner. Make sure that the solvent or carb cleaner is safe for oxygen sensor systems and catalytic converters. **Caution:** *Do not clean the Throttle Position (TP) sensor or the solenoid motor with solvent. Also, do NOT use a metal brush to clean the bore of the throttle body, which is protected*

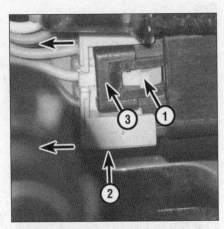

12.5c To disconnect the throttle body electrical connector on a V8, disengage the release tab (1) by depressing it, slide the white lock (2) out of the connector, then depress the release tab (3) and pull off the connector

by a special coating. Scrubbing the bore with a stiff brush could ruin the coating. Instead, wipe out the bore with a clean shop rag and a little carburetor cleaner.

Removal and installation

Refer to illustrations 12.5a, 12.5b, 12.5c, 12.6, 12.7, 12.8 and 12.9

Warning: *Wait until the engine is completely cool before beginning this procedure.*

Note: *The photos accompanying this Section depict the throttle body on a V8 engine, but the throttle body used on V6 engines is virtually identical.*

3   Disconnect the cable from the negative battery terminal (see Chapter 5, Section 1).

4   Remove the air intake duct (see Section 9).

5   Disconnect the throttle body electrical connector **(see illustrations)**.

12.6 To disconnect the EVAP purge line from the throttle body, push the lock tang with your finger then pull off the connector

12.7 To detach the throttle body on a V6 model, remove the two upper mounting bolts and the two lower mounting nuts

6   On V8 models, disconnect the EVAP purge line from the throttle body **(see illustration)**.

7   On V6 models, drain the engine coolant (see Chapter 1). Remove the heater inlet and outlet pipe retaining nuts from the two lower throttle body mounting studs, loosen the hose clamps that secure the pipes to the two heater coolant hoses and set the two pipes aside. Then remove the two upper mounting bolts and the two lower mounting nuts **(see illustration)**.

8   On V8 models, remove the four throttle body mounting bolts **(see illustration)** and remove the throttle body.

9   Remove the O-ring type throttle body gasket **(see illustration)** and inspect it. If the gasket isn't cracked, torn or otherwise deteriorated, it's okay to reuse it. But if it's damaged or worn, replace it. (If the vehicle is fairly old, it's a good idea to replace this gasket regardless of its apparent condition.)

10   If necessary, clean the throttle body as outlined in Step 2.

11   Installation is the reverse of removal. Be sure to install the throttle body gasket, then install the throttle body and tighten the throttle body mounting bolts to the torque listed in this Chapter's Specifications. On V6 models, refill the cooling system (see Chapter 1).

12   Start the engine, then verify that the throttle body operates correctly and that there are no air leaks.

13   Fuel rail and injectors - removal and installation

Refer to illustrations 13.4, 13.7a, 13.7b, 13.7c, 13.9, 13.10, 13.11 and 13.12

1   Relieve the fuel system pressure (see Section 2).

2   Equalize tank pressure by removing the fuel filler cap.

3   Disconnect the cable from the negative battery terminal (see Chapter 5, Section 1).

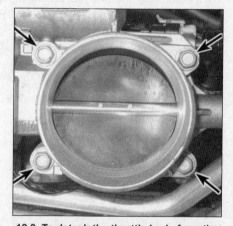

12.8 To detach the throttle body from the intake manifold on a V8 model, remove these four bolts

4   Disconnect the fuel line from the fuel rail **(see illustration)**.

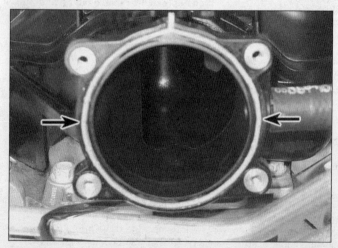

12.9 Remove and inspect the throttle body's O-ring type gasket; if it's in good condition it's okay to reuse it, but if it's cracked, torn or otherwise deteriorated, replace it

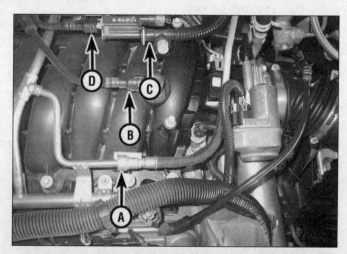

13.4 On V8 models, disconnect the quick-connect fitting for the fuel line (A), the Positive Crankcase Ventilation (PCV) system (B) and the inlet (C) and outlet (D) fittings at the EVAP canister purge solenoid valve (see Section 4 and illustration 12.6)

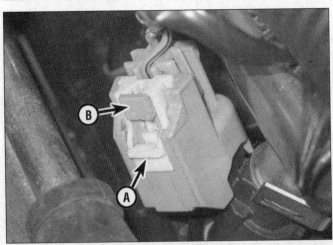

13.7a To disconnect a fuel injector electrical connector, slide the lock (A) up until it stops, then depress the release tab (B) and pull the connector straight up

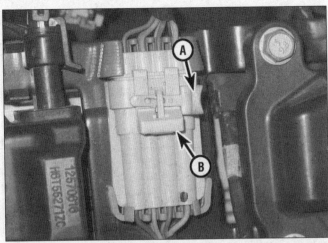

13.7b To disconnect the electrical connector for the ignition coil harness, pull out the lock (A), lift up on the tab (B) and separate the connector halves (V8 models)

13.7c After disconnecting the coil and fuel injector connectors, detach the clips for the harnesses from the brackets on each fuel rail

13.9 Fuel rail mounting bolts (V8 engine)

5   On V6 models, remove the upper intake manifold (see Chapter 2A).

6   On V6 models, remove the mounting bracket bolt for the fuel injector harness to detach the injector harness from the manifold. Then disconnect the electrical connectors from the Camshaft Position (CMP) sensor and the Engine Coolant Temperature (ECT) sensor (see Chapter 6).

7   On V8 models, disconnect the electrical connectors from the:
*   Alternator (see Chapter 5).
*   Electronic throttle body **(see illustration 12.5b)**
*   Evaporative Emissions System (EVAP) purge solenoid (see Chapter 6)
*   Manifold Absolute Pressure (MAP) sensor (see Chapter 6)
*   Valve Lifter Oil Manifold (VLOM) oil pressure sensor (see Chapter 6)
*   VLOM solenoid terminal (see Chapter 6)
*   Fuel injectors **(see illustration)**
*   Ignition coil harnesses for front and rear cylinder banks **(see illustrations)**

8   Disconnect the electrical connectors from the ignition coils and the fuel injectors and set the harnesses aside.

9   Remove the fuel rail mounting bolts **(see illustration)**.

10   Carefully disengage the injectors from the intake manifold and lift the fuel rail and

all six injectors from the engine as a single assembly **(see illustration)**. **Note:** *If you have difficulty freeing the right rear injector from its mounting hole, remove the alternator (see Chapter 5), the drivebelt idler pulley and the alternator mounting bracket.*

11   Remove each injector retainer **(see**

13.10 Disengage the fuel injectors from the intake manifold, then lift the fuel rail and the injectors as a single assembly (V8 shown)

13.11 Carefully pry off each injector retaining clip with a small screwdriver, then pull the injector out of the fuel rail

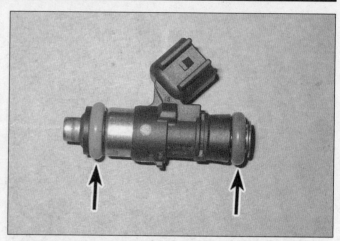

13.12 Carefully remove the O-rings from each fuel injector, then install new O-rings. When installing the new O-rings, coat them with a little clean engine oil to protect them from damage

illustration) and remove the injectors from the fuel rail.

12   Remove and discard the old injector O-rings **(see illustration)**. Always install new O-rings on the injectors before reassembling the injectors and the fuel rail.

13   To ensure that the new injector O-rings are not damaged when the injectors are installed into the fuel rail and into the intake manifold, lubricate them with clean engine oil.

14   Installation is otherwise the reverse of removal. Be sure to tighten the fuel rail mounting bolts securely.

15   Start the engine and verify that there are no fuel leaks.

14   Exhaust system servicing - general information

Inspection

Warning: *Inspect and repair exhaust system components only after allowing the exhaust components to cool completely. This applies particularly to the catalytic converter, which operates at very high temperatures. Also, when working under the vehicle, make sure it is securely supported on jackstands.*

1   The exhaust system consists of the exhaust manifold(s), the catalytic converter(s), the exhaust pipes, the muffler, and all brackets, hangers and clamps that support the exhaust system. Inspect the exhaust system regularly to ensure that it remains safe and quiet. Look for any damaged or bent parts, open seams, holes, loose connections, excessive corrosion or other defects which could allow exhaust fumes to enter the vehicle. Also check the catalytic converter(s) when you inspect the exhaust system. Inspect the catalytic converter heat shield(s) for cracks, dents and loose or missing fasteners. If a heat shield is damaged, the converter might also be damaged. Damaged or deteriorated exhaust system components should not be repaired; they should be replaced with new parts.

2   Before trying to disassemble any exhaust components, spray the fasteners with a penetrating oil to help ease removal. If the exhaust system components are extremely corroded or rusted together, welding equipment will probably be required to remove them. The convenient way to accomplish this is to have a muffler repair shop remove the corroded sections with a cutting torch. If, however, you want to save money by doing it yourself (and you don't have a welding outfit with a cutting torch), simply cut off the old components with a hacksaw. If you have compressed air, special pneumatic cutting chisels can also be used. If you decide to tackle the job at home, be sure to wear safety goggles to protect your eyes from metal chips and work gloves to protect your hands.

3   Here are some simple guidelines to follow when repairing the exhaust system:

a) *Work from the back to the front when removing exhaust system components.*

b) *Apply penetrating oil to the exhaust system component fasteners to make them easier to remove.*

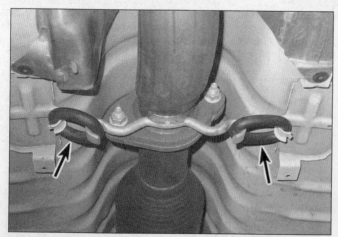

14.4a Rubber exhaust hangers at the flange between the front exhaust pipe/catalyst assembly and the rear exhaust pipe assembly

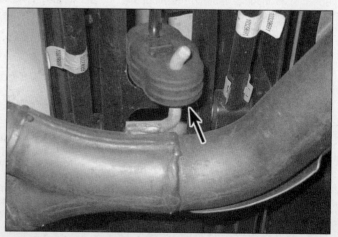

14.4b Typical rubber exhaust hanger for the rear exhaust pipe assembly (other rear pipe hanger not shown)

c) Use new gaskets, hangers and clamps when installing exhaust systems components.

d) Apply anti-seize compound to the threads of all exhaust system fasteners at reassembly.

e) Be sure to allow sufficient clearance between newly installed parts and all points on the underbody to avoid overheating the floor pan and possibly damaging the interior carpet and insulation. Pay particularly close attention to the catalytic converter and heat shield.

Component replacement

Rubber exhaust hangers

Refer to illustrations 14.4a, 14.4b and 14.4c

4   The exhaust system is attached to the body with rubber hangers **(see illustrations)**. Anytime you must raise the vehicle to perform any under-vehicle service, make sure that you

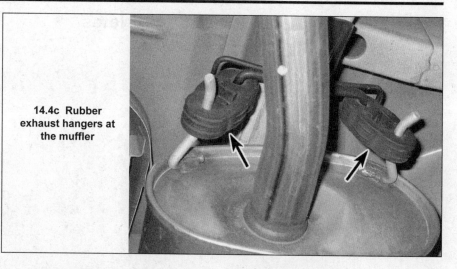

14.4c Rubber exhaust hangers at the muffler

inspect the exhaust hangers. Look for cracks, tears and deterioration. If a rubber hanger is worn or damaged, replace it.

Catalytic converters

5   The procedures for replacing the catalytic converter is in Chapter 6.

Notes

Chapter 5
Engine electrical systems

Contents

Specifications

General

Firing order
V6 engines	1-2-3-4-5-6
V8 engine	1-8-7-2-6-5-4-3

Cylinder numbering (from drivebelt end to transaxle end)

V6 engines
Rear bank	1-3-5
Front bank	2-4-6

V8 engine
Rear bank	2-4-6-8
Front bank	1-3-5-7

Ignition timing .... Not adjustable

Torque specifications

Ft-lbs

Starter motor mounting bolts
V6 engines	32
V8 engine	37

1 General information, precautions and battery disconnection

The engine electrical systems include all ignition, charging and starting components. Because of their engine-related functions, these components are discussed separately from chassis electrical devices such as the lights, the instruments, etc. (see Chapter 12).

Precautions

Always observe the following precautions when working on the electrical system:

a) Be extremely careful when servicing engine electrical components. They are easily damaged if checked, connected or handled improperly.

b) Never leave the ignition switched on for long periods of time when the engine is not running.

c) Never disconnect the battery cables while the engine is running.

d) *Maintain correct polarity when connecting battery cables from another vehicle during jump starting - see the "Booster battery (jump) starting" Section at the front of this manual.*

e) *Always disconnect the negative cable from the battery before working on the electrical system, but read the following battery disconnection procedure first.*

It's also a good idea to review the safety-related information regarding the engine electrical systems located in the "Safety first!" Section at the front of this manual, before beginning any operation included in this Chapter.

Battery disconnection

Warning: *On 2006 and later models with OnStar, make absolutely sure the ignition key is in the Off position and Retained Accessory Power (RAP) has been depleted before disconnecting the cable from the negative battery terminal. Also, never remove the OnStar fuse with the ignition key in any position other than Off. If these precautions are not taken, the OnStar system's back-up battery will be activated, and remain activated, until it goes dead. If this happens, the OnStar system will not function as it should in the event that the main vehicle battery power is cut off (as might happen during a collision).*

Note: *To disconnect the battery for service procedures requiring power to be cut from the vehicle, first open the driver's door to disable Retained Accessory Power (RAP), then loosen the cable end bolt and disconnect the cable from the negative battery terminal. Isolate the cable end to prevent it from coming into accidental contact with the battery terminal.*

The battery is located in the engine compartment on all vehicles covered by this manual. To disconnect the battery for service procedures that require battery disconnection, simply disconnect the cable from the negative battery terminal. Make sure that you isolate the cable to prevent it from coming into contact with the battery negative terminal.

Some vehicle systems (radio, alarm system, power door locks, etc.) require battery power all the time, either to enable their operation or to maintain control unit memory (Powertrain Control Module, automatic transaxle control module, etc.), which would be lost if the battery were to be disconnected. So before you disconnect the battery, note the following points:

a) *Before connecting or disconnecting the cable from the negative battery terminal, make sure that you turn the ignition key and the lighting switch to their OFF positions. Failure to do so could damage semiconductor components.*

b) *On a vehicle with power door locks, it is a wise precaution to remove the key from the ignition and to keep it with you, so that it does not get locked inside if the power door locks should engage accidentally when the battery is reconnected!*

c) *After the battery has been disconnected, then reconnected (or a new battery has been installed), the Transaxle Control Module (TCM) will need some time to relearn its adaptive strategy. As a result, shifting might feel firmer than usual. This is a normal condition and will not adversely affect the operation or service life of the transaxle. Eventually, the TCM will complete its adaptive learning process and the shift feel of the transaxle will return to normal.*

d) *The engine management system's PCM has some learning capabilities that allow it to adapt or make corrections in response to minor variations in the fuel system in order to optimize driveability and idle characteristics. However, the PCM might lose some or all of this information when the battery is disconnected. The PCM must go through a relearning process before it can regain its former driveability and performance characteristics. Until it relearns this lost data, you might notice a difference in driveability, idle and/or shift feel.*

Memory savers

Devices known as "memory savers" (typically, small 9-volt batteries) can be used to avoid some of the above problems. A memory saver is usually plugged into the cigarette lighter, and then you can disconnect the vehicle battery from the electrical system. The memory saver will deliver sufficient current to maintain security alarm codes and - maybe, but don't count on it! - PCM memory. It will also run "unswitched" (always on) circuits such as the clock and radio memory, while isolating the car battery in the event that a short circuit occurs while the vehicle is being serviced. **Warning:** *If you're going to work around any airbag system components, disconnect the battery and do not use a memory saver. If you do, the airbag could accidentally deploy and cause personal injury.* **Caution:** *Because memory savers deliver current to operate unswitched circuits when the battery is disconnected, make sure that the circuit that you're going to service is actually open before working on it!*

2   Battery - emergency jump starting

Refer to the *Booster battery (jump) starting* procedure at the front of this manual.

3   Battery - check and replacement

Warning: *Hydrogen gas is produced by the battery, so keep open flames and lighted cigarettes away from it at all times. Always wear eye protection when working around a battery. Rinse off spilled electrolyte immediately with large amounts of water.*

3.1a Use a battery hydrometer to draw electrolyte from the battery cell; this hydrometer is equipped with a thermometer to make temperature corrections

Check

Refer to illustrations 3.1a, 3.1b and 3.1c

1   A battery cannot be accurately tested until it is at or near a fully charged state. Disconnect the negative battery cable from the battery and perform the following tests:

a) ***Battery state of charge test*** *- Visually inspect the indicator eye (if equipped) on the top of the battery. If the indicator eye is dark in color, charge the battery as described in Chapter 1. If the battery is equipped with removable caps, check the battery electrolyte. The electrolyte level should be above the upper edge of the plates. If the level is low, add distilled water. DO NOT OVERFILL. The excess electrolyte may spill over during periods of heavy charging. Test the specific gravity of the electrolyte using a hydrometer* **(see illustration)**. *Remove the caps and extract a sample of the electrolyte and observe the float inside the barrel of the hydrometer. Follow the instructions from the tool manufacturer and determine the specific gravity of the electrolyte for each cell. A fully charged battery will indicate approximately 1.270 (green zone) at 68-degrees F (20-degrees C). If the specific gravity of the electrolyte is low (red zone), charge the battery as described in Chapter 1.*

b) ***Open circuit voltage test*** *- Using a digital voltmeter, perform an open circuit voltage test* **(see illustration)**. *Connect the negative probe of the voltmeter to the negative battery post and the positive probe to the positive battery post. The battery voltage should be greater than 12.5 volts. If the battery is less than the specified voltage, charge the battery before proceeding to the next test. Do not proceed with the battery load test until the battery is fully charged.*

c) ***Battery load test*** *- An accurate check of the battery condition can only be performed with a load tester (available at*

3.1b To test the open-circuit voltage of the battery, connect the black probe of a voltmeter to the negative terminal and the red probe to the positive terminal of the battery; if the battery is fully charged, the voltmeter should indicate above 12.5 volts (depending on the outside air temperature)

3.1c Some battery load testers are equipped with an ammeter, which enables you to impose a precise load on the battery (less expensive testers, like this one, have only a load switch and a voltmeter)

most auto parts stores). This test evaluates the ability of the battery to operate the starter and other accessories during periods of heavy amperage draw (load). Connect a battery load-testing tool to the battery terminals **(see illustration)**. Load test the battery according to the tool manufacturer's instructions. This tool increases the load demand (amperage draw) on the battery. Maintain the load on the battery for 15 seconds and observe that the battery voltage does not drop below 9.6 volts. If the battery condition is weak or defective, the tool will indicate this condition immediately. **Note:** Cold temperatures will cause the minimum voltage reading to drop slightly. Follow the chart given in the tool manufacturer's instructions to compensate for cold climates. Minimum load voltage for

freezing temperatures (32-degrees F/0-degrees C) should be approximately 9.1 volts.

d) **Battery drain test** - This test will indicate whether there's a constant drain on the vehicle's electrical system that can cause the battery to discharge. Make sure all accessories are turned off. If the vehicle has an underhood light, verify that it's working properly, then disconnect it. Connect one lead of a digital ammeter to the disconnected negative battery cable clamp and the other lead to the negative battery post. A drain of approximately 100 milliamps or less is considered normal (due to the engine control computers, clocks, digital radios and other components that normally cause a key-off battery drain). An excessive drain (approximately 500 milliamps or more)

will cause the battery to discharge. The problem circuit or component can be located by removing the fuses, one at a time, until the excessive drain stops and normal drain is indicated on the meter.

Replacement

Refer to illustrations 3.2, 3.3, 3.6 and 3.8

2   Remove the right front diagonal brace **(see illustration)**.
3   Disconnect the cable from the negative battery terminal **(see illustration)**. **Warning:** *ALWAYS disconnect the negative cable FIRST and connect it last, or you might accidentally short the battery with the tool you're using to loosen the cable clamps.*
4   Open the red plastic cover protecting the positive battery terminal and disconnect the cable from the positive terminal.

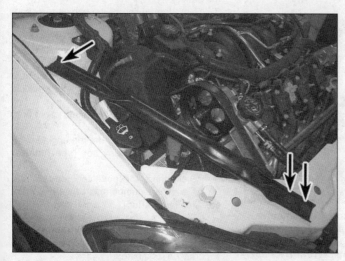

3.2 To remove the right front diagonal brace, remove these bolts

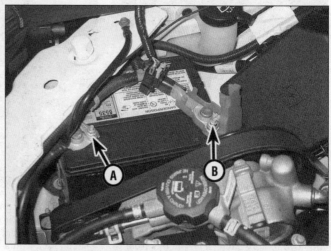

3.3 Loosen the nut and disconnect the cable from the negative terminal of the battery (A) first, then lift up the cover and disconnect the cable from the positive terminal (B)

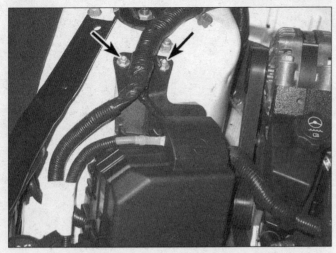

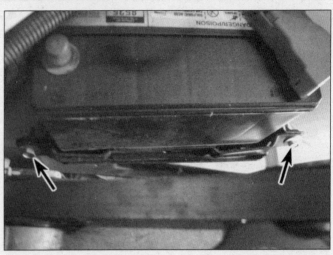

3.6 To detach the engine compartment fuse and relay box from the right strut tower, remove these two nuts, then carefully lift up the fuse and relay box and set it aside

3.8 To remove the battery from a V8 model, remove the battery hold-down strap by removing the two retaining bolts (V6 models use a conventional hold-down clamp bolt and clamp)

5   On V6 models, remove the battery insulator.

6   On V8 models, detach the engine compartment fuse and relay box **(see illustration)** and set it aside to provide clearance for lifting out the battery.

7   On V6 engines, remove the hold-down clamp bolt and clamp.

8   On V8 engines, remove the hold-down strap bolts **(see illustration)** and remove the strap.

9   Lift out the battery. Use a battery lifting strap that attaches to the battery posts to lift the battery safely and easily.

10   Installation is the reverse of removal.
Warning: *When connecting the battery cables, always connect the positive cable first and the negative cable last to avoid a short circuit caused by the tool used to tighten the cable clamps.*

4   Battery cables - replacement

Check

Note 1: *The negative and positive battery cables are part of a single assembly on all models. In other words, you can't just replace one or the other cable. If either cable needs to be replaced you must replace the entire negative and positive cable assembly.*
Note 2: *The photos accompanying this section depict the negative and positive battery cable assembly on a V8 model. However, the negative and positive battery cable assembly on V6 models is similar.*

1   Periodically inspect the entire length of each battery cable for damage, cracked or burned insulation and corrosion. Poor battery cable connections can cause starting problems and decreased engine performance.

2   Check the cable-to-terminal connections at the ends of the cables for cracks, loose wire strands and corrosion. The presence of white, fluffy deposits under the insulation at the cable terminal connection is a sign that the cable is corroded and should be replaced. Check the terminals for distortion, missing mounting bolts and corrosion (see Chapter 1 for further information regarding battery cable maintenance).

Replacement

Refer to illustrations 4.3a, 4.3b, 4.6, 4.7, 4.9 and 4.10

3   Disconnect the instrument panel electrical connector from the battery current sensor **(see illustrations)**.

4   When removing the cables always disconnect the negative cable from the negative battery post first and hook it up last or the tool used to loosen the cable clamps may short the battery.

5   Note the routing of the cables to ensure correct installation. Disconnect the old cables from the battery terminals (see Section 3), then disconnect the rest of the negative and positive battery cable assembly as follows.

6   Disconnect the battery cable electrical connector from the instrument panel electrical connector **(see illustration)**.

7   Disconnect the upper ground cable from the body **(see illustration)**.

8   Remove the cover from the engine compartment fuse and relay box **(see illustration 4.6)**.

9   Disconnect the positive battery cable from the engine compartment fuse and relay box **(see illustration)**.

10   Disconnect the positive cable from the starter motor solenoid **(see illustration)**.

11   Raise the front of the vehicle and place it securely on jackstands.

12   Disconnect the lower ground cable from the engine-to-transaxle bolt and nut right

4.3a The instrument panel electrical connector is plugged into the battery current sensor, which is located on the positive battery cable, a few inches from the positive battery terminal

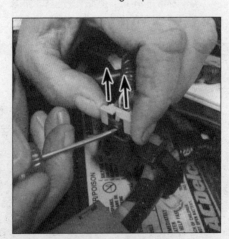

4.3b To disconnect the electrical connector from the battery current sensor, depress the locking tab of the white plastic lock with a small screwdriver and pull the lock out, then depress the locking lever and unplug the connector

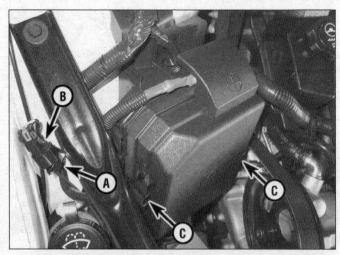

4.6 Disconnect the battery cable lead (A) from the instrument panel electrical connector (B), then pull back on the tabs (C) and remove the cover

4.7 To disconnect the upper ground cable from the body, remove this bolt

below the starter motor.

13   Tracing the length of each negative and positive battery cable, detach or disengage the cable locator pins and remove the cable assembly.

14   There are other, smaller cables that are also part of the negative and positive cable system for the battery, alternator and starter motor, but they're an integral part of various other engine harnesses, and are therefore not easily replaced because they're taped and/or cable-tied together. Before you can remove these other cables you'll have to cut off the electrical tape and/or cable ties. Be extremely careful when cutting off electrical tape; you might create driveability problems if you accidentally cut or damage one of the small wires in some of the harnesses. Instead, remove the battery to give yourself some room to work (see Section 3). Then locate the point at which the cables are bundled into another harness

and the point at which they emerge from the harness down below, then cut off whatever holds the cables together. Some cables are also secured by clips or locator pins to various engine compartment components. You can usually detach these clips without damaging them. If you do damage a clip when disengaging it, replace it with a new clip when you install the new cable.

15   Positive cables are almost always red and larger in cross-section; ground cables are usually black and smaller in cross-section. Because this cable assembly includes a lot of stuff besides just the negative and positive battery cables, it is vitally important that you replace this cable assembly with an identical assembly because every cable is custom fitted with respect to length, gauge, etc.

16   Clean the threads of the starter solenoid and/or ground connection with a wire brush to remove rust and corrosion. Apply a light coat

of battery terminal corrosion inhibitor or petroleum jelly to the threads to prevent future corrosion.

17   Attach the lower ends of the cables first, then connect the upper ends. And don't reconnect the ground cable to the negative battery post until you're completely finished. Before connecting a new cable to the battery, make sure that it reaches the battery post without having to be stretched.

18   Reattach the new cables to whatever harness they were previously attached to with new cables ties and/or electrical tape. If either cable is supposed to be secured by any brackets or clips, make sure that you reattach them.

19   Don't forget to install all locator pins and positioning clips.

20   After all cables are completely installed, reconnect the ground cable to the negative battery post (see Section 3).

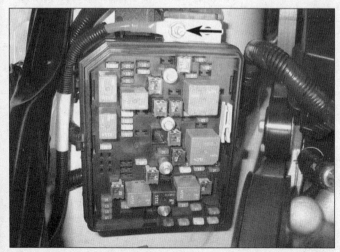

4.9 To disconnect the battery positive cable from the engine compartment fuse and relay box, remove this nut

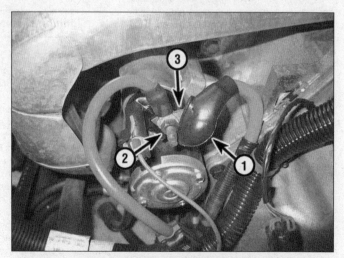

4.10 To disconnect the positive cable from the starter solenoid, pull back the boot (1), remove the nut (2) and pull the cable eyelet (3) off the stud terminal

5   Ignition system - general information

The ignition system consists of the ignition control module(s), the ignition coil pack(s), the spark plugs, the Camshaft Position (CMP) sensor (V6 models only), the Crankshaft Position (CKP) sensor, the knock sensor(s) and the Powertrain Control Module (PCM).

V6 models

V6 models use three ignition coils; each coil fires two spark plugs via spark plug wires. The three coils and the ignition control module are combined into one integral coil pack unit mounted on the left end of the rear valve cover. V6 models do not have a separate ignition control module (GM calls it an ignition coil driver module); it's an integral part of the coil pack. If a coil pack or its ignition module fails, you must replace the entire unit.

Each coil fires two spark plugs. One coil fires the No. 1 and No. 4 cylinders; the second coil fires the No. 2 and No. 5 cylinders; the third coil fires the No. 3 and No. 6 cylinders. When the piston in cylinder No. 1 is on the compression stroke, the piston in cylinder No. 4 is on the exhaust stroke. When the coil fires cylinder No. 1, most of the spark voltage goes to that cylinder because the pressure - and therefore the resistance - is high in that cylinder (the higher the resistance, the higher the voltage needed to jump the gap from the spark plug's center electrode to ground). Conversely, the piston in cylinder No. 4, which is on the exhaust stroke, produces no pressure, and therefore little resistance, so little voltage is needed to jump the gap from the spark plug's center electrode to ground. The ignition coils for cylinders 2 and 5 and 3 and 6 work the same way. This design is known as a "waste spark" ignition.

V8 models

V8 models have eight ignition coils; each coil fires its corresponding spark plug, in firing order, via a very short spark plug wire. Each coil is located on the valve cover, directly above the plug that it fires. Each gang of four coils is mounted on a bracket that is bolted to the valve cover. If you need to remove the valve cover, you can remove all four coils and the mounting bracket as a single assembly. If a coil fails, you can remove and replace it without having to replace the entire coil assembly for that cylinder head. There is no separate ignition control module; each coil has its own integral module (GM calls it an ignition coil driver module).

All models

Each ignition coil has a terminal for voltage supply (12 volts) and a terminal for ground. The Powertrain Control Module (PCM) supplies a low reference circuit and an ignition control (IC) circuit, which controls the ground path for the primary winding in the coil. Each coil contains an ignition coil driver module (ignition control module). When the PCM

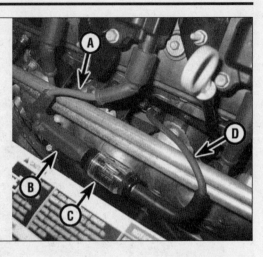

6.3 Here's the setup used for checking to see if the ignition coil is sending power to the spark plug. If the coil is delivering power to the plug, the tester will flash (this type of spark tester is available at most auto parts stores):

A   *Spark plug wire*
B   *Spark plug wire boot (metal heat shield removed so that the tester will fit)*
C   *Calibrated spark tester body*
D   *Spark tester plug wire (connect boot on lower end to spark plug)*

commands the IC circuit to come on by closing the ground path, current flows through the primary coil windings during the dwell period (the time that it takes for the primary coil to absorb as much voltage as it can, which is known as saturation). When the primary coil is saturated, the PCM turns off the IC circuit by opening the ground path. The magnetic field produced by the primary coil windings collapses across the secondary coil windings, which induces a high voltage across the spark plug electrodes. The primary coils are current limited to protect them from damage in the event that the IC circuit should be on too long.

The PCM uses inputs from a variety of information sensors to control ignition timing: Camshaft Position (CMP) sensor, Crankshaft Position (CKP) sensor, Engine Coolant Temperature (ECT) sensor, Intake Air Temperature (IAT) sensor, knock sensors, Mass Air Flow (MAF) sensor, transmission gear position sensor or Transmission Range (TR) sensor and Vehicle Speed Sensor (VSS). For more information on these other sensors, refer to Chapter 6.

6   Ignition system - check

Refer to illustration 6.3

Warning: *Because of the very high voltage generated by the ignition system (as much as 40,000 volts), use extreme care when you're servicing ignition components such as the ignition coil pack and spark plugs.*

Note 1: *The ignition system components are difficult to diagnose. In the event of ignition system failure, if the checks do not clearly indicate the source of the ignition system problem, have the vehicle tested by a dealer service department or other qualified auto repair facility.*

Note 2: *For the following test, you'll need a calibrated spark tester (available at auto parts stores). Don't use the old-fashioned type of spark tester that looks like a spark plug with an alligator clip on it. This type of tester disables the spark plug for the plug wire that you're testing, which might set a Diagnostic*

Trouble Code for a misfire. Instead, use the type of spark tester shown in **illustration 6.3**. *This newer type of tester enables you to check for spark without disabling the spark plug for the plug wire that you're testing.*

1   If a malfunction occurs and the vehicle won't start, do not immediately assume that the ignition system is causing the problem. First, check the following items:

a) *Make sure the battery cable clamps, where they connect to the battery, are clean and tight.*

b) *Test the condition of the battery (see Section 3). If it does not pass all the tests, replace it with a new battery.*

c) *Check the wiring and connections for the ignition control module and for the ignition coil pack. Inspect the spark plug wires; make sure that they're in good shape and tightly connected to the coil pack and to the spark plugs.*

d) *Check the related fuses inside the fuse box (see Chapter 12). If they're burned, determine the cause and repair the circuit.*

2   If the engine turns over but won't start, verify that there is sufficient secondary ignition voltage to fire the spark plug as follows.

3   Disconnect the spark plug wire from the spark plug for the No. 1 cylinder, then connect a calibrated spark tester between the spark wire and the spark plug **(see illustration)**.

4   Crank the engine while watching the tester. If the tester flashes, sufficient voltage is reaching the spark plug to fire it. **Caution:** *Do NOT crank the engine or allow it to run for more than five seconds; running the engine for more than five seconds might set a Diagnostic Trouble Code (DTC) for a cylinder misfire.*

5   Repeat this test for each cylinder.

6   Proceed on this basis until you have verified that there's a good spark from each coil terminal. If there is, then you have verified that the coil(s) are functioning correctly.

7   If all the coils are firing correctly but the engine has a misfire, then one or more of the plugs might be fouled. Remove and check the spark plugs or install new ones (see Chapter 1). Also inspect the boots carefully for corrosion (high resistance) or deterioration of the insulation (low resistance). If any of the boots

look damaged or deteriorated, replace them as a set.

8   No further testing of the ignition system is possible without special diagnostic equipment.

7   Ignition coil pack - removal and installation

V6 models

Refer to illustrations 7.2 and 7.5

1   Disconnect the cable from the negative battery terminal (see Section 3).

2   Disconnect the Manifold Absolute Pressure (MAP) sensor electrical connector **(see illustration)**.

3   Disconnect the electrical connector from the ignition coil pack.

4   Disconnect the spark plug wires from the ignition coil.

5   Remove the ignition coil pack mounting bolts **(see illustration)** and remove the ignition coil pack assembly.

6   Before installing the boots on the ignition coil pack, coat the interior of each boot with silicone dielectric compound.

7   Installation is otherwise the reverse of removal.

V8 models

Refer to illustration 7.10

8   Disconnect the cable from the negative battery terminal (see Section 3).

9   Remove the engine cover.

10   Disconnect the electrical connector from the ignition coil **(see illustration)**.

11   Disconnect the spark plug wire from the coil.

12   Remove the two ignition coil mounting bolts **(see illustration 7.10)** and remove the coil.

13   Installation is the reverse of removal.

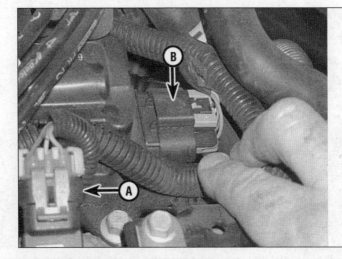

7.2 **On V6 models, disconnect the MAP sensor electrical connector (A), then disconnect the electrical connector (B) from the coil pack (the connector is disconnected from the coil as described in illustration 4.3b)**

8   Charging system - general information and precautions

The charging system supplies electrical power for the ignition system, the lights, the radio, the electronic control systems and all other electrical components on the car. The charging system consists of the battery, the alternator (with an integral voltage regulator), the Powertrain Control Module (PCM), the charge indicator lamp on the instrument panel cluster, a fusible link (located inline between the starter solenoid terminal and the alternator) and the wiring between all the components.

The alternator generates alternating current (AC), which is rectified to direct current (DC) to charge the battery and supply power to other electrical systems. The alternator is driven by a drivebelt at the front of the engine (right side of the vehicle) and is located at the right rear corner of all engines. The voltage regulator limits the alternator charging voltage by regulating the current supplied to the alternator field circuit. The regulator is a sol-

id-state electronic assembly mounted inside the alternator. The regulator is not separately replaceable on these vehicles. If it's defective, you must replace the alternator.

Inspect the alternator drivebelt, battery and all charging system wires and connections at the intervals listed in Chapter 1.

Be very careful when making any circuit connections and note the following:

a) *Never start the engine with a battery charger connected.*

b) *Never disconnect a battery cable with the engine running.*

c) *Always disconnect both battery cables before using a battery charger: negative cable first, positive cable last.*

9   Charging system - check

Refer to illustrations 9.2 and 9.3

1   If the charging system malfunctions, don't immediately assume that the alternator is causing the problem. First check the following items:

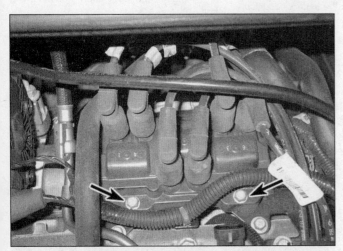

7.5 **To detach the ignition coil pack on a V6 model, remove the two coil mounting bolts from the front side of the coil pack and the two mounting nuts (not shown) on the backside of the coil pack**

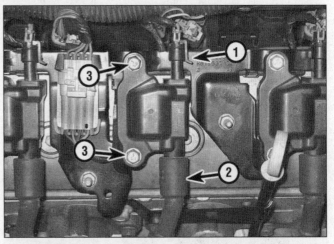

7.10 **To detach an ignition coil from the coil mounting bracket on a V8 model, disconnect the electrical connector (1), disconnect the spark plug wire (2), then remove the ignition coil mounting bolts (3)**

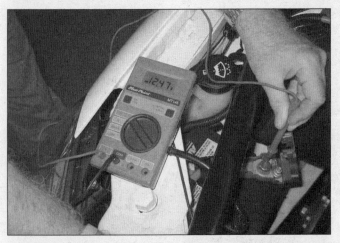

9.2 To measure standing voltage, put your multimeter in the volts mode, connect the positive probe of the meter to the positive battery terminal and the negative probe to the negative terminal and note the reading, which should be 12.6 volts if the battery is fully charged

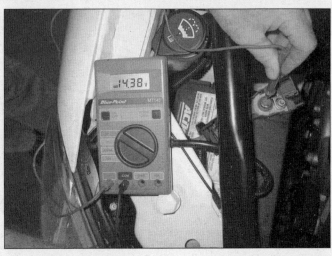

9.3 To measure charging voltage, turn on the engine and note the reading again, which should then be about 13.5 volts to 14.5 volts

a) *Ensure that the battery cable connections at the battery are clean and tight.*
b) *If the battery is not a maintenance-free type, check the electrolyte level and specific gravity. If the electrolyte level is low, add distilled water. If the specific gravity is low, charge the battery.*
c) *Check the alternator wiring and connections.*
d) *Check the drivebelt condition and tension (see Chapter 1).*
e) *Check the alternator mounting bolts for looseness.*
f) *Run the engine and check the alternator for abnormal noise.*

2 Use a voltmeter to check the battery voltage with the engine off. If the battery has a full charge, it should be 12.6 volts **(see illustration)**.

3 Start the engine and check the battery voltage again. It should now be approximately 13.5 to 14.5 volts **(see illustration)**

4 If the voltage didn't increase, inspect the condition of the fusible link that's located near the starter. If the fusible link is melted, replace the fusible link (available at dealer parts departments). The correct size of the fusible link should be printed on the outside of the link. Make sure that you obtain the correct fusible link for the application. After replacing the fusible link, check the charging voltage again.

5 If the voltage reading is more or less than the specified charging voltage, the voltage regulator is defective. Replace the alternator (the voltage regulator cannot be replaced separately).

6 The charging system (battery) light on the instrument cluster lights up when the ignition key is turned to ON, but it should go out when the engine starts.

7 If the charging system light stays on after the engine has been started, there is a problem with the charging system. Before replacing the alternator, check the battery condition,

alternator belt tension and electrical cable connections.

8 If replacing the alternator doesn't restore voltage to the specified range, have the charging system tested by a dealer service department or other qualified repair shop.

10   Alternator - removal and installation

V6 models

Refer to illustrations 10.3 and 10.5

1 Disconnect the cable from the negative battery terminal (see Section 3).

2 Remove the accessory drivebelt (see Chapter 1).

3 Disconnect the electrical connectors from the alternator **(see illustration)**.

4 Remove the front alternator mounting bolt.

10.3 To remove the alternator from a V6 engine, disconnect the electrical connector (A) and the battery cable (B) from the alternator, remove the front mounting bolt (C) . . .

10.5 . . . then remove the two rear mounting bolts (one bolt not visible)

10.10a On a V8 engine, remove this nut (A) and disconnect the battery cable from the B+ stud terminal, then disconnect the electrical connector (B)

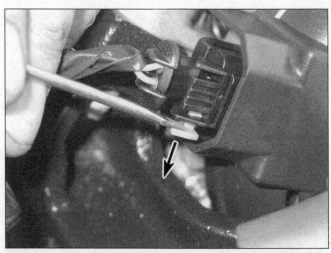

10.10b To disconnect the electrical connector from the alternator on a V8 model, unlock the connector by sliding the lock tab down, then pull off the connector

5   Remove the alternator rear mounting bolts **(see illustration)**. On 3.9L models, the right bolt (the one nearest the pulley) is a stud bolt. A clip for the power steering line is secured to this stud bolt by a nut. On these models you'll have to remove the nut and detach the power steering line clip from the stud before you can remove the stud.

6   Remove the alternator.

7   Installation is the reverse of removal. Be sure to tighten the alternator mounting bolts securely.

V8 models

Refer to illustrations 10.10a, 10.10b and 10.11

8   Disconnect the cable from the negative battery terminal (see Section 3).

9   Remove the accessory drivebelt (see Chapter 1).

10   Disconnect the electrical connectors from the alternator **(see illustrations)**.

11   Remove the four alternator mounting bolts **(see illustration)**.

12   Remove the alternator.

13   Installation is the reverse of removal. Be sure to tighten the alternator mounting bolts securely.

11   Starting system - general information and precautions

The starting system consists of the battery, the ignition switch, the Transmission Range (TR) switch, the Body Control Module (BCM), the Powertrain Control Module (PCM), the starter motor solenoid, the starter motor and the wires that connect these components. The solenoid is located on top of and is an integral part of the starter motor. The starter is located on the left rear side of the block on V6 models and on the left front side of the block on V8 models.

The starter motor can be operated only when the shift lever is in PARK or NEUTRAL. When the ignition key is turned to the START position, it sends a signal to the Body Control Module (BCM), which sends a signal to the Powertrain Control Module (PCM). The PCM uses the TR switch inside the transmission to verify that the transmission is in PARK or NEUTRAL, then sends battery voltage to the control circuit of the starter relay, which closes the starter circuit and supplies battery voltage to the S terminal on the starter solenoid.

Always observe the following precautions when working on the starting system:

a) *Excessive cranking of the starter motor can overheat it and cause serious damage. Never operate the starter motor for more than 15 seconds at a time without pausing for at least two minutes to allow it to cool.*

b) *The starter is connected directly to the battery and could arc or cause a fire if mishandled, overloaded or short-circuited.*

c) *Always detach the cable from the negative battery terminal before working on the starting system.*

12   Starter motor and circuit - check

Refer to illustrations 12.3 and 12.4

1   If a malfunction occurs in the starting circuit, do not immediately assume that the starter is causing the problem. First, check the following items:

a) *Make sure that the battery cable clamps are clean and tight where they connect to the battery.*

b) *Check the condition of the battery cables (see Section 4). Replace any defective battery cables with new parts.*

c) *Test the condition of the battery (see Section 3). If it does not pass all the tests, replace it with a new battery.*

d) *Check the starter solenoid wiring and connections. Refer to the wiring diagrams at the end of Chapter 12.*

e) *Check the starter mounting bolts for tightness.*

f) *Make sure that the shift lever is in PARK or NEUTRAL.*

10.11 To detach the alternator from a V8 model, remove these four bolts

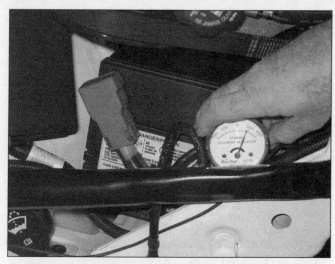

12.3 Use an inductive-type ammeter to measure the current draw. The advantage of this simple meter is that you can place it directly on the positive or negative (shown) battery cable, whichever is easier to access

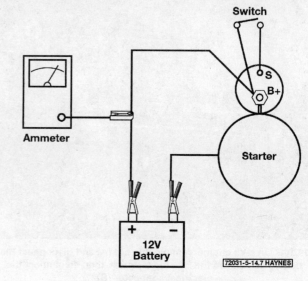

12.4 Starter motor bench testing details

2   If the starter motor does not operate when the ignition switch is turned to the START position, check for battery voltage to the solenoid. Connect a test light or voltmeter to the starter solenoid switched terminal (the small wire) while an assistant turns the ignition switch to the START position. If voltage is not available, check the starting system circuit (see the wiring diagrams at the end of Chapter 12). If voltage is available but the starter motor does not operate, remove the starter (see Section 13) and bench test it (see Step 4).

3   If the starter turns over slowly, check the starter cranking voltage and the current draw from the battery (this test must be performed with the starter on the engine). Crank the engine over (for 10 seconds or less) and observe the battery voltage. It should not drop below 8.5 volts. Also, observe the current draw using an inductive type ammeter **(see illustration)**. It should not exceed 400 amps or drop below 250 amps. **Caution:** *The battery cables might overheat because of the large amount of current being drawn from the bat-*

tery. Discontinue the testing until the starting system has cooled down. If the starter motor cranking amp values are not within the correct range, replace it with a new unit. There are several conditions that may affect the starter cranking potential. The battery must be in good condition and the battery cold-cranking rating must not be under-rated for the particular application. Be sure to check the battery specifications carefully. The battery terminals and cables must be clean and not corroded. Also, in cases of extreme cold temperatures, make sure the battery and/or engine block is warmed before performing the tests.

4   If the starter is receiving voltage but does not activate, remove and check the starter/ solenoid assembly on the bench **(see illustration)**. Most likely the solenoid is defective. In some rare cases, the engine may be seized so be sure to try and rotate the crankshaft pulley (see Chapter 2) before proceeding. With the starter/solenoid assembly mounted in a vise on the bench, install one jumper cable from the negative battery terminal to the body

of the starter. Install the other jumper cable from the positive battery terminal to the B+ terminal on the starter. Install a starter switch and apply battery voltage to the solenoid S terminal (for 10 seconds or less) and see if the solenoid plunger, shift lever and overrunning clutch extends and rotates the pinion drive. If the pinion drive extends but does not rotate, the solenoid is operating but the starter motor is defective. If there is no movement but the solenoid clicks, the solenoid and/or the starter motor is defective. If the solenoid plunger extends and rotates the pinion drive, the starter/solenoid assembly is working properly.

13   Starter motor - removal and installation

V6 models

Refer to illustration 13.5

1   Disconnect the cable from the negative battery terminal (see Section 3).

2   Raise the front of the vehicle and support it securely on jackstands.

3   Remove the under-engine splash shield.

4   Disconnect the battery cable (the larger cable) and the starter control cable (the smaller cable) from the starter solenoid terminals.

5   Remove the driveplate/torque converter access cover **(see illustration)**.

6   Remove the starter motor mounting bolts and remove the starter motor.

7   Installation is the reverse of removal. Be sure to tighten the starter motor mounting bolts to the torque listed in this Chapter's Specifications.

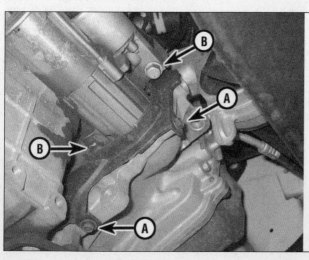

13.5 Starter motor mounting details (V6 models)

A   *Driveplate/torque converter access cover bolts*

B   *Starter mounting bolts*

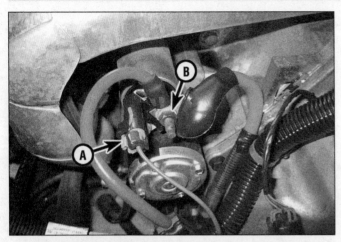

13.10 Starter motor electrical connections (V8 models)

A   *Disconnect the electrical connector*
B   *Pull back the boot and remove the nut, then disconnect the cables from the BAT terminal*

13.11 To detach the starter motor from a V8 engine, remove these two bolts (use a long extension and a universal joint adapter on the socket to access these bolts)

V8 models

Refer to illustrations 13.10 and 13.11

8   Disconnect the cable from the negative battery terminal (see Section 3).
9   Remove the air filter housing (see Chapter 4).

10   Disconnect the battery cable (the larger cable) and the starter control cable (the smaller cable) from the starter motor solenoid terminals **(see illustration)**.
11   Remove the starter motor mounting bolts **(see illustration)** and remove the starter motor.

12   Installation is the reverse of removal. Be sure to tighten the starter motor mounting bolts to the torque listed in this Chapter's Specifications.

Notes

Chapter 6
Emissions and engine control systems

Contents

Specifications

Torque specifications

Note: *One foot-pound (ft-lb) of torque is equivalent to 12 inch-pounds (in-lbs) of torque. Torque values below approximately 15 ft-lbs are expressed in inch-pounds, because most foot-pound torque wrenches are not accurate at these smaller values.*

Ft-lbs (unless otherwise indicated)

Engine coolant temperature sensor .... 180 in-lbs
Knock sensor retaining bolt 18
Oxygen sensors 30
Valve Lifter Oil Manifold (VLOM) assembly mounting bolts 18

1 General information

Refer to illustration 1.7

The emission control systems and components are an integral part of the engine management system, which is called the Sequential Fuel Injection (SFI) system (see Chapter 4 for more information on the SFI system). The SFI system also includes all the government-mandated diagnostic features of the second generation of on-board diagnostics, which is known as On-Board Diagnostics II (OBD-II).

At the center of the SFI and OBD-II systems is the on-board computer, which is known as the Powertrain Control Module (PCM). Using a variety of information sensors, the PCM monitors all of the important engine operating parameters (temperature, speed, load, etc.). It also uses an array of out-

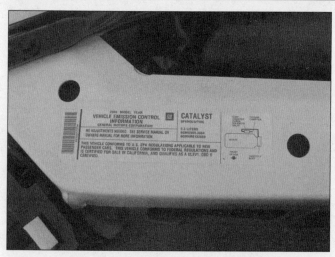

1.7 The Vehicle Emissions Control Information (VECI) label is located on the radiator crossmember

2.1 Simple code readers are an economical way to extract trouble codes when the CHECK ENGINE light comes on

put actuators (such as the ignition coils, fuel injectors and various solenoids and relays) to respond to and alter these parameters as necessary to maintain optimal performance, economy and emissions. The principal emission control systems used on the vehicles covered in this manual include the:

Camshaft Actuator System (V6 models)
Catalytic converter
Displacement on Demand (DOD) system
(V8 models)
Evaporative Emission Control (EVAP)
system
Exhaust Gas Recirculation (EGR) system
Intake Manifold Tuning (IMT) Valve
system (2006 3.9L V6 models)
Positive Crankcase Ventilation (PCV)
system
Throttle Actuator Control (TAC) system

The Sections in this Chapter include general descriptions and component replacement procedures for most of the information sensors and output actuators, as well as the important components that are part of the systems listed above. Refer to Chapter 4 for more information on the air intake, fuel and exhaust systems, and to Chapter 5 for information on the ignition system. Refer to Chapter 1 for any scheduled maintenance for emission-related systems and components.

The procedures in this Chapter are intended to be practical, affordable and within the capabilities of the home mechanic. The diagnosis of most engine and emission control functions and driveability problems requires specialized tools, equipment and training. When servicing emission devices or systems becomes too difficult or requires special test equipment, consult a dealer service department.

Although engine and emission control systems are very sophisticated on late-model vehicles, you can do most of the regular maintenance and some servicing at home with common tune-up and hand tools and

relatively inexpensive meters. Because of the Federally mandated warranty that covers the emission control system, check with a dealer about warranty coverage before working on any emission-related systems. After the warranty has expired, you may wish to perform some of the component replacement procedures in this Chapter to save money. Remember that the most frequent cause of emission and driveability problems is a loose electrical connector or a broken wire or vacuum hose, so always check the electrical connections, the electrical wiring and the vacuum hoses first.

Pay close attention to any special precautions given in this Chapter. Remember that illustrations of various systems might not exactly match the system installed on the vehicle on which you're working because of changes made by the manufacturer during production or from year to year.

A Vehicle Emission Control Information (VECI) label **(see illustration)** is located in the engine compartment. This label contains emission-control and engine tune-up specifications and adjustment information. It also includes a vacuum hose routing diagram for emission-control components. When servicing the engine or emission systems, always check the VECI label in your vehicle. If any information in this manual contradicts what you read on the VECI label on your vehicle, always defer to the information on the VECI label.

---

2   On-Board Diagnostic (OBD) system and Diagnostic Trouble Codes (DTCs)

Scan tool information

Refer to illustrations 2.1 and 2.2

1   Hand-held scanners are handy for analyzing the engine management systems used on late-model vehicles. Because extracting

the Diagnostic Trouble Codes (DTCs) from an engine management system is now the first step in troubleshooting many computer-controlled systems and components, even the most basic generic code readers are capable of accessing a computer's DTCs **(see illustration)**. More powerful scan tools can also perform many of the diagnostics once associated with expensive factory scan tools. If you're planning to obtain a generic scan tool for your vehicle, make sure that it's compatible with OBD-II systems. If you don't plan to purchase a code reader or scan tool and don't have access to one, you can have the codes extracted by a dealer service department or by an independent repair shop.

2   With the advent of the Federally mandated emission control system known as On-Board Diagnostics-II (OBD-II), specially designed scanners were developed. Several tool manufacturers have released OBD-II scan tools for the home mechanic **(see illustration)**. **Note:** *An aftermarket generic scanner should work with any model covered by this manual. Before purchasing a generic scan tool, verify that it will work properly with the OBD-II system you want to scan. If necessary, of course, you can always have the codes extracted by a dealer service department or an independent repair shop with a professional scan tool. Some auto parts stores even provide this service for free.*

OBD-II system general description

3   All vehicles covered by this manual are equipped with the OBD-II system. This system consists of the on-board computer, known as the Powertrain Control Module (PCM), and information sensors that monitor various functions of the engine and send a constant stream of data to the PCM during engine operation. Unlike earlier on-board diagnostics systems, the OBD-II system doesn't just monitor everything, store Diagnostic Trouble

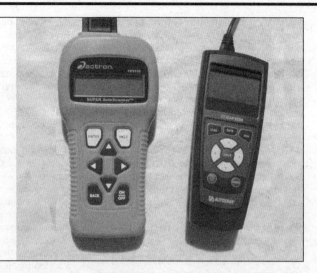

2.2 Scanners like these from Actron and AutoXray are powerful diagnostic aids - they can tell you just about anything that you want to know about your engine management system

Codes (DTCs) and illuminate a Malfunction Indicator Light (MIL) when there's a problem. It even predicts the probable failure of systems and components when their data starts to become suspicious!

4   The PCM is the brain of the electronically controlled OBD-II system. It receives data from a number of information sensors and switches. Based on the data that it receives from the sensors, the PCM constantly alters engine operating conditions to optimize driveability, performance, emissions and fuel economy. It does so by turning on and off and by controlling various output actuators such as relays, solenoids, valves and other devices. The PCM is mounted in the left front corner of the engine compartment, in the bottom of the air filter housing.

5   If your vehicle is still under warranty, virtually every fuel, ignition and emission control component in the OBD-II system is covered by a Federally mandated extended emissions warranty that is longer than the warranty covering the rest of the vehicle. Vehicles sold in California and in some other states have even longer emissions warranties than other states. Read your owner's manual for the terms of the warranty protecting the emission-control systems on your vehicle. It isn't a good idea to do-it-yourself at home while the vehicle emission systems are still under warranty because owner-induced damage to the PCM, the sensors and/or the control devices might VOID this warranty. So as long as the emission systems are still warranted, take the vehicle to a dealer service department if there's a problem.

Information sensors

6   **Accelerator Pedal Position (APP) sensor** - The APP sensor, which is located at the top of the accelerator pedal, is part of the electronic throttle control system. None of the vehicles covered in this manual use a conventional accelerator cable. The APP sensor constantly monitors the angle of the accelerator pedal and sends this data to the PCM, which controls an output actuator known as the throttle motor (located in the throttle body) to open or close the throttle plate inside the

throttle body to the correct position. The APP sensor actually consists of two identical sensors known as "potentiometers," variable resistors, each of which receives a 5-volt reference and a low reference voltage from the PCM and returns a signal voltage to the PCM that's proportional to the angle of the accelerator pedal. One of the potentiometers is redundant, and serves as a back-up in the event that the primary potentiometer fails. The PCM compares the signal outputs from both potentiometers to assess the accuracy of the primary potentiometer's signal. The APP sensor is an integral component of the accelerator pedal assembly. If it's defective, replace the accelerator pedal assembly.

7   **Camshaft Position (CMP) sensor** - The CMP sensor produces a signal that the PCM uses to monitor the position of the camshaft. This data enables the CMP sensor to identify the number 1 cylinder so that it can time the firing order of the spark plugs and the firing sequence of the fuel injectors. On V6 engines the CMP sensor is located in the valley between the heads, on top of and at the front of the block, right behind the timing chain cover and ahead of the intake manifold. On V8 engines the CMP sensor is located on the upper part of the timing chain cover.

8   **Crankshaft Position (CKP) sensor** - The CKP sensor produces a signal that the PCM uses to determine the position of the crankshaft. The PCM uses data from the CKP sensor (and from the CMP sensor on V6 models) to synchronize ignition timing with fuel injector timing, to control spark knock and to detect misfires. On V6 models, the CKP sensor is located on the backside (firewall side) of the engine block. On V8 engines the CKP sensor is located on the backside (firewall side) of the engine block, near the flywheel.

9   **Engine Coolant Temperature (ECT) sensor** - The ECT sensor is a thermistor (temperature-sensitive variable resistor) that sends a voltage signal to the PCM, which uses this data to determine the temperature of the engine coolant. The ECT sensor tells the PCM when the engine is sufficiently warmed up to go into closed loop, helps the PCM con-

trol the air/fuel mixture ratio and ignition timing, and also helps the PCM determine when to turn the Exhaust Gas Recirculation (EGR) system on and off. On V6 models, the ECT sensor is located at the left end of the front cylinder head. On V8 engines, the ECT sensor is located on the front cylinder head, at the right front corner, above the spark plug.

10   **Fuel tank pressure sensor** - The fuel tank pressure sensor measures the fuel tank pressure when the PCM tests the EVAP system. It's also used to control fuel tank pressure by signaling the EVAP system to purge the tank when the pressure becomes excessive. The fuel tank pressure sensor is located on top of the fuel tank, on the mounting flange of the fuel pump/fuel level sending unit module.

11   **Intake Air Temperature (IAT) sensor** - The IAT sensor monitors the temperature of the air entering the engine and sends a signal to the PCM. The IAT sensor is an integral component of the Mass Air Flow (MAF) sensor, which is located between the air filter housing and the air intake duct on all models. For more information, see *Mass Air Flow (MAF) sensor* below.

12   **Knock sensor** - The knock sensor is a "piezoelectric" crystal that oscillates in proportion to engine vibration. (The term piezoelectric refers to the property of certain crystals that produce a voltage when subjected to a mechanical stress.) The oscillation of the piezoelectric crystal produces a voltage output that is monitored by the PCM, which retards the ignition timing when the oscillation exceeds a certain threshold. When the engine is operating normally, the knock sensor oscillates consistently and its voltage signal is steady. When detonation occurs, engine vibration increases, and the oscillation of the knock sensor exceeds a design threshold. (Detonation is an uncontrolled explosion, after the spark occurs at the spark plug, which spontaneously combusts the remaining air/fuel mixture, resulting in a pinging or knocking sound.) If allowed to continue, the engine can be damaged. On all models, the two knock sensors are located on the front and rear sides of the block, right below the exhaust manifolds.

13   **Manifold Absolute Pressure (MAP) sensor** - The MAP sensor monitors the pressure or vacuum downstream from the throttle plate, inside the intake manifold. The MAP sensor measures intake manifold pressure and vacuum on the absolute scale, i.e. from zero instead of from sea-level atmospheric pressure (14.7 psi). The MAP sensor converts the absolute pressure into a variable voltage signal that changes with the pressure. The PCM uses this data to determine engine load so that it can alter the ignition advance and fuel enrichment. On V6 models, the MAP sensor is located at the upper left rear corner of the intake manifold. On V8 models, the MAP sensor is located on the intake manifold, right behind the throttle body.

14   **Mass Air Flow (MAF) sensor** - The MAF sensor is the means by which the PCM

measures the amount of intake air drawn into the engine. It uses a hot-wire sensing element to measure the amount of air entering the engine. The wire is constantly maintained at a specified temperature above the ambient temperature of the incoming air by electrical current. As intake air passes through the MAF sensor and over the hot wire, it cools the wire, and the control system immediately corrects the temperature back to its constant value. The current required to maintain the constant value is used by the PCM to determine the amount of air flowing through the MAF sensor. The MAF sensor also includes an integral Intake Air Temperature (IAT) sensor. The two components cannot be serviced separately; if either sensor is defective, replace the MAF sensor. On all models, the MAF sensor is located between the air filter housing and the air intake duct. The MAF sensor is also referred to as an MAF/IAT sensor because it also incorporates the Intake Air Temperature (IAT) sensor.

15   **Oxygen sensors** - An oxygen sensor is a galvanic battery that generates a small variable voltage signal in proportion to the difference between the oxygen content in the exhaust stream and the oxygen content in the ambient air. The PCM uses the voltage signal from the upstream oxygen sensor to maintain a stoichiometric air/fuel ratio of 14.7:1 by constantly adjusting the on-time of the fuel injectors. There are two oxygen sensors on all models: one upstream sensor in the rear exhaust manifold, right above the flange, and a downstream sensor in the exhaust pipe right behind the catalytic converter.

16   **Throttle Position (TP) sensor** - The TP sensor is a potentiometer that receives a constant voltage input from the PCM and sends back a proportional voltage signal that varies in relation to the opening angle of the throttle plate inside the throttle body. This voltage signal tells the PCM when the throttle is closed, half-open, wide open or anywhere in between. The PCM uses this data, along with information from other sensors, to calculate injector pulse width (the interval of time during which an injector solenoid is energized by the PCM). There are actually two TP sensors on the electronic throttle body. One TP sensor has a signal that's above four volts when the throttle plate is closed, and which decreases as the throttle plate opens. The other sensor has a signal that's below one volt when the throttle plate is closed, and which increases as the throttle plate opens. The PCM compares the two signals to make sure that the primary sensor is functioning correctly. The TP sensors are an integral part of the electronic throttle body and cannot be serviced separately.

17   **Transmission speed sensors** - The Input Shaft Speed (ISS) sensor is located inside the transaxle, so you cannot replace it at home. The Vehicle Speed Sensor (VSS) is a magnetic pick-up coil located on the right side of the automatic transaxle, near the inner CV joint. The VSS provides the PCM with information about the rotational speed of the output shaft in the transmission. The PCM

uses this information to control the torque converter and to calculate speed scheduling and the correct operating pressure for the transaxle.

18   **Valve Lifter Oil Manifold (VLOM) oil pressure sensor** - The VLOM oil pressure sensor is located on the VLOM itself, which is located on top of the block, between the two cylinder heads. The oil pressure sensor, which is part of the Displacement on Demand (DOD) system used on V8 engines, monitors the oil pressure inside the DOD system and sends this information to the PCM, which controls the DOD system. For more information about the DOD system, see Section 18.

Powertrain Control Module (PCM)

19   The PCM, which is located at the left front corner of the engine compartment, inside the air filter housing, is the brain of the engine management system. It monitors the data input of all the information sensors, processes this information by comparing it to the operational *map* (program) for the engine management system, then sends command decisions to the output actuators, which execute those commands. These decisions are made so quickly (in milliseconds) that the entire process is virtually undetectable. As a result, driveability is smooth and seamless.

Output actuators

20   **Camshaft actuator solenoid** - The PCM-controlled camshaft actuator solenoid controls the flow of oil into the camshaft actuator system. When the PCM sends a pulse-width modulated voltage signal to the camshaft actuator solenoid, oil flows through one of two passages into the *cam phaser*. When oil is directed through one passage the cam phaser advances the camshaft; when it's directed through the other passage the cam phaser retards the camshaft. The camshaft actuator solenoid and the cam phaser are components of the camshaft actuator system, which lowers emissions, increases fuel economy and improves engine idle stability. For more information about the camshaft actuator system, see Section 17.

21   **EVAP canister purge solenoid** - The EVAP canister purge solenoid (or purge valve) controls the flow of fuel vapors (unburned hydrocarbons) from the EVAP canister to the intake manifold. The EVAP canister purge solenoid is normally closed. But when ordered to do so by the PCM, it allows intake manifold vacuum to draw the fuel vapors that are stored in the EVAP canister into the intake manifold, where they're mixed with intake air, then burned along with the normal air/fuel mixture. On V6 models, the purge valve is located at the left rear corner of the intake manifold, right in front of the throttle body. (The intake manifolds on 3.5L and 3.9L V6 engines look different, but the location of the canister purge valve is the same on both manifolds.) On V8 models, the canister purge valve is located on top of the intake manifold.

22   **EVAP canister vent solenoid** - The EVAP canister vent solenoid is normally open, to allow outside air to flow through the vent, through the EVAP canister and into the fuel tank, which maintains atmospheric pressure inside the fuel tank. But when energized by the PCM, the vent solenoid closes and seals off the EVAP system for inspection and maintenance tests and for OBD-II leak and pressure tests. The EVAP canister vent solenoid is located behind the left rear wheel well fender liner. You have to raise the vehicle to access the vent solenoid, but you don't have to remove the rear wheel well fender liner.

23   **Fuel injectors** - The fuel injectors, which spray a fine mist of fuel into the intake ports, where it is mixed with incoming air, are inductive coils under PCM control. The injectors are installed in the intake manifold. For more information about the injectors, see Chapter 4.

24   **Ignition coils** - The ignition coils are under the control of the Powertrain Control Module (PCM). V6 models use a coil pack, which consists of three ignition coils. V8 models use an individual coil for each cylinder. For more information about the ignition coils, see Chapter 5.

25   **Intake Manifold Tuning (IMT) valve solenoid** - The IMT valve solenoid is part of the IMT valve system, a variable air induction tuning system that improves performance and efficiency over a wider operating range on 2006 3.9L V6 models. The PCM uses the IMT valve motor to alter the configuration of the intake manifold. When the IMT valve is closed, the intake manifold is divided into two smaller plenums; when the IMT valve is open the intake manifold is one large plenum. The two smaller plenums improve torque during low-speed, high-load conditions. The single larger plenum increases horsepower during high-speed, high-load conditions. For more information on the IMT valve system, refer to Section 19.

26   **Throttle actuator motor** - The throttle actuator motor, which is an electric motor that opens and closes the throttle plate in response to commands from the PCM, is located inside the electronic throttle body. It cannot be serviced separately from the throttle body. For more information about the throttle actuator and the Throttle Actuator Control (TAC) system, refer to Section 20.

27   **Valve Lifter Oil Manifold (VLOM) solenoids** - The VLOM solenoids are components of the Displacement on Demand (DOD) system used on V8 engines. The PCM-controlled VLOM solenoids control the flow of engine oil to special hydraulic lifters used to activate and deactivate cylinders 4 and 6 on the rear cylinder bank and cylinders 1 and 7 on the front bank. The VLOM solenoids are located on the underside of the VLOM itself, which is located on top of the engine block, between the cylinder heads. You have to remove the intake manifold to access anything on the VLOM. For more information about the VLOM solenoids and the DOD system, refer to Section 18.

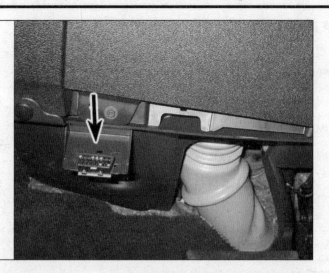

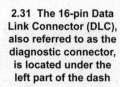

2.31 The 16-pin Data Link Connector (DLC), also referred to as the diagnostic connector, is located under the left part of the dash

28   **Secondary Air Injection Reaction (AIR) system** - 2009 and later 3.5L models are equipped with an AIR system that reduces the amount of unburned hydrocarbons (HC) and carbon monoxide (CO) in the exhaust gases by injecting outside air into the hot exhaust gases flowing from the exhaust manifolds. The AIR system uses an electric air pump mounted on top of the transaxle to inject air into the exhaust system. The AIR system can be monitored and diagnosed using a scan tool to access the trouble codes.

Obtaining and clearing Diagnostic Trouble Codes (DTCs)

29   All models covered by this manual are equipped with on-board diagnostics. When the PCM recognizes a malfunction in a moni-

tored emission control system, component or circuit, it turns on the Malfunction Indicator Light (MIL) on the dash. The PCM will continue to display the MIL until the problem is fixed and the Diagnostic Trouble Code (DTC) is cleared from the PCM's memory. You'll need a scan tool to access any DTCs stored in the PCM.

30   Before outputting any DTCs stored in the PCM, thoroughly inspect ALL electrical connectors and hoses. Make sure that all electrical connections are tight, clean and free of corrosion. And make sure that all hoses are correctly connected, fit tightly and are in good condition (no cracks or tears). Also, make sure that the engine is tuned up. A poorly running engine is probably one of the biggest causes of emission-related malfunctions. Often, simply giving the engine a good tune-up will correct the problem.

Accessing the DTCs

Refer to illustration 2.31

31   On these models, all of which are equipped with On-Board Diagnostic II (OBD-II) systems, the Diagnostic Trouble Codes (DTCs) can only be accessed with a code reader or a scan tool **(see illustrations 2.1 and 2.2)**. Simply plug the connector of the tool into the Data Link Connector (DLC) or diagnostic connector **(see illustration)**, which is located under the lower edge of the dash, just to the right of the steering column. Then follow the instructions included with the scan tool to extract the DTCs.

32   Once you have outputted all of the stored DTCs look them up on the accompanying DTC chart.

33   After troubleshooting the source of each DTC, make any necessary repairs or replace the defective component(s).

Clearing the DTCs

34   Clear the DTCs with the scan tool in accordance with the instructions provided by the scan tool's manufacturer.

Diagnostic Trouble Codes

35   The accompanying tables are a list of the Diagnostic Trouble Codes (DTCs) that can be accessed by a do-it-yourselfer working at home (there are many, many more DTCs available to dealerships with proprietary scan tools and software, but those codes cannot be accessed by a generic scan tool). If, after you have checked and repaired the connectors, wire harness and vacuum hoses (if applicable) for an emission-related system, component or circuit, the problem persists, have the vehicle checked by a dealer service department or other qualified repair shop.

OBD-II Diagnostic Trouble Codes (DTCs)

Note: *Not all trouble codes apply to all models.*

Code	Probable cause
P0010	Camshaft Position (CMP) actuator solenoid control circuit
P0011	Camshaft Position (CMP) system performance
P0016	Crankshaft Position (CKP) sensor/Camshaft Position (CMP) sensor correlation
P0030	Oxygen sensor heater control circuit (bank 1, sensor 1)
P0036	Oxygen sensor heater control circuit (bank 1, sensor 2)
P0050	Oxygen sensor heater control circuit (bank 2, sensor 1)
P0053	Oxygen sensor heater resistance, (bank 1, sensor 1)
P0054	Oxygen sensor heater resistance, (bank 1, sensor 2)
P0068	Throttle body air flow performance

OBD-II Diagnostic Trouble Codes (DTCs) (continued)

Note: *Not all trouble codes apply to all models.*

Code	Probable cause
P0101	Mass Air Flow (MAF) sensor performance
P0102	Mass Air Flow (MAF) sensor circuit, low frequency
P0103	Mass Air Flow (MAF) sensor circuit, high frequency
P0106	Manifold Absolute Pressure (MAP) sensor performance
P0107	Manifold Absolute Pressure (MAP) sensor circuit, low voltage
P0108	Manifold Absolute Pressure (MAP) sensor circuit, high voltage
P0112	Intake Air Temperature (IAT) sensor circuit, low voltage
P0113	Intake Air Temperature (IAT) sensor circuit, high voltage
P0116	Engine Coolant Temperature (ECT) sensor performance
P0117	Engine Coolant Temperature (ECT) sensor circuit, low voltage
P0118	Engine Coolant Temperature (ECT) sensor circuit, high voltage
P0120	Throttle Position (TP) sensor 1 circuit
P0121	Throttle Position (TP) sensor 1 performance
P0122	Throttle Position (TP) sensor 1 circuit, low voltage
P0123	Throttle Position (TP) sensor 1 circuit, high voltage
P0128	Engine coolant temperature below thermostat-regulated temperature
P0131	Oxygen sensor circuit, low voltage (bank 1, sensor 1)
P0132	Oxygen sensor circuit, high voltage (bank 1, sensor 1)
P0133	Oxygen sensor circuit, slow response (bank 1, sensor 1)
P0134	Oxygen sensor circuit, insufficient activity (bank 1, sensor 1)
P0135	Oxygen sensor heater performance (bank 1, sensor 1)
P0136	Oxygen sensor circuit (sensor 2) (5.3L V8)
P0137	Oxygen sensor circuit, low voltage (bank 1, sensor 2)
P0138	Oxygen sensor circuit, high voltage (bank 1, sensor 2)
P0140	Oxygen sensor circuit, insufficient activity (bank 1, sensor 2)
P0141	Oxygen sensor heater performance (bank 1, sensor 2)
P0171	Fuel trim system lean (bank 1)
P0172	Fuel trim system rich (bank 1)

Code	Probable cause
P0201	Injector no. 1 circuit malfunction
P0202	Injector no. 2 circuit malfunction
P0203	Injector no. 3 circuit malfunction
P0204	Injector no. 4 circuit malfunction
P0205	Injector no. 5 circuit malfunction
P0206	Injector no. 6 circuit malfunction
P0207	Injector no. 7 circuit malfunction
P0208	Injector no. 8 circuit malfunction
P0218	Transmission fluid temperature too high
P0220	Throttle Position (TP) sensor 2 circuit
P0222	Throttle Position (TP) sensor 2 circuit, low voltage
P0223	Throttle Position (TP) sensor 2 circuit, high voltage
P0230	Fuel pump relay control circuit
P0300	Engine misfire detected
P0301	Engine misfire detected (cylinder 1)
P0302	Engine misfire detected (cylinder 2)
P0303	Engine misfire detected (cylinder 3)
P0304	Engine misfire detected (cylinder 4)
P0305	Engine misfire detected (cylinder 5)
P0306	Engine misfire detected (cylinder 6)
P0307	Engine misfire detected (cylinder 7)
P0308	Engine misfire detected (cylinder 8)
P0315	Crankshaft Position (CKP) system, system variation not learned
P0324	Knock control system error
P0325	Knock sensor (KS) module performance or knock sensor circuit
P0326	Knock sensor (KS) performance (bank 1)
P0327	Knock sensor (KS) circuit, low frequency (bank 1)
P0328	Knock sensor no. 1 circuit, high input (bank 1 or single sensor)
P0332	Knock sensor (KS) circuit, low frequency (bank 2)
P0333	Knock sensor no. 2 circuit, high input (bank 2)

OBD-II Diagnostic Trouble Codes (DTCs) (continued)

Note: *Not all trouble codes apply to all models.*

Code	Probable cause
P0335	Crankshaft Position (CKP) sensor circuit
P0336	Crankshaft Position (CKP) sensor performance
P0340	Camshaft Position (CMP) sensor circuit
P0341	Camshaft Position (CMP) sensor performance
P0351	Ignition coil 1 control circuit
P0352	Ignition coil 2 control circuit
P0353	Ignition coil 3 control circuit
P0354	Ignition coil 4 control circuit
P0355	Ignition coil 5 control circuit
P0356	Ignition coil 6 control circuit
P0357	Ignition coil 7 control circuit
P0358	Ignition coil 8 control circuit
P0411	Secondary air injection system, incorrect flow detected
P0412	Secondary air injection system switching valve A, circuit malfunction
P0418	Secondary air injection system, relay A circuit malfunction
P0420	Catalyst system, low efficiency (bank 1)
P0442	Evaporative Emission (EVAP) system, small leak detected
P0443	Evaporative Emission (EVAP) system, purge solenoid control circuit
P0446	Evaporative Emission (EVAP) vent system performance
P0449	Evaporative Emission (EVAP) vent solenoid control circuit
P0451	Fuel Tank Pressure (FTP) sensor performance
P0452	Fuel Tank Pressure (FTP) sensor circuit, low voltage
P0453	Fuel Tank Pressure (FTP) sensor circuit, high voltage
P0454	Fuel Tank Pressure (FTP) sensor circuit intermittent
P0455	Evaporative Emission (EVAP) system, large leak detected
P0461	Fuel level sensor circuit performance
P0462	Fuel level sensor circuit, low voltage
P0463	Fuel level sensor circuit, high voltage

Code	Probable cause
P0464	Fuel level sensor circuit intermittent
P0480	Cooling fan relay 1 control circuit
P0481	Cooling fan relays 2 and 3 control circuit
P0496	EVAP system flow during non-purge
P0506	Idle speed low
P0507	Idle speed high
P0513	Theft deterrent key incorrect
P0521	Engine oil pressure (EOP) sensor, performance
P0522	Engine oil pressure (EOP) sensor circuit, low voltage
P0523	Engine oil pressure (EOP) sensor circuit, high voltage
P0532	Air conditioning refrigerant pressure sensor circuit, low voltage
P0533	Air conditioning refrigerant pressure sensor circuit, high voltage
P0556	Brake booster pressure sensor performance
P0557	Brake booster pressure sensor circuit, low voltage
P0558	Brake booster pressure sensor circuit, high voltage
P0562	System voltage low
P0563	System voltage high
P0575	Cruise control switch signal circuit
P0601	Powertrain or Transmission Control Module Read Only Memory (ROM)
P0602	Powertrain or Transmission Control Module not programmed
P0603	Powertrain or Transmission Control Module long-term memory reset
P0604	Powertrain or Transmission Control Module Random Access Memory
P0606	Powertrain Control Module (PCM) internal performance
P0607	Powertrain Control Module (PCM) performance
P060D	Accelerator Pedal Position (APP) system control module performance
P060E	Throttle Position (TP) system control module performance
P0615	Starter relay control circuit
P0621	Alternator L-terminal circuit
P0622	Alternator F-terminal circuit
P062F	Powertrain Control Module (PCM) long-term memory performance

OBD-II Diagnostic Trouble Codes (DTCs) (continued)

Note: *Not all trouble codes apply to all models.*

Code	Probable cause
P062F	Transmission Control Module (TCM) EEPROM error
P0633	Theft deterrent key not programmed
P0641	5-volt reference circuit
P0645	Air conditioning clutch relay control circuit
P0650	Malfunction Indicator Light (MIL) control circuit
P0651	5-volt reference 2 circuit
P0660	Intake Manifold Tuning (IMT) valve solenoid control circuit
P0685	Engine controls ignition relay control circuit
P0689	Engine controls ignition relay feedback circuit, low voltage
P0690	Engine controls ignition relay feedback circuit, high voltage
P0700	Transmission Control Module (TCM) requested MIL illumination
P0703	Brake switch circuit 2
P0711	Transmission Fluid Temperature (TFT) sensor performance
P0712	Transmission Fluid Temperature (TFT) sensor circuit, low voltage
P0713	Transmission Fluid Temperature (TFT) sensor circuit, high voltage
P0716	Input speed sensor performance
P0717	Input Speed Sensor (ISS) circuit, low voltage
P0722	Output Speed Sensor (OSS) circuit, low voltage
P0723	Output Speed Sensor (OSS) circuit, intermittent
P0741	Torque Converter Clutch (TCC) system, stuck off
P0742	Torque Converter Clutch (TCC) system, stuck on
P0751	1-2 Shift Solenoid (SS) valve performance, no 1st or 4th gear
P0752	1-2 Shift Solenoid (SS) valve performance, no 2nd or 3rd gear
P0756	2-3 Shift Solenoid (SS) valve performance, no 1st or 2nd gear
P0757	2-3 Shift Solenoid (SS) valve performance, no 3rd or 4th gear
P0758	2-3 Shift Solenoid (SS) control circuit
P0842	Transmission Fluid Pressure (TFP) sensor circuit, low voltage
P0843	Transmission Fluid Pressure (TFP) sensor circuit, high voltage

Code	Probable cause
P0851	Park/Neutral Position (PNP) switch - input circuit low
P0852	Park/Neutral Position (PNP) switch - input circuit high
P0961	Line Pressure Control (PC) solenoid system performance
P0973	1-2 Shift Solenoid (SS) control circuit, low voltage
P0974	1-2 Shift Solenoid (SS) control circuit, high voltage
P0976	2-3 Shift Solenoid (SS) control circuit, low voltage
P0977	2-3 Shift Solenoid (SS) control circuit, high voltage

3   Accelerator Pedal Position (APP) sensor - replacement

Refer to illustration 3.2

Note: *The APP sensor is located at the top of the accelerator pedal arm. The APP sensor and the accelerator pedal are a one-piece assembly and are replaced as a unit.*

1   Remove the knee bolster (see Chapter 11).

2   Locate the APP sensor at the top of the accelerator pedal assembly **(see illustration)**.

3   Disconnect the electrical connector from the APP sensor.

4   Remove the APP sensor mounting bolts and remove the APP sensor and accelerator pedal as a single assembly.

5   Installation is the reverse of removal. Tighten the APP sensor assembly mounting bolts securely.

4   Camshaft Position (CMP) sensor - replacement

V6 models

Refer to illustration 4.1

Note: *The CMP sensor is located at the front and on top of the block, right behind the timing chain cover.*

1   Disconnect the CMP sensor electrical connector **(see illustration)**.

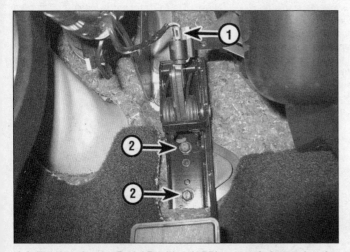

3.2 The Accelerator Pedal Position (APP) sensor is located at the top of the accelerator pedal arm. The accelerator pedal and the APP sensor are a one-piece assembly. To remove the APP sensor/pedal assembly:

1   Disconnect the electrical connector
2   Remove the two APP sensor/pedal assembly mounting bolts

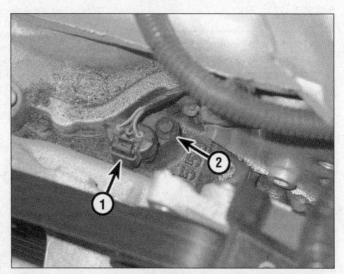

4.1 To remove the Camshaft Position (CMP) sensor from a V6 engine, disconnect the electrical connector (1), then remove the sensor mounting bolt (2)

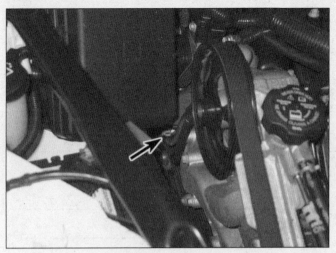

4.6a On V8 engines, the Camshaft Position (CMP) sensor is located on the front of the timing chain cover

4.6b Here's a view of the CMP sensor location with the engine removed

2   Remove the CMP sensor retaining bolt.
3   Remove the CMP sensor.
4   Remove and discard the old CMP sensor O-ring.
5   Installation is the reverse of removal. Be sure to use a new O-ring, lubricate it with a film of clean engine oil, and tighten the CMP sensor bolt securely.

V8 models

Refer to illustrations 4.6a, 4.6b and 4.7

6   Using a flashlight, locate the CMP sensor on the timing chain cover **(see illustrations)**.
7   Disconnect the electrical connector from the CMP sensor **(see illustration)**.
8   Remove the CMP sensor retaining bolt and remove the CMP sensor.
9   Installation is the reverse of removal. Lubricate the O-ring with clean engine oil and be sure to tighten the CMP sensor bolt securely.

---

5   Crankshaft Position (CKP) sensor - replacement

V6 models

Refer to illustration 5.4
Note: *The CKP sensor is located on the back-side (firewall side) of the engine block. If the Malfunction Indicator Light (MIL) comes on after replacing the CKP sensor and starting the engine, drive the vehicle to a dealer and have the service department perform a crankshaft position variation learn procedure with a factory scan tool.*
1   Raise the vehicle and place it securely on jackstands.
2   Disconnect the electrical connector from the CKP sensor.
3   Remove the CKP sensor mounting bolt.
4   Remove and discard the old CKP sensor O-ring **(see illustration)**.
5   Installation is the reverse of removal. Be sure to use a new O-ring and tighten the CKP sensor mounting bolt securely.

V8 models

Refer to illustration 5.8
Note: *The CKP sensor is located on the back-side (firewall side) of the engine block, near the flywheel. If the Malfunction Indicator Light (MIL) comes on after replacing the CKP sensor and starting the engine, take the vehicle to a dealer and have the service department perform a crankshaft position variation learn procedure with a factory scan tool.*
6   Raise the vehicle and place it securely on jackstands.

7   Remove the rear exhaust manifold (see Chapter 2B).
8   Disconnect the electrical connector from the CKP sensor **(see illustration)**.
9   Remove the CKP sensor mounting bolt and remove the CKP sensor.
10   Installation is the reverse of removal. Be sure to tighten the CKP sensor mounting bolt securely.

---

6   Engine Coolant Temperature (ECT) sensor - replacement

Warning: *Wait until the engine is completely cool before beginning this procedure.*

V6 models

Refer to illustration 6.4
Note: *The ECT sensor is located on the left end of the front cylinder head.*
1   Drain the cooling system to a level that's below the level of the ECT sensor (see Chapter 1).

5.4 Be sure to remove the old O-ring from the CKP sensor; always install the sensor with a new O-ring (even if you're installing the old sensor)

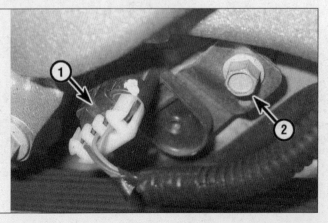

4.7 To remove the CMP sensor from the timing chain cover on a V8 engine, disconnect the electrical connector (1) and remove the sensor mounting bolt (2)

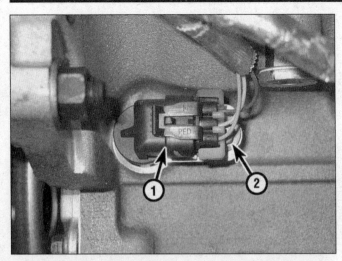

5.8 To remove the CKP sensor from a V8 engine, disconnect the electrical connector (1) and remove the sensor mounting bolt (2)

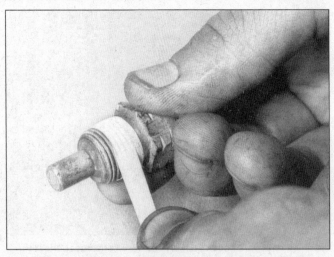

6.4 Before installing the ECT sensor, wrap the threads of the sensor with Teflon tape to prevent leaks

2   Disconnect the electrical connector from the ECT sensor.
3   Unscrew and remove the ECT sensor.
4   Wrap the threads of the new ECT sensor with Teflon tape **(see illustration)**.
5   Installation is the reverse of removal. Be sure to tighten the ECT sensor to the torque listed in this Chapter's Specifications.
6   Refill the cooling system when you're done (see Chapter 1).

V8 models

Refer to illustration 6.8
Note: *The ECT sensor is located at the right end of the front cylinder head, above the No. 1 spark plug.*
7   Drain the cooling system to a level that's below the level of the ECT sensor (see Chapter 1).

8   Disconnect the electrical connector from the ECT sensor **(see illustration)**.
9   Unscrew the ECT sensor and remove it.
10   Wrap the threads of the ECT sensor with Teflon tape **(see illustration 6.4)**.
11   Installation is the reverse of removal. Be sure to tighten the ECT sensor to the torque listed in this Chapter's Specifications.
12   Refill the cooling system when you're done (see Chapter 1).

7   Intake Air Temperature (IAT) sensor - replacement

The IAT sensor is an integral component of the Mass Air Flow (MAF) sensor (see Section 10).

8   Knock sensor - replacement

Note: *There are two knock sensors, one for each side of the block. They're located in the upper middle part of each side of the block, right below the exhaust manifolds.*

V6 models

Refer to illustration 8.2
1   Raise the front of the vehicle and place it securely on jackstands. If you're removing the knock sensor from the rear cylinder bank (bank 1) on a 3.9L V6 engine, remove the catalytic converter.
2   Disconnect the electrical connector from the knock sensor **(see illustration)**.
3   Remove the knock sensor retaining bolt and remove the knock sensor.
4   Installation is the reverse of removal. Be sure to tighten the knock sensor retaining bolt

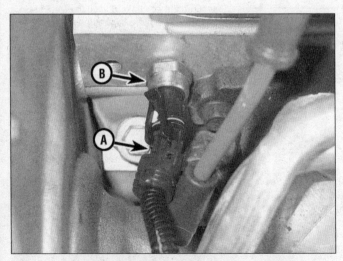

6.8 Disconnect the electrical connector (A) from the ECT sensor (B), then unscrew and remove the sensor (V8 engine)

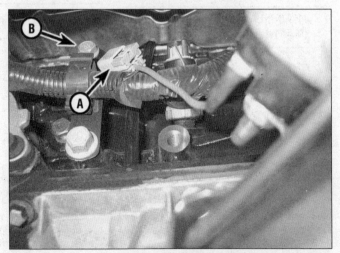

8.2 To detach either of the knock sensors on a V6, disconnect the electrical connector (A), then remove the retaining bolt (B) (knock sensor on the back of the block shown; knock sensor on the front of the block identical)

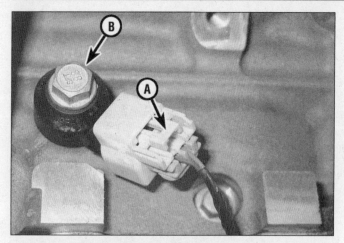

8.7 To remove a knock sensor on a V8 engine, disconnect the electrical connector (A), then remove the retaining bolt (B)

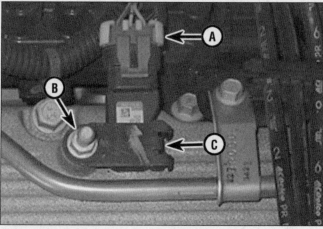

9.1 To remove the MAP sensor from the intake manifold on a V6 engine, disconnect the electrical connector (A), remove the retaining bolt (B), remove the hold-down clamp (C), then pull the sensor straight up

to the torque listed in this Chapter's Specifications.

V8 models

Refer to illustration 8.7

Warning: *Wait until the engine is completely cool before beginning this procedure.*
5   Drain the cooling system (see Chapter 1).
6   Raise the front of the vehicle and place it securely on jackstands.
7   Disconnect the knock sensor electrical connector **(see illustration)**.
8   Remove the knock sensor retaining bolt and remove the knock sensor.
9   Installation is the reverse of removal. Be sure to tighten the knock sensor retaining bolt to the torque listed in this Chapter's Specifications.
10   Refill the cooling system (see Chapter 1).

9   Manifold Absolute Pressure (MAP) sensor - replacement

V6 models

Refer to illustrations 9.1 and 9.3

Note: *The MAP sensor is located on top of and at the left rear corner of the intake manifold.*
1   Disconnect the MAP sensor electrical connector **(see illustration)**.
2   Remove the MAP sensor retaining bolt and the hold-down clamp, then remove the MAP sensor.
3   Remove the old sealing grommet **(see illustration)** from the MAP sensor and inspect it. If the grommet is cracked, torn or otherwise deteriorated, replace it.
4   When installing the MAP sensor, use a little clean engine oil on the grommet so that it doesn't tear when pushing the MAP sensor into its mounting hole. Installation is the reverse of removal.

V8 models

Refer to illustration 9.6

Note: *The MAP sensor is located on the intake manifold, right behind the throttle body.*
5   Remove the engine cover.
6   Disconnect the MAP sensor electrical connector **(see illustration)**.
7   Pull the sensor straight up to remove it.
8   Remove the old sealing grommet **(see illustration 9.3)** from the MAP sensor and inspect it. If the grommet is cracked, torn or otherwise deteriorated, replace it.
9   When installing the MAP sensor, use a little clean engine oil on the grommet so that it doesn't tear when pushing the MAP sensor into its mounting hole. Installation is otherwise the reverse of removal.

10   Mass Air Flow (MAF) sensor - replacement

Refer to illustrations 10.1 and 10.4

Note: *The MAF sensor is located between the air filter housing and the air intake duct. The same unit is used on all models.*
1   Disconnect the electrical connector from

9.3 Remove and inspect the old MAP sensor sealing grommet. If it's cracked, torn or otherwise deteriorated, replace it

the MAF sensor **(see illustration)**.
2   Loosen the hose clamp screw that secures the air intake duct to the MAF sensor.
3   Remove the air filter housing cover and MAF sensor (see Chapter 1).
4   Remove the MAF sensor mounting screws **(see illustration)** and remove the MAF sensor from the filter housing cover.
5   Installation is the reverse of removal.

9.6 To remove the MAP sensor from a V8 engine, disconnect the electrical connector (A) by prying up the locking tab on the connector, then pull the sensor (B) straight up while wiggling it side to side

10.1 Disconnect the electrical connector from the MAF sensor (A) and loosen the hose clamp screw (B) that secures the air intake duct to the MAF sensor

10.4 To detach the MAF sensor from the air filter housing cover, remove these two screws

11   Oxygen sensors - general information and replacement

General information

1   An oxygen sensor is a galvanic battery that produces a very small voltage output in response to the amount of oxygen in the exhaust gases. This voltage signal is the input side of the feedback loop between the oxygen sensor and the Powertrain Control Module (PCM). Without it, the PCM would be unable to correct the injector on-time (which determines the air/fuel ratio) to maintain the perfect (known as stoichiometric) air/fuel ratio of 14.7:1 that the catalyst needs for optimal operation.

2   All vehicles covered by this manual have On-Board Diagnostics II (OBD-II) engine management systems, which means they have the ability to verify the accuracy of the basic feedback loop between the oxygen sensor and the PCM. They accomplish this by using an oxygen sensor ahead of the catalytic converter and another oxygen sensor behind the catalytic converter. By comparing the amount of oxygen in the post-catalyst exhaust gas to the oxygen content of the exhaust gas before it enters the catalyst, the PCM can determine the efficiency of the converter.

3   All models covered by this manual have two heated oxygen sensors: one upstream sensor (ahead of the catalytic converter) and a downstream oxygen sensor (after the catalyst). The upstream sensor is located on the rear exhaust manifold, right above the flange. The downstream sensor is located under the vehicle, in the exhaust pipe right behind the catalytic converter. You'll have to raise the vehicle to access the downstream sensor.

All models

4   The upstream and downstream oxygen sensors on all models are heated to speed up the warm-up time during which the sensors are unable to produce an accurate voltage signal. The circuit for each oxygen sensor heater is controlled by the PCM, which opens the ground side of the circuit to shut off the heater as soon as the sensor reaches its normal operating temperature.

5   Special care must be taken whenever a sensor is serviced.

a) *Oxygen sensors have a permanently attached pigtail and an electrical connector that cannot be removed. Damaging or removing the pigtail or electrical connector will render the sensor useless.*

b) *Keep grease, dirt and other contaminants away from the electrical connector and the louvered end of the sensor.*

c) *Do not use cleaning solvents of any kind on an oxygen sensor.*

d) *Oxygen sensors are extremely delicate. Do not drop a sensor, throw it around or handle it roughly.*

e) *Make sure that the silicone boot on the sensor is installed in the correct position. Otherwise, the boot might melt and it might prevent the sensor from operating correctly.*

Replacement

Note: *Because it is installed in the exhaust manifold or exhaust pipe, both of which contract as they cool down, an oxygen sensor can be very difficult to loosen when the engine is cold. Rather than risk damage to the sensor or its mounting threads, start and run the engine for a minute or two, then shut it off. Be careful not to burn yourself during the following procedure.*

Upstream oxygen sensor

Refer to illustrations 11.7 and 11.8

Note: *The upstream oxygen sensor is located on the rear exhaust manifold, right above the flange. You can access it from above, but there's not a lot of room to work. You'll also need an oxygen sensor socket.*

6   If you don't have enough room to work, remove the ignition coil assembly from the rear valve cover (V6 models, see *Ignition coil pack - removal and installation* in Chapter 5; V8 models, see *Spark plug check and replacement* in Chapter 1).

7   If necessary, detach the locator clip for the upstream oxygen sensor electrical connector from its mounting stud **(see illustration)**, then disconnect the connector.

11.7 If necessary, detach the locator clip for the upstream oxygen sensor electrical connector from its mounting stud, then disconnect the connector (V8 shown)

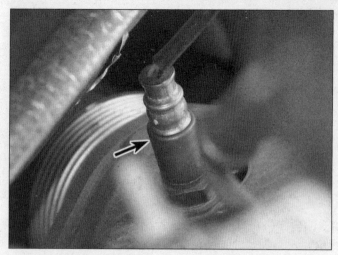

11.8 Using an oxygen sensor socket, unscrew the upstream oxygen sensor from the exhaust manifold

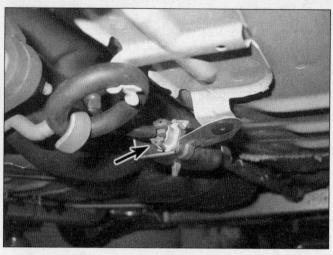

11.12 Locate the downstream oxygen sensor connector, then disconnect it

8   Using an oxygen sensor socket (available at most auto parts stores), unscrew the upstream oxygen sensor **(see illustration)**. If the sensor is difficult to loosen, spray some penetrant onto the sensor threads and allow it to soak in for awhile.
9   If you're going to install the old sensor, apply anti-seize compound to the threads of the sensor to facilitate future removal. If you're going to install a new oxygen sensor, it's not necessary to apply anti-seize compound to the threads. The threads on new sensors already have anti-seize compound on them.
10   Installation is otherwise the reverse of removal. Be sure to tighten the sensor to the torque listed in this Chapter's Specifications.

Downstream oxygen sensor

Refer to illustrations 11.12 and 11.13
Note: *The downstream oxygen sensor is located on top of the exhaust pipe right behind*

the catalytic converter.
11   Raise the vehicle and place it securely on jackstands.
12   Locate the downstream oxygen sensor **(see illustration)** then trace the sensor electrical lead to the connector and disconnect it.
13   Unscrew the downstream oxygen sensor **(see illustration)** with an oxygen sensor socket. If the sensor is difficult to loosen, spray some penetrant onto the sensor threads and allow it to soak in for awhile.
14   If you're going to install the old sensor, apply anti-seize compound to the threads of the sensor to facilitate future removal. If you're going to install a new oxygen sensor, it's not necessary to apply anti-seize compound to the threads. The threads on new sensors already have anti-seize compound on them.
15   Installation is otherwise the reverse of removal. Be sure to tighten the sensor to the torque listed in this Chapter's Specifications.

12   Vehicle Speed Sensor (VSS) - replacement

Refer to illustrations 12.2, 12.3a and 12.3b
Note: *There are two transmission speed sensors: the Input Shaft Speed (ISS) sensor and the Vehicle Speed Sensor (VSS). The ISS is located inside the transaxle and cannot be replaced at home. It must be replaced by a dealer service department or by a qualified transmission shop. This Section covers the VSS, which is located on the upper right end of the transaxle, near the right inner CV joint.*
1   Loosen the right front wheel lug nuts, raise the front of the vehicle and place it securely on jackstands. Remove the right front wheel.
2   Disconnect the electrical connector from the VSS **(see illustration)**.
3   Remove the VSS hold-down bolt **(see**

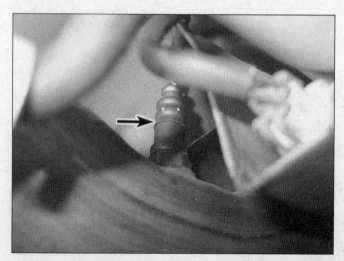

11.13 Using an oxygen sensor socket, unscrew the downstream oxygen sensor from the exhaust pipe

12.2 Disconnect the electrical connector from the Vehicle Speed Sensor (VSS)

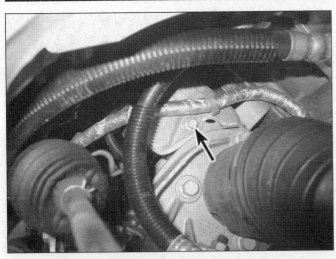

12.3a Unscrew this bolt and remove the shield . . .

12.3b . . . then remove the hold-down bolt and pull the sensor out of the transaxle housing

illustrations) and remove the VSS from the transaxle.

4   Remove the old O-ring from the VSS and discard it. Be sure to use a new O-ring when installing the VSS (even if you're planning to reuse the old VSS sensor).

5   Installation is the reverse of removal. Be sure to tighten the VSS hold-down bolt securely.

13 Powertrain Control Module (PCM) and Transmission Control Module (TCM) - removal and installation

Refer to illustrations 13.3, 13.4, 13.5, 13.7 and 13.8

Caution: *To avoid electrostatic discharge damage to the PCM, handle the PCM only*
by its case. Do not touch the electrical termi-nals during removal and installation. If avail-able, ground yourself to the vehicle with an anti-static ground strap, available at computer supply stores.

Note 1: *The PCM and TCM are mounted inside the air filter housing, which is located on the left side of the engine compart-ment.*

Note 2: *The procedures in this section apply only to disconnecting, removing and installing the PCM and TCM that are already installed in your vehicle. If, for example, you need to remove the air filter housing, you will have to disconnect the PCM and TCM and pull the PCM/TCM harness out of the air filter hous-ing. Or, if you need to replace the air filter housing, you will have to remove the PCM and the TCM from the old filter housing and install them in the new filter housing. If, how-*
ever, you need to replace the PCM or TCM, it must be programmed with new software and calibrations. This procedure requires the use of GM's TECH-2 scan tool and GM's lat-est PCM-programming software, so you WILL NOT BE ABLE TO REPLACE THE PCM OR TCM AT HOME.

1   Disconnect the cable from the negative terminal of the battery (see Chapter 5, Sec-tion 1).

2   Remove the air filter element (see Chap-ter 1), then remove the upper portion of the air filter housing.

3   The PCM and the TCM are installed in the floor of the air filter housing **(see illustration)**.

4   Lift the TCM out of the air filter housing, then disconnect the electrical connector **(see illustration)** and remove the TCM.

5   Lift the PCM out of the air filter housing, then disconnect the electrical connectors from

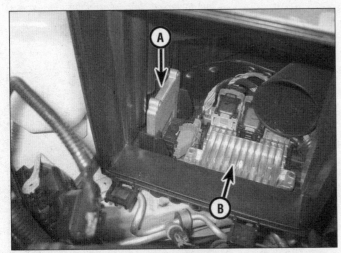

13.3 The TCM (A) and the PCM (B) are located inside the air filter housing

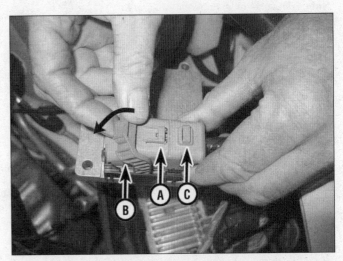

13.4 To unlock the electrical connector from the TCM, depress the release tab (A) and pivot the lock (B) to its release position. When connecting the connector, be sure to pivot the lock back to its locked position between the release tab and the locator tab (C)

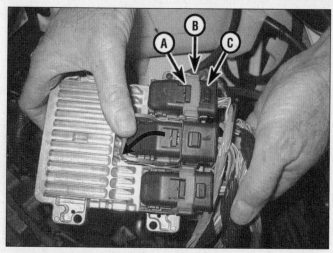

13.5 To unlock the three electrical connectors from the PCM, depress each release tab (A) and pivot the lock (B) to its release position. When connecting the three connectors, be sure to pivot the locks back to their locked position between the release tabs and the locator tabs (C)

13.7 When installing the PCM into the air filter housing, make sure that it snaps into place between the locator tabs

the PCM **(see illustration)** and remove the PCM.

6   When connecting the electrical connectors to the PCM and the TCM, make sure that the locks are fully seated between their locator tabs.

7   When installing the PCM into the air filter housing, make sure that it snaps into place between the locator tabs **(see illustration)**.

8   When installing the TCM into the filter housing, make sure that it's secured by the two locator ribs **(see illustration)**.

9   Installation is otherwise the reverse of removal.

14 Catalytic converter - description, check and replacement

Note: *Because of a Federally-mandated extended warranty which covers emission-related components such as the catalytic converter, check with a dealer service department before replacing the converter at your own expense.*

Description

1   A catalytic converter (or catalyst) is an emission control device in the exhaust system that reduces certain pollutants in the exhaust gas stream. There are two types of converters. An oxidation catalyst reduces hydrocarbons (HC) and carbon monoxide (CO). A reduction catalyst reduces oxides of nitrogen (NOx). Catalysts that can reduce all three pollutants are known as three-way catalysts. The models covered by this manual are equipped with three-way catalysts.

Check

2   The test equipment for a catalytic converter (a loaded-mode dynamometer and a five-gas analyzer) is expensive. If you sus-

pect that the converter on your vehicle is malfunctioning, take it to a dealer or authorized emission inspection facility for diagnosis and repair.

3   Whenever you raise the vehicle to service underbody components, inspect the converter for leaks, corrosion, dents and other damage. Carefully inspect the welds and/or flange bolts and nuts that attach the front and rear ends of the converter to the exhaust system. If you note any damage, replace the converter.

4   Although catalytic converters don't break too often, they can become plugged up. The easiest way to check for a restricted converter is to use a vacuum gauge to diagnose the effect of a blocked exhaust on intake vacuum.

a) *Connect a vacuum gauge to an intake manifold vacuum source (see Chapter 2).*

b) *Warm the engine to operating temperature, place the transaxle in Park (automatic models) or Neutral (manual models) and apply the parking brake.*

c) *Note the vacuum reading at idle and write it down.*

d) *Quickly open the throttle to near its wide-open position and then quickly get off the throttle and allow it to close. Note the vacuum reading and write it down.*

e) *Do this test three more times, recording your measurement after each test.*

f) *If your fourth reading is more than one in-Hg lower than the reading that you noted at idle, the exhaust system might be restricted (the catalytic converter could be plugged, OR an exhaust pipe or muffler could be restricted).*

Replacement

Refer to illustrations 14.7 and 14.8

Note: *The catalytic converter is located underneath the vehicle, at the lower end of the downpipe connected to the rear exhaust manifold flange.*

5   Raise the vehicle and place it securely on jackstands.

13.8 When installing the TCM into the air filter housing, make sure that it's secured by these two locator ribs

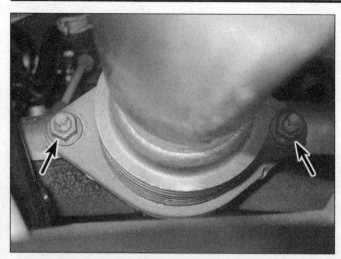

14.7 To disconnect the upper flange of the catalyst/exhaust pipe assembly from the exhaust manifold flange, remove these two nuts

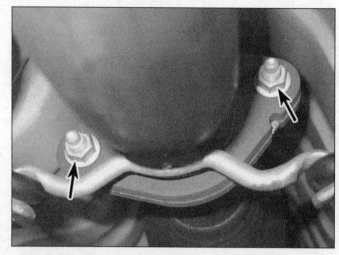

14.8 To disconnect the rear flange of the catalyst/exhaust pipe assembly from the rest of the exhaust pipe assembly, remove these two nuts

6   Disconnect the electrical connector for the downstream oxygen sensor and remove the sensor **(see illustrations 11.12 and 11.13)**.

7   Remove the two nuts **(see illustration)** that secure the upper flange of the catalyst/exhaust pipe assembly to the exhaust manifold flange.

8   Remove the two nuts **(see illustration)** that secure the rear flange of the catalyst/exhaust pipe assembly to the rest of the exhaust system and remove the catalyst/exhaust pipe assembly.

9   Remove and discard the old flange gaskets from both mounting flanges. Be sure to use new gaskets at both mounting flanges. Also use new fasteners at both flanges.

10   Coat the threads of the nuts and bolts with anti-seize compound to facilitate future removal. Tighten the nuts that secure the catalyst/exhaust pipe assembly to the exhaust manifold securely. Installation is otherwise the reverse of removal

15   Evaporative emissions control (EVAP) system - description and component replacement

Description

1   The Evaporative Emissions Control (EVAP) system prevents fuel system vapors (which contain unburned hydrocarbons) from escaping into the atmosphere. On warm days, vapors trapped inside the fuel tank expand until the pressure reaches a certain threshold, at which point the fuel vapors are routed from the fuel tank through the fuel vapor vent valve and the fuel vapor control valve to the EVAP canister, where they're stored temporarily, until they can be consumed by the engine during normal operation. When the conditions are right (engine warmed up, vehicle up to speed, moderate or heavy load on the engine, etc.)

the Powertrain Control Module (PCM) opens the canister purge solenoid, which allows the fuel vapors to be drawn from the canister into the intake manifold, where they mix with the air/fuel mixture before being consumed in the combustion chambers. This system is complex and virtually impossible to troubleshoot without the right tools and training. However, the following description should give you a good idea of how it works:

2   The EVAP canister is located under the vehicle, on top of the fuel tank. The EVAP canister, which contains activated charcoal, is the repository for storing the fuel vapors. You'll have to raise the vehicle and lower the fuel tank to inspect or replace the canister (or the fuel tank pressure sensor) but the canister is designed to be maintenance-free and should last the life of the vehicle.

3   The fuel tank pressure sensor, which is located on top of the mounting flange for the in-tank fuel pump/fuel level sending unit module, monitors the pressure inside the tank, and transmits its measurement to the PCM during an OBD-II leak test.

4   The EVAP canister vent solenoid, which is mounted behind the left rear wheel well fender liner, is normally open. But it seals off the EVAP system for inspection and maintenance (I/M 240) testing and for OBD-II leak and pressure tests.

5   The EVAP canister purge solenoid, which is under the control of the Powertrain Control Module (PCM), regulates the flow of vapors being purged from the EVAP canister into the intake manifold. The canister purge solenoid is normally closed. It opens only when directed to do so by the PCM, which uses the availability of intake manifold vacuum and data from various information sensor inputs to determine when and how long to open the valve. The interval of time during which the purge valve is opened by the PCM is known as its duty cycle. On V6 engines the purge valve is located on the left end of the intake manifold,

near the throttle body. On V8 engines, it's located on top of the intake manifold.

General system checks

6   The most common symptom of a faulty EVAP system is a strong fuel odor (particularly during hot weather). If you smell fuel while driving or (more likely) right after you park the vehicle and turn off the engine, check the fuel filler cap first. Make sure that it's screwed onto the fuel filler neck all the way. If the odor persists, inspect all EVAP hose connections, both in the engine compartment and under the vehicle. You'll have to raise the vehicle and place it securely on jackstands to inspect most of the EVAP system, since it's located under the vehicle. Be sure to inspect each hose attached to the canister for damage and leakage along its entire length. Repair or replace as necessary. Inspect the canister for damage and look for fuel leaking from the bottom. If fuel is leaking or the canister is otherwise damaged, replace it.

7   Poor idle, stalling, and poor driveability can be caused by a defective fuel vapor vent valve or canister purge solenoid, a damaged canister, cracked hoses, or hoses connected to the wrong tubes. Fuel loss or fuel odor can be caused by fuel leaking from fuel lines or hoses, a cracked or damaged canister, or a defective vapor valve.

8   To check for excessive fuel vapor pressure in the fuel tank, remove the gas cap and listen for the sound of pressure release. If the fuel tank emits a whooshing sound when you open the filler cap, fuel tank vapor pressure is excessive. Inspect the canister vapor hoses and the canister inlet port for blockage or collapsed hoses. Also inspect the vapor vent valve. A complete test can only be done with a proprietary OBD-II scan tool, which will run a series of checks to detect excessive pressure. You'll have to take the vehicle to a dealer service department or other qualified repair shop to have the EVAP system professionally diagnosed.

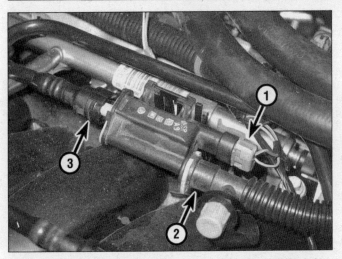

15.14 To remove the EVAP canister purge valve from a V8 engine, disconnect the electrical connector (1), disconnect the quick-connect fitting for the EVAP purge inlet line (2) and the quick-connect fitting for the EVAP purge outlet line (3) . . .

15.16 . . . then slide the purge valve straight up to disengage it from its mounting bracket

Component replacement

EVAP canister purge solenoid

V6 engines

Note: *The EVAP canister purge solenoid is located at the left front corner of the intake manifold, in front of the throttle body.*

9   Disconnect the canister purge solenoid electrical connector.

10   Disconnect the EVAP purge line quick-connect fitting from the canister purge solenoid. Cap the line to prevent dirt, dust and moisture from entering the EVAP system while the line is open. If you're unfamiliar with quick-connect fittings, refer to Section 4 in Chapter 4.

11   Remove the canister purge solenoid mounting bolt and remove the purge solenoid.

12   Installation is the reverse of removal.

V8 engines

Refer to illustrations 15.14 and 15.16

Note: *The EVAP canister purge valve is located on top of the rear part of the intake manifold.*

13   Remove the engine cover.

14   Disconnect the electrical connector from the EVAP canister purge valve **(see illustration)**.

15   Disconnect the EVAP purge line quick-connect fittings from the canister purge solenoid. Cap both lines to prevent dirt, dust and moisture from entering the EVAP system while the line is open.

16   To remove the canister purge valve simply slide it straight up off its mounting bracket **(see illustration)**.

17   Installation is the reverse of removal.

EVAP canister vent solenoid

Refer to illustration 15.19

Note: *The EVAP canister vent solenoid is located in the void behind the left rear wheel well.*

18   Raise the vehicle and place it securely on jackstands.

19   Disconnect the electrical connector from the vent solenoid **(see illustration)**.

20   Disconnect the EVAP hose from the vent solenoid.

21   To disengage the vent solenoid from its

mounting bracket, slide it straight up.

22   Installation is the reverse of removal.

EVAP canister

Note: *The EVAP canister is located on top of the fuel tank.*

23   Raise the vehicle and place it securely on jackstands.

24   Remove the fuel tank (see Chapter 4).

25   Disconnect all electrical connectors from the EVAP canister.

26   Clearly label all EVAP hoses connected to the EVAP canister, then disconnect the hoses from the canister.

27   Detach the EVAP canister from its mounting bracket.

28   Installation is otherwise the reverse of removal.

Fuel tank pressure sensor

Note: *The fuel tank pressure sensor is located on top of the fuel pump/fuel level sensor module mounting flange.*

29   Raise the vehicle and place it securely on jackstands.

30   Remove the fuel tank (see Chapter 4).

31   Disconnect the electrical connector from the fuel tank pressure sensor.

32   Remove the fuel tank pressure sensor from the fuel pump/fuel level sensor module mounting flange.

33   Installation is the reverse of removal.

---

16   Positive Crankcase Ventilation (PCV) system - description, check and component replacement

---

Description

Refer to illustration 16.2

1   The Positive Crankcase Ventilation (PCV) system reduces hydrocarbon emissions by scavenging crankcase vapors, which are rich in unburned hydrocarbons.

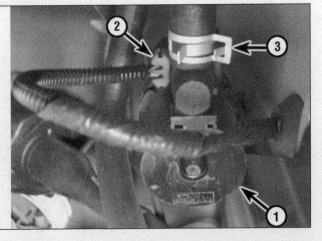

15.19 To remove the EVAP canister vent solenoid (1), disconnect the electrical connector (2), loosen the spring-type hose clamp (3) and pull off the EVAP hose, then slide the vent solenoid straight up to disengage it from its mounting bracket

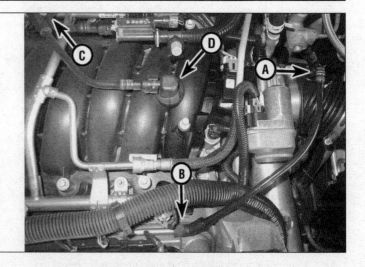

16.2 Typical PCV system on a V8 engine:

A   *Fresh air is drawn from the air intake duct through the fresh air inlet hose . . .*
B   *. . . into the crankcase, via a pipe on the front valve cover*
C   *Crankcase vapors are drawn from the crankcase through a pipe on the rear valve cover (under the alternator, but not visible here), then through the crankcase ventilation hose . . .*
D   *. . . and into the intake manifold, where they're mixed with the incoming air/fuel mixture and consumed*

2   The PCV system **(see illustration)** uses a fixed orifice, which is located on top of the intake manifold. There are two hoses in this system. The fresh air inlet hose carries outside air from the air intake duct to a pipe on the front valve cover, then into the crankcase, where it mixes with blow-by gases and crankcase vapors. These vapors are drawn from the crankcase through a pipe on the rear valve cover (under the alternator), through the crankcase ventilation hose (PCV hose), then into the intake manifold, where they mix with the incoming air. The PCV valve is located in the PCV hose, in the hose that connects the rear valve cover to the intake manifold.

Check

3   Without a properly functioning crankcase ventilation system, an engine can be damaged. So anytime you're servicing the engine, be sure to inspect the PCV system hoses for cracks, tears and other damage. Disconnect the hoses and check for damage and obstructions. If a hose is clogged, clean it out. If you're unable to clean it satisfactorily, replace it.
4   A plugged PCV hose might cause any or all of the following conditions: A rough idle, stalling or a slow idle speed, oil leaks or sludge in the engine. So if the engine is running roughly, stalling and idling at a lower than normal speed, losing oil, has oil in the throttle body or air intake manifold plenum, or has a build-up of sludge, a PCV system hose might be clogged. Repair or replace the hoses as necessary. Make sure that it's clean by blowing it out with compressed air.
5   A leaking PCV hose might cause any or all of the following conditions: a rough idle, stalling or a high idle speed. So if the engine is running roughly, stalling and idling at a higher than normal speed, a PCV system hose might be leaking. Repair or replace the hose.
6   Here's an easy functional check of the PCV system:
a)   *Disconnect the PCV hose from the front valve cover (V6 models) or from the rear valve cover (V8 models).*

b)   *Start the engine and let it warm up to its normal idle.*
c)   *Verify that there is vacuum at the PCV hose. If there is no vacuum, look for a plugged hose or manifold port.*
d)   *Remove the engine oil dipstick and install a vacuum gauge on the upper end of the dipstick tube.*
e)   *Block off the PCV fresh air inlet hose.*
f)   *Run the engine at 1500 rpm for 30 seconds, then read the vacuum gauge while the engine is running at 1500 rpm.*
g)   *If there's vacuum present, the crankcase ventilation system is operating correctly.*
h)   *If there's NO vacuum present, the engine might be drawing in outside air. The PCV system won't function correctly unless the engine is a sealed system. Inspect the valve cover gaskets and the oil pan gasket for leaks.*
i)   *If the vacuum gauge indicates positive pressure, look for a plugged hose or engine blow-by.*

7   If the PCV system is functioning correctly, but there's evidence of engine oil in the throttle body or air filter housing, it could be caused by excessive crankcase pressure. Have the crankcase pressure tested by a dealer service department or other repair shop.
8   In this type of PCV system, excessive blow-by (caused by worn rings, pistons and/or cylinders, or by constant heavy loads) is discharged into the intake manifold and consumed. If you discover heavy sludge deposits or a dilution of the engine oil, even though the PCV system is functioning correctly, look for other causes (see *Troubleshooting* and refer to Chapter 2C) and correct them as soon as possible.

Component replacement
V6 models

Fresh air inlet hose

9   Disconnect the fresh air inlet hose from the air intake duct **(see illustration 16.2)**.
10   Disconnect the fresh air inlet hose from the rear valve cover.

11   Installation is otherwise the reverse of removal.

Crankcase ventilation hose (PCV hose)

12   Disconnect the crankcase ventilation hose from the front valve cover **(see illustration 16.2)**.
13   Disconnect the crankcase ventilation hose from the intake manifold.
14   Installation is otherwise the reverse of removal.

PCV fixed orifice

15   The PCV fixed orifice cannot be replaced. If it becomes necessary to clean it, flush the orifice with solvent and compressed air. In extreme cases, the valve cover may be removed (see Chapter 2) to gain access to its rear.

V8 models

Fresh air inlet hose

16   Disconnect the fresh air inlet hose from the air intake duct.
17   Disconnect the fresh air inlet hose from the pipe on the front valve cover.
18   Installation is the reverse of removal.

Crankcase ventilation hose (PCV hose)

19   Disconnect the crankcase ventilation hose from the pipe on the rear valve cover.
20   Disconnect the crankcase ventilation hose from the intake manifold.
21   Installation is the reverse of removal.

17   Camshaft actuator system (V6 models) - description and component replacement

Description

1   The camshaft actuator system, which is used on V6 engines, reduces emissions, improves engine torque, increases fuel mileage and stabilizes engine idle by controlling the amount of intake and exhaust valve overlap.

18.7 To remove the VLOM oil filter and O-ring, disconnect the electrical connector from the VLOM oil pressure sensor . . .

18.8 . . . unscrew the sensor with a deep socket and remove the sensor and washer . . .

2   The camshaft actuator system consists of the Powertrain Control Module (PCM), the camshaft actuator solenoid and the *cam phaser*, which is a variable camshaft timing sprocket. The actuator solenoid opens and closes two passages through which oil flows to the hydraulically operated variable camshaft timing sprocket on the front end of the camshaft. The PCM uses a pulse-width modulated signal to control the camshaft actuator solenoid, which responds by directing oil through one of the two passages feeding oil to the variable cam timing sprocket. When oil is directed by the solenoid through one passage, the variable cam sprocket advances the camshaft timing; when oil is directed through the other passage, the sprocket retards cam timing.

Component replacement

Variable camshaft timing sprocket
3   To replace the variable camshaft timing sprocket, refer to *Timing chain and sprockets - removal, inspection and installation* in Chapter 2B.

Camshaft actuator solenoid
Note: *The camshaft actuator solenoid is located on the upper front part of the timing chain cover, directly in front of the camshaft.*
4   Remove the engine cover.
5   Remove the air intake duct and air filter housing (see Chapter 4).
6   Remove the engine mount strut bracket.
7   Disconnect the electrical connector from the camshaft actuator solenoid.
8   Remove the camshaft actuator solenoid mounting bolts and remove the solenoid.
9   Remove and discard the old O-ring.
10   Installation is the reverse of removal. Be sure to use a new O-ring and tighten the solenoid mounting bolts securely.

18   Displacement on Demand (DOD) system (V8 models) - description and component replacement

Description
1   The Displacement on Demand (DOD) system, which GM refers to as the Cylinder Deactivation (Active Fuel Management) system on 2007 and later models, improves fuel economy and lowers emissions by deactivating four of the engine's eight cylinders. During starting, idling and medium or heavy throttle conditions, the engine operates normally. But during light-load cruising, the Powertrain Control Module (PCM) deactivates cylinders one and seven in the front cylinder bank and cylinders two and four in the rear cylinder bank, effectively turning the engine into a V4.
2   The DOD system consists of the Valve Lifter Oil Manifold (VLOM) assembly and eight specially designed valve lifters (four intake and four exhaust) for the DOD cylinders. The VLOM assembly consists of four electrically-operated solenoids. Each solenoid directs the flow of pressurized engine oil to the DOD intake and exhaust valve lifters. An oil pressure sensor, which is mounted on the left end of the VLOM assembly, monitors engine oil pressure and functions as an information sensor for the PCM. An oil filter, which is located directly below the oil pressure sensor, helps control contamination inside the DOD hydraulic system. An oil pressure relief valve, which is located at the left rear corner of the oil pan, regulates engine oil pressure to the lubrication system and to the VLOM assembly.
3   When operating in V8 mode, the DOD valve lifters function just like conventional lifters. The solenoids in the VLOM assembly are in their closed position and no pressurized oil is directed to the valve lifters. Spring-loaded

locking pins in the lifters extend outward, mechanically locking the pin housings to the outer bodies of the valve lifters.
4   When the conditions are right, the PCM grounds each solenoid control circuit in firing order sequence, which allows current to flow through the solenoid windings. When the solenoid windings are energized, the normally-closed solenoid valves open, which directs pressurized engine oil through the VLOM assembly into eight vertical oil passages in the engine block lifter valley. The eight vertical passages, two per cylinder, direct pressurized oil to the lifter bores of the DOD cylinders. The pressurized oil forces the locking pins inside the lifters inward, locking up the pushrods and preventing them from traveling up and down. The outer bodies of the lifters continue moving up and down independently of the pin housings.
5   When the PCM turns off the DOD system, the solenoids in the VLOM assembly close, blocking the flow of pressurized oil to the valve lifters. The oil pressure within the lifters decreases and the locking pins again move out to mechanically lock up the pin housing with the outer lifter body.

Component replacement

VLOM oil pressure sensor and oil filter
Refer to illustrations 18.7, 18.8 and 18.9
6   Remove the engine cover.
7   Disconnect the electrical connector from the VLOM oil pressure sensor **(see illustration)**.
8   Remove the VLOM oil pressure sensor **(see illustration)** and remove the sensor washer.
9   Remove the oil filter and the filter O-ring **(see illustration)**. If the filter is plugged or the O-ring is cracked, torn or otherwise deterio-

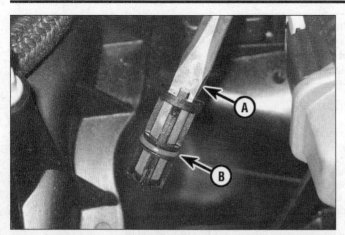

18.9 . . . then, carefully wedge the tip of a screwdriver (A) into the top of the oil filter and pull out the filter. Inspect the condition of the mesh screen of the filter and the condition of the O-ring (B). If either is damaged, replace the filter and O-ring as a set

18.14 Disconnect the electrical connector from the VLOM solenoid

rated, replace the filter and O-ring as a set.
10   Installation is the reverse of removal.

Valve Lifter Oil Manifold (VLOM) assembly

Refer to illustrations 18.14, 18.15 and 18.16
11   Remove the engine cover.
12   Disconnect the electrical connector from the VLOM oil pressure sensor **(see illustration 18.7)**.
13   Remove the intake manifold (see Chapter 2B).
14   Disconnect the electrical connector from the VLOM solenoid terminal **(see illustration)**.
15   Remove the VLOM assembly mounting bolts **(see illustration)** and remove the VLOM assembly. **Caution:** *Be careful not to lose the small sleeves located in the mounting bolt holes of the VLOM assembly.*

16   Inspect the VLOM assembly gasket **(see illustration)**. If it's cracked, torn or otherwise deteriorated, replace it.
17   Installation is the reverse of removal. Be sure to tighten the VLOM assembly mounting bolts to the torque listed in this Chapter's Specifications.

19   Intake Manifold Tuning (IMT) valve system - description and component replacement

Description

Note: *The IMT system is used only on 3.9L V6 models.*
1   When intake air is drawn into the cylinders at idle or at low engine speeds, less air is needed because the cylinders don't need

to be filled so often or so quickly. So at idle and at low engine speeds, the air drawn into an engine with smaller intake runners will have a higher velocity than one with larger intake runners. However, at higher engine speeds, smaller intake runners would prevent the cylinders from filling quickly enough and would therefore limit power. Most intake manifold designs are a compromise between the conflicting demands of low and high engine speeds.
2   The Intake Manifold Tuning (IMT) Valve system helps to maintain a uniformly higher intake air velocity throughout the engine's operating range. Higher intake air velocity promotes better vaporization of the fuel sprayed into the stream of incoming air by the fuel injectors, which means more complete combustion, more power, better fuel economy and fewer emissions.

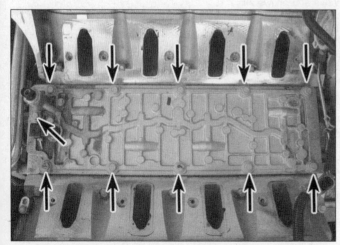

18.15 To detach the VLOM assembly from the engine, remove these mounting bolts

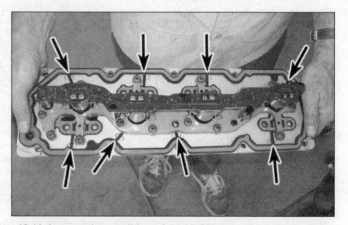

18.16 Inspect the condition of the VLOM assembly gasket. If it's cracked, torn or otherwise deteriorated, replace it. To remove the original gasket from the VLOM assembly, carefully cut the eight retaining straps at the indicated points to separate the outer gasket (the part that you're going to replace) from the rest of the original gasket (which you're not going to replace, and which doesn't need to be replaced)

3   The IMT Valve system consists of the Powertrain Control Module (PCM), a special intake manifold with an IMT valve inside the manifold, and a PCM-controlled solenoid that opens and closes the IMT valve. When the IMT valve is open, the intake manifold is configured as one large plenum. When the IMT valve is closed, the intake manifold is divided into smaller plenums.

4   When the engine is operating at a lower speed but under a higher load, the IMT valve is closed, so incoming air is directed through a longer path. Directing incoming air through a longer path increases torque.

5   When the engine speed and load are both high, the IMT valve is open, which creates a shorter intake path. Directing incoming air through a shorter intake path increases horsepower.

Component replacement

Intake Manifold Tuning (IMT) valve solenoid

Note: *The IMT valve solenoid is located on the intake manifold.*

6   Disconnect the electrical connector from the IMT valve solenoid.

7   Remove the IMT valve solenoid mounting screws and remove the solenoid.

8   Installation is the reverse of removal. Tighten the solenoid screws securely.

Intake manifold

9   Refer to Chapter 2B.

20   Throttle Actuator Control (TAC) system - description

The Throttle Actuator Control (TAC) system, which is used on all vehicles, is an electronic throttle control system - there is no mechanically actuated accelerator cable. When the engine is running, the TAC system constantly monitors the position of the accelerator pedal and responds by constantly altering the position of the throttle plate inside the throttle body. The TAC system also handles cruise control functions.

The TAC system consists of three principal components: the Accelerator Pedal Position (APP) sensor, the Powertrain Control Module (PCM) and the throttle body. The replacement procedure for the APP sensor is covered in Section 3, the removal and installation procedure for the PCM is covered in Section 13 and the removal and installation procedure for the throttle body is covered in Chapter 4.

21   Secondary Air Injection Reaction (AIR) system - general description, check and component replacement

General description

Note: *2009 and later 3.5L V6 engines are equipped with a Secondary Air Injection (AIR) system.*

1   The air injection exhaust emission control system reduces the level of unburned hydrocarbons (HC) and carbon monoxide (CO) in the exhaust by injecting outside air into the hot exhaust gases flowing through the exhaust manifolds. When fresh air is mixed with the hot exhaust gases, oxidation is increased, reducing the concentration of hydrocarbons and carbon monoxide and converting them into harmless carbon dioxide and water.

2   The AIR system consists of the electric AIR pump, the control solenoid, the control relays, the pressure sensor, the shut-off valve, the check valves, and the hoses and pipes connecting all of these components. **Note:** *The AIR control solenoid, the shut-off valve and the pressure sensor are replaced as a complete unit.*

3   **AIR pump** - The AIR pump draws in filtered, outside air and pumps it into the exhaust manifolds. The pump is turned on and off by a relay. The ground path for the PCM-controlled pump relay is through the PCM. When the PCM closes the ground path, battery voltage is applied to the pump.

4   **AIR control solenoid** - The AIR control solenoid activates the AIR shut-off valve. When the PCM turns on the AIR system, it grounds the two AIR relays and the control solenoid, which allows the opening of the AIR shut-off valve.

5   **AIR shut-off valve** - The AIR shut-off valve is actuated by the AIR control solenoid. When the AIR system is operating, the PCM supplies a ground to the solenoid, which opens the AIR shut-off valve and allows air from the AIR pump to reach the check valves.

6   **AIR pump and AIR control solenoid relays** - The relays supply battery voltage and high current to the AIR pump and the AIR control solenoid. The PCM commands the relay ON by supplying a ground circuit.

7   When the coolant temperature is 45-degrees F or more, or when the vehicle is decelerating (high intake vacuum, rich air/fuel mixture, lots of unburned hydrocarbons and carbon monoxide in the exhaust), the PCM energizes the AIR pump relay, which energizes the electric clutch, at which point the pump begins pumping air into the exhaust system.

8   The PCM may turn off the AIR pump when the system is in closed-loop operation, when one or more Diagnostic Trouble Codes

(DTCs) are set by the PCM, when the system is in the power-enrichment mode for too long, when intake manifold vacuum is low or when the rise in intake vacuum is too quick (rapid deceleration).

Check

9   Checking the PCM-controlled, electric-pump-equipped AIR systems is beyond the scope of the home mechanic. Have the AIR system checked out by a dealer service department or other qualified repair shop.

Component replacement

10   Disconnect the cable from the negative battery terminal (see Chapter 5).

AIR shut-off valve

11   Remove the exhaust crossover pipe from the rear of the cylinder heads directly above the transaxle bellhousing.

12   Disconnect the quick-connect fittings from the upper section of the inlet hose on the AIR shut-off valve. Refer to Chapter 4 for information on removing plastic quick-connect fittings similar to the fuel line fittings.

13   Remove the inlet hose mounting bolt from the upper section near the AIR shut-off valve.

14   Disconnect the electrical connector from the shut-off valve.

15   Raise the vehicle and support it securely on jackstands.

16   Working below the engine, remove the mounting nuts from the AIR shut-off valve extension pipe to the reactor pipe. **Note:** *The AIR control solenoid, the shut-off valve and the pressure sensor are replaced as a complete unit.*

17   Working on the upper section of the engine, remove the AIR shut-off valve mounting bolts from the mounting bracket.

18   Installation is the reverse of removal. Tighten all fasteners securely.

AIR pump

19   Remove the air filter housing (see Chapter 4).

20   Disconnect the quick-connect fittings from the upper section of the inlet hose. Refer to Chapter 4 for information on disconnecting plastic quick-connect fittings similar to the fuel line fittings.

21   Raise the vehicle and support it securely on jackstands.

22   Disconnect the quick-connect fittings from the lower section of the inlet hose from the AIR pump.

23   Disconnect the electrical connectors from the AIR pump and from the AIR solenoid valve.

24   Remove the AIR pump mounting nuts, then remove the pump from the transaxle bracket.

25   Installation is the reverse of removal. Tighten all fasteners securely.

Chapter 7
Automatic transaxle

Contents

Specifications

Torque specifications
Ft-lbs

Transaxle-to-engine bolts 66
Driveplate-to-torque converter bolts 46
Fluid pan bolts .... See Chapter 1

1 General information

The vehicles covered by this manual are equipped with the 4T65-E Hydra-matic automatic transaxle, an electronically-controlled four speed model.

Due to the complexity of the clutches and the hydraulic control system, and because of the special tools and expertise required to perform an automatic transaxle overhaul, it is not included in this manual. Therefore, the procedures in this Chapter are limited to general diagnosis, adjustment and transaxle removal and installation.

If the transaxle requires major repair work it should be left to a dealer service department or an automotive or transmission repair shop. You can, however, remove and install the transaxle yourself and save the expense, even if the repair work is done by a transmission specialist.

Adjustments that the home mechanic may perform include those involving the shift cable and the Brake Transmission Shift Interlock (BTSI) system.

2   Diagnosis - general

Note: *Automatic transaxle malfunctions may be caused by five general conditions: poor engine performance, improper adjustments, hydraulic malfunctions, mechanical malfunctions or malfunctions in the Powertrain Control Module or its signal network. Diagnosis of these problems should always begin with a check of the easily repaired items: fluid level and condition (see Chapter 1), and shift cable adjustment (see Section 4). Next, perform a road test to determine if the problem has been corrected or if more diagnosis is necessary. Because the transaxle relies on many sensors in the engine control system, and since the transaxle shift points are controlled by the Powertrain Control Module, you'll also want to check to see if any trouble codes have been stored in the PCM (see Chapter 6 for a list of trouble codes and how to extract them). If the problem persists after the preliminary tests and corrections are completed, additional diagnosis should be done by a dealer service department or transmission repair shop. Refer to the Troubleshooting Section at the front of this manual for transaxle problem diagnosis.*

Preliminary checks

1   Drive the vehicle to warm the transaxle to normal operating temperature.
2   Check the fluid level as described in Chapter 1:

   a) *If the fluid level is unusually low, add enough fluid to bring the level within the designated area of the dipstick, then check for external leaks.*

   b) *If the fluid level is abnormally high, drain off the excess, then check the drained fluid for contamination by coolant. The presence of engine coolant in the automatic transmission fluid indicates that a failure has occurred in the internal radiator walls that separate the coolant from the transmission fluid (see Chapter 3).*

   c) *If the fluid is foaming, drain it and refill the transaxle, then check for coolant in the fluid or a high fluid level.*

3   Check the engine idle speed. **Note:** *If the engine is malfunctioning, do not proceed with the preliminary checks until it has been repaired and runs normally.*
4   Inspect the shift cable (see Section 4). Make sure that it's properly adjusted and that it operates smoothly.
5   Check the Transaxle Range (TR) sensor adjustment (see Chapter 6).

Fluid leak diagnosis

6   Most fluid leaks are easy to locate visually. Repair usually consists of replacing a seal or gasket. If a leak is difficult to find, the following procedure may help.
7   Identify the fluid. Make sure it's transmission fluid and not engine oil or brake fluid (automatic transmission fluid is a deep red color).

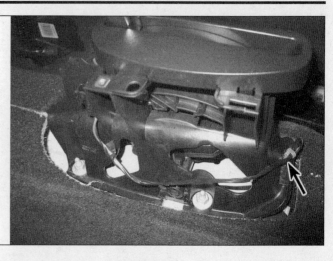

3.2 Disconnect the wiring from the shifter assembly

8   Try to pinpoint the source of the leak. Drive the vehicle several miles, then park it over a large sheet of cardboard. After a minute or two, you should be able to locate the leak by determining the source of the fluid dripping onto the cardboard.
9   Make a careful visual inspection of the suspected component and the area immediately around it. Pay particular attention to gasket mating surfaces. A mirror is often helpful for finding leaks in areas that are hard to see.
10   If the leak still cannot be found, clean the suspected area thoroughly with a degreaser or solvent, then dry it.
11   Drive the vehicle for several miles at normal operating temperature and varying speeds. After driving the vehicle, visually inspect the suspected component again.
12   Once the leak has been located, the cause must be determined before it can be properly repaired. If a gasket is replaced but the sealing flange is bent, the new gasket will not stop the leak. The bent flange must be straightened.
13   Before attempting to repair a leak, check to make sure that the following conditions are corrected or they may cause another leak. **Note:** *Some of the following conditions cannot be fixed without highly specialized tools and expertise. Such problems must be referred to a transmission shop or a dealer service department.*

Gasket leaks

14   Check the pan periodically. Make sure the bolts are tight, no bolts are missing, the gasket is in good condition and the pan is flat (dents in the pan may indicate damage to the valve body inside).
15   If the pan gasket is leaking, the fluid level or the fluid pressure may be too high, the vent may be plugged, the pan bolts may be too tight, the pan sealing flange may be warped, the sealing surface of the transaxle housing may be damaged, the gasket may be damaged or the transaxle casting may be cracked or porous. If sealant instead of gasket material has been used to form a seal between the pan and the transaxle housing, it may be the wrong sealant.

Seal leaks

16   If a transaxle seal is leaking, the fluid level or pressure may be too high, the vent may be plugged, the seal bore may be damaged, the seal itself may be damaged or improperly installed, the surface of the shaft protruding through the seal may be damaged or a loose bearing may be causing excessive shaft movement.
17   Make sure the dipstick tube seal is in good condition and the tube is properly seated. Periodically check the area around the speedometer gear or sensor for leakage. If transmission fluid is evident, check the O-ring for damage. Also inspect the driveaxle oil seals for leakage.

Case leaks

18   If the case itself appears to be leaking, the casting is porous and will have to be repaired or replaced.
19   Make sure the oil cooler hose fittings are tight and in good condition.

Fluid comes out vent pipe or fill tube

20   If this condition occurs, the transaxle is overfilled, there is coolant in the fluid, the case is porous, the dipstick is incorrect, the vent is plugged or the drain back holes are plugged.

3   Shift lever - removal and installation

Refer to illustrations 3.2, 3.3a and 3.3b
Warning: *The models covered by this manual are equipped with a Supplemental Restraint System (SRS), more commonly known as airbags. Always disarm the airbag system before working in the vicinity of any airbag system component to avoid the possibility of accidental deployment of the airbag, which could cause personal injury (see Chapter 12). Do not use a memory saving device to preserve the PCM's memory when working on or near airbag system components.*
1   Remove the top console cover plate (see Chapter 11).
2   Unplug the console wiring harness and set it aside **(see illustration)**.

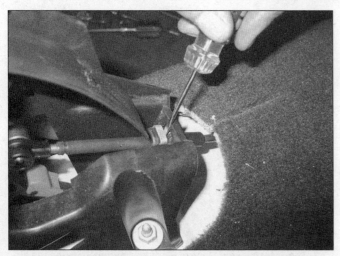

3.3a Use a small screwdriver to release the shifter cable from its mount . . .

3.3b . . . then pry the cable end from the mounting stud

3   Disconnect the shifter cable (see illustrations).
4   Disconnect the lamp from the shifter base.
5   Remove the four mounting nuts from their studs and lift the shifter assembly out.
6   Installation is the reverse of removal.

4   Shift cable - replacement and adjustment

Warning: *The models covered by this manual are equipped with a Supplemental Restraint System (SRS), more commonly known as airbags. Always disarm the airbag system before working in the vicinity of any airbag system component to avoid the possibility of accidental deployment of the airbag, which could cause personal injury (see Chapter 12). Do not use a memory saving device to preserve the PCM's memory when working on or near airbag system components.*

4.4 To disengage the shift cable from the cable bracket on the transaxle, remove this clip then squeeze the two locking tangs and pull the cable housing from the bracket

Replacement

Refer to illustration 4.4

1   Refer to Chapter 4 and remove the throttle body air inlet duct.
2   Release the cable from all retaining clips and retainers.
3   Pry the cable end off of the transaxle selector lever ball stud.
4   Disconnect the cable from the retaining bracket near the lever by squeezing the tabs on the cable housing (see illustration).
5   Refer to Section 3 and disconnect the cable from the shift lever.
6   Tie a piece of wire or cord to the end of the cable before removing it completely. This will allow you to fish the new cable through easier.
7   Slide the cable out the front of the shifter assembly, under the carpet and out through the firewall.
8   Installation is the reverse of removal. Be sure to adjust the new cable after installing it.

Adjustment

2006 models

9   Detach the cable from the manual lever on the transaxle. Place the manual lever on the transaxle in the Neutral position; this is accomplished by rotating the lever clockwise from the Park position, through Reverse and into Neutral.
10   Place the shift lever inside the car in Neutral.
11   Pull up on the cable adjuster tab at the cable bracket on the transaxle, then connect the cable to the manual lever on the transaxle. The cable will automatically adjust itself. Push the adjuster tab back into place.
12   Make sure the engine will start in the Park and Neutral positions only.
13   If the engine can be started in any position other than Park or Neutral, check the adjustment of the Transmission Range Sensor (see Chapter 6), then adjust and check the shift cable again.

2007 and later models

14   Place the shift lever inside the vehicle to Park. Set the parking brake.
15   Pull back the white part of the plastic connector and pull up on the center tabs of the lock button.
16   Without grabbing the shift cable end, release the cable end; this will allow the cable spring to adjust and tension the cable.
17   Pull the white part of the plastic connector back to its original position and push the lock button back into place.
18   If the engine can be started in any other position other than Park or Neutral, the cable must be adjusted. Check that all the gear positions can be selected. If any cannot, then the cable needs to be adjusted.

5   Brake Transmission Shift Interlock (BTSI) system - description and component replacement

Warning: *The models covered by this manual are equipped with a Supplemental Restraint System (SRS), more commonly known as airbags. Always disarm the airbag system before working in the vicinity of any airbag system component to avoid the possibility of accidental deployment of the airbag, which could cause personal injury (see Chapter 12). Do not use a memory saving device to preserve the PCM's memory when working on or near airbag system components.*

Description

1   The Brake Transmission Shift Interlock (BTSI) system prevents the shift lever from being moved out of Park unless the brake pedal is depressed simultaneously. It also prevents the ignition key from being removed from the ignition switch unless the shift lever is in the Park position. When the car is started, the BTSI (Brake Transmission Shift Interlock) solenoid is

6.4 The driveaxle oil seal can generally be pried out with a large screwdriver, but in some cases a slide hammer with a hooked end will have to be used

7.3 The Transmission Control Module is mounted inside the air cleaner housing - it is the module at the side of the housing

energized, locking the shift lever in Park; when the brake pedal is depressed, the solenoid is de-energized, unlocking the shift lever so that it can be moved into some other gear.

BTSI solenoid replacement
Early models
2   Remove the center console (see Chapter 11).
3   Unplug the electrical connector from the BTSI solenoid.
4   Pry off each end of the BTSI solenoid assembly from the ball sockets and remove it from the shift lever base.
5   Installation is the reverse of removal.

Late models
6   The shift interlock solenoid is an integral part of the shifter assembly. Refer to Section 3 for information on replacement of the shifter.

---

6   Driveaxle oil seals - replacement

Removal

Refer to illustration 6.4

1   Oil leaks frequently occur due to wear of the driveaxle oil seals. Replacement of these seals is relatively easy, since the repairs can be performed without removing the transaxle from the vehicle.
2   The driveaxle oil seals are located in the sides of the transaxle, where the driveaxles are attached. If leakage at the seal is suspected, raise the vehicle and support it securely on jackstands. If the seal is leaking, fluid will be found on the sides of the transaxle.
3   Remove the driveaxles (see Chapter 8).
4   Pry the oil seal from the transaxle, taking care to avoid damaging the aluminum bore **(see illustration)**. Usually, a large flat-blade screwdriver will suffice, however a slide hammer with a hook end may be required on the right side on some models.

Installation
5   Note how deep the seal is installed, then use a screwdriver or prybar to carefully pry the oil seal out of the transaxle bore. If the oil seal cannot be removed with a screwdriver or prybar, a special oil seal removal tool (available at most auto parts stores) will be required.
6   Compare the old seal to the new one to be sure it's the correct one.
7   Coat the outside and inside diameters of the new seal with a small amount of transmission fluid.
8   Using a seal installation tool, install the new oil seal. Drive it into the bore squarely and make sure it's seated to the original depth.
9   Install the driveaxle (see Chapter 8).
10   Installation is the reverse of removal. Check the transaxle fluid level, adding as necessary (see Chapter 1).

---

7   Transmission Control Module (TCM) - removal and installation

---

Refer to illustrations 7.3 and 7.4
Caution: *The TCM is an Electro-Static Dis-charge (ESD) sensitive electronic device, meaning a static electricity discharge from your body could possibly damage electrical components. Be sure to properly ground yourself and the TCM before handling it. Avoid touching the electrical terminals of the TCM.*
Note: *The procedures in this section apply only to removing and installing the TCM that is already installed in your vehicle. If you need a new TCM, it must be programmed with new software and calibrations. This procedure requires the use of GM's TECH-2 scan tool and GM's latest TCM-programming software, so you WILL NOT BE ABLE TO REPLACE THE TCM AT HOME.*
1   Disconnect the cable from the negative terminal of the battery (see Chapter 5, Section 1).
2   Refer to Chapter 4 and remove the upper section of the air cleaner housing. This will expose the electronic modules in the base of the air cleaner housing.
3   Slide the TCM out of its retainer **(see illustration)**.
4   Swing the lever to the fully released position **(see illustration)**. Pull the connector off of the TCM.
5   Installation is the reverse of removal.

7.4 Pull the safety lever out; this will release it so that it can be fully rotated and allow the connector to be detached from the TCM

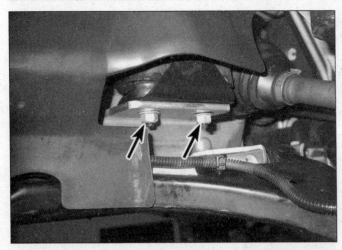

8.10 The transaxle mount is bolted to the subframe at this point - the subframe must be removed from the vehicle to allow the transaxle to be lowered

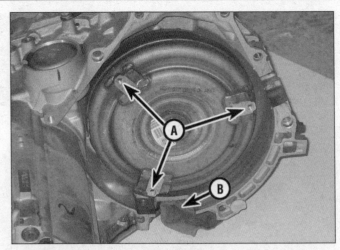

8.12 The driveplate is bolted to the torque converter at three points (A) - rotate the engine by turning the crankshaft with a large ratchet and socket, then remove the bolts through the access hole (B)

8 Automatic transaxle - removal and Installation

Refer to illustrations 8.10, 8.12, 8.13a, 8.13b and 8.18

Removal

1   Disconnect the cable from the negative battery terminal (see Chapter 5, Section 1). Loosen the front wheel lug nuts.
2   Remove the engine cover from its mounting studs.
3   Remove the air inlet duct from the throttle body and the air cleaner housing (see Chapter 4).
4   Label and then disconnect all transaxle wiring and grounds that are accessible from the top.
5   Use a screwdriver to pry the transaxle shifter cable from the lever on top of the transaxle. Disconnect the cable from the bracket and move it out of the way.

6   Raise the vehicle high enough to easily remove the transaxle and jack from below. Support it securely on jackstands.
7   Attach an engine support fixture or an engine hoist to the engine and raise it enough to support its weight. **Note 1:** *The engine must remain supported while the transaxle is out of the vehicle.* **Note 2:** *If you use an engine hoist, position it with its legs inserted under the passenger side. This will give enough room to maneuver the transaxle out using a floor jack.*
8   Remove the upper transaxle-to-engine bolts.
9   Remove the front wheels and both inner fender splash shields (see Chapter 11).
10   Remove the subframe (see Chapter 10) **(see illustration)**.
11   Remove the starter (see Chapter 5).
12   Remove the torque converter bolt access cover, then remove the driveplate-to-torque converter bolts **(see illustration)**. Use a ratchet and socket on the crankshaft balancer

bolt to rotate the torque converter for access to all three bolts.
13   Disconnect the transaxle cooler lines from the transaxle. On V8 models, pull off the plastic covers from the fittings, then use a small screwdriver to pry out the small wire retaining clips **(see illustrations)**. Note how the protrusions of the clips seat into slots in the fittings.
14   Remove both driveaxles (see Chapter 8). **Note:** *With the subframe removed, you will be able to pull out on the steering knuckles far enough to remove the driveaxles (it won't be necessary to separate the control arm ball-joints from the steering knuckles as described in Chapter 8).*
15   Disconnect the vehicle speed sensor. It is located under a heat shield near the steering gear on V8 models.
16   Support the transaxle with a jack, preferably one made for this purpose. Transmission jacks are commonly available at equipment rental yards. These jacks are equipped with

8.13a There is a plastic cover over the transaxle cooler line ends; pry it loose with a small screwdriver

8.13b The retaining clips engage in small slots; they must be installed with their protrusions securely snapped into the slots

8.18 The transaxle is quite tall so make sure you have plenty of clearance under the front of the vehicle to remove it

safety chains; use these chains to secure the transaxle to the jack.

17   Remove the lower transaxle-to-engine mounting bolts.

18   Remove the transaxle by sliding it away from the engine and then lowering it **(see illustration)**.

Installation

19   Installation is the reverse of removal, with attention paid to the following points:

a) *Before installing the transaxle, make sure the torque converter is completely seated. To do this, push in on the converter while turning it. If it wasn't seated, it will "clunk" into place (it may even "clunk" more than once).*

b) *Apply a film of multi-purpose grease to the nose of the converter.*

c) *When mating the transaxle to the engine, make sure the transaxle seats against the engine completely before tightening the bolts; if it doesn't, figure out why. Don't use the bolts to draw the transaxle into place, as you could break something.*

d) *Tighten all transaxle-to-engine bolts to the torque listed in this Chapter's Specifications.*

e) *Tighten the torque converter-to-driveplate bolts to the torque listed in this Chapter's Specifications.* **Note:** *Install all of the bolts before tightening any of them.*

f) *Tighten the subframe mounting bolts to the torque listed in the Chapter 10 Specifications. Also tighten the intermediate shaft pinch bolt, the control arm*

balljoint-to-steering knuckle nuts and the tie-rod end-to-steering knuckle nuts to the torque values listed in the Chapter 10 Specifications.

g) *Tighten the transmission (powertrain) mounting fasteners securely.*

h) *Tighten the wheel lug nuts to the torque listed in the Chapter 1 Specifications.*

i) *The front end alignment should be checked and, if necessary, adjusted.*

j) *Adjust the shift cable (see Section 4).*

k) *Check the transaxle fluid level and add fluid, as necessary, to bring it to the appropriate level (see Chapter 1).*

9   Automatic transaxle overhaul - general information

In the event of a fault occurring, it will be necessary to establish whether the fault is electrical, mechanical or hydraulic in nature, before repair work can be contemplated. Diagnosis requires detailed knowledge of the transaxle's operation and construction, as well as access to specialized test equipment, and so is deemed to be beyond the scope of this manual. It is therefore essential that problems with the automatic transaxle are referred to a dealer service department or other qualified repair facility for assessment.

Note that a faulty transaxle should not be removed before the vehicle has been assessed by a knowledgeable technician equipped with the proper tools, as troubleshooting must be performed with the transaxle installed in the vehicle.

Chapter 8
Driveaxles

Contents

Specifications

Inner CV joint boot length	3.75 inches

Torque specifications

	Ft-lbs
Driveaxle/hub nut	118
Wheel lug nuts	See Chapter 1

1 Driveaxles - general information and inspection

1   Power is transmitted from the transaxle to the wheels through a pair of driveaxles. The inner end of each driveaxle is connected to the transaxle, directly splined to the differential side gears. The outer ends of the driveaxles are splined to the axle hubs and locked in place by a large nut.

2   The inner ends of the driveaxles are equipped with sliding constant velocity joints, which are capable of both angular and axial motion. Each inner joint assembly consists of a tripod bearing and a joint tulip (housing) in which the joint is free to slide in-and-out as the driveaxle moves up-and-down with the wheel. The joints can be disassembled and cleaned in the event of a boot failure, but if any parts are damaged, the joints must be replaced as a unit (see Section 3).

3   Each outer joint, which consists of ball bearings running between an inner race and an outer race (housing), is capable of angular but not axial movement.

4   The boots should be inspected periodically for damage and leaking lubricant. Torn CV joint boots must be replaced immediately or the joints can be damaged. Boot replacement involves removal of the driveaxle (see Section 2). **Note:** *Some auto parts stores carry "split" type replacement boots, which can be installed without removing the drive-axle from the vehicle. This is a convenient alternative; however, the driveaxle should be removed and the CV joint disassembled and cleaned to ensure the joint is free from con-taminants such as moisture and dirt which will accelerate CV joint wear.* The most common symptoms of worn or damaged CV joints, besides lubricant leaks, are a clicking noise in turns, a clunk when accelerating after coasting and vibration at highway speeds. To check for wear in the CV joints and driveaxle shafts, grasp each axle (one at a time) and rotate it in both directions while holding the CV joint housings, feeling for play indicating worn splines or sloppy CV joints. Also check the driveaxle shafts for cracks, dents and distortion.

2.2 To prevent the hub from turning while you're loosening the driveaxle hub nut, wedge a prybar between two of the wheel studs

2.6 To loosen the driveaxle from the hub splines, tap the end of the driveaxle with a soft-faced hammer

2   Driveaxles - removal and installation

Warning: *The manufacturer recommends replacing the driveaxle/hub nuts with new ones whenever they are removed.*

Removal

Refer to illustrations 2.2, 2.6 and 2.9

1   Loosen the front wheel lug nuts, raise the vehicle and support it securely on jackstands. Remove the wheel.

2   Remove the driveaxle/hub nut with a large socket and breaker bar **(see illustration).**

3   It's not absolutely necessary that you drain the transaxle lubricant prior to removing a driveaxle, but if the mileage on the odometer indicates that the transaxle is nearing the lubricant-change interval prescribed in Chapter 1, now is a good time to do it.

4   Disconnect the tie-rod end from the steering knuckle, and the stabilizer link from the lower control arm (see Chapter 10).

5   Separate the steering knuckle from the strut (see Chapter 10).

6   To loosen the driveaxle from the hub splines, tap the end of the driveaxle with a soft-faced hammer **(see illustration).** If the driveaxle is stuck in the hub splines and won't move, it may be necessary to push it from the hub with a puller.

7   Pull out on the steering knuckle and detach the driveaxle from the hub. Suspend the outer end of the driveaxle on a bungee cord or piece of wire.

8   Before you remove the driveaxle, look for lubricant leakage in the area around the differential seal. If there's evidence of a leak, you'll want to replace the seal after removing the driveaxle (see Chapter 7).

9   Position a prybar against the inner joint and carefully pry the joint from the transaxle **(see illustration).** Do not use the driveaxle to pull on the inner joint. Doing so might damage the inner joint components. Remove the driveaxle assembly, being careful not to over-extend the inner joint or damage the axleshaft boots.

10   Should it become necessary to move the vehicle while the driveaxle is out, place a large bolt with two large washers (one on each side of the hub) through the hub and tighten the nut securely.

Installation

11   Installation is the reverse of removal, but with the following additional points:

a)   Apply a film of multi-purpose grease around the splines of the joints.

b)   When installing the driveaxle, hold the driveaxle straight out, then push it in sharply to seat the driveaxle set-ring. To make sure the set-ring is properly seated, attempt to pull the inner CV joint housing out of the transaxle by hand. If the set-ring is properly seated, the inner joint will not move out.

c)   Clean all foreign matter from the drive-axle outer CV joint threads and coat the splines with multi-purpose grease. Guide the driveaxle into the hub splines and install the new driveaxle/hub nut. Tighten the nut securely but not to the specified torque at this time.

d)   Reconnect the steering knuckle and tie-rod end, then tighten the suspension fasteners to the torque listed in the Chapter 10 Specifications.

e)   Tighten the driveaxle/hub nut to the torque listed in this Chapter's Specifications.

f)   Install the wheel and lug nuts, then lower the vehicle.

g)   Tighten the wheel lug nuts to the torque listed in the Chapter 1 Specifications.

h)   Add transaxle lubricant if it was drained or if any fluid spilled out (see Chapter 1).

2.9 Using a prybar, carefully pry the joint from the transaxle

3   Driveaxle boot replacement

Note: *If the CV joint boots must be replaced, explore all options before beginning the job. Complete rebuilt driveaxles are available on an exchange basis, which eliminates much time and work. Whichever route you choose to take, check on the cost and availability of parts before disassembling the vehicle.*

1   Remove the driveaxle (see Section 2).

3.3a Cut off the boot retaining clamps and discard them

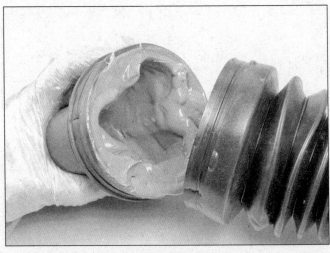

3.3b Slide the housing and bushing off the spider assembly

2   Place the driveaxle in a vise lined with rags to avoid damage to the axleshaft. Check the CV joint for excessive play in the radial direction, which indicates worn parts. Check for smooth operation throughout the full range of motion for each CV joint. If a boot is torn, disassemble the joint, clean the components and inspect for damage due to loss of lubrication and possible contamination by foreign matter.

Inner CV joint

Refer to illustrations 3.3a through 3.3t

3   To replace the inner boot, refer to the accompanying illustrations **(see illustrations 3.3a through 3.3t).**

3.3c Slide the boot towards the center of the driveaxle

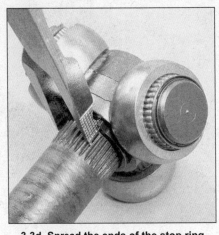

3.3d Spread the ends of the stop ring apart and slide it towards the center of the shaft

3.3e Slide the spider assembly back to expose the retaining ring, then pry off the ring

3.3f Carefully tap the spider off the axleshaft with a brass punch (but don't hit it so hard that it flies off, or you'll be picking up needle bearings!)

3.3g When you slide the spider off the driveaxle, hold the bearings in place with your hand; even better, use tape or a cloth wrapped around the spider bearing assembly to retain them

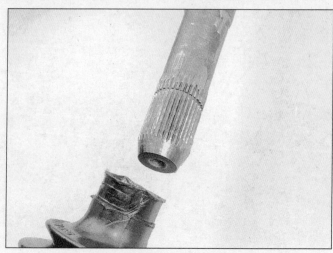

3.3h Slide the boot and the stop ring off the axleshaft

3.3i Clean all of the old grease out of the housing and spider assembly, then remove each bearing, one at time

3.3j Carefully disassemble each section of the spider assembly, clean the needle bearings with solvent and inspect the rollers, spider cross, bearings and housing for scoring, pitting and other signs of abnormal wear

3.3k Apply a coat of CV joint grease to the inner bearing surfaces to hold the needle bearings in place, then slide the bearing over them

3.3l Wrap the axleshaft splines with tape to avoid damaging the boot, then slide the small clamp and boot onto the axleshaft

3.3m Slide the spider stop ring onto the axleshaft, past the groove in which it seats

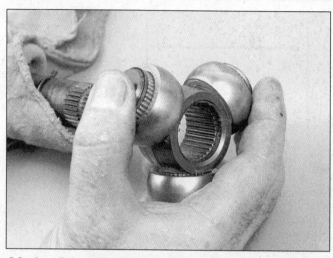

3.3n Install the spider bearing with the recess in the counterbore facing the end of the driveaxle

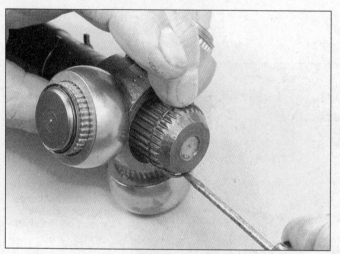

3.3o Install the spider retaining ring, then slide the spider assembly against it and install the stop ring in its groove

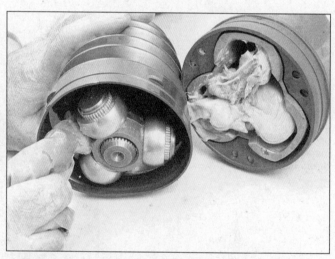

3.3p Pack the housing with half of the grease furnished with the new boot and place the remainder in the boot

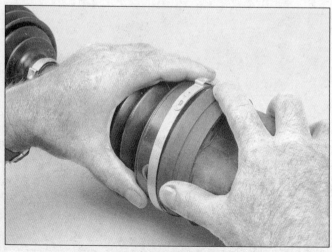

3.3q Install the bushing to the tripot housing, then with the retaining clamps in place (but not tightened), install the tripot housing

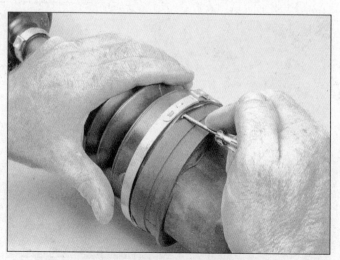

3.3r Seat the boot in the housing and axle seal grooves - a small screwdriver can make the job easier (make sure the boot isn't dimpled, stretched or out of shape)

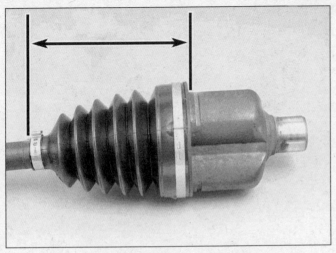

3.3s Adjust the CV joint to the length listed in this Chapter's Specifications

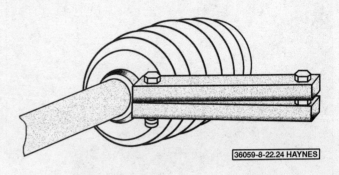

36059-8-22.24 HAYNES

3.3t With the joint at the proper length, equalize the pressure in the boot by inserting a small screwdriver between the boot and the housing, then secure the boot clamps with a clamp crimping tool (available at auto parts stores)

Outer CV joint

Refer to illustrations 3.4a through 3.4q

4   Refer to the accompanying illustrations and perform the outer CV joint boot replacement procedure **(see illustrations 3.4a through 3.4q).**

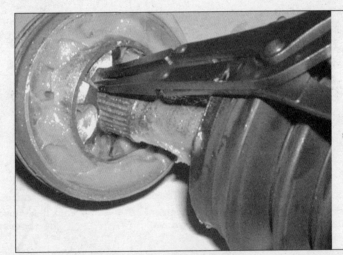

3.4a Cut off the boot retaining clamps, and slide the boot back, spread apart the ends of the internal snapring, then slide the CV joint off the shaft

3.4b Press down on the inner race far enough to allow a ball bearing to be removed - if it's difficult to tilt, gently tap the cage and inner race with a brass punch and hammer

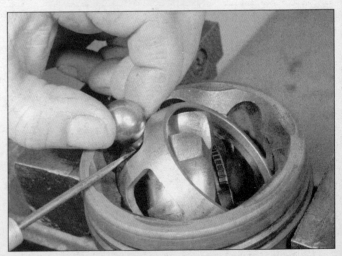

3.4c Pry the balls out of the cage, one at a time

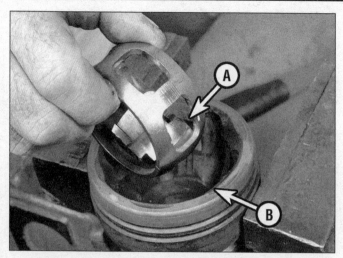

3.4d Tilt the inner race and cage 90-degrees, then align the windows in the cage (A) with the lands of the housing (B) and rotate the inner race up and out of the outer race

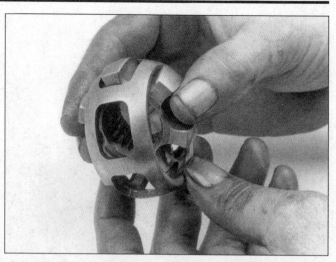

3.4e Align the inner race lands with the cage window and rotate the inner race out of the cage

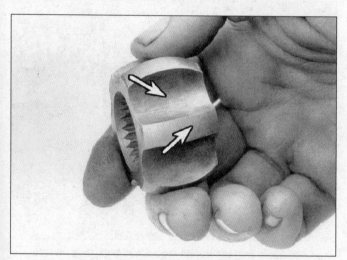

3.4f After cleaning the components with solvent, check the inner race lands and grooves for pitting and score marks

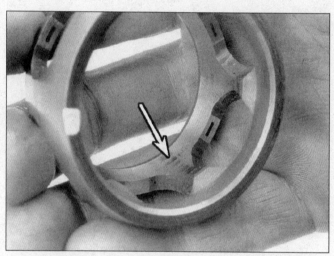

3.4g Check the cage for cracks, pitting and score marks - shiny spots are normal and don't affect operation

3.4h With the race and cage tilted at 90-degrees, lower the assembly into the housing

3.4i Rotate the assembly by gently tapping with a hammer and brass punch . . .

3.4j . . . then press the balls into the cage windows, repeating until all of the balls are installed

3.4k Use needle-nose pliers to lower a new snap-ring into the groove . . .

3.4l . . . then seat it into the groove with snap-ring pliers

3.4m Apply grease through the splined hole, then insert a wooden dowel (with a diameter slightly less than that of the axle) through the splined hole and push down - the dowel will force the grease into the joint. Repeat until the bearing is completely packed

3.4n Install the small clamp and the boot on the driveaxle and apply grease to the inside of the axle boot . . .

3.4o . . . until the level is up to the end of axle

3.4p Position the CV joint assembly on the driveaxle, aligning the splines, then use a soft-face hammer to drive the joint onto the driveaxle until the snap-ring is seated in the groove

3.4q Seat the inner end of the boot in the groove and install the retaining clamp, then do the same on the other end of the boot - tighten boot clamps with the special tool (see illustration 3.3t)

Notes

Chapter 9
Brakes

Contents

Specifications

General

Brake fluid type	See Chapter 1

Disc brakes

Brake pad minimum thickness	See Chapter 1
Disc lateral runout limit	0.002 inch
Disc minimum thickness	Cast into disc
Rear Disc/Drum diameter	Cast into disc
Parallelism (thickness variation) limit	0.001 inch

Torque specifications

Ft-lbs (unless otherwise indicated)

Note: *One foot-pound (ft-lb) of torque is equivalent to 12 inch-pounds (in-lbs) of torque. Torque values below approximately 15 foot-pounds are expressed in inch-pounds, because most foot-pound torque wrenches are not accurate at these smaller values.*

ABS hydraulic control unit mounting bracket bolts	89 in-lbs
Brake hose banjo fitting bolt	40
Caliper mounting bolts/guide pins	
Front	26
Rear	32
Caliper mounting bracket bolts	
Front	133
Rear	88
Master cylinder mounting nuts	24
Wheel lug nuts	See Chapter 1

1   General information

The vehicles covered by this manual are equipped with hydraulically operated front and rear disc brakes. Disc brake systems are self-adjusting and automatically compensate for pad wear.

Hydraulic system

The hydraulic system consists of two separate circuits. The master cylinder has separate reservoir chambers for each circuit, and, in the event of a leak or failure in one hydraulic circuit, the other circuit will remain operative. A warning indicator will light up on the instrument panel when a substantial amount of brake fluid is lost, showing that a failure has occurred. A dual proportioning valve in the circuit provides brake balance between the front and rear brakes. Models that are equipped with ABS (Anti-Lock Brake System - see Section 2) do not require a proportioning valve.

Power brake booster

The power brake booster is mounted on the firewall in the engine compartment. It utilizes engine manifold vacuum and atmospheric pressure to provide assistance to the hydraulically operated brakes, resulting in less brake pedal effort.

Parking brake

The parking brake system mechanically operates the rear brakes through the use of cables and a foot operated pedal. On most models, the cables pull on levers and actuators that expand parking brake shoes in the center portion (drum) of the rear brake disc. Some later models are equipped with parking brake actuators integrated into the rear brake calipers. The parking brake cables pull on levers that turn a jackscrew in each caliper piston, pushing the pistons outward and applying clamping force through the brake pads.

Service

After completing any operation involving disassembly of any part of the brake system, always test drive the vehicle to check for proper braking performance before resuming normal driving. When testing the brakes, perform the tests on a clean, dry, flat surface. Conditions other than these can lead to inaccurate test results.

Test the brakes at various speeds with both light and heavy pedal pressure. The vehicle should stop evenly without pulling to one side or the other. Avoid locking the brakes, because this slides the tires and diminishes braking efficiency and control of the vehicle.

Tires, vehicle load and wheel alignment are factors which also affect braking performance.

Precautions

There are some general cautions and warnings involving the brake system on this vehicle:

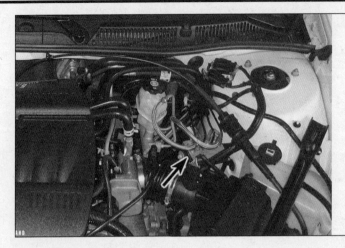

2.2 Location of the ABS hydraulic unit

a) *Use only brake fluid conforming to DOT 3 specifications.*
b) *The brake pads and linings contain fibers that are hazardous to your health if inhaled. Whenever you work on brake system components, clean all parts with brake system cleaner. Do not allow the fine dust to become airborne. Also, wear an approved filtering mask.*
c) *Safety should be paramount whenever any servicing of the brake components is performed. Do not use parts or fasteners that are not in perfect condition, and be sure that all clearances and torque specifications are adhered to. If you are at all unsure about a certain procedure, seek professional advice. Upon completion of any brake system work, test the brakes carefully in a controlled area before putting the vehicle into normal service. If a problem is suspected in the brake system, don't drive the vehicle until it's fixed.*

2   Anti-lock Brake System (ABS) - general information

General information

Refer to illustration 2.2

Note: *Vehicles equipped with ABS are also equipped with a Traction Control System (TCS) which helps limit wheel spin when slippery road conditions are encountered.*

1   The Anti-lock Brake System is designed to maintain vehicle steerability, directional stability and optimum deceleration under severe braking conditions on most road surfaces. It does so by monitoring the rotational speed of each wheel and controlling the brake line pressure to each wheel during braking. This prevents the wheels from locking up.

2   The ABS system has three main components - the wheel speed sensors, the electronic control unit (ECU) and the hydraulic unit **(see illustration)**. Four wheel speed sensors - one at each wheel - send a variable voltage signal to the control unit, which monitors these signals, compares them to its program and determines

whether a wheel is about to lock up. When a wheel is about to lock up, the control unit signals the hydraulic unit to reduce hydraulic pressure (or not increase it further) at that wheel's brake caliper. Pressure modulation is handled by electrically-operated solenoid valves.

3   If a problem develops within the system, an "ABS" warning light will glow on the dashboard. Sometimes, a visual inspection of the ABS system can help you locate the problem. Carefully inspect the ABS wiring harness. Pay particularly close attention to the harness and connections near each wheel. Look for signs of chafing and other damage caused by incorrectly routed wires. If a wheel sensor harness is damaged, it must be replaced. **Warning:** *Do NOT try to repair an ABS wiring harness. The ABS system is sensitive to even the smallest changes in resistance. Repairing the harness could alter resistance values and cause the system to malfunction. If the ABS wiring harness is damaged in any way, it must be replaced.* **Caution:** *Make sure the ignition is turned off before unplugging or reattaching any electrical connections.*

Diagnosis and repair

4   If a dashboard warning light comes on and stays on while the vehicle is in operation, the ABS system requires attention. Although special electronic ABS diagnostic testing tools are necessary to properly diagnose the system, you can perform a few preliminary checks before taking the vehicle to a dealer service department.

a) *Check the brake fluid level in the reservoir.*
b) *Verify that the computer electrical connectors are securely connected.*
c) *Check the electrical connectors at the hydraulic control unit.*
d) *Check the fuses.*
e) *Follow the wiring harness to each wheel and verify that all connections are secure and that the wiring is undamaged.*

5   If the above preliminary checks do not rectify the problem, the vehicle should be diagnosed by a dealer service department or other qualified repair shop. Due to the complex nature of this system, all actual repair work must be done by a qualified automotive technician.

3.5 On front brakes and rear brakes with parking brake shoes (instead of actuator-type calipers), depress the caliper pistons into the bottom of their bores with a large C-clamp

3.6a Always wash the brakes with brake cleaner before disassembling anything

Wheel speed sensor - removal and installation

6   The wheel speed sensors are integrated into the wheel bearing and hub assemblies. Refer to Chapter 10 for replacement of these components.

3   Disc brake pads - replacement

Refer to illustration 3.5

Warning: *Disc brake pads must be replaced on both front or both rear wheels at the same time - never replace the pads on only one wheel. Also, the dust created by the brake system is harmful to your health. Never blow it out with compressed air and don't inhale any of it. An approved filtering mask should be worn when working on the brakes. Do not, under any circumstances, use petroleum-based solvents to clean*

brake parts. Use brake system cleaner only! **Note:** *This procedure applies to front and rear disc brakes.*

1   Remove the cap from the brake fluid reservoir and remove about two-thirds of the fluid. **Caution:** *Brake fluid will damage paint. Cover all painted surfaces around the work area and be careful not to spill fluid during this procedure. Clean any spilled fluid immediately and rinse the area with lots of water.*

2   Loosen the wheel lug nuts, raise the end of the vehicle you're working on and support it securely on jackstands. Block the wheels at the opposite end.

3   Remove the wheels. Work on one brake assembly at a time, using the assembled brake for reference if necessary.

4   Inspect the brake disc carefully as outlined in Section 5. If machining is necessary, follow the information in that Section to remove the disc, at which time the pads can be removed as well.

5   On front brakes and rear brakes with parking brake shoes (instead of actuator-type calipers), push the piston back into its bore to provide room for the new brake pads. A C-clamp can be used to accomplish this **(see illustration)**. As the piston is depressed to the bottom of the caliper bore, the fluid in the master cylinder will rise. Make sure that it doesn't overflow. If necessary, siphon off some of the fluid. **Caution:** *Do not attempt to depress the piston into the caliper on later models with parking brake actuator-type calipers.*

Front

Refer to illustrations 3.6a through 3.6n

6   Follow the accompanying photos **(illustrations 3.6a through 3.6n)** for the actual pad replacement procedure. Be sure to stay in order and read the caption under each illustration. Once you have installed the new pads, proceed to Step 9.

3.6b Hold the guide pin with one wrench while removing the lower caliper mounting bolt with another . . .

3.6c . . . then, being careful not to damage the seal on the upper caliper guide pin, pivot the caliper up and secure it with a piece of wire

3.6d Remove the outer brake pad from the mounting bracket . . .

3.6e . . . then remove the inner pad

3.6f Remove both pad support plates

3.6g Install new pad support plates

3.6h Remove the upper and lower guide pins from the caliper mounting bracket and clean the old grease off them (the upper guide pin can be removed by pulling the caliper from the mounting bracket with the pin still attached to the caliper)

3.6i Inspect the guide pins for wear or damage and replace them if necessary. Lubricate the guide pins with high-temperature brake grease and install them

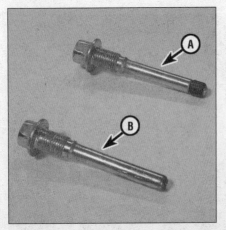

3.6j Reinstall the upper (A) and lower (B) guide pins, making sure the guide pin with the bushing on the end (A) is installed in the top position

3.6k Compare the new pads with the old ones to make sure that they are the same, then install the inner pad. Make sure that the ends of the pad are fully engaged with the pad support plates. A wear indicator is attached to the inboard pad

3.6l Install the outer pad

3.6m Place the caliper over the new pads and back onto the mounting bracket

3.6n Install the caliper mounting bolt(s) and tighten them to the torque listed in this Chapter's Specifications

3.8a Remove the upper caliper guide pin and wipe the old grease from it. Inspect it for wear or damage and replace it if necessary . . .

3.8b . . . then, being careful not to damage the seal on the lower caliper guide pin, pivot the caliper down and secure it with a piece of wire

3.8c Remove the outer brake pad from the mounting bracket . . .

3.8d . . . then remove the inner pad

Rear

Refer to illustrations 3.8a through 3.8n

7   On rear brakes with parking brake shoes (instead of actuator-type calipers), using a C-clamp, depress the caliper piston into its bore **(see illustration 3.5)**. On all models, wash the brake assembly with brake cleaner **(see illustration 3.6a)**. **Caution:** *Do not attempt to depress the piston into the caliper on later models with parking brake actuator-type calipers.*

8   Follow the accompanying photos **(illustrations 3.8a through 3.8n)** for the actual pad replacement procedure. Be sure to stay in order and read the caption under each illustration. Once you have installed the new pads, proceed to Step 9.

Front or rear brake pads

9   Install the wheel and lug nuts, lower the vehicle and tighten the lug nuts to the torque listed in the Chapter 1 Specifications.

10   Apply and release the brake pedal several times to bring the pads into contact with the brake discs. Check the brake fluid level and add fluid, if necessary (see Chapter 1).

11   Check the operation of the brakes in an isolated area before driving the vehicle in traffic.

3.8e Remove both pad support plates

3.8f Install new pad support plates

3.8g Compare the new pads with the old ones to make sure that they are the same, then install the inner pad. Make sure that the ends of the pad are fully engaged with the pad support plates

3.8h Install the outer pad. A wear indicator is fixed to the outboard pad and placed so it's at the bottom when installed

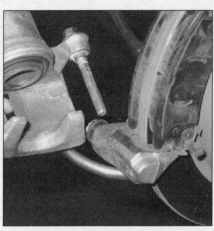

3.8i Move the caliper away from the mounting bracket so that the lower guide pin slides completely out. Wipe the old grease off, inspect it for wear or damage and replace it if necessary

3.8j On later models with parking brake actuator style rear calipers, retract the caliper piston by rotating it into its bore. Here, a special caliper piston tool is being used

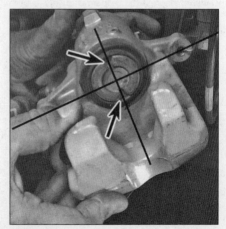

3.8k Once retracted, align the notches perpendicular to the mounting bolt holes (the notches must align with the pins on the brake shoe backing plates)

3.8l Lubricate it with high-temperature brake grease and reinstall the caliper by sliding the guide pin back into the caliper mounting bracket

3.8m Place the caliper over the new pads, being careful not to damage the guide pin seals

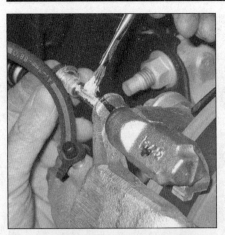

3.8n Lubricate and install the upper caliper guide pin and tighten it to the torque listed in this Chapter's Specifications

4.3 Brake caliper mounting details (front shown - rear is similar):

1   Brake line fitting
2   Caliper mounting bolts
3   Caliper mounting bracket bolts

4   Disc brake caliper - removal and installation

Warning: *Dust created by the brake system is harmful to your health. Never blow it out with compressed air and don't inhale any of it. An approved filtering mask should be worn when working on the brakes. Do not, under any circumstances, use petroleum-based solvents to clean brake parts. Use brake system cleaner only.*

Note 1: *If replacement is indicated (usually because of fluid leakage), it is recommended that the calipers be replaced, not overhauled. New and factory rebuilt units are available on an exchange basis, which makes this job quite easy. Always replace the calipers in pairs - never replace just one of them.*

Note 2: *This procedure applies to front and rear disc brakes.*

Removal

Refer to illustration 4.3

1   Loosen the wheel lug nuts, raise the end of the vehicle you're working on and support it securely on jackstands. Block the wheels at the opposite end. Remove the wheels.

2   Depress the caliper piston with a C-clamp just enough to allow the pad to clear the disc **(see illustration 3.5). Caution:** *Do not attempt to depress the piston into the caliper on later models with parking brake actuator-type calipers.*

3   Disconnect the brake line from the caliper and plug it to keep contaminants out of the brake system and to prevent losing any more brake fluid than is necessary **(see illustration). Note:** *If you're simply removing the caliper for access to other components, don't disconnect the brake line from the caliper.*

4   Remove the caliper mounting bolts (or guide pins on rear calipers). **Note:** *On front calipers, hold the guide pin with a wrench to remove the mounting bolts (see illustration 3.6b).*

5   Detach the caliper from its mounting bracket.

Installation

6   Install the caliper by reversing the removal procedure. Remember to replace the copper sealing washers on either side of the brake line fitting with new ones. Tighten the caliper mounting bolts and the brake line banjo fitting bolt to the torque listed in this Chapter's Specifications.

7   Bleed the brake system (see Section 10).

8   Install the wheels and lug nuts and lower the vehicle. Tighten the wheel lug nuts to the torque listed in the Chapter 1 Specifications. Check the operation of the brakes thoroughly before placing the vehicle into normal service.

5   Brake disc - inspection, removal and installation

Warning: *Dust created by the brake system is harmful to your health. Never blow it out with compressed air and don't inhale any of it. An approved filtering mask should be worn when working on the brakes. Do not, under any circumstances, use petroleum-based solvents to clean brake parts. Use brake system cleaner only.*

Inspection

Refer to illustrations 5.4, 5.5a, 5.5b, 5.6a and 5.6b

Note: *The manufacturer may have installed a thin plate (with a small V-notch pointing to one of the wheel studs) between the disc and the hub flange as a method to correct disc runout. Before removing the plate from the hub, make sure that you place a match mark on the stud that the V-notch points to. If the disc is going to be machined or replaced, it's possible that the plate can be removed and discarded. Check the disc runout on the machined or replacement disc with the plate and disc installed. If there is excessive runout, remove the plate and check the disc runout again.*

1   Loosen the wheel lug nuts, raise the vehicle and support it securely on jackstands. Remove the wheel.

2   Remove the brake caliper as outlined in Section 4. It's not necessary to disconnect the

brake hose for this procedure. After removing the caliper mounting bolts, suspend the caliper out of the way with a piece of wire. Don't let the caliper hang by the hose and don't stretch or twist the hose.

3   Reinstall the lug nuts (inverted) to hold the disc against the hub. It may be necessary to install washers between the disc and the lug nuts to take up space.

4   Visually check the disc surface for score marks, cracks and other damage. Light scratches and shallow grooves are normal after use and may not always be detrimental to brake operation. Deep score marks or cracks may require disc refinishing by an automotive machine shop or disc replacement **(see illustration)**. Be sure to check both sides of the disc. If pulsating has been noticed during application of the brakes, suspect disc runout. **Note:** *The most common symptoms of damaged or worn brake discs are pulsation in the brake pedal when the brakes are applied or loud grinding noises caused from severely worn brake pads. If these symptoms are extreme, it is very likely that the disc(s) will need to be replaced.*

5   To check disc runout, place a dial indicator at a point about 1/2-inch from the outer

5.4 The brake pads on this vehicle were obviously neglected, as they wore down completely and cut deep grooves into the disc - wear this severe means the disc must be replaced

5.5a To check disc runout, mount a dial indicator as shown and rotate the disc

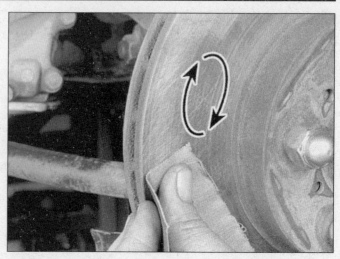

5.5b Using a swirling motion, remove the glaze from the disc surface with sandpaper or emery cloth

edge of the disc **(see illustration)**. Set the indicator to zero and turn the disc. An indicator reading that exceeds 0.003 of an inch could cause pulsation upon brake application and will require disc refinishing by an automotive machine shop or disc replacement. **Note:** *If disc refinishing or replacement is not necessary, you can deglaze the brake pad surface on the disc with emery cloth or sandpaper (use a swirling motion to ensure a non-directional finish)* **(see illustration)**.

6   The disc must not be machined to a thickness less than the specified minimum refinish thickness. The minimum wear (or discard) thickness is cast into either the front or backside of the disc **(see illustration)**. The disc thickness can be checked with a micrometer **(see illustration)**.

Removal and installation

7   Remove the caliper mounting bracket **(see illustration 4.3)**.
8   Mark the disc in relation to the hub so

that it can be installed in its original position on the hub. Remove the bolt securing the disc to the hub flange and then remove the disc. If the disc appears to be stuck to the hub, use a mallet to knock it loose. **Note:** *Be sure to look for a thin plate that may be installed between the brake disc and hub flange and refer to the* **Note** *at the beginning of this Section.*
9   Clean the hub flange and the inside of the brake disc thoroughly, removing any rust or corrosion, then install the disc onto the hub assembly and tighten the retaining bolt securely.
10   Install the caliper mounting bracket and tighten the bolts to the torque listed in this Chapter's Specifications.
11   Place the caliper over the disc and onto the mounting bracket. Install the caliper mounting bolts (or guide pins on rear brakes) and tighten them to the torque listed in this Chapter's Specifications.
12   Install the wheel and lower the vehicle to the ground. Tighten the wheel lug nuts to

the torque listed in the Chapter 1 Specifications. Depress the brake pedal a few times to bring the brake pads into contact with the disc. Bleeding of the system will not be necessary unless the brake hose was disconnected from the caliper. Check the operation of the brakes thoroughly before placing the vehicle into normal service.

6   Parking brake shoes - replacement

Refer to illustrations 6.4, 6.5, 6.7, 6.8a, 6.8b, 6.9a and 6.9b

Warning 1: *Dust created by the brake system is harmful to your health. Never blow it out with compressed air and don't inhale any of it. An approved filtering mask should be worn when working on the brakes. Do not, under any circumstances, use petroleum-based solvents to clean brake parts. Use brake system cleaner only.*

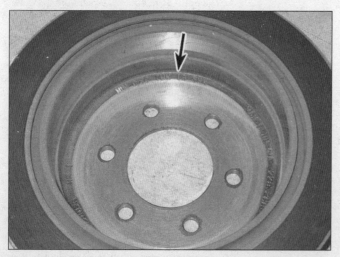

5.6a Here's an example of how the minimum thickness specification is cast into a disc (this specification is an example only - check your disc for the actual specification)

5.6b Use a micrometer to measure disc thickness

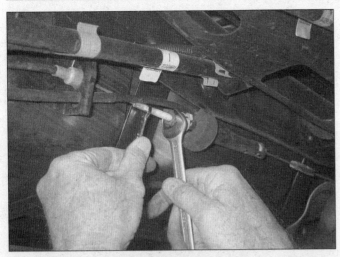

6.4 Hold the cable end with a small wrench while moving the adjustment nut towards the equalizer to loosen the cable

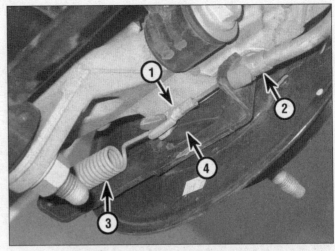

6.5 Parking brake cable connection details:

1	Brake cable end	3	Brake cable return spring
2	Brake cable fitting at cable bracket	4	Parking brake actuator lever

Warning 2: *The parking brake shoes must be replaced on both wheels at the same time - never replace the shoes on only one wheel. To avoid mixing up parts, work on one brake assembly at a time.*

1   Loosen the wheel lug nuts, raise the rear of the vehicle and support it securely on jackstands. Block the front wheels to keep the vehicle from rolling and release the parking brake.

2   Remove the rear wheels.

3   Remove the brake caliper (see Section 4) and the brake disc (see Section 5).

4   Loosen the parking brake cable at the equalizer **(see illustration)**.

5   Detach the brake cable and spring from the actuator lever, then separate the cable from the bracket **(see illustration)**.

6   Remove the rear wheel hub and bearing mounting bolts (see Chapter 10). **Note:** *The wheel hub and bearing, backing plate, parking brake shoes and related components are removed as an assembly during wheel bearing removal.*

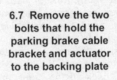

6.7 Remove the two bolts that hold the parking brake cable bracket and actuator to the backing plate

7   Remove the cable bracket from the backing plate **(see illustration)**.

8   Adjust the actuator to separate it from the brake shoe lining assembly **(see illustra-** **tion)**. Remove the small actuator lever and seal, then remove the actuator from the backing plate **(see illustration)**.

9   Remove the brake shoe lining assembly

6.8a Turn the adjuster wheel on the actuator to release the tension on the brake shoe lining assembly

6.8b Remove the actuator from the backing plate

6.9a Slide the brake shoe lining assembly away from the clip on the backing plate

6.9b The brake shoe lining assembly is removed from around the wheel bearing and hub assembly

from the backing plate and from around the wheel bearing and hub **(see illustrations)**.

10   Installation is the reverse of removal noting the following points:

a) *Tighten the parking brake cable bracket mounting bolts to the torque listed in this Chapter's Specifications.*

b) *Be sure to tighten the wheel bearing and hub assembly mounting bolts to the torque listed in the Chapter 10 Specifications, the caliper mounting bolts and mounting bracket bolts to the torque listed in this Chapter's Specifications, and the wheel lug nuts to the torque listed in the Chapter 1 Specifications.*

c) *Adjust the parking brake (see Section 7).*

11   Press and release the parking brake pedal several times and confirm that the parking brake is working properly.

7   Parking brake - adjustment

Refer to illustration 7.5

1   The parking brake pedal, when properly adjusted, should travel about six to eight clicks when set. If it travels much less than specified, there's a chance the parking brake might not be releasing completely and the parking brake shoes might be dragging on the drum. If the pedal travels more than specified, the parking brake may not hold the vehicle adequately on an incline, allowing the car to roll.

2   There are two areas of adjustment for the parking brake: the wheel adjuster on the actuator at the shoes and the adjusting nut on the brake cable at the brake cable equalizer. Perform the adjustment at the actuator first.

3   Loosen the wheel lug nuts, raise the rear of the vehicle and support it securely on jackstands. Block the front wheels to keep the vehicle from rolling and release the parking brake.

4   Remove the rear brake disc (see Section 5).

5   Turn the actuator adjustment wheel so that the parking brake shoe just contacts the drum portion of the rear disc when the disc is installed **(see illustration)**. **Note:** *If the parking brake shoe lining appears severely worn, damaged, or contaminated with oil, replace the shoe lining assembly* (see Section 6).

6   Place the disc on the hub and rotate it to confirm that it turns freely. If it does not, remove the disc, back-off the adjustment slightly and then recheck it. **Note:** *Install the disc retaining screw or place nuts on two wheel studs to hold the disc against the hub flange while checking the disc rotation.*

7   Adjust the actuator on both wheels. Make sure that each wheel turns freely before continuing the following Steps.

8   Install the discs (see Section 5), calipers (see Section 4) and wheels. Tighten the caliper mounting bracket bolts and guide pins to the torque listed in this Chapter's Specifications. Keep the vehicle supported on jackstands.

9   Turn the adjuster nut on the parking brake cable at the equalizer **(see illustration 6.4)** in small increments while spinning each wheel. When either wheel starts to

drag, back off the adjuster nut one complete turn. **Note:** *Moving the nut towards the cable end will take up slack in the cable (making it shorter). Moving the nut towards the equalizer will loosen the cable (making it longer).*

10   Set and release the parking brake a few times noting the number of clicks as the pedal goes down.

11   With the brake released, spin the wheels again to confirm that neither of the parking brakes are dragging. Re-adjust the brake cable if necessary.

12   Lower the vehicle and tighten the lug nuts to the torque specifications in Chapter 1.

13   Press and release the parking brake pedal again and confirm that the parking brake is working properly.

8   Master cylinder - removal and installation

Removal

Refer to illustration 8.2

1   Depress the brake pedal several times with the engine off to deplete the vacuum reserve from the power brake booster.

7.5 Turn this wheel to increase or decrease the clearance of the brake shoes to the drum portion of the rear disc

8.2 Brake master cylinder mounting details:

1   Brake line fittings (use a flare-nut wrench on these fittings)
2   Mounting nuts
3   Fluid level sensor electrical connector

8.9 The best way to bleed air from the master cylinder before installing it on the vehicle is with a pair of bleeder tubes that direct brake fluid into the reservoir during bleeding

2   The master cylinder is located in the engine compartment, mounted to the power brake booster **(see illustration)**.

3   Remove as much fluid as you can from the reservoir with a syringe, such as an old turkey baster. **Warning 1:** *If a baster is used, never again use it for the preparation of food.* **Warning 2:** *Don't depress the brake pedal until the reservoir has been refilled, otherwise air may be introduced into the brake hydraulic system.*

4   Place rags under the fluid fittings and prepare caps or plastic bags to cover the ends of the lines once they are disconnected. **Caution:** *Brake fluid will damage paint. Cover all painted surfaces around the work area and be careful not to spill fluid during this procedure.*

5   Loosen the fittings at the ends of the brake lines where they enter the master cylinder. To prevent rounding-off the corners on these nuts, use a flare-nut wrench. Pull the brake lines slightly away from the master cylinder and plug the ends to prevent contamination.

6   Disconnect the electrical connector for the brake fluid level sensor on the reservoir, and then remove the nuts attaching the master cylinder to the power booster. Pull the master cylinder off the studs and out of the engine compartment. Again, be careful not to spill the fluid as this is done.

7   If a new master cylinder is being installed, it may be necessary to transfer the old reservoir to the new master cylinder. Tap the retaining pins out with a hammer and punch to remove the old reservoir. **Note:** *Be sure to install new seals when transferring the reservoir and carefully remove the fluid level sensor by pressing the small tabs with needle-nose pliers.*

Installation

Refer to illustrations 8.9 and 8.18

8   Bench bleed the new master cylinder

before installing it. Mount the master cylinder in a vise, with the jaws of the vise clamping on the mounting flange.

9   Attach a pair of master cylinder bleeder tubes to the outlet ports of the master cylinder **(see illustration)**.

10   Fill the reservoir with brake fluid of the recommended type (see Chapter 1).

11   Slowly push the pistons into the master cylinder (a large Phillips screwdriver can be used for this) - air will be expelled from the pressure chambers and into the reservoir. Because the tubes are submerged in fluid, air can't be drawn back into the master cylinder when you release the pistons.

12   Repeat the procedure until no more air bubbles are present.

13   Remove the bleed tubes, one at a time, and install plugs in the open ports to prevent fluid leakage and air from entering. Install the reservoir cap.

14   Install the master cylinder onto the power brake booster and tighten the mounting nuts only finger tight at this time.

15   Carefully thread the brake line fittings into the master cylinder by hand until you know they are started straight. Since the master cylinder is still a bit loose, it can be moved slightly in order for the fittings to thread in easily. **Caution:** *Do not strip the threads as the fittings are tightened.*

16   Fully tighten the mounting nuts, then the brake line fittings. Tighten the nuts to the torque listed in this Chapter's Specifications.

17   Connect the electrical connector for the brake fluid level sensor on the reservoir.

18   Fill the master cylinder reservoir with fluid, then bleed the master cylinder and the brake system as described in Section 10. To bleed the cylinder on the vehicle, have an assistant depress the brake pedal and hold the pedal to the floor. Loosen the fitting to allow air and fluid to escape, then close the fitting. Repeat this procedure on both fittings

8.18 Have an assistant depress the brake pedal and hold it down, then loosen the fitting nut, allowing the air and fluid to escape; repeat this procedure on both fittings until the fluid is clear of air bubbles

until the fluid is clear of air bubbles **(see illustration)**. **Caution:** *Have plenty of rags on hand to catch the fluid - brake fluid will ruin painted surfaces. After the bleeding procedure is completed, rinse the area under the master cylinder with a lot of clean water.*

19   Test the operation of the brake system thoroughly before placing the vehicle into normal service. **Warning:** *Do not operate the vehicle if you are in doubt about the effectiveness of the brake system. It is possible for air to become trapped in the anti-lock brake system hydraulic control unit, so, if the pedal continues to feel spongy after repeated bleedings or the BRAKE or ANTI-LOCK light stays on, have the vehicle towed to a dealer service department or other qualified shop to be bled with the aid of a scan tool.*

9.3 Brake hose fitting details:

1   *Metal tube nut (use a flare-nut wrench here)*
2   *Retaining clip*
3   *Brake hose fitting (use a back-up wrench here)*

10.8 When bleeding the brakes, a hose is connected to the bleed screw at the caliper or wheel cylinder and submerged in brake fluid - air will be seen as bubbles in the tube and container (all air must be expelled before moving to the next wheel)

9   Brake hoses and lines - inspection and replacement

1   About every six months, with the vehicle raised and placed securely on jackstands, the flexible hoses which connect the steel brake lines with the front and rear brake assemblies should be inspected for cracks, chafing of the outer cover, leaks, blisters and other damage. These are important and vulnerable parts of the brake system and an inspection should be thorough. A light and mechanics mirror may be needed to see all areas of the flexible hoses. If a hose exhibits any of the above defects, replace it with a new one.

Flexible hoses

Refer to illustration 9.3

2   Clean all dirt away from the ends of the hose. Follow the path of the hose from the metal line to the brake caliper and remove any brackets that may secure sections of the hose to other components.
3   To disconnect a brake hose from the brake line, unscrew the metal tube nut with a flare-nut wrench while holding the flats of the hose fitting with wrench. Plug or cap all openings to prevent contamination. Remove the hose from the frame bracket and remove the retaining clip from the hose fitting **(see illustration)**.
4   Disconnect the hose fitting from the caliper, discarding the sealing washers on either side of the fitting.
5   Using new sealing washers, attach the new brake hose to the caliper or wheel cylinder.
6   To reattach a brake hose to the metal line, insert the end of the hose through the frame bracket, make sure the hose is routed properly and isn't twisted. Install the retaining clip on the hose fitting at the frame bracket and then carefully thread the metal tube nut into the hose fitting. Tighten the tube nut securely with a flare-nut wrench.

7   Install any other hose brackets that may secure the hose to other components. Carefully check to make sure the suspension or steering components don't make contact with the hose. Have an assistant push down on the vehicle and also turn the steering wheel lock-to-lock during inspection. **Note***: If your replacement hose is matched to the original one and routed in the same way, you should not experience any problems with the hose making contact with other components.*
8   After installation, check the master cylinder fluid level and add fluid as necessary. Bleed the brake system as outlined in Section 10 and test the brakes carefully before placing the vehicle into normal operation.

Metal brake lines

9   When replacing brake lines, be sure to use the correct parts. Don't use copper tubing for any brake system components. Purchase steel brake lines from a dealer parts department or auto parts store.
10   Prefabricated brake line, with the tube ends already flared and fittings installed, is available at auto parts stores and dealer parts departments. These lines can be bent to the proper shapes using a tubing bender.
11   When installing the new line make sure it's well supported in the brackets and has plenty of clearance between moving or hot components.
12   After installation, check the master cylinder fluid level and add fluid as necessary. Bleed the brake system as outlined in Section 10 and test the brakes thoroughly before placing the vehicle into normal operation.

10   Brake hydraulic system - bleeding

Refer to illustration 10.8
Warning 1: *If air has found its way into the hydraulic control unit, the system must be bled*

with the use of a specialized scan tool. If the brake pedal feels "spongy" even after bleeding the brakes, or the ABS light or BRAKE warning light on the instrument panel stays on, or if you have any doubts whatsoever about the effectiveness of the brake system, have the vehicle towed to a dealer service department or other repair shop equipped with this tool.
Warning 2: *Wear eye protection when bleeding the brake system. If the fluid comes in contact with your eyes, immediately rinse them with water and seek medical attention.*
Caution: *Brake fluid will damage paint. If fluid gets on any painted surface, rinse it off immediately with plenty of water.*
Note: *Bleeding the brake system is necessary to remove any air that's trapped in the system when it's opened during removal and installation of a hose, line, caliper or master cylinder.*
1   It will probably be necessary to bleed the system at all four brakes if air has entered the system due to a low fluid level, or if the brake lines have been disconnected at the master cylinder.
2   If a brake line was disconnected only at a wheel, then only that caliper or wheel cylinder must be bled.
3   If a brake line is disconnected at a fitting located between the master cylinder and any of the brakes, that part of the system served by the disconnected line must be bled, beginning with the fitting closest to the master cylinder and then working downstream, bleeding each fitting of each component as described in Step 18 of Section 8. This includes the proportioning valve or the ABS modulator assembly.
4   Remove vacuum from the brake power booster by applying the brake several times with the engine off.
5   Remove the master cylinder reservoir cap and fill the reservoir with brake fluid. Reinstall the cap. **Note:** *Check the fluid level often during the bleeding operation and add fluid as necessary to prevent the fluid level from falling low enough to allow air bubbles into the*

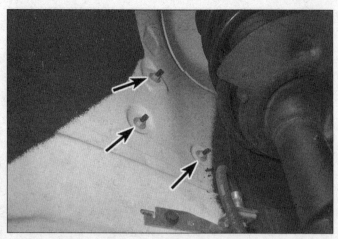

11.9a Mounting fasteners for the ABS hydraulic control unit in the wheel well

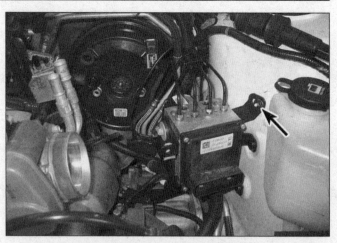

11.9b Mounting fastener for the ABS hydraulic control unit in the engine compartment

master cylinder.

6   Have an assistant on hand, as well as a supply of new brake fluid, an empty clear plastic container, a length of plastic, rubber or vinyl tubing to fit over the bleeder valve and a wrench to open and close the bleeder valve.

7   Beginning at the right rear wheel, loosen the bleeder screw slightly, then tighten it to a point where it's snug but can still be loosened quickly and easily.

8   Place one end of the tubing over the bleeder screw fitting and submerge the other end in brake fluid in the container **(see illustration)**.

9   Have the assistant slowly depress the brake pedal and hold it in the depressed position.

10   While the pedal is held depressed, open the bleeder screw just enough to allow a flow of fluid to leave the valve. Watch for air bubbles to exit the submerged end of the tube. When the fluid flow slows after a couple of seconds, tighten the screw and have your assistant release the pedal.

11   Repeat Steps 9 and 10 until no more air is seen leaving the tube, then tighten the bleeder screw and proceed to the left front wheel, the left rear wheel and the right front wheel, in that order, and perform the same procedure. Be sure to check the fluid in the master cylinder reservoir frequently.

12   Never use old brake fluid. It contains moisture that can boil, rendering the brake system inoperative.

13   Refill the master cylinder with fluid at the end of the operation.

14   Check the operation of the brakes thoroughly. The pedal should feel solid when depressed, with no sponginess. If necessary, repeat the entire process. **Warning:** *Do not operate the vehicle if you are in doubt about the effectiveness of the brake system. It is possible for air to become trapped in the anti-lock brake system hydraulic control unit, so, if the pedal continues to feel spongy after repeated bleedings or the BRAKE or ANTI-LOCK light stays on, have the vehicle towed to a dealer service department or*

other qualified shop to be bled with the aid of a scan tool.

11   Power brake booster - removal and installation

Warning: *The ABS hydraulic control unit, if equipped, must be moved aside in order to remove the power brake booster. It's important to note that if the ABS hydraulic control unit is removed, and the hydraulic lines are detached from it (opening the circuit), then air can be introduced into the system. If air has found its way into the hydraulic control unit, the system must be bled with the use of a specialized scan tool. If the brake pedal feels "spongy" even after bleeding the brakes, or the ABS light or BRAKE warning light on the instrument panel stays on, or if you have any doubts whatsoever about the effectiveness of the brake system, have the vehicle towed to a dealer service department or other qualified repair shop equipped with this tool.*
Note: *The power brake booster is not serviceable. If it has failed, replace it with a new or rebuilt unit.*

Operating check

1   Depress the brake pedal several times with the engine off and make sure that there is no change in the pedal reserve distance.

2   Depress the pedal and start the engine. If the pedal goes down slightly, operation is normal.

Airtightness check

3   Start the engine and turn it off after one or two minutes. Depress the brake pedal several times slowly. If the pedal goes down farther the first time but gradually rises after the second or third depression, the booster is airtight.

4   Depress the brake pedal while the engine is running, then stop the engine with the pedal depressed. If there is no change in the pedal reserve travel after holding the pedal for 30 seconds, the booster is airtight.

Removal and installation

Refer to illustrations 11.9a, 11.9b, 11.15, 11.16, 11.18a and 11.18b

5   Turn the ignition key to the OFF position and press the brake pedal several times to remove vacuum in the power brake booster.

6   Set the parking brake and loosen the lug nuts on the left-front wheel. Raise the left-front part of the vehicle and support it securely on a jackstand. Remove the left-front wheel. **Note:** *Raise the vehicle just high enough to remove the wheel.*

7   Remove the top engine cover (see Chapter 2).

8   Remove the air filter housing (see Chapter 4).

9   Remove the ABS hydraulic control unit mounting bracket fasteners and carefully place the unit aside **(see illustrations)**. **Caution:** *In this step, the brake lines from the hydraulic control unit can stay connected, but be extremely careful not to bend or kink any of the lines while moving it aside. Also, make certain that the electrical connector and harness are not damaged when the unit is moved.*

10   Remove the master cylinder from the power booster (see Section 8). **Note:** *In this step, the brake lines from the master cylinder to the hydraulic control unit can stay connected.*

11   On all V8 models and 2004 through 2008 V6 models, remove the exhaust crossover pipe from between the manifolds (see Chapter 2). On 2009 and later V6 engines, drain the cooling system (see Chapter 3) and remove the heater pipes that run under the throttle body. **Warning:** *Wait until the engine is completely cool before performing this step.*

12   Remove the check valve from the power brake booster; simply pull it out of the rubber grommet and move the vacuum hose aside.

13   Disconnect the electrical connector from the brake booster, if equipped.

14   Remove the brake pedal position sensor (see Section 12).

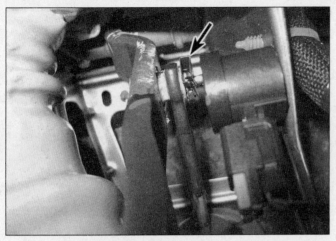

11.15 The location of the brake booster pushrod-to-pedal arm retaining clip (replace)

11.16 On V8 engine models, remove these two coolant pipe bracket bolts

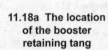 

11.18a The location of the booster retaining tang

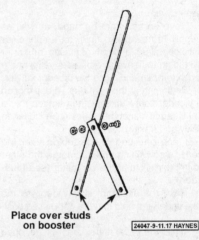

Place over studs on booster

24047-9-11.17 HAYNES

11.18b A tool can be fabricated out of strap steel to enable you to unlock the booster from its bracket

15   Remove the retaining clip securing the booster pushrod to the brake pedal arm **(see illustration)**. **Note:** *The clip is self-locking and will be damaged when it is removed. You will need a replacement clip for installation.*

16   In the engine compartment, on V8 engine models, remove the mounting bolts for the coolant pipe brackets so they can be moved aside when removing the booster **(see illustration)**.

17   Working inside of the vehicle, remove the pushrod from the brake pedal arm.

18   Turn the booster counterclockwise (as you are facing it) to move the retaining tang down and out of the bracket on the firewall. This will release the booster from its mount **(see illustration)**. A special tool is available that bolts to the front of the booster and allows you to turn the booster with a ratchet or breaker bar. If you don't have access to one of these tools, you can fabricate a substitute out of two lengths of strap steel bolted together **(see illustration)**. **Caution:** *Avoid excessive sideways movement and force on the push-rod.*

19   Carefully guide the booster unit out of the engine compartment.

20   Installation is the reverse of removal noting the following points:

a) *Make sure the booster retaining tang engages its bracket completely, and the tang at the base of the booster (where it contacts the firewall) engages securely and completely with the bracket on the firewall.*

b) *Install a new retaining clip to secure the brake booster pushrod to the brake pedal arm.*

c) *Install the brake pedal position sensor (see Section 12).*

d) *Tighten the master cylinder mounting fasteners to the torque listed in this Chapter's Specifications.*

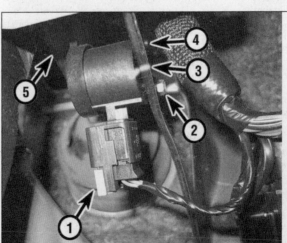

12.2 Brake pedal position sensor mounting details:

1   *Electrical connector*
2   *Mounting fasteners*
3   *Index mark (made before sensor removal)*
4   *Small mounting pin*
5   *Sensor lever (engaged with brake pedal arm)*

21   Test the operation of the brakes thoroughly before placing the vehicle into normal service. Refer to the **Warning** at the beginning of this Section.

12   Brake pedal position sensor - replacement

Refer to illustration 12.2

Note: *The manufacturer states that a special scan tool is necessary for calibrating this component when its installed. They also state that a new component and mounting bolt are installed whenever it is removed.*

1   These model vehicles do not utilize a typical brake light switch; they are equipped with a Brake Pedal Position Sensor.
2   Disconnect the brake pedal position sensor electrical connector **(see illustration)**.
3   Mark the relationship of the sensor to its mount and then remove its mounting bolt **(see illustration 12.2)**.
4   Carefully remove the sensor.
5   Installation is the reverse of removal.

Replace the sensor in its original position by using the index marks made in Step 3.
Note: *If the sensor requires calibration after it's installed, the circuit may set a diagnostic trouble code (DTC) and a warning lamp may illuminate on the dash. The vehicle will need to be taken to a dealership service department or other qualified repair shop to calibrate the sensor and clear any codes. For more information on diagnostic trouble codes, see Chapter 6.*

Notes

Chapter 10
Suspension and steering systems

Contents

Specifications

General
Power steering fluid type .... See Chapter 1

Torque specifications
Ft-lbs (unless otherwise indicated)

Note: *One foot-pound (ft-lb) of torque is equivalent to 12 inch-pounds (in-lbs) of torque. Torque values below approximately 15 ft-lbs are expressed in inch-pounds, since most foot-pound torque wrenches are not accurate at these smaller values.*

Front suspension
Strut
Damper shaft nut	52
Strut upper mounting nut	24
Strut-to-steering knuckle nuts**	96

Stabilizer bar
Stabilizer bar link nuts	17
Stabilizer bar bracket bolts	31

Control arm
Mounting fasteners**	92

Balljoint-to-steering knuckle castle nut
Step 1	15
Step 2	Tighten an additional 120-degrees, then align the cotter pin hole (make sure the nut is tightened to at least 41 ft-lbs)

Hub and bearing assembly bolts*	96

Subframe
Subframe-to-body bolts
Front	107
Rear	118
Driveaxle/hub nut	See Chapter 8

Torque specifications (continued)　　　　　　　　　　**Ft-lbs** (unless otherwise indicated)

Note: One foot-pound (ft-lb) of torque is equivalent to 12 inch-pounds (in-lbs) of torque. Torque values below approximately 15 ft-lbs are expressed in inch-pounds, since most foot-pound torque wrenches are not accurate at these smaller values.

Rear suspension

Rear suspension support	81
Suspension arms 1 and 2	
Arm-to-rear knuckle fasteners	111
Arm-to-suspension support fasteners	100
Trailing arm	
Trailing arm-to-rear knuckle fasteners	177
Trailing arm bracket-to-body bolts	38
Trailing arm-to-bracket through-bolt	77
Hub and bearing assembly bolts	55
Stabilizer bar	
Stabilizer bar link nuts	
Upper	38
Lower	37
Stabilizer bar bracket bolts	35
Strut	
Damper shaft nut	55
Strut upper mounting nuts	33
Strut-to-steering knuckle nuts**	89

Steering system

Power steering pump mounting bolts	18
Steering gear mounting nuts/bolts	66
Tie-rod end-to-steering knuckle nut	
Step 1	22
Step 2	Tighten an additional 120-degrees, then align the cotter pin hole
Intermediate shaft coupler-to-steering gear input shaft pinch-bolt	35
Intermediate shaft coupler-to-steering column pinch-bolt/nut	46
Steering column mounting fasteners	18
Steering wheel mounting nut	30

*Fastener must be replaced

**According to the manufacturer, the lower strut mounting nuts must develop 27 in-lbs of torque prior to seating. If they do not, they must be replaced.

1　General information

Refer to illustrations 1.1 and 1.2

The front suspension is a MacPherson strut design. The upper end of each strut is attached to the vehicle's body strut support. The lower end of the strut is connected to the upper end of the steering knuckle. The steering knuckle is attached to a balljoint mounted on the outer end of the suspension control arm. A stabilizer bar connected to each control arm and mounted to the suspension crossmember reduces body roll during cornering **(see illustration)**.

The rear suspension utilizes struts with coil-over springs, trailing arms and two lower arms (on each side). A stabilizer bar is clamped to a suspension support and connected to the rear strut by two links **(see illustration)**.

The power-assisted rack-and-pinion steering gear is attached to the front suspension subframe. The steering gear moves the tie-rods, which are attached to the steering knuckles. The steering column is designed to collapse in the event of an accident.

Frequently, when working on the suspension or steering system components, you may come across fasteners which seem impossible to loosen. These fasteners on the underside of the vehicle are continually subjected to water, road grime, mud, etc., and can become rusted or "frozen" in place, making them extremely difficult to remove. In order to unscrew these stubborn fasteners without damaging them (or other components), be sure to use lots of penetrating oil and allow it to soak in for a while. Using a wire brush to clean exposed threads will also ease removal of the nut or bolt and prevent damage to the threads. Sometimes a sharp blow with a hammer and punch will break the bond between a nut and bolt threads, but care must be taken to prevent the punch from slipping off the fastener and ruining the threads. Heating the stuck fastener and surrounding area with a torch sometimes helps too, but isn't recommended because of the obvious dangers associated with fire. Long breaker bars and extension, or "cheater," pipes will increase leverage, but never use an extension pipe on a ratchet - the ratcheting mechanism could be damaged. Sometimes tightening the nut or bolt first will help to break it loose. Fasteners that require drastic measures to remove should always be replaced with new ones.

Most of the procedures in this Chapter involve raising the vehicle and working underneath it; a suitable jack and a good pair of jackstands will be needed. A hydraulic floor jack is the preferred type of jack to lift the vehicle, and it can also be used to support certain components during various operations. **Warning 1:** *Never, under any circumstances, rely on a jack to support the vehicle while working on it.* **Warning 2:** *Whenever any of the suspension or steering fasteners are loosened or removed they must be inspected and, if necessary, replaced with new ones of the same part number or of original equipment quality and design. Torque specifications must be followed for proper reassembly and component retention. Never attempt to heat or straighten any suspension or steering components. Instead, replace any bent or damaged parts with new ones.*

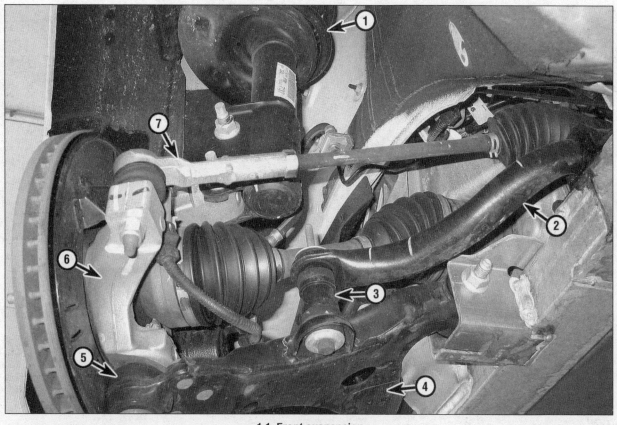

1.1 Front suspension

1	Strut and spring assembly	4	Control arm	6	Steering knuckle
2	Stabilizer bar	5	Balljoint	7	Tie-rod end
3	Stabilizer bar link				

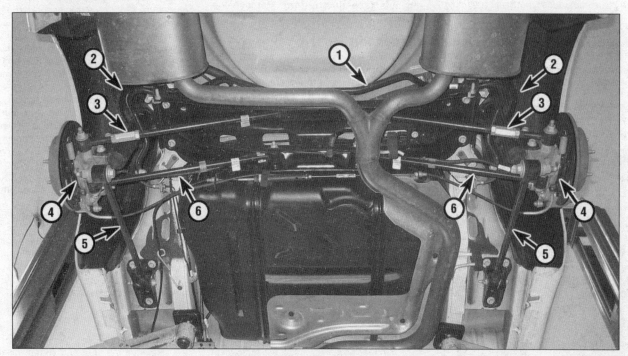

1.2 Rear suspension

1	Stabilizer bar	3	Suspension arm 2	5	Trailing arm
2	Strut and spring assembly	4	Rear knuckle	6	Suspension arm 1

2.2 Mark the relationship of the strut to the steering knuckle and mark the fasteners on each side of the strut bracket

2.3 Pound the bolt out of the steering knuckle. Use a punch if necessary

2   Strut assembly - removal, inspection and installation (front)

Warning: *Always replace the struts and/or coil springs in pairs - never replace just one strut or one coil spring (this could cause dangerous handling peculiarities).*

Removal

Refer to illustrations 2.2, 2.3 and 2.5

1   Loosen the wheel lug nuts, raise the front of the vehicle and support it securely on jackstands. **Note:** *Support the vehicle by placing the jackstands under the frame (unibody) and not under any of the suspension components or subframe.* Remove the front wheels.
2   Mark the relationship of the strut to the knuckle (these marks will be used during installation to ensure that the camber angle is returned to its original setting) **(see illustration).**
3   Remove the strut-to-knuckle nuts while holding the oval shaped bolt heads with a wrench. Remove the bolts by striking the

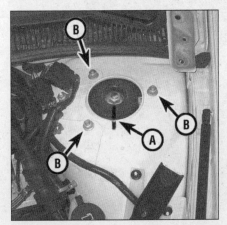

2.5 Mark the strut in relation to the strut tower (A), then remove the mounting fasteners (B) while supporting the strut

end with a hammer to push them out of the knuckle and strut **(see illustration). Caution:** *Do not attempt to turn the strut mounting bolts. These bolts are serrated to fit tightly when seated against the strut mounting flange and in the holes of the knuckle.*
4   Separate the strut from the steering knuckle. Be careful not to overextend the inner CV joint. Also, don't let the steering knuckle fall outward, as the brake hose could be damaged. If necessary, support the lower control arm with a jack.
5   Support the strut and spring assembly with one hand and remove the upper mounting nuts **(see illustration).** Remove the assembly from the fenderwell.

Inspection

6   Check the strut body for leaking fluid, dents, cracks and other obvious damage that would warrant repair or replacement.
7   Check the coil spring for chips or cracks in the spring coating (this can cause premature spring failure due to corrosion). Inspect the spring seat for cuts, hardness and general deterioration.
8   If any undesirable conditions exist, proceed to the strut disassembly procedure (see Section 3).

Installation

9   Noting the index mark made earlier, guide the strut assembly up into the fenderwell and insert the upper mounting studs through the holes in the strut tower. Once the studs protrude from the strut tower, install the nuts so the strut won't fall back through. It's best to use an assistant, as the strut is quite heavy and awkward.
10   Slide the steering knuckle into the strut flange and install the two bolts using a soft-face hammer or mallet. Install the nuts, align the marks made in Step 2, then tighten the nuts to the torque listed in this Chapter's Specifications. **Warning:** *Do not use the mounting nuts if they do not meet the condi-*

tions stated in this Chapter's Torque Specifications.
11   Install the wheel and lug nuts, then lower the vehicle and tighten the lug nuts to the torque listed in the Chapter 1 Specifications.
12   Tighten the upper mounting nuts to the torque listed in this Chapter's Specifications.
13   Have the front wheel alignment checked and, if necessary, adjusted.

3   Strut/coil spring - replacement

Note: *You'll need a spring compressor for this procedure. Spring compressors can usually be rented at most auto parts stores or equipment yards.*

1   If the struts or coil springs exhibit the tell-tale signs of wear (leaking fluid, loss of damping capability, chipped, sagging or cracked coil springs) explore all options before beginning any work. The strut/coil spring components are not serviceable and must be replaced if a problem develops. However, strut assemblies, complete with springs, may be available on an exchange basis (which eliminates much time and work). Whichever route you choose to take, check on the cost and availability of parts before disassembling your vehicle. **Warning:** *Disassembling a strut is potentially dangerous and utmost attention must be directed to the job, or serious injury may result. Use only a high-quality spring compressor and carefully follow the manufacturer's instructions furnished with the tool. After removing the coil spring from the strut assembly, set it aside in a safe, isolated area.*

Disassembly

Refer to illustrations 3.3, 3.5, 3.6 and 3.8

2   Remove the strut and spring assembly (see Section 2). Mount the strut clevis bracket portion of the strut assembly in a vise. **Caution:** *Do not clamp any other portion of the strut assembly in the vise as it will be dam-*

3.3 Install the spring compressor following the tool manufacturer's instructions; compress the spring until all pressure is relieved from the upper spring seat (you can verify this by wiggling the spring)

3.5 Remove the upper mount after taking off the damper shaft nut

3.6 Remove the upper spring seat

aged. Line the vise jaws with wood or rags to prevent damage to the unit and don't tighten the vise excessively.

3   Following the tool manufacturer's instructions, install the spring compressor (which can be obtained at most auto parts stores or equipment yards on a daily rental basis) on the spring and compress it sufficiently to relieve all pressure from the upper spring seat **(see illustration)**. This can be verified by wiggling the spring.

4   Hold the damper shaft from turning with an appropriate tool, and unscrew the damper shaft nut.

5   Remove the nut and upper mount **(see illustration)**. Lay the parts out in the exact order in which they are removed. Check the rubber portion of the upper mount for cracking and general deterioration. If there is any separation of the rubber, replace it.

6   Remove the upper spring seat from the damper shaft **(see illustration)**. Check the rubber portion of the spring seat for cracking

and hardness; replace it if necessary. Inspect the bearing in the spring seat for smooth operation. If it doesn't turn smoothly, replace it.

7   Slide the dust boot and rubber bump stop off the damper shaft. Check the bump stop for cracking and general deterioration. If there is any deterioration of the rubber, replace it.

8   Carefully lift the compressed spring from the assembly **(see illustration)** and set it in a safe place. **Warning:** *When removing the compressed spring, lift it off carefully and set it in a safe place. Keep the ends of the spring away from your body.* **Note:** *If you are disassembling both struts, mark the springs LEFT and RIGHT so you don't mix them up (they're different).*

Reassembly

Refer to illustration 3.10

9   Extend the damper rod to its full length and install the rubber bump stop and dust boot.

10   Carefully place the compressed coil spring onto the lower seat of the damper, with

the end of the spring resting against the raised stop **(see illustration)**.

11   Install the upper insulator and spring seat.

12   Install the upper mount and mounting nut and then tighten it to the torque listed in this Chapter's Specifications.

13   Remove the spring compressor tool.

14   Install the strut/spring assembly (see Section 2).

4   Stabilizer bar, bushings and links (front) - removal and installation

Refer to illustrations 4.2, 4.3 and 4.5

Note 1: *Stabilizer bar removal involves lowering the rear of the subframe. The stabilizer bar bushings and links can be replaced without removing the bar from the vehicle. If the bar is damaged, it is most likely the result of an accident that was severe enough to damage other major components (such as the subframe itself). Keep in mind that damage this severe will require the services of an auto body shop.*

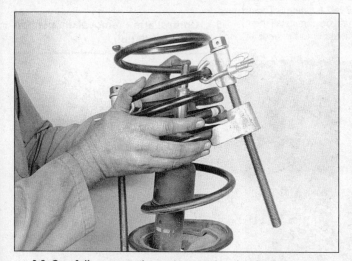

3.8 Carefully remove the compressed spring from the strut

3.10 When installing the spring, make sure the end rests against the raised stop

4.2 Hold the link (bolt) at the bottom while removing the nut at the top

4.3 Stabilizer bar bracket bolts

Note 2: *The manufacturer recommends using new subframe mounting bolts.*

1   Loosen the front wheel lug nuts, raise the front of the vehicle, support it securely on jackstands and remove the front wheels. **Note:** *Support the vehicle by placing the jackstands under the frame (unibody) and not under any of the suspension components or subframe.*

2   Remove the stabilizer link nut above the stabilizer bar by holding the link bolt at the control arm bracket **(see illustration)**. Remove the links. **Note:** *If you are only removing the links, disassemble and reassemble them one side at a time so that one side can serve as a reference for the other.*

3   Remove the bolts from the stabilizer bar bushing brackets **(see illustration)**. Remove the brackets from the bushings, prying them off if necessary. Remove the bushings from the bar, noting the direction of the split in the bushings made for their removal.

4   Remove the pinch-bolt from the intermediate shaft coupler to the steering gear input shaft (see Section 18).

5   Support the rear part of the subframe with a floor jack, then remove the two rear subframe mounting bolts **(see illustra-**

tion). **Warning:** *Do not work below any part of the subframe unless it is supported by jackstands.*

6   Slowly and carefully lower the subframe with the floor jack just enough to remove the stabilizer bar. At the same time, make sure the steering gear input shaft and shaft coupler separate without binding. Also, check for any wiring harnesses or hoses that may come under tension as the subframe is lowered and detach them if necessary. **Warning:** *Lowering the subframe more than necessary could damage other components, so be careful not to lower it too much.*

7   Carefully remove the bar.

8   Inspect the link and bar bushings for cracks and tears. If any are broken, damaged, distorted or worn, replace them.

9   Install the stabilizer bar (if removed) and bushings. Clean the areas on the stabilizer bar where the bushings are located. Lubricate the inside and outside of the bushings with vegetable oil (used in cooking) to simplify reassembly. **Caution:** *Don't use petroleum or mineral-based lubricants or brake fluid - they will lead to deterioration of the bushings.* These bushings are split so that you can install them without having to slide them onto the ends of

the stabilizer bar. Install the bushings with the slit in each bushing facing towards the rear of the vehicle.

10   Install the brackets and bolts, tightening the bolts to the torque listed in this Chapter's Specifications.

11   Slowly and carefully raise the subframe with the floor jack while guiding the steering gear input shaft into the shaft coupler. Install the pinch-bolt and tighten it to the torque listed in this Chapter's Specifications (if removed).

12   Install the rear subframe mounting bolts and tighten them to the torque listed in this Chapter's Specifications (if necessary).

13   Make sure that any wire harnesses or brackets that were removed to lower the subframe are reattached.

14   Install the links, tightening the link nuts to the torque listed in this Chapter's Specifications.

15   Install the wheels and lug nuts, then lower the vehicle. Tighten the wheel lug nuts to the torque listed in the Chapter 1 Specifications.

---

5   Control arm - removal, inspection and installation

Removal

Refer to illustrations 5.1 and 5.5

Note: *Due to the design of the front suspension, the manufacturer makes a special tool to separate the balljoint (on the control arm) from the steering knuckle without causing damage to the balljoint and boot. The tool can be ordered from a dealer service department but the cost is typically high. A picklefork balljoint separator tool (see illustration 6.7) can be used if you are replacing the control arm because the arm comes equipped with a new balljoint. Otherwise, use the following alternative because the picklefork method will damage the balljoint and boot. If you are removing the control arm to service the drive-*

4.5 Place a floor jack under the rear part of the subframe (A), then remove the two rear subframe bolts (B) and lower it just enough to remove the stabilizer bar

5.1 Mark the relationship of the control arm to the subframe bracket when the vehicle is at normal ride height

5.5 Control arm mounting details:

1   *Front pivot mounting nut and bolt*
2   *Rear mounting bolt*

axle or other components, separate it from the subframe and leave the balljoint attached to the steering knuckle while supporting it. Or, remove the control arm and steering knuckle together.

1   With the vehicle at normal ride height, mark the relationship of the control arm to the front mounting bracket (where it attaches to the subframe) **(see illustration)**. **Note:** *If you are replacing the control arm, transfer this mark to the replacement arm when the old one is removed.*

2   Loosen the wheel lug nuts on the side to be disassembled. Apply the parking brake, raise the front of the vehicle, support it securely on jackstands and remove the wheel.

3   Remove the stabilizer bar link from the control arm (see Section 4).

4   Remove the steering knuckle (see Section 7) or separate the balljoint from the steering knuckle (see the **Note** above).

5   Remove the fasteners that attach the control arm to the subframe **(see illustration)**.

6   Separate the control arm from the subframe.

Inspection

7   Check the control arm for distortion and the bushings for wear, replacing parts as necessary. Do not attempt to straighten a bent control arm. If the bushings are cracked or show signs of wear, take the control arm to an automotive machine shop and have the bushings replaced.

Installation

8   Installation is the reverse of removal; tighten all of the fasteners to the torque values listed in this Chapter's Specifications. **Note:** *Before tightening the control arm pivot bolt (front), raise the outer end of the control arm with a floor jack and match the reference marks made in step one to simulate normal ride height.* **Warning:** *Do not use the mount-*

ing fasteners if they do not meet the conditions stated in this Chapter's Torque Specifications.

9   Install the wheel and lug nuts, lower the vehicle and tighten the lug nuts to the torque listed in the Chapter 1 Specifications.

10   It's a good idea to have the front wheel alignment checked and, if necessary, adjusted after this job has been performed.

6   Balljoints - check and replacement

Check

1   Raise the front of the vehicle and support it securely on jackstands. Apply the parking brake and block the rear wheels to keep the vehicle from rolling off the jackstands.

2   Place a large prybar under the balljoint and resting on the wheel, then try to pry the balljoint up while feeling for movement between the balljoint and steering knuckle. Now, pry between the control arm and the steering knuckle and try to lever the control arm down while feeling for movement between

the balljoint and steering knuckle. If excessive movement is evident (over 0.125 of an inch) in either check, the balljoint is worn. Install a dial indicator and measure the amount of movement to be certain.

3   Have an assistant grasp the tire at the top and bottom and move the top of the tire in-and-out. Touch the balljoint stud nut. If excessive movement is evident (over 0.125 of an inch), the balljoint or knuckle is worn. Install a dial indicator and measure the amount of movement to be certain.

Replacement

Refer to illustration 6.6, 6.7 and 6.9

4   With the vehicle at normal ride height, mark the relationship of the control arm to the front mounting bracket (where it attaches to the subframe) **(see illustration 5.1)**.

5   Loosen the wheel lug nuts on the side to be disassembled. Apply the parking brake, raise the front of the vehicle, support it securely on jackstands and remove the wheel.

6   Remove the cotter pin from the ballstud and loosen the castle nut **(see illustration)**.

6.6 Balljoint mounting details:

1   *Cotter pin and castellated nut*
2   *Mounting rivets*

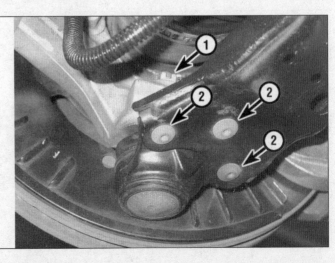

6.7 A picklefork balljoint separator tool can be used to separate the ballstud from the steering knuckle (but it will most likely damage the boot)

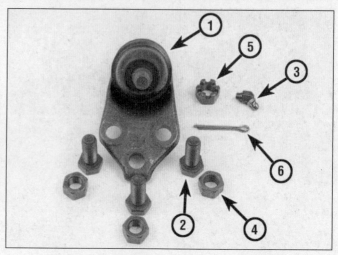

6.9 Replacement balljoint details (typical shown):

1 Replacement balljoint	4 Mounting nut
2 Mounting bolt	5 Castellated nut
3 Grease fitting	6 Cotter pin

7   Separate the balljoint from the steering knuckle **(see illustration)**.
8   Remove the control arm from the sub-frame (see Section 5).
9   Drill out the three rivets securing the balljoint, remove the balljoint and clean the control arm. Install the new balljoint against the mating surface of the control arm and secure it with the supplied fasteners (nuts and bolts are normally supplied with the new balljoint). Tighten the balljoint fasteners to the torque specified in the balljoint replacement kit instructions **(see illustration)**.
10   Install the control arm to the subframe and leave the fasteners loose.
11   Place the ballstud into the steering knuckle. Install the castle nut and tighten it to the torque listed in this Chapter's Specifications. Install a new cotter pin. **Note:** *If necessary, tighten the nut a little more to allow insertion of the cotter pin. Never loosen the nut to align the cotter pin holes.*

12   Using a jack, raise the control arm under the balljoint to simulate normal ride height and then tighten the control arm fasteners to the torque listed in this Chapter's Specifications. **Warning:** *Do not use the mounting fasteners if they do not meet the conditions stated in this Chapter's Torque Specifications.*
13   Install the wheel and lug nuts, lower the vehicle and tighten the lug nuts to the torque listed in the Chapter 1 Specifications.

---

7   Steering knuckle - removal and installation

Warning: *Dust created by the brake system is harmful to your health. Never blow it out with compressed air and don't inhale any of it. Do not, under any circumstances, use petroleum-based solvents to clean brake parts. Use brake system cleaner only.*

Removal

Refer to illustration 7.10

1   Loosen the wheel lug nuts, raise the front of the vehicle and support it securely on jackstands. Remove the wheel.
2   Disconnect the ABS wheels speed sensor electrical connector and detach it from its bracket. Also, detach the ABS wire harness from the control arm, if equipped **(see illustration 8.2)**.
3   Remove the driveaxle/hub nut (see Chapter 8).
4   Remove the brake caliper, the caliper mounting bracket and the brake disc from the hub (see Chapter 9). **Caution:** *Suspend the caliper to the strut coil spring using a piece of wire. DO NOT let the caliper hang by the brake hose.*
5   Remove the hub and bearing assembly (see Section 8). **Caution:** *Suspend the drive-axle using a piece of wire or cord. DO NOT let it hang freely or damage to the CV joint may occur.*
6   Detach the tie-rod end from the steering knuckle (see Section 16).
7   Mark the strut to the steering knuckle then remove the strut-to-steering knuckle bolts **(see illustrations 2.3a and 2.3b)**. **Note:** *Refer to Section 2 for special information regarding the removal of these fasteners.*
8   Separate the strut from the steering knuckle and suspend it with cord or wire so that it does not fall outward.
9   Remove the cotter pin from the ballstud on the balljoint and loosen the castle nut **(see illustration 6.6)**.
10   Use a balljoint separator tool to detach the balljoint from the steering knuckle **(see illustration)**. **Caution:** *Do not use a picklefork balljoint separator tool or damage to the balljoint and boot will occur.*
11   Remove the steering knuckle.

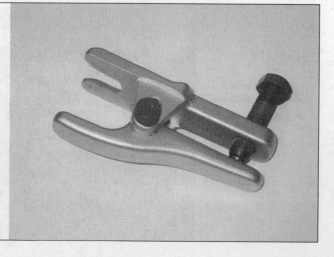

7.10 A balljoint separator tool like this one is available at most automotive parts stores and will not damage the balljoint boot when used correctly

8.2 Disconnect the ABS wheel speed sensor harness connector and remove it from the bracket

8.5 Hub and bearing assembly mounting bolt locations

Installation

12   Guide the knuckle into the strut mounting flange and insert the mounting fasteners. Do not tighten the nuts yet. **Note:** *Since the strut mounting bolts are serrated and designed to fit tightly into the steering knuckle and strut flange, use a soft-face hammer or mallet to install them.*

13   Guide the driveaxle in place and install the hub and bearing assembly leaving the mounting fasteners finger tight at this time. **Note:** *Be sure that the wire harness for the ABS wheel speed sensor is in the correct position, if equipped.*

14   Attach the ballstud to the steering knuckle and tighten the castle nut to the torque listed in this Chapter's Specifications, then install a new cotter pin. **Note:** *If necessary, tighten the nut a little more to allow insertion of the cotter pin. Never loosen the nut to align the cotter pin holes.*

15   Attach the tie-rod to the steering knuckle and tighten the tie-rod nut to the torque listed in this Chapter's Specifications.

16   Align the steering knuckle using the marks on the strut flange, then tighten the nuts to the torque listed in this Chapter's Specifications. **Warning:** *Do not use the mounting fasteners if they do not meet the conditions stated in this Chapter's Torque Specifications.*

17   Tighten the hub and bearing assembly mounting bolts to the torque listed in this Chapter's Specifications.

18   Install and connect the electrical connector for the ABS wheel speed sensor, if equipped.

19   Place the brake disc on the hub and install the caliper mounting bracket and caliper (see Chapter 9).

20   Install the driveaxle/hub nut and tighten it to the torque listed in the Chapter 8 Specifications.

21   Install the wheel and lug nuts.

22   Lower the vehicle and tighten the lug nuts to the torque listed in the Chapter 1 Specifications.

23   Have the front-end alignment checked and, if necessary, adjusted.

8   Hub and bearing assembly (front) - removal and installation

Removal

Refer to illustrations 8.2 and 8.5

1   Loosen the wheel lug nuts, raise the front of the vehicle and support it securely on jackstands. Remove the wheel.

2   Disconnect the ABS wheel speed sensor electrical connector and detach it from its bracket, if equipped **(see illustration)**.

3   Remove the driveaxle/hub nut (see Chapter 8).

4   Remove the brake caliper, the caliper mounting bracket and the brake disc from the hub (see Chapter 9). **Caution:** *Suspend the caliper to the strut coil spring with a piece of wire. DO NOT let the caliper hang by the brake hose.*

5   Remove the hub/bearing assembly mounting bolts from the back of the steering knuckle **(see illustration)**. Discard the mounting bolts.

6   Remove the hub/bearing assembly from the steering knuckle. **Note:** *If the driveaxle splines stick in the hub, push the driveaxle out of the hub with a two-jaw puller.*

Installation

Warning: *The manufacturer states that new hub/bearing mounting bolts must be used for installation.*

7   Make sure that the mounting surface inside the steering knuckle and on the driveaxle splines is smooth and free of burrs and nicks prior to installing the hub/bearing assembly.

8   Lubricate the driveaxle splines with multi-purpose grease. Install the hub/bearing assembly onto the driveaxle and into the steering knuckle until it is fully seated on the steering knuckle.

9   Install the hub/bearing assembly to the steering knuckle using NEW mounting bolts. Tighten the bolts to the torque listed in this Chapter's Specifications. On ABS equipped vehicles, connect the wheel speed sensor harness connector and secure it to its bracket.

10   Install the brake disc, the caliper mounting bracket and the caliper; tighten the fasteners to the torque values listed in the Chapter 9 Specifications.

11   Install the driveaxle/hub nut and tighten it to the torque listed in the Chapter 8 Specifications. **Note:** *Have an assistant apply the brakes while tightening the driveaxle/hub nut.*

12   Install the wheel and lug nuts, remove the jackstands and lower the vehicle.

13   Tighten the lug nuts to the torque listed in the Chapter 1 Specifications.

9   Strut assembly - removal, inspection and installation (rear)

Warning: *Always replace the struts and/or coil springs in pairs - never replace just one strut or one coil spring (this could cause dangerous handling peculiarities).*

Note: *For procedures regarding coil spring replacement on the rear struts, see Section 3 of this Chapter.*

Removal

Refer to illustrations 9.1 and 9.5

1   In the trunk compartment, move the side trim away to expose the strut upper mounting fasteners. Pull the rubber cap off the top of the strut, if equipped, then loosen, but do not

9.1 Location of the rear strut upper mounting fasteners

9.5 Location of the rear strut lower mounting fasteners

remove, the mounting fasteners **(see illustration)**.

2   Loosen the rear wheel lug nuts. Block the front wheels to keep the vehicle from rolling, then raise the rear of the vehicle and support it securely on jackstands. Remove the rear wheels.

3   Detach the stabilizer bar link from the strut (see Section 11).

4   Mark the relationship of the strut to the knuckle (these marks will be used during installation to ensure that the camber angle is returned to its original setting) **(see illustration 2.2)**.

5   Remove the strut-to-knuckle nuts while holding the oval shaped bolt heads with a wrench. Remove the bolts by striking the end with a hammer to push them out of the knuckle and strut **(see illustration 2.3 and the accompanying illustration)**. **Caution:** *Do not attempt to turn the strut mounting bolts. These bolts are serrated to fit tightly when seated against the strut mounting flange and in the holes of the knuckle.*

6   Separate the strut from the rear knuckle, then remove the upper mounting nuts and remove the strut. Secure the rear knuckle so that it does not fall outward and damage the brake hose or ABS wire harness, if equipped.

Inspection

7   Check the strut body for leaking fluid, dents, cracks and other obvious damage that would warrant repair or replacement.

8   Check the coil spring for chips or cracks in the spring coating (this can cause premature spring failure due to corrosion). Inspect the spring seat for cuts, hardness and general deterioration.

9   If any undesirable conditions exist, proceed to the strut disassembly procedure (see Section 3).

Installation

10   Guide the knuckle into the strut flange while placing the upper part of the strut in position where it mounts to the body. Install the upper mounting nuts finger-tight to hold the strut in place. Install the two bolts using a soft-face hammer or mallet. Install the nuts, align the marks made in Step 4, then tighten the nuts to the torque listed in this Chapter's Specifications. **Warning:** *Do not use the mounting nuts if they do not meet the conditions stated in this Chapter's Torque Specifications.*

11   Install the stabilizer bar link (see Section 11).

12   Install the wheel and lug nuts, then lower the vehicle and tighten the lug nuts to the torque listed in the Chapter 1 Specifications.

13   Tighten the upper mounting nuts to the torque listed in this Chapter's Specifications.

14   Have the wheel alignment checked and, if necessary, adjusted.

10   Hub and bearing assembly (rear) - removal and installation

Refer to illustrations 10.3, 10.5a and 10.5b

Warning: *Dust created by the brake system is harmful to your health. Never blow it out with compressed air and don't inhale any of it. Do not, under any circumstances, use petroleum-based solvents to clean brake parts. Use brake system cleaner only.*

1   Loosen the rear wheel lug nuts. Block the front wheels to keep the vehicle from rolling, then raise the rear of the vehicle and support it securely on jackstands. Remove the rear wheels.

2   Remove the brake caliper, the caliper mounting bracket and the brake disc from the hub (see Chapter 9). **Caution:** *Suspend the caliper to the strut coil spring with a piece of wire. DO NOT let the caliper hang by the brake hose.*

3   On ABS equipped vehicles, disconnect the wire harness for the wheel speed sensor **(see illustration)**.

4   Detach the parking brake cable from the actuator and the bracket attached to the rear backing plate (see Chapter 9).

5   Remove the hub mounting bolts and detach the hub assembly and parking brake assembly from the knuckle **(see illustrations)**. **Note:** *The wheel bearing and hub, backing plate, parking brake shoes and related components are removed as an assembly during wheel bearing removal.*

6   Remove the parking brake shoe and related components, then remove the hub and bearing (see Chapter 9).

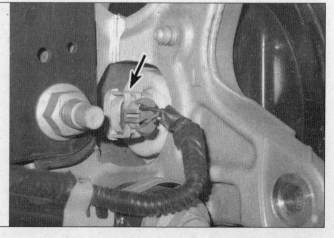

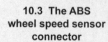

10.3 The ABS wheel speed sensor connector

10.5a Turn the hub to access the hub mounting bolts through the holes in the hub flange

10.5b Remove the hub and parking brake assembly together

7   Installation is the reverse of removal noting the following points:

a) *Be sure that the hub and bearing is installed in the correct direction for the ABS wheel speed sensor electrical connector, if equipped.*

b) *Tighten the NEW hub and bearing mounting bolts to the torque listed in this Chapter's Specifications.*

c) *Adjust the parking brake (see Chapter 9).*

8   Install the wheel and lug nuts, lower the vehicle and tighten the lug nuts to the torque listed in the Chapter 1 Specifications.

11 Stabilizer bar, bushings and links (rear) - removal and installation

Refer to illustrations 11.2 and 11.3

1   Loosen the rear wheel lug nuts. Block the front wheels to keep the vehicle from rolling, then raise the rear of the vehicle and support it securely on jackstands. Remove the rear wheels.

2   Detach the stabilizer bar links from the stabilizer bar (and also the rear struts to remove one or both links entirely) **(see illustration)**.

3   Remove the stabilizer bar bushing bracket fasteners **(see illustration)**.

4   Pull the brackets off the stabilizer bar, then remove the bar.

5   Inspect the bushings for cracks, hardness and other signs of deterioration. If the bushings are damaged, replace them.

6   Installation is the reverse of removal, noting the following points:

a) *Lubricate the inside and outside of the bushings with vegetable oil (used in cooking) to simplify reassembly.* **Caution:** *Don't use petroleum or mineral-based lubricants or brake fluid - they will lead to deterioration of the bushings. These bushings are split so that you can install them without having to slide them onto the ends of the stabilizer bar.)*

b) *Tighten the link and bracket fasteners to the torque values listed in this Chapter's Specifications.*

7   Install the wheel and lug nuts, lower the vehicle and tighten the lug nuts to the torque listed in the Chapter 1 Specifications.

12 Suspension arms (rear) - removal and installation

1   Loosen the rear wheel lug nuts. Block the front wheels to keep the vehicle from rolling, then raise the rear of the vehicle and support it securely on jackstands. Place the jackstands on the unibody portion of the chassis, not on any of the rear suspension components. Remove the rear wheels.

Suspension arm 1

Refer to illustrations 12.5, 12.6, 12.7 and 12.9

2   Remove the rear portion of the exhaust system (see Chapter 4).

3   Detach the stabilizer bar link from the stabilizer bar (see Section 11).

4   Remove the ABS wiring harness clips from the arm, if equipped.

11.2 Rear stabilizer bar link and mounting fasteners

11.3 Rear stabilizer bar bracket mounting nut

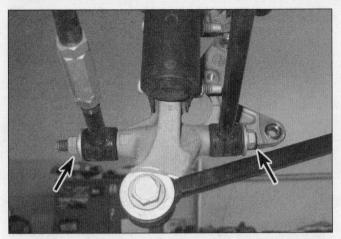

12.5 Suspension arm mounting fasteners at the knuckle

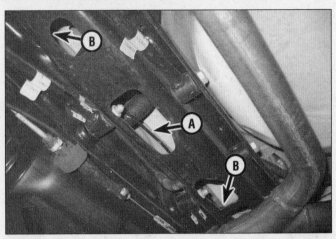

12.6 A brake line (A) is attached to the top of the rear suspension support with two small plastic clips (B - vicinity shown)

5   Remove the mounting fasteners for both suspension arms (1 and 2) at the rear knuckle, then detach both arms from the knuckle **(see illustration)**.
6   Detach the hydraulic brake line from the top of the rear suspension support. The plastic retainers can be pushed from the bottom to separate them from the support **(see illustration)**.
7   Place a floor jack beneath the rear suspension support and raise it until it just contacts the support at its center **(see illustration)**.
8   Remove the mounting bolts for the rear suspension support on the same side that the arm is being removed from. Loosen the mounting bolts on the opposite side of the support about one-half inch. This will allow the rear suspension support to pivot downward for access to the suspension arm mounting fasteners **(see illustration 12.7)**. **Note:** *Only remove the bolts on one side at a time (right or left) so that the rear suspension support is kept stable.*
9   Slowly and carefully lower the rear suspension support with the floor jack just

enough to get access to the suspension arm's mounting fasteners **(see illustration)**. **Caution:** *Do not lower the support to the point that the attached brake cables or wiring harnesses come under tension. Detach the brake cables from the parking brake actuators (see Chapter 9) and remove the wiring harnesses if necessary.*
10   Place a jackstand under the rear suspension support, then remove the floor jack.
11   Remove the mounting fasteners that hold the suspension arm to the rear suspension support, then remove the arm.
12   Inspect the suspension arm bushings for signs of deterioration. If they are in need of replacement, take the arm to an automotive machine shop to have the bushings replaced.
13   Installation is the reverse of removal. Tighten the mounting fasteners to the torque listed in this Chapter's Specifications.

Suspension arm 2

Refer to illustration 12.19
Note: *This suspension arm incorporates a toe*

adjustment mechanism that does not need to be disturbed during removal and installation.
14   Detach the stabilizer bar link from the stabilizer bar (see Section 11).
15   Remove the mounting fasteners for both suspension arms (1 and 2) at the rear knuckle, then detach the arm from the knuckle **(see illustration 12.5)**.
16   Detach the hydraulic brake line from the top of the rear suspension support. The plastic retainers can be pushed from the bottom to separate them from the support **(see illustration 12.6)**.
17   Place a floor jack beneath the rear suspension support and raise it until it just contacts the support at its center **(see illustration 12.7)**.
18   Remove the mounting bolts for the rear suspension support on the same side that the arm is being removed from. Loosen the mounting bolts on the opposite side of the support about one-half inch. This will allow the rear suspension support pivot downward for access to the suspension arm mounting fasteners **(see illustration 12.7)**. **Note:** *Only*

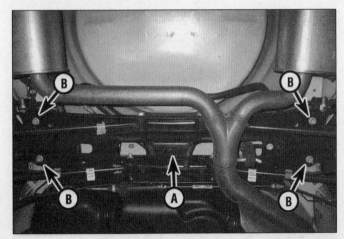

12.7 Rear suspension support (A) and mounting fasteners (B). Remove the support mounting fasteners on only one side (right or left) while loosening the fasteners on the other

12.9 Suspension arm 1 inner mounting fasteners

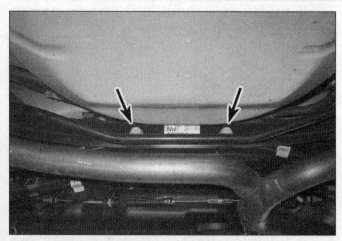

12.19 The suspension arm 2 mounting fasteners

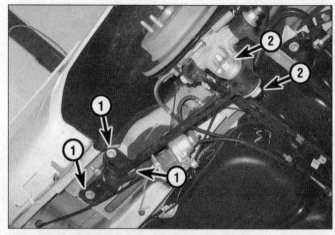

12.24 Trailing arm mounting details:

1   *Bracket-to-body mounting bolts*
2   *Trailing arm-to-knuckle fasteners*

remove the bolts on one side at a time (right or left) so that the rear suspension support is kept stable.

19   Slowly and carefully lower the rear suspension support with the floor jack just enough to get access to the suspension arm's mounting fasteners **(see illustration)**. **Caution:** *Do not lower the support to the point that the attached brake cables or wiring harnesses come under tension.*

20   Place a jackstand under the rear suspension support, then remove the floor jack.

21   Remove the mounting fasteners that hold the suspension arm to the rear suspension support, then remove the arm.

22   Inspect the suspension arm bushings for signs of deterioration. If they are in need of replacement, take the arm to an automotive machine shop to have the bushings replaced.

23   Installation is the reverse of removal. Tighten the mounting fasteners to the torque listed in this Chapter's Specifications.

Trailing arm

Refer to illustration 12.24

24   Remove the trailing arm bracket-to-body mounting bolts **(see illustration)**.

25   Remove the trailing arm-to-knuckle mounting fasteners and then remove the trailing arm **(see illustration 12.24)**.

26   Remove the trailing arm bracket from the trailing arm, if necessary.

27   Inspect the trailing arm bushing for signs of deterioration. If it is in need of replacement, take the trailing arm to an automotive machine shop to have the bushing replaced.

28   Installation is the reverse of removal. Tighten the mounting fasteners to the torque listed in this Chapter's Specifications.

All components

29   After the removal and installation of any of the rear suspension components, it's a good idea to have the wheel alignment checked and, if necessary, adjusted.

13 Knuckle (rear) - removal and installation

Warning: *Dust created by the brake system is harmful to your health. Never blow it out with compressed air and don't inhale any of it. Do not, under any circumstances, use petroleum-based solvents to clean brake parts. Use brake system cleaner only.*

1   Loosen the rear wheel lug nuts. Block the front wheels to keep the vehicle from rolling, then raise the rear of the vehicle and support it securely on jackstands. Remove the rear wheels.

2   Remove the hub and bearing assembly (see Section 10).

3   Remove the trailing arm-to-knuckle fasteners (see Section 12).

4   Detach both suspension arms (1 and 2) from the knuckle (see Section 12).

5   Remove the lower strut mounting fasteners (see Section 9).

6   Remove the knuckle.

7   Installation is the reverse of removal. Tighten all mounting fasteners to the torque values listed in this Chapter's Specifications.

8   Install the wheel and lug nuts, lower the vehicle and tighten the lug nuts to the torque listed in the Chapter 1 Specifications.

9   After the removal and installation of any of the rear suspension components, it's a good idea to have the wheel alignment checked and, if necessary, adjusted.

14 Steering wheel - removal and installation

Warning 1: *These models are equipped with a Supplemental Restraint System (SRS), more commonly known as airbags. Always disable the airbag system before working in the vicinity of any airbag system component to avoid the possibility of accidental deployment of the airbag(s), which could cause per-*

sonal injury (see Chapter 12).

Warning 2: *Do not use a memory saving device to preserve the PCM or radio memory when working on or near airbag system components.*

Removal

Refer to illustrations 14.3, 14.4a, 14.4b, 14.5, 14.6 and 14.9

1   Park the vehicle with the wheels pointing straight ahead. Disconnect the cable from the negative terminal of the battery (see Chapter 5, Section 1).

2   Disable the airbag system (see Chapter 12).

3   Remove the airbag module by inserting a thin round tool directly into the hole. Push slightly on the tool to release the retainer while gently pulling the airbag module towards you **(see illustration)**. Repeat this procedure on the other side of the steering wheel (there is

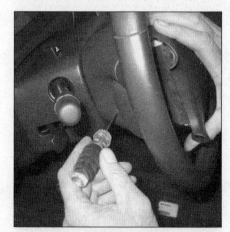

14.3 The airbag module is secured by spring clips that engage two posts on the airbag (one post per side); to release them, insert a thin blunt rod into the small hole on one side while gently pulling the airbag away from the steering wheel. Repeat this procedure on the other side

14.4a Lift up the small locks on both connectors . . .

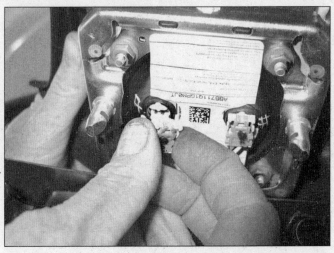

14.4b . . . then squeeze the sides of the connectors to release them from the module

one hole on each side).

4   With the airbag module released, disconnect the electrical connectors and remove the airbag module **(see illustrations)**. **Warning:** *When carrying the airbag module, keep the driver's side of it away from your body, and when you set it down (in an isolated area), have the driver's side facing up.*

5   Detach the clockspring wire harness from the steering wheel hub and disconnect the electrical connector for the steering wheel switches **(see illustration)**.

6   Note the index mark on the steering wheel hub and the steering shaft and confirm that they are in the 12 o'clock position **(see illustration)**.

7   Remove the steering wheel nut from the steering shaft.

8   Lift the steering wheel off the shaft. If is does not come off easily, remove it by installing a two-jaw puller; placing the puller jaws in the holes on the hub **(see illustration 14.6)**. **Caution 1:** *Be careful not to damage the airbag clockspring when installing the two-jaw*

puller. The jaws of the puller need to be thin enough to fit between the steering wheel hub and the airbag clockspring or the clockspring could be damaged.* **Caution 2:** *While the steering wheel is removed, DO NOT turn the steering shaft. Damage to the clockspring will occur if it's installed and the steering shaft is not centered.*

9   If it is necessary to remove the clockspring, remove the upper and lower steering column covers (see Chapter 11). Remove the snap-ring, detach the clockspring from the steering column and disconnect the electrical connectors from the back of it **(see illustration)**. **Caution:** *Use electrical tape to keep the clockspring rings aligned to one another until it is reinstalled. Otherwise, the clockspring will need to be re-centered.* **Note:** *It is not necessary to remove the clockspring to re-center it but it may be necessary to remove the steering column covers.*

Installation

10   When installing the clockspring, make sure that the wheels are pointing straight ahead, the steering shaft is lined up in the 12 o'clock position and that the airbag clockspring

is centered. This shouldn't be a problem as long as you have not turned the steering shaft from its centered position. If for some reason the shaft was turned, re-center it by placing the front wheels in the straight ahead position and align the index mark on the shaft to the 12 o'clock position. **Note:** *A gap in the splines on the steering shaft will be in the 12 o'clock position also.*

11   Center the clockspring as follows:

a) *Rotate the clockspring clockwise until it stops (don't apply too much force, though).*

b) *Rotate the clockspring counterclockwise about 2-1/2 turns and confirm that the two small arrows on the clockspring are aligned* **(see illustration 14.9)**.

12   The remainder of the installation is the reverse of removal, noting the following points:

a) *Make sure that the airbag clockspring is centered and the steering shaft is in the 12 o'clock position before installing the steering wheel.*

b) *When installing the steering wheel, align the index mark on the steering wheel hub*

14.5 Unclip the clockspring wiring harness (A) from the steering wheel hub and disconnect the electrical connector for the steering wheel switches (B)

14.6 Steering wheel hub details:

1   *Index mark on the steering wheel hub (at the 12 o'clock position)*

2   *Index mark on the steering shaft (at the 12 o'clock position)*

3   *Use these holes when using a puller tool to remove the steering wheel. DO NOT damage the clockspring that is directly beneath the hub*

14.9 Clockspring mounting details:

1   *Snap-ring that secures the clockspring to the steering shaft*
2   *Index marks that are used for centering the clockspring*

15.7 Remove the knee bolster support mounting fasteners

with the mark on the shaft **(see illustration 14.6)**. *This will align the block-tooth on the steering wheel hub with the gap on the steering shaft splines and ensure that the steering wheel is in the proper position on the steering shaft.*

c) *Install the steering wheel nut and tighten it to the torque listed in this Chapter's Specifications.*
d) *Install the airbag module on the steering wheel and push it into place until the retaining posts engage with the retaining springs.*
e) *Enable the airbag system (see Chapter 12).*

15 Steering column - removal and installation

Warning 1: *These models are equipped with airbags. Always disable the airbag system*

before working in the vicinity of any airbag system component to avoid the possibility of accidental deployment of the airbag(s), which could cause personal injury (see Chapter 12). **Warning 2:** *Do not use a memory saving device to preserve the PCM's memory when working on or near airbag system components.*

Removal

Refer to illustrations 15.7, 15.8, 15.9, 15.10 and 15.12

1   Park the vehicle with the wheels pointing straight ahead. Disconnect the cable from the negative terminal of the battery (see Chapter 5, Section 1).
2   Disable the airbag system (see Chapter 12).
3   Remove the steering column covers (see Chapter 11).
4   Remove the steering wheel (see Section 14).

5   Remove the airbag clockspring (see Section 14).
6   Remove the insulating panel from below the dash (see Chapter 11).
7   Remove the knee bolster (see Chapter 11) and the knee bolster support from under the steering column **(see illustration)**.
8   Disconnect the electrical connectors from the steering column switches and remove the wiring harness from the column **(see illustration)**.
9   Move the boot seal away from the intermediate shaft coupler **(see illustration)**.
10   Mark the relationship of the steering column shaft to the intermediate shaft coupler, then remove the pinch-bolt by removing the nut first **(see illustration)**.
11   Check for any remaining electrical connectors or wiring harnesses that would interfere with removal.
12   Remove the steering column mounting fasteners, then carefully guide the column

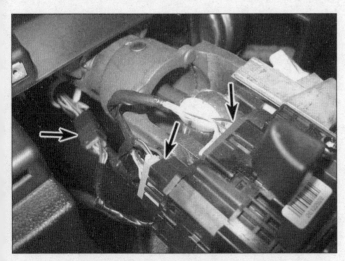

15.8 Disconnect all electrical connectors and move the wiring harnesses away from the steering column

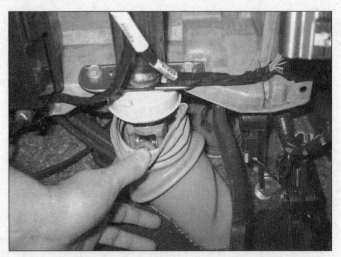

15.9 Move the intermediate shaft boot away from the coupler for access

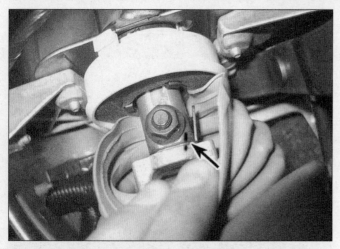

15.10 Mark the relationship of the steering shaft to the intermediate shaft coupler, then remove the coupler pinch-bolt by removing the nut first

15.12 Steering column mounting fastener locations

out from the instrument panel **(see illustration)**. **Note:** *If you are replacing the steering column, remove any components that will be used on the replacement column. For removal and installation of the electrical components (near the top of the column), refer to Chapter 12.*

Installation

13   Guide the column into position, connecting the steering shaft with the intermediate shaft coupler. Be sure to align the marks made in Step 8.

14   Install the mounting fasteners and tighten the bolts (first) then the nuts (second) to the torque listed in this Chapter's Specifications.

15   Install the intermediate shaft coupler pinch-bolt and nut and tighten the nut to the torque listed in this Chapter's Specifications.

16   The remainder of the installation is the reverse of the removal procedure. Refer to Section 14 for the clockspring, steering wheel and airbag module installation details.

16   Tie-rod ends - removal and installation

Removal

Refer to illustrations 16.2, 16.3 and 16.4

1   Loosen the wheel lug nuts, raise the front of the vehicle and support it securely on jackstands. Apply the parking brake and block the rear wheels to keep the vehicle from rolling off the jackstands. Remove the wheel.

2   Loosen the tie-rod end jam nut **(see illustration)**.

3   Mark the relationship of the tie-rod end to the threaded portion of the tie-rod. This will ensure the toe-in setting is restored when reassembled **(see illustration)**.

4   Loosen the tie-rod end ballstud nut a few turns, then install a puller to loosen the ballstud from the steering knuckle arm **(see illustration)**.

5   With the ballstud loose, remove the ball-

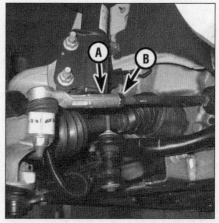

16.2 Using two wrenches, hold the tie-rod end (A) and loosen the jam nut (B)

stud nut and then completely separate the tie-rod end from the steering knuckle arm.

6   Unscrew the tie-rod end from the tie-rod.

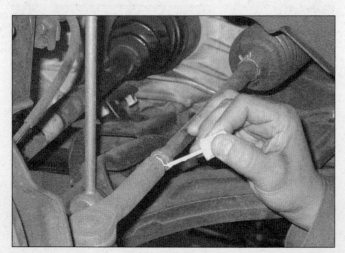

16.3 Mark the position of the tie-rod end in relation to the threads (typical shown)

16.4 Loosen the tie-rod end ballstud from the steering knuckle arm with a puller

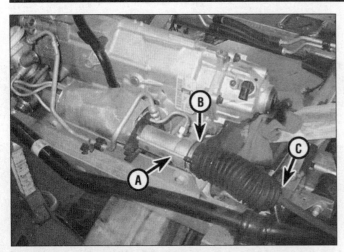

17.7 Location of the steering gear breather tube (A) (if equipped), the boot inner clamp (B) and the boot outer clamp (C) (engine, transmission and subframe removed for clarity)

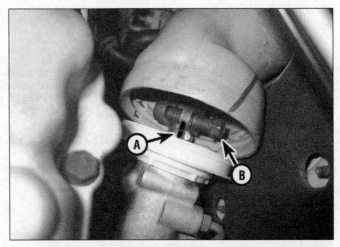

18.5 Pull the flexible boot away from the steering gear input shaft. Mark the relationship of the intermediate shaft coupler to the steering gear input shaft (A) and remove the coupler pinch-bolt (B)

Installation

7   Thread the tie-rod end onto the tie-rod to the marked position and insert the tie-rod end ballstud into the steering knuckle arm. Install the nut onto the ballstud and tighten it to the torque listed in this Chapter's Specifications.

8   Tighten the jam nut securely and install the wheel. Lower the vehicle and tighten the lug nuts to the torque listed in the Chapter 1 Specifications.

9   Have the front end alignment checked and, if necessary, adjusted.

17   Steering gear boots - removal and installation

Refer to illustration 17.7

Warning: *Make sure the steering shaft is not turned while the steering gear is detached or you could damage the airbag system clockspring. To prevent the shaft from turning, place the ignition key in the LOCK position or thread the seat belt through the steering wheel and clip it into place.*

Note 1: *Steering gear boot removal and installation involves lowering the rear of the subframe.*

Note 2: *The manufacturer recommends using new subframe mounting bolts.*

1   Loosen the front wheel lug nuts, raise the front of the vehicle, support it securely on jackstands and remove the front wheels. **Note:** *Support the vehicle by placing the jackstands under the frame (unibody) and not under any of the suspension components or subframe.*

2   Disconnect the stabilizer links from the stabilizer bar (see Section 4).

3   Remove the tie-rod end and jam nut (see Section 16).

4   Remove the pinch-bolt from the intermediate shaft coupler to the steering gear input shaft (see Section 18).

5   Support the rear part of the subframe with a floor jack, then remove the two rear subframe mounting bolts **(see illustration 4.5)**. **Warning:** *Do not work below any part of the subframe unless it is supported by jackstands.*

6   Slowly and carefully lower the subframe with the floor jack just enough to gain access to the inner clamps that secure the boots. At the same time, make sure the steering gear input shaft and shaft coupler separate without binding. Also, check for any wiring harnesses or hoses that may come under tension as the subframe is lowered and detach them if necessary. **Warning:** *Lowering the subframe more than necessary could damage other components so be careful not to lower it too much.*

7   Mark the steering gear housing with the position of the small breather tube that fits in the boot, if equipped **(see illustration)**.

8   Remove the outer steering gear boot clamp with a pair of pliers **(see illustration 17.7)**. Cut off the inner boot clamp with diagonal cutters and slide the boot off the rod.

9   Before installing the new boot, wrap the threads and spines on the end of the steering rod with a layer of tape so the small end of the new boot isn't damaged.

10   Slide the new boot into position on the steering gear. Make sure that the breather tube is connected and in the right position, if equipped. With the boot properly positioned on the housing and seated to the steering rod, install new clamps. **Note:** *Refer to Chapter 8 regarding boot clamps and tools needed to install them.*

11   Slowly and carefully raise the subframe with the floor jack while guiding the steering gear input shaft into the shaft coupler. Install the pinch-bolt and tighten the nut to the torque listed in this Chapter's Specifications.

12   Install the rear subframe mounting bolts and tighten them to the torque listed in this Chapter's Specifications.

13   Make sure that any wire harnesses or

brackets that were removed to lower the subframe are reattached.

14   Remove the tape and install the tie-rod end (see Section 16).

15   Install the stabilizer bar links (see Section 4).

16   Install the wheel and lug nuts. Lower the vehicle and tighten the lug nuts to the torque listed in the Chapter 1 Specifications.

17   Have the front end alignment checked and, if necessary, adjusted.

18   Steering gear - removal and installation

Warning: *Make sure the steering shaft is not turned while the steering gear is detached or you could damage the airbag system clockspring. To prevent the shaft from turning, place the ignition key in the LOCK position or thread the seat belt through the steering wheel and clip it into place.*

Note 1: *Steering gear removal and installation involves lowering the rear of the subframe.*

Note 2: *The manufacturer recommends using new subframe mounting bolts.*

Removal

Refer to illustrations 18.5 and 18.9

1   Loosen the front wheel lug nuts, raise the front of the vehicle and support it securely on jackstands. Remove both front wheels.

2   Remove the power steering fluid from the power steering reservoir. This can be accomplished with a suction gun or large syringe, or by disconnecting the fluid hose and draining the fluid into a container.

3   Disconnect the stabilizer links from the stabilizer bar (see Section 4).

4   Detach the tie-rod ends from the steering knuckles (see Section 16).

5   Move the boot covering the steering gear input shaft off the steering gear housing for access **(see illustration)**.

6   Mark the relationship of the intermediate shaft coupler to the steering gear input shaft. Remove the coupler pinch-bolt and detach the coupler **(see illustration 18.5)**.

7   Support the rear part of the subframe with a floor jack, then remove the two rear sub-frame mounting bolts **(see illustration 4.5)**. **Warning:** *Do not work below any part of the subframe unless it is supported by jackstands.*

8   Slowly and carefully lower the subframe with the floor jack just enough to remove the steering gear from the left side of the vehicle. At the same time, make sure the steering gear input shaft and shaft coupler separate without binding. Also, check for any wiring harnesses or hoses that may come under tension as the subframe is lowered and detach them if necessary. **Warning:** *Lowering the subframe more than necessary could damage other components so be careful not to lower it too much.*

9   Place a drain pan under the steering gear and detach the power steering pressure and return lines using a flare-nut wrench **(see illustration)**. Cap all openings to prevent excessive fluid loss and contamination. **Note:** *The lines are secured to the subframe by small plastic retainers.*

10   Remove the steering gear mounting fasteners **(see illustration 18.9)**.

11   Carefully guide the steering gear through the left wheel opening and out of the vehicle.

Installation

12   Installation is the reverse of removal, noting the following points:

a)   *Tighten the steering gear mounting fasteners to the torque listed in this Chapter's Specifications*

b)   *Slowly and carefully raise the subframe with the floor jack while guiding the steering gear input shaft into the intermediate shaft coupler.*

c)   *Install the rear subframe mounting bolts and tighten them to the torque listed in this Chapter's Specifications.*

d)   *Make sure that any wire harnesses or brackets that were removed to lower the subframe are reattached.*

18.9 Steering gear mounting details (engine, transmission and subframe removed for clarity)

1   *Return line fitting*
2   *Pressure line fitting*
3   *Mounting bolts (nuts are on other end)*

e)   *Install the pinch-bolt for the intermediate shaft coupler and tighten it to the torque listed in this Chapter's Specifications.*

f)   *Fill the power steering pump with the recommended fluid (see Chapter 1), bleed the system (see Section 20) and recheck the fluid level, if applicable.*

g)   *Run the engine and check for proper operation and leaks. Shut off the engine and recheck fluid levels, if applicable.*

h)   *Install the wheel and lug nuts. Lower the vehicle and tighten the lug nuts to the torque listed in the Chapter 1 Specifications.*

i)   *Have the front end alignment checked and, if necessary, adjusted.*

19   Power steering pump - removal and installation

Removal

Refer to illustrations 19.3 and 19.4

1   Use a large syringe or suction gun and remove as much fluid out of the power steering fluid reservoir as possible. Place a drain pan under the vehicle to catch any fluid that spills out when the hoses are disconnected.

2   Remove the drivebelt (see Chapter 1).

3   Disconnect the return hose from the power steering pump. Then, using a flare-nut wrench, unscrew the pressure line fitting from the pump **(see illustration)**.

4   Remove the mounting bolts securing the pump to the mounting bracket and remove the pump **(see illustration)**. **Note:** *The power steering pump pulley has holes that allow access to the pump mounting bolts on the other side of the pulley. Also, it may be necessary to remove the pulley in some applications. Pulley removal and installation tools are available at most auto parts stores. When installing the pulley, the hub of the pulley should be flush (even) with the end of the pump shaft.*

Installation

Note: *If you're installing a new pump, it may be necessary to transfer the old pulley to the new pump (see **Note** above).*

5   Installation is the reverse of removal,

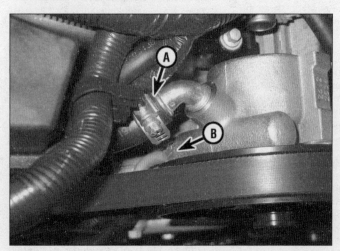

19.3 Power steering return hose (A) and pressure line (B)

19.4 Power steering pump mounting fasteners (one hidden from view)

21.5 Engine splash shield and fasteners

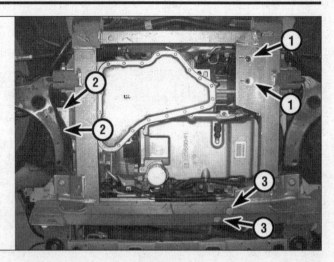

21.10 Subframe mounting details (V8 model shown, others are similar):

1   Transaxle mount-to-subframe fasteners
2   Right engine mount-to-subframe fasteners (one hidden)
3   Front engine mount-to-subframe fasteners (access through holes)

noting the following points:

a) Tighten the mounting bolts to the torque listed in this Chapter's Specifications and tighten the line and hose fittings securely.
b) Install the drivebelt as outlined in Chapter 1.
c) Fill the power steering reservoir with the recommended fluid (see Chapter 1). Bleed the power steering hydraulic system as described in Section 20.

20 Power steering system - bleeding

1   The power steering system must be bled whenever a line is disconnected. Bubbles can be seen in power steering fluid that has air in it and the fluid will often have a tan or milky appearance. Low fluid level can cause air to mix with the fluid, resulting in a noisy pump as well as foaming of the fluid.
2   Open the hood and check the fluid level in the reservoir, adding the specified fluid necessary to bring it up to the proper level (see Chapter 1).
3   Raise the front of the vehicle and support it securely on jackstands.

4   Turn the ignition key ON but leave the engine OFF. Slowly turn the steering wheel completely from left-to-right.
5   Check the fluid level again.
6   Start the engine and verify that there is no noise coming from the power steering system as the wheels are turned.
7   Lower the vehicle, check the fluid level, turn the steering wheel and confirm that the power steering system is working properly.

21 Subframe - removal and installation

Refer to illustrations 21.5, 21.10, 21.11, 21.12 and 21.14

Note: The manufacturer recommends using new subframe mounting bolts.
1   With the vehicle at normal ride height, mark the relationship of the control arm to the front mounting bracket (where it attaches to the subframe) (see illustration 5.1).
2   Disconnect the cable from the negative battery terminal (see Chapter 5, Section 1).
3   Loosen the front wheel lug nuts, raise

the front of the vehicle and support it securely on jackstands. Remove both front wheels. Note: The jackstands must be placed away from the subframe and not used on any part of the front suspension.
4   Attach an engine support fixture to the top of the engine or attach an engine hoist to support the engine and transaxle (see Chapter 2).
5   Remove the engine splash shield that's attached to the bottom of the front bumper cover - refer to Bumper Covers - removal and installation in Chapter 11. Also, remove the small splash shields above each side of the subframe (see illustration).
6   Disconnect the front ABS wheels speed sensors and detach the wire harness from the control arms and the subframe (if equipped) (see illustration 8.2). Carefully secure the harnesses aside.
7   Disconnect the stabilizer bar links from the stabilizer bar (see Section 4).
8   Pivot the stabilizer bar up for access, then remove the power steering gear mounting fasteners. Tie the gear to the exhaust manifold to secure it. Note: The tie-rod ends and intermediate steering shaft coupler can stay attached to the steering gear when the gear is secured to the exhaust.
9   Detach the control arms from the subframe and secure the ends so that the arms do not hang loosely by the lower balljoints (see Section 5). Note: The front mounting point of each control arm must be pulled away from the subframe when it's lowered to clear its mounting bracket on the subframe.
10   Remove the fasteners that attach the engine and transaxle mounts to the subframe (see illustration).
11   Remove the power steering fluid lines routed along the subframe and secure them to the engine (see illustration). Note: The lines run from the power steering gear to the front of the engine on the right side of the subframe.
12   Carefully mark the position of the subframe in relation to the vehicle chassis (see illustration).
13   Thoroughly check for wiring harnesses or anything else that may be attached to the

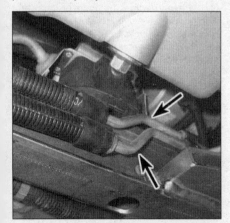

21.11 Power steering fluid lines at the front part of the subframe just below the front engine mount (V8 model shown, others are similar)

21.12 Mark the relationship of the subframe to the body (A) on both right corners of the subframe and note the alignment holes (B) - one corner shown

subframe. Detach them before continuing on to the next step.

14   Position one jack on each side of the subframe to support it. Place them midway between the front and rear mounting points **(see illustration)**.

15   Remove the subframe mounting bolts **(see illustration 21.14)**.

16   Slowly lower the floor jacks until the subframe is clear of the vehicle and the floor jacks are down fully.

17   Inspect the subframe mounting bushings for cracks, hardness and other signs of deterioration. If the bushings are damaged, replace them. **Note**: *A special tool may be necessary to remove and install the bushings. Most automotive repair shops that specialize in front-end alignment and suspension repair will have the ability to press the bushings out and install new bushings.*

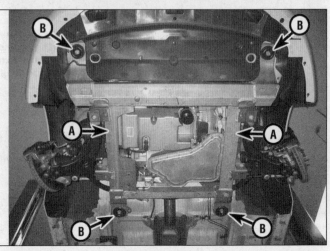

21.14 Place the floor jacks on each side of the subframe (A), then remove the subframe mounting bolts (B)

Installation

18   Installation is the reverse of removal, noting the following points:

a) *Raise and support the subframe with the floor jacks while guiding the subframe into position and onto the studs for the engine and transaxle mounts. Install the subframe mounting bolts until they are all finger tight.*

b) *Align the subframe using the reference marks made earlier and by using a punch or drift in the alignment holes provided. Tighten the subframe mounting bolts to the torque listed in this Chapter's Speci-*

fications **(see illustration 21.12)**.

c) *Tighten the engine and transaxle mount fasteners to the torque values listed in the Chapter 2 and Chapter 7 Specifications.*

d) *Tighten the control arm and steering gear mounting fasteners to the torque values listed in this Chapter's Specifications. Raise the control arm to normal ride height before tightening the mounting fasteners.*

e) *Reconnect the negative battery cable (see Chapter 5, Section 1).*

f) *Have the front end alignment checked and, if necessary, adjusted.*

22   Wheels and tires - general information

Refer to illustration 22.1

1   All vehicles covered by this manual are equipped with metric-sized fiberglass or steel belted radial tires **(see illustration)**. Use of other size or type of tires may affect the ride and handling of the vehicle. Don't mix different types of tires, such as radials and bias belted, on the same vehicle as handling may be seriously affected. It's recommended that tires be replaced in pairs on the same axle, but if only one tire is being replaced, be sure it's the same size, structure and tread design as the other.

2   Because tire pressure has a substantial effect on handling and wear, the pressure on all tires should be checked at least once a month or before any extended trips (see Chapter 1).

3   Wheels must be replaced if they are bent, dented, leak air, have elongated bolt holes, are heavily rusted, out of vertical symmetry or if the lug nuts won't stay tight. Wheel repairs that use welding or peening are not recommended.

4   Tire and wheel balance is important in the overall handling, braking and performance of the vehicle. Unbalanced wheels can adversely affect handling and ride characteristics as well as tire life. Whenever a tire is installed on a wheel, the tire and wheel should be balanced by a shop with the proper equipment.

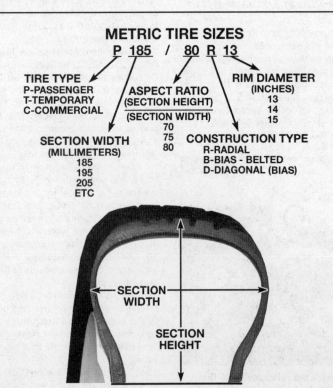

METRIC TIRE SIZES

P 185 / 80 R 13

TIRE TYPE
P-PASSENGER
T-TEMPORARY
C-COMMERCIAL

ASPECT RATIO
(SECTION HEIGHT)
―――――――――
(SECTION WIDTH)
70
75
80

RIM DIAMETER
(INCHES)
13
14
15

SECTION WIDTH
(MILLIMETERS)
185
195
205
ETC

CONSTRUCTION TYPE
R-RADIAL
B-BIAS - BELTED
D-DIAGONAL (BIAS)

SECTION WIDTH

SECTION HEIGHT

22.1 Metric tire size code

23   Wheel alignment - general information

Refer to illustration 23.1

A wheel alignment refers to the adjustments made to the wheels so they are in proper angular relationship to the suspension and the ground. Wheels that are out of proper alignment not only affect vehicle control, but also increase tire wear. The front end angles normally measured are camber, caster and toe-in **(see illustration)**. Toe-in and camber are adjustable; if the caster is not correct, check for bent components. Rear toe-in and camber are also adjustable.

Getting the proper wheel alignment is a very exacting process, one in which complicated and expensive machines are necessary to perform the job properly. Because of this, you should have a technician with the proper equipment perform these tasks. We will, however, use this space to give you a basic idea of what is involved with a wheel alignment so you can better understand the process and deal intelligently with the shop that does the work.

Toe-in is the turning in of the wheels. The purpose of a toe specification is to ensure parallel rolling of the wheels. In a vehicle with zero toe-in, the distance between the front edges of the wheels will be the same as the distance between the rear edges of the wheels. The actual amount of toe-in is normally only a fraction of an inch. On the front end, toe-in is controlled by the tie-rod end position on the tie-rod. On the rear end, it's controlled by the position of the suspension toe link on the chassis. Incorrect toe-in will cause the tires to wear improperly by making them scrub against the road surface.

Camber is the tilting of the wheels from vertical when viewed from one end of the vehicle. When the wheels tilt out at the top, the camber is said to be positive (+). When the wheels tilt in at the top the camber is negative (-). The amount of tilt is measured in degrees from vertical and this measurement is called the camber angle. This angle affects the amount of tire tread which contacts the road and compensates for changes in the suspension geometry when the vehicle is cornering or traveling over an undulating surface. Camber can be adjusted on the front end, but will require a modification of the lower strut-to-knuckle bolt hole on the strut. The strut must be disconnected from the steering knuckle, the lower mounting bolt holes elongated (from side-to-side), then reassembled. The relationship of the steering knuckle to the strut can then be altered. On the rear end, camber is controlled by the position of the lower control arm on the subframe.

Caster is the tilting of the front steering axis from the vertical. A tilt toward the rear is positive caster and a tilt toward the front is negative caster.

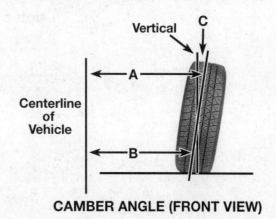

CAMBER ANGLE (FRONT VIEW)

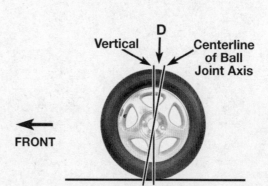

CASTER ANGLE (SIDE VIEW)

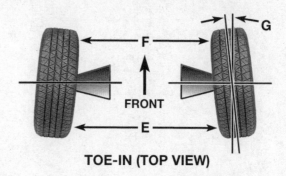

TOE-IN (TOP VIEW)

23.1 Camber, caster and toe-in angles

A minus B = C (degrees camber)
D = degrees caster

E minus F = toe-in (measured in inches)
G = toe-in (expressed in degrees)

Notes

Chapter 11
Body

Contents

1   General information

The Chevrolet Impala and Monte Carlo models covered by this manual feature unibody construction, in which the major body components, floor pan and front and rear frame side rails are welded together to create a rigid structure which supports the remaining body components, drivetrain, front and rear suspension and other components.

Certain components are particularly vulnerable to accident damage and can be unbolted and repaired or replaced. Among these parts are the body moldings, bumpers, front fenders, doors, the hood and trunk lid. Only general body maintenance practices and body panel repair procedures within the scope of the do-it-yourselfer are included in this Chapter.

Although all models are very similar, some procedures may differ somewhat from one body to another.

2   Body - maintenance

1   The condition of your vehicle's body is very important, because the resale value depends a great deal on it. It's much more difficult to repair a neglected or damaged body than it is to repair mechanical components. The hidden areas of the body, such as the wheel wells, the frame and the engine compartment, are equally important, although they don't require as frequent attention as the rest of the body.
2   Once a year, or every 12,000 miles, it's a good idea to have the underside of the body steam cleaned. All traces of dirt and oil will be removed and the area can then be inspected carefully for rust, damaged brake lines, frayed electrical wires, damaged cables and other problems.
3   At the same time, clean the engine and the engine compartment with a steam cleaner or water-soluble degreaser.

4   The wheel wells should be given close attention, since undercoating can peel away and stones and dirt thrown up by the tires can cause the paint to chip and flake, allowing rust to set in. If rust is found, clean down to the bare metal and apply an anti-rust paint.
5   The body should be washed about once a week. Wet the vehicle thoroughly to soften the dirt, then wash it down with a soft sponge and plenty of clean soapy water. If the surplus dirt is not washed off very carefully, it can wear down the paint.
6   Spots of tar or asphalt thrown up from the road should be removed with a cloth soaked in solvent.
7   Once every six months, wax the body and chrome trim. If a chrome cleaner is used to remove rust from any of the vehicle's plated parts, remember that the cleaner also removes part of the chrome, so use it sparingly. After cleaning chrome trim, apply paste wax to preserve it.

3 Vinyl trim - maintenance

Don't clean vinyl trim with detergents, caustic soap or petroleum-based cleaners. Plain soap and water works just fine, with a soft brush to clean dirt that may be ingrained. Wash the vinyl as frequently as the rest of the vehicle. After cleaning, application of a high-quality rubber and vinyl protectant will help prevent oxidation and cracks. The protectant can also be applied to weatherstripping, vacuum lines and rubber hoses, which often fail as a result of chemical degradation, and to the tires.

4 Upholstery and carpets - maintenance

1   Every three months, remove the floormats and clean the interior of the vehicle (more frequently if necessary). Use a stiff whiskbroom to brush the carpeting and loosen dirt and dust, then vacuum the upholstery and carpets thoroughly, especially along seams and crevices.

2   Dirt and stains can be removed from carpeting with basic household or automotive carpet shampoos available in spray cans. Follow the directions and vacuum again, then use a stiff brush to bring back the nap of the carpet.

3   Most interiors have cloth or vinyl upholstery, either of which can be cleaned and maintained with a number of material-specific cleaners or shampoos available in auto supply stores. Follow the directions on the product for usage, and always spot-test any upholstery cleaner on an inconspicuous area (bottom edge of a backseat cushion) to ensure that it doesn't cause a color shift in the material.

4   After cleaning, vinyl upholstery should be treated with a protectant. **Note:** *Make sure the protectant container indicates the product can be used on seats - some products may make a seat too slippery.* **Caution:** *Do not use protectant on vinyl-covered steering wheels.*

5   Leather upholstery requires special care. It should be cleaned regularly with saddle-soap or leather cleaner. Never use alcohol, gasoline, water, nail polish remover or thinner to clean leather upholstery.

6   After cleaning, regularly treat leather upholstery with a leather conditioner, rubbed in with a soft cotton cloth. Never use car wax on leather upholstery.

7   In areas where the interior of the vehicle is subject to bright sunlight, cover leather seating areas of the seats with a sheet if the vehicle is to be left out for any length of time.

5 Body repair - minor damage

Repair of scratches

1   If the scratch is superficial and does not penetrate to the metal of the body, repair is very simple. Lightly rub the scratched area with a fine rubbing compound to remove loose paint and built-up wax. Rinse the area with clean water.

2   Apply touch-up paint to the scratch, using a small brush. Continue to apply thin layers of paint until the surface of the paint in the scratch is level with the surrounding paint. Allow the new paint at least two weeks to harden, then blend it into the surrounding paint by rubbing with a very fine rubbing compound. Finally, apply a coat of wax to the scratch area.

3   If the scratch has penetrated the paint and exposed the metal of the body, causing the metal to rust, a different repair technique is required. Remove all loose rust from the bottom of the scratch with a pocket knife, then apply rust inhibiting paint to prevent the formation of rust in the future. Using a rubber or nylon applicator, coat the scratched area with glaze-type filler. If required, the filler can be mixed with thinner to provide a very thin paste, which is ideal for filling narrow scratches. Before the glaze filler in the scratch hardens, wrap a piece of smooth cotton cloth around the tip of a finger. Dip the cloth in thinner and then quickly wipe it along the surface of the scratch. This will ensure that the surface of the filler is slightly hollow. The scratch can now be painted over as described earlier in this Section.

Repair of dents

See photo sequence

4   When repairing dents, the first job is to pull the dent out until the affected area is as close as possible to its original shape. There is no point in trying to restore the original shape completely as the metal in the damaged area will have stretched on impact and cannot be restored to its original contours. It is better to bring the level of the dent up to a point which is about 1/8-inch below the level of the surrounding metal. In cases where the dent is very shallow, it is not worth trying to pull it out at all.

5   If the back side of the dent is accessible, it can be hammered out gently from behind using a soft-face hammer. While doing this, hold a block of wood firmly against the opposite side of the metal to absorb the hammer blows and prevent the metal from being stretched.

6   If the dent is in a section of the body which has double layers, or some other factor makes it inaccessible from behind, a different technique is required. Drill several small holes through the metal inside the damaged area, particularly in the deeper sections. Screw long, self tapping screws into the holes just enough for them to get a good grip in the metal. Now the dent can be pulled out by pulling on the protruding heads of the screws with locking pliers.

7   The next stage of repair is the removal of paint from the damaged area and from an inch or so of the surrounding metal. This is easily done with a wire brush or sanding disk in a drill motor, although it can be done just as effectively by hand with sandpaper. To complete the preparation for filling, score the surface of the bare metal with a screwdriver or the tang of a file or drill small holes in the affected area. This will provide a good grip for the filler material. To complete the repair, see the Section on *Filling and painting.*

Repair of rust holes or gashes

8   Remove all paint from the affected area and from an inch or so of the surrounding metal using a sanding disk or wire brush mounted in a drill motor. If these are not available, a few sheets of sandpaper will do the job just as effectively.

9   With the paint removed, you will be able to determine the severity of the corrosion and decide whether to replace the whole panel, if possible, or repair the affected area. New body panels are not as expensive as most people think and it is often quicker to install a new panel than to repair large areas of rust.

10   Remove all trim pieces from the affected area except those which will act as a guide to the original shape of the damaged body, such as headlight shells, etc. Using metal snips or a hacksaw blade, remove all loose metal and any other metal that is badly affected by rust. Hammer the edges of the hole on the inside to create a slight depression for the filler material.

11   Wire brush the affected area to remove the powdery rust from the surface of the metal. If the back of the rusted area is accessible, treat it with rust inhibiting paint.

12   Before filling is done, block the hole in some way. This can be done with sheet metal riveted or screwed into place, or by stuffing the hole with wire mesh.

13   Once the hole is blocked off, the affected area can be filled and painted. See the following subsection on *Filling and painting.*

Filling and painting

14   Many types of body fillers are available, but generally speaking, body repair kits which contain filler paste and a tube of resin hardener are best for this type of repair work. A wide, flexible plastic or nylon applicator will be necessary for imparting a smooth and contoured finish to the surface of the filler material. Mix up a small amount of filler on a clean piece of wood or cardboard (use the hardener sparingly). Follow the manufacturer's instructions on the package, otherwise the filler will set incorrectly.

15   Using the applicator, apply the filler paste to the prepared area. Draw the applicator across the surface of the filler to achieve the desired contour and to level the filler surface. As soon as a contour that approximates the original one is achieved, stop working the paste. If you continue, the paste will begin to stick to the applicator. Continue to add thin layers of paste at 20-minute intervals until the level of the filler is just above the surrounding metal.

16   Once the filler has hardened, the excess can be removed with a body file. From then on, progressively finer grades of sandpaper should be used, starting with a 180-grit paper and finishing with 600-grit wet-or-dry paper. Always wrap the sandpaper around a flat rubber or wooden block, otherwise the surface of the filler will not be completely flat. During the sanding of the filler surface, the wet-or-dry paper should be periodically rinsed in water. This will ensure that a very smooth finish is produced in the final stage.

17   At this point, the repair area should be surrounded by a ring of bare metal, which in turn should be encircled by the finely feathered edge of good paint. Rinse the repair area with clean water until all of the dust produced by the sanding operation is gone.

18   Spray the entire area with a light coat of primer. This will reveal any imperfections in the surface of the filler. Repair the imperfections with fresh filler paste or glaze filler and once more smooth the surface with sandpaper. Repeat this spray-and-repair procedure until you are satisfied that the surface of the filler and the feathered edge of the paint are perfect. Rinse the area with clean water and allow it to dry completely.

19   The repair area is now ready for painting. Spray painting must be carried out in a warm, dry, windless and dust free atmosphere. These conditions can be created if you have access to a large indoor work area, but if you are forced to work in the open, you will have to pick the day very carefully. If you are working indoors, dousing the floor in the work area with water will help settle the dust which would otherwise be in the air. If the repair area is confined to one body panel, mask off the surrounding panels. This will help minimize the effects of a slight mismatch in paint color. Trim pieces such as chrome strips, door handles, etc., will also need to be masked off or removed. Use masking tape and several thickness of newspaper for the masking operations.

20   Before spraying, shake the paint can thoroughly, then spray a test area until the spray painting technique is mastered. Cover the repair area with a thick coat of primer. The thickness should be built up using several thin layers of primer rather than one thick one. Using 600-grit wet-or-dry sandpaper, rub down the surface of the primer until it is very smooth. While doing this, the work area should be thoroughly rinsed with water and the wet-or-dry sandpaper periodically rinsed as well. Allow the primer to dry before spraying additional coats.

21   Spray on the top coat, again building up the thickness by using several thin layers of paint. Begin spraying in the center of the repair area and then, using a circular motion, work out until the whole repair area and about two inches of the surrounding original paint is covered. Remove all masking material 10 to 15 minutes after spraying on the final coat of paint. Allow the new paint at least two weeks to harden, then use a very fine rubbing compound to blend the edges of the new paint

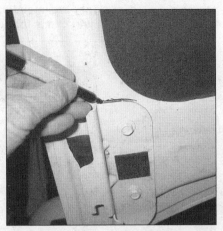

9.2 Before removing the hood, draw a mark around the hinge plate

into the existing paint. Finally, apply a coat of wax.

6   Body repair - major damage

1   Major damage must be repaired by an auto body shop specifically equipped to perform body and frame repairs. These shops have the specialized equipment required to do the job properly.

2   If the damage is extensive, the body must be checked for proper alignment or the vehicle's handling characteristics may be adversely affected and other components may wear at an accelerated rate.

3   Due to the fact that all of the major body components (hood, fenders, etc.) are separate and replaceable units, any seriously damaged components should be replaced rather than repaired. Sometimes the components can be found in a wrecking yard that specializes in used vehicle components, often at considerable savings over the cost of new parts.

7   Hinges and locks - maintenance

Once every 3000 miles, or every three months, the hinges and latch assemblies on the doors, hood and trunk should be given a few drops of light oil or lock lubricant. The door latch strikers should also be lubricated with a thin coat of grease to reduce wear and ensure free movement. Lubricate the door and trunk locks with spray-on graphite lubricant.

8   Windshield and fixed glass - replacement

Replacement of the windshield and fixed glass requires the use of special fast-setting adhesive/caulk materials and some specialized tools and techniques. These operations should be left to a dealer service department or a shop specializing in glass work.

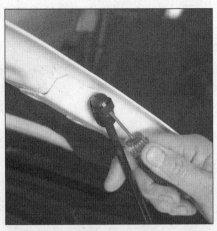

9.4a Use a small screwdriver to pry the clip out of its locking groove, then detach the end of the strut from the locating stud

9.4b Support the hood with your shoulder while removing the hood bolts

9   Hood - removal, installation and adjustment

Removal and installation

Refer to illustrations 9.2, 9.4a and 9.4b

Note: *The hood is somewhat awkward to remove and install; at least two people should perform this procedure.*

1   Open the hood, then place blankets or pads over the fenders and cowl area of the body. This will protect the body and paint as the hood is lifted off.

2   Make marks or scribe a line around the hood hinge to ensure proper alignment during installation **(see illustration)**.

3   Disconnect any cables or wires that will interfere with removal.

4   Support one side of the hood while an assistant supports the other and remove the hood support strut **(see illustration)**. Remove the hinge-to-hood bolts and lift off the hood **(see illustration)**.

5   Installation is the reverse of removal. Align the hinge bolts with the marks made in Step 2.

These photos illustrate a method of repairing simple dents. They are intended to supplement *Body repair - minor damage* in this Chapter and should not be used as the sole instructions for body repair on these vehicles.

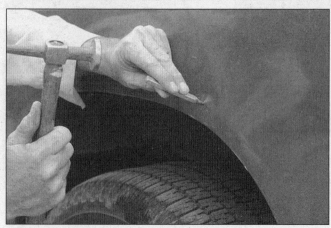

1 If you can't access the backside of the body panel to hammer out the dent, pull it out with a slide-hammer-type dent puller. In the deepest portion of the dent or along the crease line, drill or punch hole(s) at least one inch apart . . .

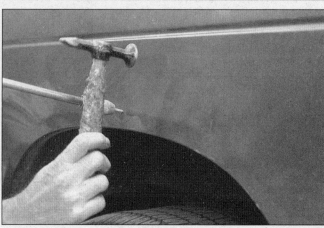

2 . . . then screw the slide-hammer into the hole and operate it. Tap with a hammer near the edge of the dent to help 'pop' the metal back to its original shape. When you're finished, the dent area should be close to its original contour and about 1/8-inch below the surface of the surrounding metal

3 Using coarse-grit sandpaper, remove the paint down to the bare metal. Hand sanding works fine, but the disc sander shown here makes the job faster. Use finer (about 320-grit) sandpaper to feather-edge the paint at least one inch around the dent area

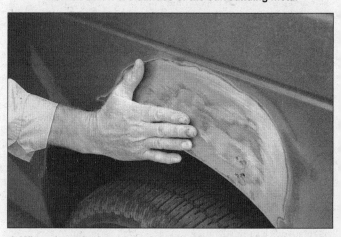

4 When the paint is removed, touch will probably be more helpful than sight for telling if the metal is straight. Hammer down the high spots or raise the low spots as necessary. Clean the repair area with wax/silicone remover

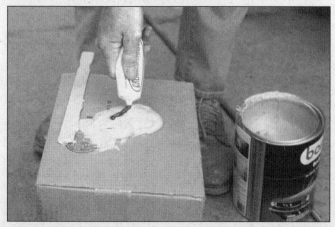

5 Following label instructions, mix up a batch of plastic filler and hardener. The ratio of filler to hardener is critical, and, if you mix it incorrectly, it will either not cure properly or cure too quickly (you won't have time to file and sand it into shape)

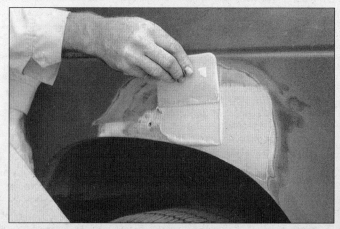

6 Working quickly so the filler doesn't harden, use a plastic applicator to press the body filler firmly into the metal, assuring it bonds completely. Work the filler until it matches the original contour and is slightly above the surrounding metal

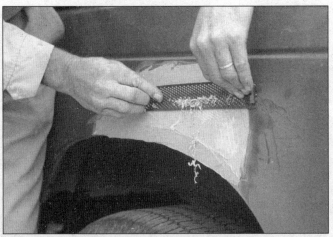

7 Let the filler harden until you can just dent it with your fingernail. Use a body file or Surform tool (shown here) to rough-shape the filler

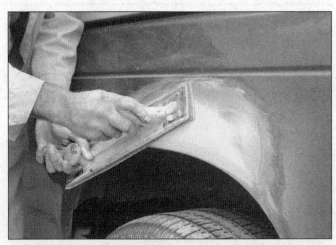

8 Use coarse-grit sandpaper and a sanding board or block to work the filler down until it's smooth and even. Work down to finer grits of sandpaper - always using a board or block - ending up with 360 or 400 grit

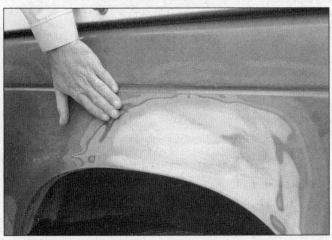

9 You shouldn't be able to feel any ridge at the transition from the filler to the bare metal or from the bare metal to the old paint. As soon as the repair is flat and uniform, remove the dust and mask off the adjacent panels or trim pieces

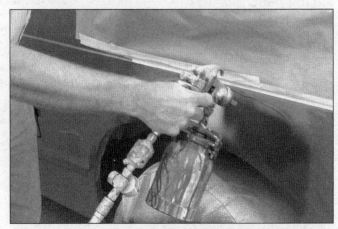

10 Apply several layers of primer to the area. Don't spray the primer on too heavy, so it sags or runs, and make sure each coat is dry before you spray on the next one. A professional-type spray gun is being used here, but aerosol spray primer is available inexpensively from auto parts stores

11 The primer will help reveal imperfections or scratches. Fill these with glazing compound. Follow the label instructions and sand it with 360 or 400-grit sandpaper until it's smooth. Repeat the glazing, sanding and respraying until the primer reveals a perfectly smooth surface

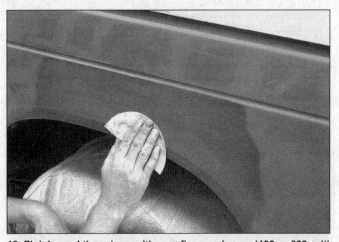

12 Finish sand the primer with very fine sandpaper (400 or 600-grit) to remove the primer overspray. Clean the area with water and allow it to dry. Use a tack rag to remove any dust, then apply the finish coat. Don't attempt to rub out or wax the repair area until the paint has dried completely (at least two weeks)

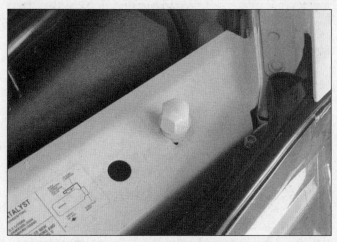

9.10 Adjust the hood closing height by turning the hood bumpers in or out

10.1 Remove the fasteners securing the radiator cover

Adjustment

Refer to illustration 9.10

6   Fore-and-aft and side-to-side adjustment of the hood is done by moving the hinge plate slot after loosening the bolts or nuts.

7   Scribe a line around the entire hinge plate so you can determine the amount of movement **(see illustration 9.2).**

8   Loosen the bolts or nuts and move the hood into correct alignment. Move it only a little at a time. Tighten the hinge bolts and carefully lower the hood to check the position.

9   If necessary after installation, the entire hood latch assembly can be adjusted up-and-down as well as from side-to-side on the radiator support so the hood closes securely and flush with the fenders.

10   Adjust the hood bumpers on the radiator support so the hood is flush with the fenders when closed **(see illustration).**

11   If the rear of the hood is too low, insert shims or washers of the correct thickness between the hood and the hinges.

12   The hood latch assembly, as well as the hinges, should be periodically lubricated with white lithium-base grease to prevent sticking and wear.

10   Hood release latch and cable - removal and installation

Latch

Refer to illustrations 10.1 and 10.2

1   Remove the radiator cover **(see illustration).**

2   Draw a mark around the latch to aid alignment when installing, then detach the latch retaining bolts from the radiator support **(see illustration)** and remove the latch.

3   Disengage the hood release cable from the latch assembly.

4   Installation is the reverse of the removal procedure.

Cable

5   Disconnect the hood release cable from the latch assembly as described above.

6   Attach a piece of stiff wire to the end of the cable, trace the cable back to the firewall and detach all cable retaining clips.

7   Working in the passenger compartment, disconnect the cable from the hood release lever.

8   Pull the old cable into the passenger compartment until you can see the stiff wire

that you attached to the cable. A grommet insulates the cable hole in the firewall from the elements. The new cable should have a new grommet, so you can remove and discard the old cable grommet. Make sure the new grommet is already on the new cable (if not, slip the old grommet onto the new cable), then detach the old cable from the wire and attach the new cable to the wire.

9   Working from the engine compartment side of the firewall, pull the wire through the cable hole in the firewall.

10   Installation is otherwise the reverse of the removal. Working from the passenger compartment side, push the grommet into place with your fingers. Make sure it's fully seated in the hole in the firewall.

11   Bumper covers - removal and installation

Front

Refer to illustrations 11.1, 11.3, 11.4 and 11.5

1   Remove the fasteners securing the upper edge of the bumper cover **(see illustration).**

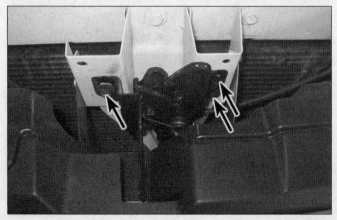

10.2 Scribe a line around the hinge to use as a reference point, then remove the retaining bolts

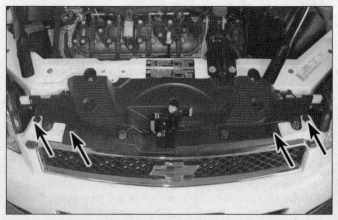

11.1 Remove the bumper cover upper fasteners

11.3 Remove the fasteners securing the engine splash shield (not all fasteners visible in photo)

11.4 Inner fenderwell splash shield fasteners

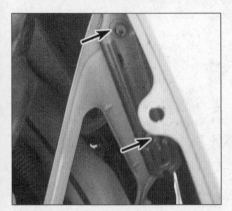

11.5 Remove the bumper cover-to-fender retaining bolts

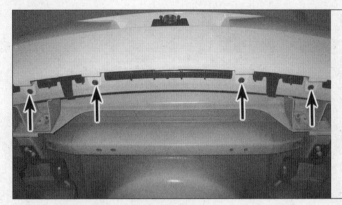

11.9 Remove the fasteners securing the bottom of the bumper

2   Raise the vehicle and support it securely on jackstands.
3   Remove the engine splash shield **(see illustration).**
4   Remove the inner fender splash shields **(see illustration).**
5   Remove the corner bumper cover retain-

ing fasteners **(see illustration).**
6   With the help of an assistant, pull the bumper cover out and away from the vehicle.
7   Installation is the reverse of removal.

Rear
Refer to illustrations 11.9, 11.10a, 11.10b, 11.11a and 11.11b
8   Raise the vehicle and support it securely

on jackstands.
9   Working under the vehicle, detach the fasteners securing the bottom of the bumper cover **(see illustration).**
10   Remove the screws securing the bumper cover in the rear wheel openings **(see illustrations).**
11   Open the trunk and remove the screws securing the upper edge of the bumper cover

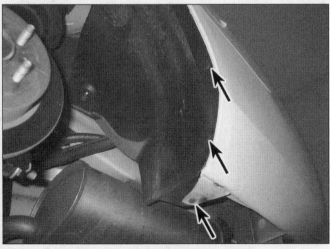

11.10a Remove the fasteners securing the inner fenderwell splash shield . . .

11.10b . . . then peel back the liner to access the bumper cover corner mounting fastener

11.11a Pull back the trunk liner . . .

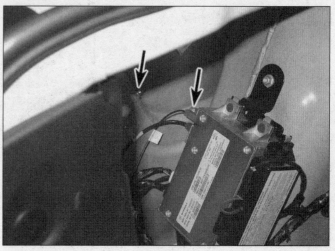

11.11b . . . then remove the fasteners securing the bumper

12.4a Remove the fender-to-door pillar bolt inside the door opening . . .

12.4b . . . and the two lower mounting bolts at the rear of the wheel opening

(see illustrations). Pull the bumper cover out and away from the vehicle.

12   Installation is the reverse of removal.

---

12 Front fender - removal and installation

Refer to illustrations 12.4a, 12.4b, 12.4c and 12.4d

1   Remove the hood (see Section 9).

2   Loosen the front wheel lug nuts, raise the vehicle and support it securely on jackstands. Remove the wheel.

3   Remove the inner fender splash shield from the wheel housings **(see illustration 11.4).**

4   Remove the fender mounting bolts **(see illustrations).**

5   Detach the fender. It's a good idea to

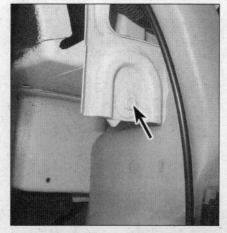

12.4c Remove the front mounting bolt inside the front of the wheel opening . . .

12.4d . . . then the fender-to-body upper mounting bolts (the left-side fender has an additional bolt for the hood support strut bracket)

13.1a Remove the fasteners inside the door handle pull

13.1b Using a trim stick, pry out the power window control switch, then unplug the electrical connector

13.2 Carefully pry off the mirror trim cover

13.3a Carefully pry off the door handle screw cover, then remove the fastener

have an assistant support the fender while it's being moved away from the vehicle to prevent damage to the surrounding body panels.
6   Installation is the reverse of removal.

13 Door trim panels - removal and installation

Refer to illustrations 13.1a, 13.1b, 13.2, 13.3a, 13.3b, 13.4, 13.5 and 13.6
1   Remove the power window control switch **(see illustrations)**.
2   Remove the outside mirror trim cover **(see illustration)**.
3   Remove the door trim panel retaining fasteners **(see illustrations)**.
4   Remove the door trim panel using a door panel removal tool **(see illustration)**.

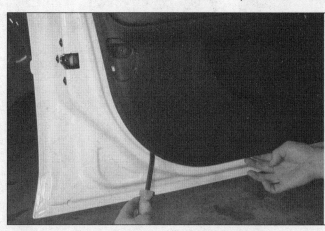

13.4 Start from the bottom of the trim panel and work around the perimeter until all the fasteners have been released from the door

13.3b Remove the door panel fastener

13.5 Disconnect the handle actuating cable

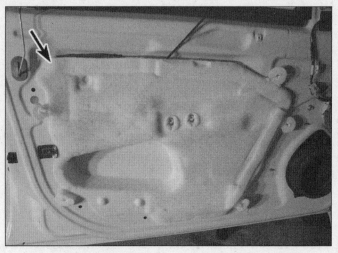

13.6 Starting at the upper corner, peel back the watershield

5   Unlatch the actuating cable from the door handle lever **(see illustration)**. Once all of the clips are disengaged, carefully detach the trim panel from the door.

6   For access to the handle, latch, lock and window regulator mechanisms, carefully peel back the watershield **(see illustration).**

7   Before installing the door trim panel, inspect the condition of all clips and reinstall any clips which may have fallen out.

8   The remainder of installation is the reverse of the removal procedure.

14   Door - removal and installation

Refer to illustration 14.6

Note: *The door is heavy and somewhat awkward to remove and install - at least two people should perform this procedure.*

1   Open the door all the way and support it on jacks or blocks covered with rags to prevent damaging the paint.

2   Remove the door trim panel and watershield as described in Section 13.

3   Unplug all electrical connections, ground wires and harness retaining clips from the door. **Note:** *It is a good idea to label all connections to aid the reassembly process.*

4   Working through the door opening, detach the rubber conduit between the body and the door. Then pull the wiring harness through the conduit hole and remove it from the door.

5   Mark around the door hinges with a pen or a scribe to facilitate realignment during reassembly.

6   With an assistant holding the door, remove the hinge-to-door bolts and lift off the door **(see illustration).**

7   Installation is the reverse of removal.

15   Door handles, key lock cylinder and latch - removal and installation

1   Raise the window, then remove the door trim panel and peel away the watershield (see Section 13).

Outside handle

Refer to illustration 15.2

2   Working through the access hole, disengage the actuating rod from the key lock cylinder **(see illustration),** and handle actuating rod from the latch.

3   Remove the door handle fasteners.

4   Remove the handle from the door.

5   Installation is the reverse of removal.

Key lock cylinder

6   Remove the outside door handle.

7   Remove the lock cylinder retaining clip from the handle, then remove the lock cylinder from the handle

8   Installation is the reverse of removal.

Door latch

Refer to illustration 15.10

9   Disengage the handles-to-latch and lock cylinder actuating rods from the latch.

10   Remove the three screws securing the latch to the door **(see illustration),** then remove the latch assembly from the door.

11   Disconnect the electrical connectors from the latch mechanism.

12   Installation is the reverse of removal.

16   Door window glass - removal and installation

Refer to illustration 16.4

1   Lower the window glass about half way down into the door.

2   Remove the door trim panel and the watershield (see Section 13).

3   Remove the window inside sealing strip.

4   Remove the window glass retainer bolts **(see illustration).**

5   Remove the glass by carefully pulling it up and out.

6   Installation is the reverse of removal.

14.6 Remove the hinge-to-door bolts

15.2 Disconnect the actuating rod from the lock cylinder

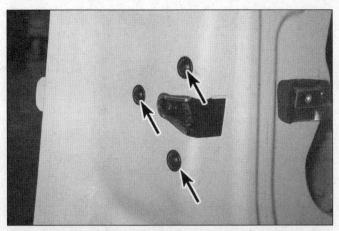

15.10 Remove the latch retaining screws from the end of the door

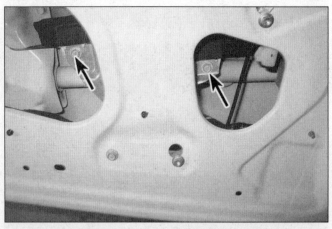

16.4 Remove the window glass retainer bolts

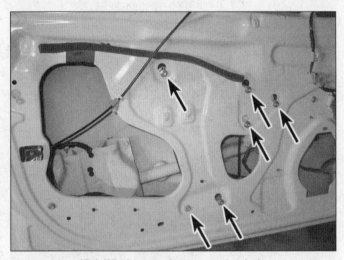

17.4 Window regulator mounting bolts

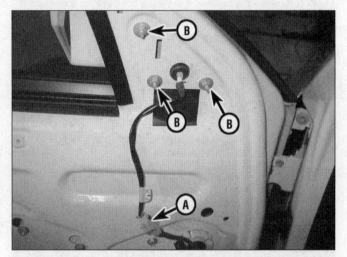

18.2 Unplug the mirror electrical connector (A), then remove the mirror retaining fasteners (B)

17 Door window glass regulator and motor - removal and installation

Refer to illustration 17.4

1   Remove the door trim panel and the watershield (see Section 13).
2   Remove the door window glass (see Section 16).
3   Unplug the electrical connector from the window regulator motor.
4   Remove the regulator mounting bolts **(see illustration).**
5   Pull the regulator assembly through the service hole in the door frame to remove it.
6   To remove the motor from the regulator assembly, simply remove the three fasteners securing it to the regulator assembly.
7   Installation is the reverse of removal.

18 Outside mirrors - removal and installation

Refer to illustrations 18.2

1   Remove the door trim panel (see Section 13).

2   Unplug the mirror electrical connector, then remove the mirror retaining fasteners **(see illustration).**
3   Detach the mirror from the vehicle.
4   Installation is the reverse of removal.

19 Trunk lid - removal and installation

Refer to illustration 19.3

Note: *The trunk lid is heavy and somewhat awkward to remove and install - at least two people should perform this procedure.*
1   Open the trunk lid and cover the edges of the trunk compartment with pads or cloths to protect the painted surfaces when the lid is removed.
2   Disconnect any cables or wire harness connectors attached to the trunk lid that would interfere with removal.
3   Make alignment marks around the hinge mounting fasteners with a marking pen **(see illustration).**
4   While an assistant supports the trunk lid, remove the lid-to-hinge fasteners on both

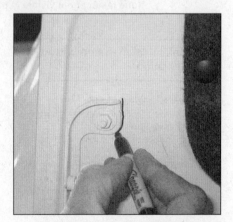

19.3 Mark around the hinge bolts for realignment purposes - then remove the retaining bolts on each side of the trunk lid

sides and lift it off.
5   Installation is the reverse of removal.
Note: *When reinstalling the trunk lid, align the lid-to-hinge fasteners with the marks made during removal.*

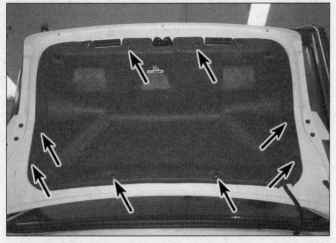

20.1 Remove the fasteners securing the trunk lid trim cover

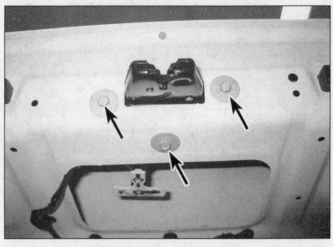

20.3 Trunk latch retaining bolts

21.2 Remove the fasteners along the top of the cowl cover
(one fastener not visible in photo)

22.3 Using a trim stick, carefully pry off the shift lever trim panel

20   Trunk lid latch - removal and installation

Refer to illustrations 20.1 and 20.3

1   Open the trunk and remove the trunk lid trim panel **(see illustration)**.
2   Disconnect the latch electrical connector.
3   Remove the trunk lid latch retaining bolts, then remove the latch **(see illustration)**.
4   Installation is the reverse of removal.

21   Cowl cover - removal and installation

Refer to illustrations 21.2

1   Remove the windshield wiper arms (see Chapter 12).
2   Remove the push pin fasteners securing the cowl cover **(see illustration)**.
3   Remove the cowl cover from the vehicle.
4   Installation is the reverse of removal.

22   Center console - removal and installation

Refer to illustrations 22.3, 22.4a, 22.4b and 22.4c
Warning: *Models covered by this manual are equipped with a Supplemental Restraint System (SRS), more commonly known as airbags. Always disable the airbag system before working in the vicinity of any airbag system component to avoid the possibility of accidental deployment of the airbag, which could cause personal injury (see Chapter 12).*

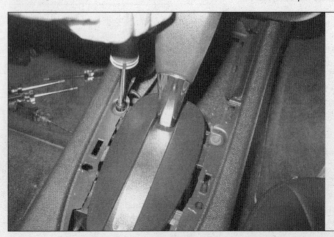

22.4a Remove the fasteners at the front of the console

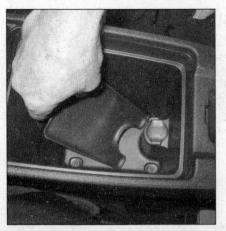

22.4b Open the lid to the console bin, and remove the mat . . .

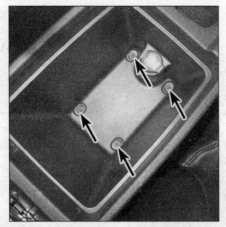

22.4c . . . then remove the four fasteners

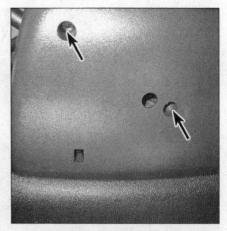

23.3 Remove the screws from the lower cover

1   Turn the ignition key to the On position, depress the brake pedal, then place the shifter in the drive position.
2   Disconnect the cable from the negative battery terminal (see Chapter 5, Section 1).
3   Remove the center console shift lever trim panel **(see illustration).**
4   Remove the console retaining screws **(see illustrations).**
5   Carefully lift the console up and over the shifter, disconnect any electrical connectors,

then remove it from the vehicle.
6   Installation is the reverse of removal.
7   Move the shift lever back into the Park position, turn the ignition key to Off, then reconnect the cable to the negative terminal of the battery.

23   Steering column covers - removal and installation

Refer to illustration 23.3
Warning: *Models covered by this manual are equipped with a Supplemental Restraint System (SRS), more commonly known as airbags. Always disable the airbag system before working in the vicinity of any airbag system component to avoid the possibility of accidental deployment of the airbag, which could cause personal injury* (see Chapter 12).
1   Disconnect the cable from the negative terminal of the battery (see Chapter 5, Section 1).
2   Remove the steering column tilt lever by pulling the lever straight out from the column.
3   Remove the steering column lower cover screws **(see illustration),** then detach the cover from the steering column.
4   Remove the upper cover screws, then

detach the cover from the steering column.
5   Installation is the reverse of removal.

24   Dashboard trim panels - removal and installation

Warning: *Models covered by this manual are equipped with a Supplemental Restraint System (SRS), more commonly known as airbags. Always disable the airbag system before working in the vicinity of any airbag system component to avoid the possibility of accidental deployment of the airbag, which could cause personal injury* (see Chapter 12).
1   Disconnect the cable from the negative battery terminal (see Chapter 5, Section 1).

Instrument cluster trim panel

Refer to illustrations 24.3a, 24.3b, 24.3c and 24.3d

2   Remove the dashboard side covers **(see illustration 24.14).**
3   Remove the fasteners securing the instrument cluster trim panel, then remove the trim panel from the instrument panel **(see illustrations)**.
4   Installation is the reverse of the removal procedure.

24.3a Remove these fasteners securing the instrument cluster bezel . . .

24.3b . . . and the fasteners at the sides of the dashboard

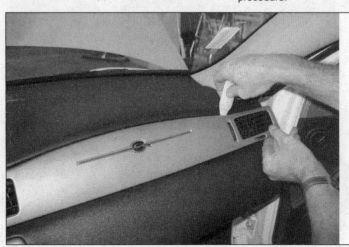

24.3c Use a trim stick to release any clips . . .

24.3d . . . then remove the panel

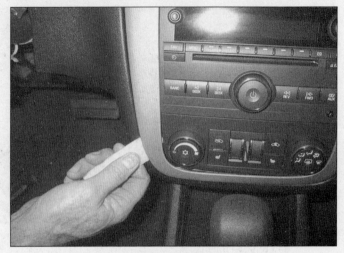

**24.5 Using a trim stick, carefully pry around the panel
to release the clips**

Center trim panel

Refer to illustration 24.5

5   Detach the clips securing the center trim panel, then remove the panel from the instrument panel **(see illustration)**.
6   Installation is the reverse of the removal procedure.

Knee bolster

Refer to illustrations 24.7 and 24.9

7   Remove the fasteners securing the knee bolster **(see illustration)**.
8   Pull the knee bolster down to release the clips from the instrument panel. Remove the knee bolster.
9   If you're removing the knee bolster support, remove the two mounting fasteners **(see illustration)**. Remove the knee bolster support.
10   Installation is the reverse of removal. Make sure the clips are engaged properly before pushing the knee bolster firmly into place.

24.7 Remove the fasteners along the bottom of the knee bolster

Glove box

Refer to illustration 24.11

11   Using a small punch, remove the glove box hinge pins **(see illustration)**.

12   Open the glove box door and squeeze the sides of the box to clear the stops. Remove the glove box.
13   Installation is the reverse of the removal procedure.

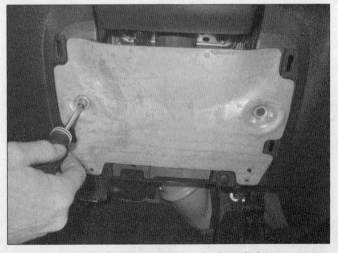

24.9 Remove the fasteners securing the knee bolster support

24.11 Using a small punch, remove the glove box hinge pins

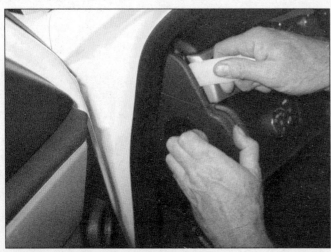

24.14 Using a trim stick, carefully pry around the side covers to release the clips

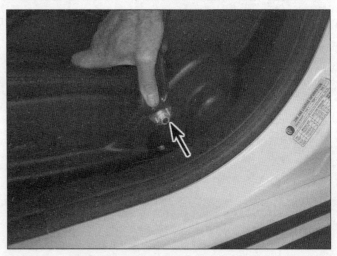

25.2a Remove the seatbelt anchor bolt

Side covers

Refer to illustration 24.14

14   Using a trim stick, carefully pry around the panels to release the clips **(see illustration)**.

15   Installation is the reverse of removal.

25 Seats - removal and installation

Front seat

Refer to illustrations 25.2a and 25.2b

Warning: *Models covered by this manual are equipped with a Supplemental Restraint System (SRS), more commonly known as airbags. Always disable the airbag system before working in the vicinity of any airbag system component to avoid the possibility of accidental deployment of the airbag, which could cause personal injury* (see Chapter 12).

1   Disconnect the cable from the negative terminal of the battery (see Chapter 5, Section 1).

2   Position the seat all the way forward to access the retaining bolts. Remove the trim cover from the side of the seat, then remove the seat belt anchor bolt **(see illustration)**. Detach any bolt trim covers and remove the retaining bolts **(see illustration)**.

3   Tilt the seat upward to access the under side. Disconnect any electrical connectors and lift the seat from the vehicle.

4   Installation is the reverse of removal.

Rear seat

Refer to illustration 25.6

5   Lift up on the rear of the seat cushion and pivot it forward.

6   Detach the retaining bolts at the lower edge of the seat back, and remove the seat belt anchor bolts **(see illustration)**.

7   Lift up on the seat back and remove it from the vehicle.

8   Installation is the reverse of removal.

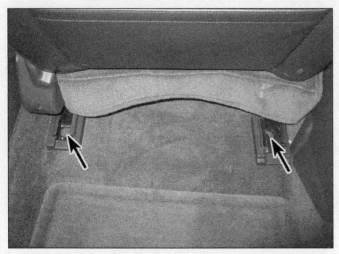

25.2b With the seat positioned all the way forward, remove the retaining bolts

25.6 Detach the retaining bolts at the lower edge of the seat back

Notes

Chapter 12
Chassis electrical system

Contents

1 General information

The electrical system is a 12-volt, negative ground type. Power for the lights and all electrical accessories is supplied by a lead/acid-type battery, which is charged by the alternator.

This Chapter covers repair and service procedures for the various electrical components not associated with the engine. Information on the battery, alternator and starter motor can be found in Chapter 5.

It should be noted that when portions of the electrical system are serviced, the negative battery cable should be disconnected from the battery to prevent electrical shorts and/or fires.

2 Electrical troubleshooting - general information

Refer to illustrations 2.5a and 2.5b

1   A typical electrical circuit consists of an electrical component, any switches, relays, motors, fuses, fusible links or circuit breakers related to that component and the wiring and connectors that link the component to both the battery and the chassis. To help you pinpoint an electrical circuit problem, wiring diagrams are included at the end of this Chapter.

2   Before tackling any troublesome electrical circuit, first study the appropriate wiring diagrams to get a complete understanding of what makes up that individual circuit. Noting whether other components related to the circuit are operating correctly, for instance, can often narrow down the location of potential trouble spots. If several components or circuits fail at one time, chances are the problem is in a fuse or ground connection, because several circuits are often routed through the same fuse and ground connections.

3   Electrical problems usually stem from simple causes, such as loose or corroded connections, a blown fuse, a melted fusible link or a failed relay. Visually inspect the condition of all fuses, wires and connections in a problem circuit before troubleshooting the circuit.

4   If test equipment and instruments are going to be utilized, use the diagrams to plan ahead of time where you will make the nec-

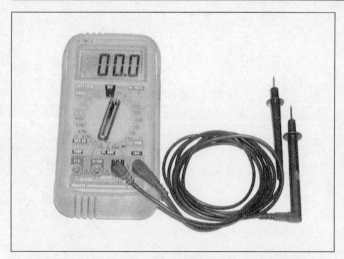

2.5a The most useful tool for electrical troubleshooting is a digital multimeter that can check volts, amps, and test continuity

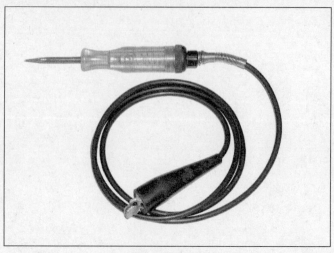

2.5b A simple test light is a very handy tool for testing voltage

essary connections in order to accurately pinpoint the trouble spot.

5   For electrical troubleshooting, you'll need a circuit tester, voltmeter or a 12-volt bulb with a set of test leads, a continuity tester and a jumper wire, preferably with a circuit breaker incorporated, which can be used to bypass electrical components **(see illustrations)**. Before attempting to locate a problem with test instruments, use the wiring diagram(s) to decide where to make the connections.

Voltage checks

Refer to illustration 2.6

6   Voltage checks should be performed if a circuit is not functioning properly. Connect one lead of a circuit tester to either the negative battery terminal or a known good ground. Connect the other lead to a connector in the circuit being tested, preferably nearest to the battery or fuse **(see illustration)**. If the bulb of the tester lights, voltage is present, which means that the part of the circuit between the connector and the battery is problem free. Continue checking the rest of the circuit in the same fashion. When you reach a point at which no voltage is present, the problem lies between that point and the last test point with voltage. Most of the time the problem can be traced to a loose connection. **Note:** *Keep in mind that some circuits receive voltage only when the ignition key is in the ACC or RUN position.*

Finding a short

7   One method of finding shorts in a live circuit is to remove the fuse and connect a test light in place of the fuse terminals (fabricate two jumper wires with small spade terminals, plug the jumper wires into the fuse box and connect the test light). There should be no voltage present in the circuit. Move the suspected wiring harness from side-to-side while watching the test light. If the bulb goes on, there is a short to ground somewhere in that area, probably where the insulation has rubbed through.

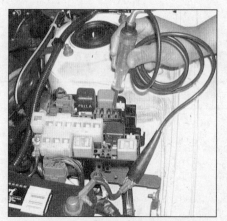

2.6 In use, a basic test light's lead is clipped to a known good ground, then the pointed probe can test connectors, wires or electrical sockets - if the bulb lights, the circuit being tested has battery voltage

Ground check

8   Perform a ground test to check whether a component is properly grounded. Disconnect the battery and connect one lead of a continuity tester or multimeter (set to the ohm scale), to a known good ground. Connect the other lead to the wire or ground connection being tested. If the resistance is low (less than 5 ohms), the ground is good. If the bulb on a self-powered test light does not go on, the ground is not good.

Continuity check

Refer to illustration 2.9

9   A continuity check determines whether there are any breaks in a circuit, i.e. whether it can no longer carry current from the voltage source to ground. With the circuit off (no power in the circuit), a self-powered continuity tester or multimeter can be used to check the circuit. Connect the test leads to both ends of the circuit (or to the power end and a good ground),

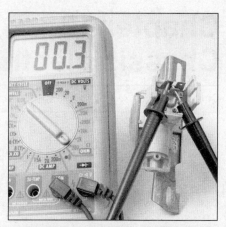

2.9 With a multimeter set to the ohm scale, resistance can be checked across two terminals - when checking for continuity, a low reading indicates continuity, a high reading or infinity indicates high resistance or lack of continuity

and if the test light comes on the circuit is passing current properly **(see illustration)**. If the resistance is low (less than 5 ohms), there is continuity; if the reading is 10,000 ohms or higher, there is a break somewhere in the circuit. The same procedure can be used to test a switch, by connecting the continuity tester to the switch terminals. With the switch turned to ON, the test light should come on (or low resistance should be indicated on a meter).

Finding an open circuit

10 When diagnosing for possible open circuits, it is often difficult to locate them by sight because the connectors hide oxidation or terminal misalignment. Merely wiggling a connector on a sensor or in the wiring harness may correct the open circuit condition. Remember this when an open circuit is indicated when troubleshooting a circuit. Intermittent problems may also be caused by oxidized

3.1a The engine compartment fuse and relay box is mounted on the right side of the engine compartment. To detach the cover from the fuse and relay box, pull the two locking tabs (A) out (away from the cover) and pull off the cover

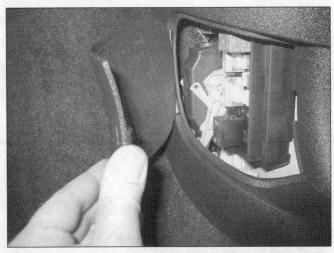

3.1b The fuse and relay box inside the vehicle is located underneath the right end of the instrument panel, behind the right kick panel. To access it, open this small door

or loose connections.

11 Electrical troubleshooting is simple if you keep in mind that all electrical circuits are basically electricity running from the battery, through the wires, switches, relays, fuses and fusible links to each electrical component (light bulb, motor, etc.) and to ground, from which it is passed back to the battery. Any electrical problem is an interruption in the flow of electricity to and from the battery.

Connectors

12 Most electrical connections on these vehicles are made with multi-wire plastic connectors. The mating halves of many connectors are secured with locking clips molded into the plastic connector shells. The mating halves of large connectors, such as some of those under the instrument panel, are held together by a bolt through the center of the connector.

13 To separate a connector with locking clips, use a small screwdriver to pry the clips apart carefully, then separate the connector halves. Pull only on the shell; never pull on the wiring harness as you may damage the individual wires and terminals inside the connectors. Look at the connector closely before trying to separate the halves. Often the locking clips are engaged in a way that is not immediately clear. Additionally, many connectors have more than one set of clips.

14 Each pair of connector terminals has a male half and a female half. When you look at the end view of a connector in a diagram, be sure to understand whether the view shows the harness side or the component side of the connector. Connector halves are mirror images of each other, and a terminal that is shown on the right side end-view of one half will be on the left side end view of the other half.

3 Fuses and fusible links - general information

Fuses

Refer to illustrations 3.1a, 3.1b and 3.2

The electrical circuits of the vehicle are protected by a combination of fuses, circuit breakers and fusible links. Fuse and relay boxes are located in the engine compartment and behind the right kick panel, under the right end of the instrument panel **(see illustrations)**. Each of the fuses is designed to protect a specific circuit, and the various circuits are identified on the fuse panel cover. If the fuse panel cover is difficult to read, or missing, you can also refer to your owner's manual, which includes a complete guide to all fuses and relays in both fuse/relay boxes.

Miniaturized fuses are employed in the fuse blocks. If an electrical component fails, always check the fuse first. The best way to check a fuse is with a test light. Check for power at the exposed terminal tips of each fuse. If power is present on one side of the

fuses but not the other, the fuse is blown. A blown fuse can also be confirmed by visually inspecting it **(see illustration)**.

Be sure to replace blown fuses with the correct type. Fuses of different ratings are physically interchangeable, but only fuses of the proper rating should be used. Replacing a fuse with one of a higher or lower value than specified is not recommended. Each electrical circuit needs a specific amount of protection. The amperage value of each fuse is molded into the fuse body.

If the replacement fuse immediately fails, don't replace it again until the cause of the problem is isolated and corrected. In most cases, this will be a short circuit in the wiring caused by a broken or deteriorated wire.

Fusible links

Some circuits are protected by fusible links. The links are used in circuits which are not ordinarily fused, or which carry high current, such as the circuit between the alternator and the starter motor. Fusible links, which are several wire gauges smaller in size than the

3.2 When a fuse blows, the element between the terminals melts

BAD   GOOD

circuit that they protect, are designed to melt if the circuit is subjected to more current than it was designed to carry. If you have to replace a blown fusible link, make sure that you replace it with one of the same specification. If the replacement fusible link blows in the same circuit, make sure that you troubleshoot the circuit in which the fusible link melted BEFORE installing another fusible link.

4   Circuit breakers - general information

Circuit breakers protect certain circuits, such as the power windows or heated seats. Depending on the vehicle's accessories, there may be one or two circuit breakers, located in the fuse/relay box in the engine compartment.

Because the circuit breakers reset automatically, an electrical overload in a circuit-breaker-protected system will cause the circuit to fail momentarily, then come back on. If the circuit does not come back on, check it immediately.

For a basic check, pull the circuit breaker up out of its socket on the fuse panel, but just far enough to probe with a voltmeter. The breaker should still contact the sockets.

With the voltmeter negative lead on a good chassis ground, touch each end prong of the circuit breaker with the positive meter probe. There should be battery voltage at each end. If there is battery voltage only at one end, the circuit breaker must be replaced.

Some circuit breakers must be reset manually.

5   Relays - general information and testing

General information

1   Several electrical accessories in the vehicle, such as the fuel injection system, horns, starter, and fog lamps use relays to transmit the electrical signal to the component. Relays use a low-current circuit (the control circuit) to open and close a high-current circuit (the power circuit). If the relay is defective, that component will not operate properly. Most relays are mounted in the engine compartment fuse/relay box, with some specialized relays located above the interior fuse box in the dash (see illustrations 3.1a, 3.1b and 3.1c). If a faulty relay is suspected, it can be removed and tested using the procedure below or by a dealer service department or a repair shop. Defective relays must be replaced as a unit.

Testing

Refer to illustrations 5.2a and 5.2b

2   Most of the relays used in these vehicles are of a type often called "ISO" relays, which refers to the International Standards Organization. The terminals of ISO relays are numbered to indicate their usual circuit connec-

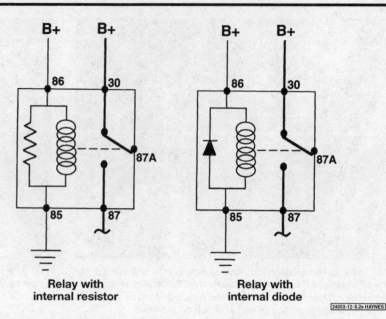

Relay with internal resistor   **Relay with internal diode**

5.2a Typical ISO relay designs, terminal numbering and circuit connections

tions and functions. There are two basic layouts of terminals on the relays used in these vehicles (see illustrations).

3   Refer to the wiring diagram for the circuit to determine the proper connections for the relay you're testing. If you can't determine the correct connection from the wiring diagrams, however, you may be able to determine the test connections from the information that follows.

4   Two of the terminals are the relay control circuit and connect to the relay coil. The other relay terminals are the power circuit. When the relay is energized, the coil creates a magnetic field that closes the larger contacts of the power circuit to provide power to the circuit loads.

5   Terminals 85 and 86 are normally the control circuit. If the relay contains a diode, terminal 86 must be connected to battery positive (B+) voltage and terminal 85 to ground. If the relay contains a resistor, terminals 85 and 86 can be connected in either direction with respect to B+ and ground.

6   Terminal 30 is normally connected to the battery voltage (B+) source for the circuit loads. Terminal 87 is connected to the circuit leading to the component being powered. If the relay has several alternate terminals for load or ground connections, they usually are numbered 87A, 87B, 87C, and so on.

7   Use an ohmmeter to check continuity through the relay control coil.

a) Connect the meter according to the polarity shown in illustration 5.2a for one check; then reverse the ohmmeter leads and check continuity in the other direction.

b) If the relay contains a resistor, resistance will be indicated on the meter, and should be the same value with the ohmmeter in either direction.

c) If the relay contains a diode, resistance should be higher with the ohmmeter in the forward polarity direction than with the meter leads reversed.

d) If the ohmmeter shows infinite resistance in both directions, replace the relay.

8   Remove the relay from the vehicle and use the ohmmeter to check for continuity between the relay power circuit terminals. There should be no continuity between terminal 30 and 87 with the relay de-energized.

9   Connect a fused jumper wire to terminal 86 and the positive battery terminal. Connect another jumper wire between terminal 85 and ground. When the connections are made, the relay should click.

10   With the jumper wires connected, check for continuity between the power circuit terminals. Now, there should be continuity between terminals 30 and 87.

11   If the relay fails any of the above tests, replace it.

Control circuits   Power circuits

5.2b Most relays are marked on the outside to easily identify the control circuits and the power circuits (four terminal type shown)

6.3 To detach the turn signal/multi-function switch from the steering column, remove the two mounting screws (A), then disconnect the two electrical connectors (B)

6.4 To disconnect the electrical connectors from the turn signal/multi-function switch, carefully pry the locking tabs loose and pull out the connectors

6 Turn signal/multi-function switch - replacement

Refer to illustrations 6.3 and 6.4

Warning: *The models covered by this manual are equipped with a Supplemental Restraint System (SRS), more commonly known as airbags. Always disarm the airbag system before working in the vicinity of any airbag system component to avoid the possibility of accidental deployment of the airbag, which could cause personal injury (see Section 24).*

1   Remove the steering wheel (see Chapter 10) and the upper and lower steering column covers (see Chapter 11).

2   Trace the electrical harnesses from the turn signal/multi-function switch down to the plastic strap that secures all the harnesses to the underside of the steering column. Remove the strap and disengage the ignition switch harnesses from the other harnesses.

3   Remove the turn signal/multi-function switch mounting screws **(see illustration)** and remove the switch.

4   Disconnect the electrical connectors from the turn signal/multi-function switch **(see illustration)**.

5   Installation is the reverse of removal.

7 Key lock cylinder and ignition switch - replacement

Warning: *The models covered by this manual are equipped with a Supplemental Restraint System (SRS), more commonly known as airbags. Always disarm the airbag system before working in the vicinity of any airbag system component to avoid the possibility of accidental deployment of the airbag, which could cause personal injury (see Section 24).*

Key lock cylinder

Refer to illustration 7.3

Caution: *The following procedure is included only as a prelude to removing the ignition switch (see below). Do NOT try to **replace** the key lock cylinder at home. If you replace the*

key lock cylinder you must have the transponder in the new key programmed by a dealer service department before the engine will start. Even if you were to use the old key in a new key lock cylinder you would still have to have it re-programmed at the dealer before the engine would start.

1   Remove the steering wheel (see Chapter 10) and the upper and lower steering column covers (see Chapter 11).

2   Insert the ignition key in the key lock cylinder and turn the key to the START position.

3   Insert a 1/8-inch awl or punch through the hole in the casting that houses the key lock cylinder, depress the lock cylinder release tab and pull out the lock cylinder **(see illustration)**.

4   Installation is the reverse of removal.

Ignition switch

Refer to illustrations 7.6 and 7.7

5   Remove the key lock cylinder (see Steps 1 through 3).

6   Remove the theft deterrent control module from the key lock cylinder housing **(see illustration)**, then trace the electrical harness

7.3 To remove the ignition key lock cylinder from the lock cylinder housing, turn the ignition key to START, then insert a 1/8-inch awl or punch (A) into the hole in the housing, depress the lock cylinder release tab and pull out the lock cylinder

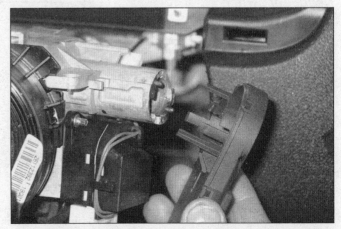

7.6 Slide off the theft control module from the key lock cylinder housing, then trace the electrical leads from the module down to the main electrical connector and the separate fused jumper connector and disconnect both of them

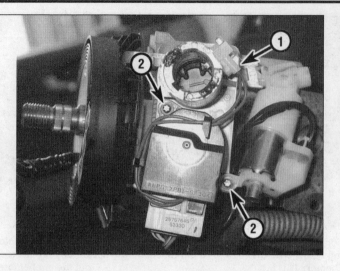

7.7 To remove the ignition switch from the key lock cylinder housing, disconnect the key alarm connector (1) from the housing, then remove the two ignition switch retaining screws (2)

8.2 To remove the headlight switch from the instrument panel, simply pop it out from the backside

from the module down to its electrical connectors and disconnect the main connector and the separate fused jumper connector.

7   Disconnect the key alarm electrical connector from the key lock cylinder housing **(see illustration)**.

8   Remove the ignition switch mounting screws and remove the ignition switch assembly. Trace the electrical harness from the switch down to its electrical connector and disconnect the connector.

9   Installation is the reverse of removal.

---

8   Dashboard switches - replacement

Warning: *The models covered by this manual are equipped with a Supplemental Restraint System (SRS), more commonly known as airbags. Always disarm the airbag system before working in the vicinity of any airbag system component to avoid the possibility of accidental deployment of the airbag, which could cause personal injury (see Section 24).*

Headlight switch

Impala models

Refer to illustrations 8.2 and 8.3

1   Remove the left instrument panel side cover (see Chapter 11).

2   Using your fingers, pop out the headlight switch **(see illustration)**.

3   Disconnect the electrical connector from the headlight switch **(see illustration)**.

4   Installation is the reverse of removal. When installing the headlight switch, make sure that it snaps back into place.

Monte Carlo models

5   Pry off the headlight switch trim bezel (see Chapter 11).

6   Disconnect the electrical connector from the headlight switch **(see illustration 8.3)**.

7   Using your fingers, pop out the headlight switch from the front side of the headlight switch trim bezel.

8   Installation is the reverse of removal. When installing the headlight switch in the trim bezel, make sure that it snaps into place.

Driver information display switch

Refer to illustration 8.9

Note: *The photo accompanying this Section depicts the driver information display switch being removed from the instrument cluster trim panel on an Impala model. The instrument cluster trim panel on a Monte Carlo is shaped differently than the cluster trim panel on an Impala, but the driver information display switch is the same unit on both models and is removed and installed from the trim panel the same way.*

9   Remove the instrument cluster trim panel (see Chapter 11), then disconnect the electrical connector from the driver information display switch **(see illustration)**.

10   Using your fingers, push out the driver information display switch from the front side of the instrument cluster trim panel.

11   Installation is the reverse of removal.

When installing the driver information display switch, make sure that the switch snaps into place.

---

9   Instrument cluster - removal and installation

Refer to illustrations 9.2a and 9.2b

Warning: *The models covered by this manual are equipped with a Supplemental Restraint System (SRS), more commonly known as airbags. Always disarm the airbag system before working in the vicinity of any airbag system component to avoid the possibility of accidental deployment of the airbag, which could cause personal injury (see Section 24).*

Note: *The photos accompanying this Section depict the instrument cluster on an Impala model. The instrument cluster on a Monte Carlo is quite similar and is removed and installed the same way.*

1   Remove the instrument cluster trim panel (see Chapter 11).

8.3 To disconnect the electrical connector from the headlight switch, depress this release tab and pull off the connector

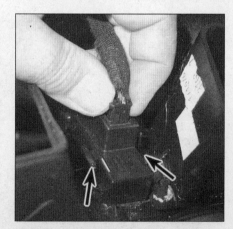

8.9 Disconnect the electrical connector from the driver information display switch, then spread the locking tabs apart and push out the switch from the front side of the panel

9.2a To remove the instrument cluster, remove these four screws (Impala shown, Monte Carlo similar)

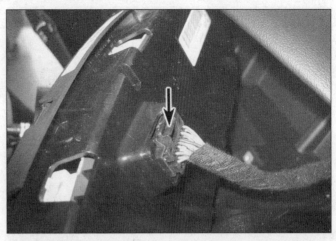

9.2b To disconnect the electrical connector from the instrument cluster, depress this release tab and pull off the connector

2   Remove the instrument cluster retaining screws **(see illustration)**, then pull out the cluster, disconnect the electrical connector **(see illustration)** and remove the cluster.
3   Installation is the reverse of removal.

10   Radio and speakers - removal and installation

Warning: *The models covered by this manual are equipped with a Supplemental Restraint System (SRS), more commonly known as air-bags. Always disarm the airbag system before working in the vicinity of any airbag system component to avoid the possibility of accidental deployment of the airbag, which could cause personal injury (see Section 24).*

Radio

Refer to illustrations 10.2, 10.3a and 10.3b

1   Remove the center trim panel (see Chapter 11).

10.2 To detach the radio unit from the instrument panel, remove these four screws

2   Remove the radio mounting screws **(see illustration)**.
3   Pull the radio out from the dash, then disconnect the electrical connectors and the antenna cable from the backside of the radio **(see illustrations)** and remove the radio from the dash.
4   Installation is the reverse of removal.

10.3a Pull out the radio and depress the release tabs on top of the electrical connectors to disconnect them

10.3b To release the antenna cable from the radio, push the antenna lead toward the radio to relieve tension on the fingers inside the connector, then pull back the spring-loaded locking ring and pull off the connector

10.6 To remove a door speaker from an Impala model, remove the screw, then disengage the flange at the bottom of the speaker from the hole (Monte Carlo models use three mounting screws instead)

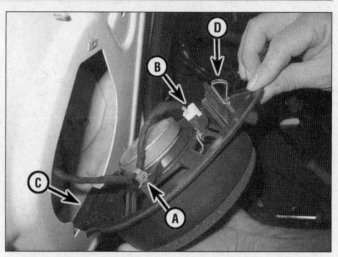

10.7 Pull out the speaker, detach the locator pin (A) for the harness clip, then disconnect the electrical connector (B). When installing the speaker, make sure that the flange (C) is positioned on the inside of the mounting hole and that the retaining clip (D) snaps into place on the inside of the hole

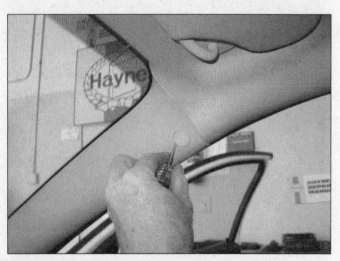

10.9a Pry out the screw trim cover at the bottom . . .

10.9b . . . then remove the screw and pull off the A-pillar trim

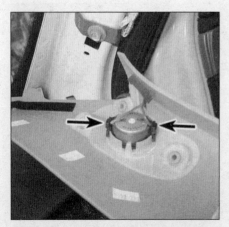

10.10 To remove a front speaker from the A-pillar trim, disengage the two locking tabs and pull out the speaker

Speakers

Door speakers

Refer to illustrations 10.6 and 10.7

5   Remove the front door trim panel (see Chapter 11).

6   Remove the speaker mounting screw **(see illustration)**. **Note:** *The photos accompanying this Section depict the front door speaker in an Impala model. But the rear door speakers, if equipped, are removed the same way. The door speakers on Monte Carlo models are also similar, but they are secured to the door with three screws instead of one.*

7   Pull out the speaker, detach the locator pin for the harness clip and disconnect the electrical connector **(see illustration)**.

8   Installation is the reverse of removal. Make sure that the speaker's lower mounting flange fits inside the speaker mounting hole

and that the retaining clip at the top of the speaker snaps into place on the inside of the hole.

Front upper speakers (Impala models)

Refer to illustrations 10.9a, 10.9b, 10.10 and 10.11

9   Remove the instrument panel end cover (see Chapter 11) and the A-pillar trim **(see illustration)**.

10   Disengage the front upper speaker's locking tabs **(see illustration)** and remove the speaker from the A-pillar trim.

11   Trace the speaker electrical lead down to the electrical connector **(see illustration)** and disconnect it. You can access the connector through the hole for the instrument panel end cover.

12   Installation is the reverse of removal.

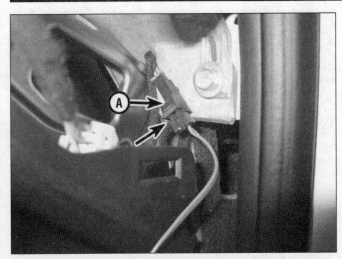

10.11 Trace the electrical lead from the front speaker down to the electrical connector (accessible through the instrument panel end cover hole), depress the release tab (A) and disconnect the connector

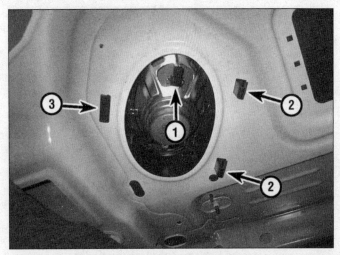

10.14 To remove a rear speaker on an Impala model, disconnect the electrical connector (1), pinch the two tabs (2) together and push them up through their slots, disengage the flange (3) from its slot, then remove the speaker from above

Rear speakers

Refer to illustration 10.14

Note: *The photo accompanying this Section depicts a typical rear speaker on an Impala model equipped with the UW6 option (custom 6-speaker system). On Impala models equipped with the UQ3 option (performance-enhanced audio speaker system), the rear speakers are slightly different than the one that you see here; they each have a mounting screw for the smaller speaker that's part of each rear speaker assembly. The rear speakers on Monte Carlo models are similar to the one that you see here.*

13   Remove the rear shelf trim panel (see Chapter 11).

14   Open the trunk and, using a flashlight, locate the rear speaker **(see illustration)** in the underside of the body located below the rear shelf trim panel.

15   Disconnect the electrical connector from the rear speaker **(see illustration 10.14)**.

16   Squeeze the two mounting tabs and push them up through their mounting holes,

12.2 . . . remove each wiper arm retaining nut, then mark the relationship of each arm to its shaft before removing the arm

12.1 To remove the windshield wiper arms, carefully pry off each trim cap with a small screwdriver . . .

then push up on the speaker and disengage the flange from its mounting slot **(see illustration 10.14)**.

17   Remove the speaker from above.

18   Installation is the reverse of removal.

11   Antenna - general information

Windshield and rear window antennas

Windshield antenna

1   On some models the antennas are mounted in the windshield and on the inside of the rear window. The windshield antenna is an integral component of the windshield; it's installed between the inner and outer layers of glass. To replace a windshield antenna you must replace the windshield.

Rear window antenna

2   The rear window antenna is a grid baked onto the glass surface, just like the rear window defroster heater grid. If the rear window antenna is damaged, you might be able

to repair it the same way that you would repair the rear window heater grid (see Section 18).

Roof-mounted antenna

3   On models with cellular navigation and/or digital satellite radio systems the antenna is mounted on the roof. To replace it you must remove the headliner and, on vehicles equipped with side-curtain airbags, the side-curtain airbag modules as well. We therefore recommend that you have this type of antenna replaced by a dealer service department or other qualified repair shop.

12   Windshield wiper motor - replacement

Refer to illustrations 12.1, 12.2, 12.4, 12.5, 12.6 and 12.7

1   Pry off the windshield wiper trim caps **(see illustration)**.

2   Remove the windshield wiper retaining nuts and washers. Mark the position of each wiper arm in relation to its shaft **(see illustration)**, then remove the wiper arms.

12.4 To detach the windshield wiper motor and linkage assembly from the cowl, remove these three bolts

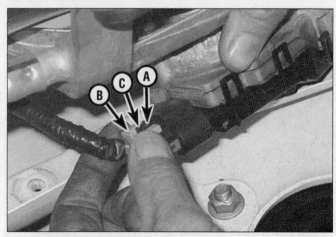

12.5 To disconnect the electrical connector from the motor, depress the tab (A) and slide the lock (B) out, then squeeze the lock tab (C) and pull the connector off the motor

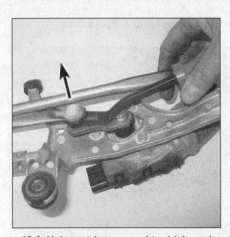

12.6 Using a trim removal tool (shown) or a large screwdriver, carefully pry the linkage arm loose from the crank arm. They're connected by a nylon spherical bearing, so the linkage arm will pop loose when you apply sufficient force

3   Remove the cowl cover (see Chapter 11).

4   Remove the three mounting bolts that secure the windshield wiper motor and linkage assembly to the cowl **(see illustration)**.

5   Lift the windshield wiper motor and linkage assembly out of the cowl area, disconnect the electrical connector from the wiper motor **(see illustration)**, then place the wiper motor and linkage assembly on a clean workbench space.

6   Using a trim removal tool or a large screwdriver, carefully pry the linkage off the wiper motor crank arm **(see illustration)**.

7   Remove the nut that attaches the actuator arm to the motor shaft **(see illustration)**.

8   Mark the relationship of the actuator arm to the motor shaft, then remove the actuator arm from the shaft.

9   Remove the motor mounting screws and remove the motor.

10   Installation is the reverse of removal. Be sure to align the marks you made on the actuator arm and the motor shaft, and on the windshield wiper arms and the wiper arm shafts.

13   Headlight housing - replacement

Refer to illustrations 13.1, 13.2, 13.4 and 13.5

1   Remove the headlight housing bolt **(see illustration)**.

2   Pull up the headlight housing retainer **(see illustration)**.

3   Pull out the headlight housing and disconnect the electrical connector.

4   When installing the headlight housing, make sure that the locator pin on the headlight housing is aligned with its corresponding grommet in the front fender **(see illustration)**.

5   When locking the retainer into place, make sure that the retainer is correctly installed and aligned with the mounting lugs on the housing **(see illustration)**.

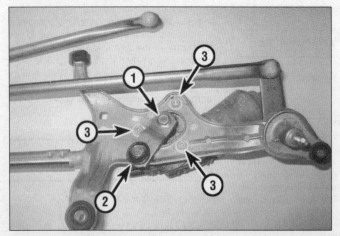

12.7 To detach the motor from the linkage assembly, remove the crank arm nut (1), mark the relationship of the crank arm to the motor shaft, remove the crank arm (2), then remove the three motor mounting screws (3)

13.1 To detach the rear part of the headlight housing, remove this bolt (Impala shown; on Monte Carlo models, the headlight housing is secured by a pair of screws located on the upper part of the housing)

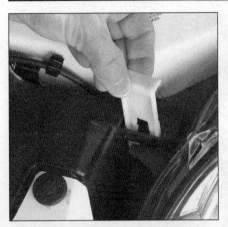

13.2 To detach the front part of the headlight housing, pull this retainer straight up (Impala model shown; Monte Carlo models similar)

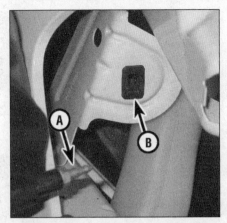

13.4 When installing the headlight housing, make sure that the locator pin (A) on the backside of the housing is aligned with the rubber grommet (B) in the fender

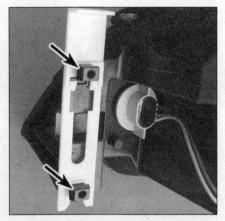

13.5 When installing the retainer, make sure it engages both lugs on the housing (headlight housing removed for clarity)

6   Installation is otherwise the reverse of removal.
7   Adjust the headlights when you're done (see Section 14).

14 Headlights - adjustment

Refer to illustrations 14.1 and 14.3

Note: *The headlights must be aimed correctly. If adjusted incorrectly they could blind the driver of an oncoming vehicle and cause a serious accident or seriously reduce your ability to see the road. The headlights should be checked for proper aim every 12 months and any time a new headlight is installed or front end bodywork is performed. It should be emphasized that the following procedure is only an interim step that will provide temporary adjustment until a properly equipped shop can adjust the headlights.*

1   The vertical adjustment screws are located behind each headlight housing **(see illustration)**. (There are no horizontal adjustment screws.)
2   There are several methods for adjusting the headlights. The simplest method requires masking tape, a blank wall and a level floor.

3   Position masking tape vertically on the wall in relation to the vehicle centerline and the centerlines of both headlights **(see illustration)**.

4   Position a horizontal tapeline in relation to the centerline of all the headlights. **Note:** *It might be easier to position the tape on the wall with the vehicle parked only a few inches away.*

14.1 Headlight vertical adjustment screw

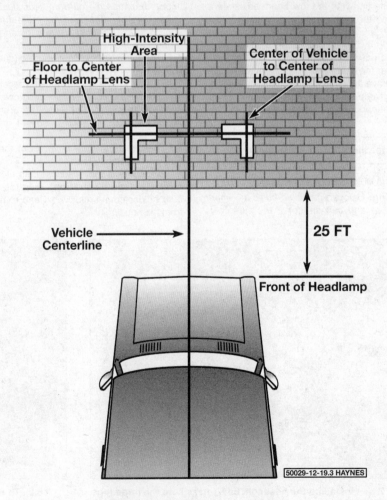

14.3 Headlight adjustment details

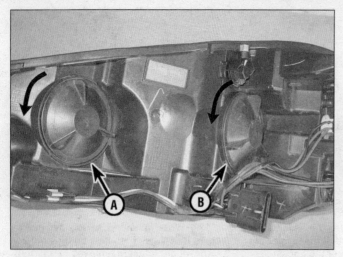

15.2 Each headlight housing has two headlight bulbs: high beam (A) and low beam (B). To remove the circular access cover for either headlight bulb, turn it counterclockwise and pull it off

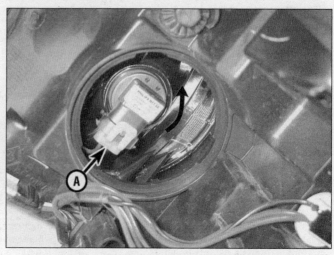

15.4 To remove a headlight bulb from the headlight housing, disconnect the electrical connector (A), then rotate the bulb counterclockwise and pull it out of the housing

5   Adjustment should be made with the vehicle parked 25 feet from the wall, sitting level, the gas tank half-full and no heavy load in the vehicle.

6   Starting with the low beam adjustment, position the high intensity zone so it is two inches below the horizontal line. Adjustment is made by turning the adjusting screw clockwise to raise the beam and counterclockwise to lower the beam.

7   Have the headlights adjusted by a dealer service department or service station at the earliest opportunity.

15   Headlight bulb - replacement

Refer to illustrations 15.2, 15.4 and 15.5

Warning: *Halogen gas-filled bulbs are under pressure and can shatter if the surface is*

scratched or the bulb is dropped. Wear eye protection and handle the bulbs carefully, grasping only the base whenever possible. Do not touch the surface of the bulb with your fingers because the oil from your skin could cause it to overheat and fail prematurely. If you do touch the bulb surface, clean it with rubbing alcohol.

1   Remove the headlight housing (see Section 13).

2   Place the headlight housing face down on a clean surface. Lay down a towel or a shop rag to protect the lens. There are two headlight bulbs in each headlight housing **(see illustration)**.

3   Remove the dust cover from the bulb that you're going to replace.

4   Disconnect the headlight bulb electrical connector **(see illustration)**, then rotate the bulb holder counterclockwise and remove it from the housing.

5   When installing the new bulb, make sure that the three lugs on the bulb holder mounting flange are aligned with the three cutouts in the plastic headlight housing **(see illustration)**, then insert the bulb into the housing and turn it clockwise. Installation is otherwise the reverse of removal. When installing the new bulb, make sure that you don't touch the glass. If you do, clean it with alcohol and a soft clean cloth before installing it.

16   Bulb replacement

Exterior lights

Front side marker light bulbs

Refer to illustration 16.2

1   Remove the headlight housing (see Section 13).

15.5 When installing the headlight bulb, make sure the three lugs on the bulb holder mounting flange are aligned with the three cutouts in the headlight housing

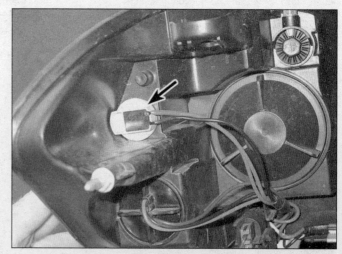

16.2 To remove the front side marker bulb holder from the headlight housing, turn it counterclockwise and pull it out of the housing

16.7 To remove the front park and turn signal bulb holder from the headlight housing, turn it counterclockwise and pull it out of the housing

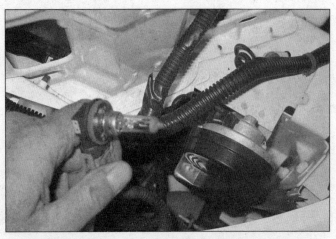

16.12 The fog light bulbs are difficult to access because they're located in the front bumper cover, below the headlight housing (which must be removed to replace the bulb). But there's just enough space to reach down, rotate the bulb holder counterclockwise and remove it from the fog light housing

2   Turn the bulb holder counterclockwise **(see illustration)** and pull it out of the headlight housing.
3   To remove the old bulb from its holder, pull it straight out.
4   To install a new bulb in the bulb holder, push it straight into the socket until it stops.
5   Installation is otherwise the reverse of removal.

Front park and turn signal bulbs

Refer to illustration 16.7

6   Remove the headlight housing (see Section 13).
7   Turn the front park and turn signal bulb holder counterclockwise **(see illustration)** and pull it out of the headlight housing.
8   To remove the old bulb from its holder, pull it straight out.
9   To install a new bulb in the bulb holder, push it straight into the socket until it stops.
10   Installation is otherwise the reverse of removal.

Fog lights

Refer to illustration 16.12

Warning: *Halogen gas-filled bulbs are under pressure and can shatter if the surface is scratched or the bulb is dropped. Wear eye protection and handle the bulbs carefully, grasping only the base whenever possible. Do not touch the surface of the bulb with your fingers because the oil from your skin could cause it to overheat and fail prematurely. If you do touch the bulb surface, clean it with rubbing alcohol.*

11   Remove the headlight housing (see Section 13).
12   Reach down and rotate the fog light bulb holder counterclockwise and pull it out of the fog light housing (see illustration).
13   Disconnect the electrical connector from the fog light bulb holder.
14   The bulb and bulb holder are a single assembly. No further disassembly is necessary. The new bulb includes its own new holder.
15   Installation is the reverse of removal.

Center high-mounted brake light

Impala models

Refer to illustration 16.17

16   Open the trunk and remove the carpet trim from the underside of the trunk lid (see Chapter 11).
17   Remove the center high-mounted brake light housing mounting nuts **(see illustration)**.
18   Remove the center high-mounted brake light assembly and disconnect the electrical connector.
19   The center high-mounted brake light housing, lens and bulb(s) are a one-piece assembly. No further disassembly is possible.
20   Installation is the reverse of removal.

Monte Carlo models

21   Open the trunk and remove the screw that secures the mounting bracket for the center high-mounted brake light. Remove the bracket.
22   Remove the center high-mounted brake light housing mounting screws.
23   Depress the retainers that secure the center high-mounted brake light housing and remove the housing from the trunk lid.
24   Disconnect the electrical connector from the center high-mounted brake light housing.
25   Installation is the reverse of removal.

License plate light bulbs

Refer to illustration 16.27

26   Access to the license plate light bulb can be gained two ways: from underneath, or by removing the license plate. It's a little quicker to lay on the ground, reach up and remove it from underneath, but if you don't feel like getting on the ground, go ahead and remove the license plate.

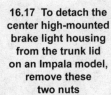

16.17 To detach the center high-mounted brake light housing from the trunk lid on an Impala model, remove these two nuts

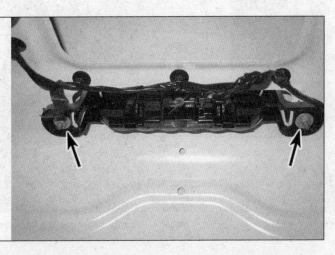

16.27 To remove the bulb holder from the license plate light housing, rotate the bulb holder counterclockwise and pull it out

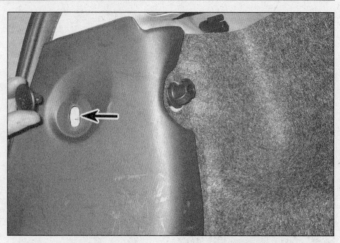

16.28 Unscrew the knob from this stud, remove the plastic trim panel, then peel back the carpet from the rear corner of the trunk (Impala model shown, Monte Carlo models similar)

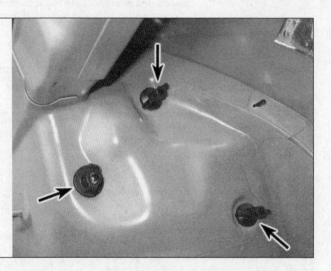

16.29 To detach the taillight housing from the body, remove these three wing nuts (Impala model shown, Monte Carlo models similar)

27   Remove the bulb holder from the license plate light housing **(see illustration)**. To remove the old bulb from its holder, simply pull it straight out. Installation is the reverse of removal.

Taillight bulbs

Refer to illustrations 16.28, 16.29, 16.30a, 16.30b and 16.31

Note: *The accompanying photos depict the taillight housing on an Impala model. The*

taillight housing on a Monte Carlo model is removed the same way, and it also has three light bulbs, but the back-up lights on Monte Carlos are in separate housings, which are located in the rear bumper cover.

28   Open the trunk. Remove the carpeting retainer **(see illustration)** and peel back the carpeting.

29   To detach the taillight housing from the vehicle, remove the plastic wing nuts **(see illustration)**.

30   Pull out the taillight housing and disconnect the electrical connector **(see illustrations)**.

31   Lay the taillight housing on a clean surface and refer to the accompanying taillight bulb guide **(see illustration)**.

32   To remove a bulb holder from the taillight housing, turn it counterclockwise and pull it out of the housing.

33   To remove an old bulb from its holder, pull it straight out.

34   To install a new bulb in its holder, push it straight into the socket until it stops.

35   Installation is the reverse of removal.

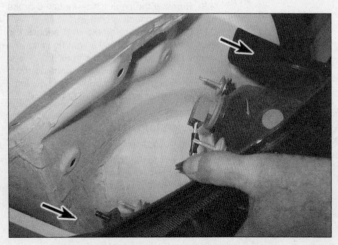

16.30a Carefully pull out the taillight housing . . .

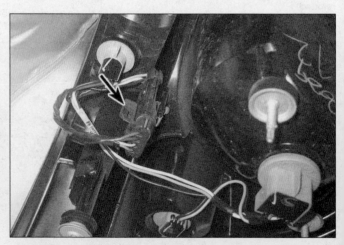

16.30b . . . and disconnect the harness electrical connector

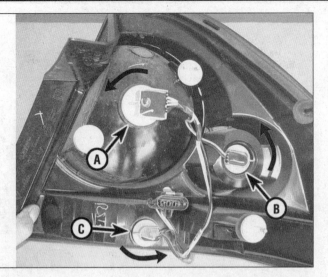

16.31 There are three bulbs in an Impala taillight housing:

A   Brake light/taillight/turn signal bulb
B   Rear sidemarker light bulb
C   Back-up light bulb

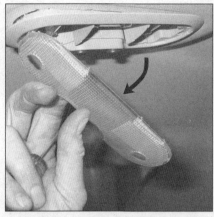

16.42 Using a small screwdriver, carefully pry loose the dome light lens at the left (driver's) end and swing it down to access the dome light bulbs

Back-up light bulbs (Monte Carlo models)

Note: *The back-up lights on Monte Carlo models are located in the rear bumper cover.*
36   Remove the two screws from the back-up light housing.
37   Pull the back-up light housing out of the rear bumper cover.
38   To remove the back-up light bulb holder, rotate it counterclockwise and pull it out of the housing.
39   To remove the old bulb from its holder, pull it straight out.
40   To install a new bulb in the holder, push it straight into the socket until it stops.
41   The remainder of installation is the reverse of removal.

Interior lights
Dome light bulbs

Refer to illustration 16.42

42   Pry off the dome light or lens **(see illustration)**.
43   Remove the bad light bulb by pulling it

straight down. **Warning:** *If it's necessary to pry a bulb out, pry only on the metal terminal ends.*
44   To install a new bulb, push it up between the conductors until it snaps into place.
45   When installing the lens, make sure that it snaps into place.

Reading light bulbs

Refer to illustration 16.47

46   Carefully pry off the reading light lens.
47   To remove a reading light bulb **(see illustration)**, simply pull it straight out.
48   To install a new reading light bulb, push it into the socket until it stops.
49   When installing the lens, make sure that the three mounting tabs on the lens are aligned with their corresponding slots in the mirror housing and that the lens snaps into place.

Instrument panel courtesy light bulb

Refer to illustration 16.50

50   The instrument panel courtesy light bulb **(see illustration)** is located in the insulator

panel under the glove box. To remove the bulb, simply pull it straight out of its socket.
51   Installation is the reverse of removal.

---

17   Horn - replacement

Note: *The horns are located at the right front corner of the vehicle, in a void below the right headlight housing and behind the right end of the bumper cover.*
1   Remove the right (passenger's side) headlight housing (see Section 13).
2   Locate the horns at the right front corner of the vehicle.
3   Disconnect the electrical connector from the horns.
4   Remove the horn mounting bracket bolt and remove the two horns and the mounting bracket as a single assembly.
5   Once the horns and mounting bracket are removed, you can detach either or both horns as necessary from the mounting bracket by unbolting them.
6   Installation is the reverse of removal.

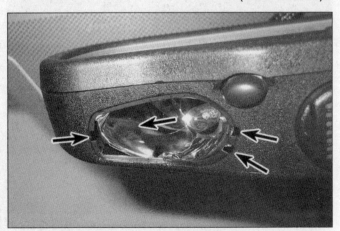

16.47 To replace either of the reading light bulbs, simply pull the bulb straight out. When installing the lens, make sure that the three mounting tabs on the lens are correctly engaged with the three slots in the mirror housing

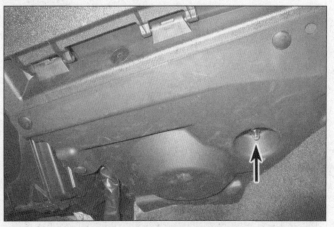

16.50 The instrument panel courtesy light bulb is located in the insulator panel below the glove box. To remove it, pull it straight out of its socket

18.4 When measuring the voltage at the rear window defogger grid, wrap a piece of aluminum foil around the positive probe of the voltmeter and press the foil against the wire with your finger

18.5 To determine if a heating element has broken, check the voltage at the center of each element; if the voltage is 5 or 6-volts, the element is unbroken, but if the voltage is 10 or 12-volts, the element is broken between the center and the ground side. If there is no voltage, the element is broken between the center and the positive side

18 Rear window defogger - check and repair

1   The rear window defogger consists of a number of horizontal elements baked onto the glass surface.
2   Small breaks in the element can be repaired without removing the rear window.

Check

Refer to illustrations 18.4, 18.5 and 18.7

3   Turn the ignition switch and defogger system switches to the ON position. Using a voltmeter, place the positive probe against the defogger grid positive terminal and the negative probe against the ground terminal. If battery voltage is not indicated, check the fuse, defogger switch and related wiring. If voltage is indicated, but all or part of the defogger doesn't heat, proceed with the following tests.

4   When measuring voltage during the next two tests, wrap a piece of aluminum foil around the tip of the voltmeter positive probe and press the foil against the heating element with your finger **(see illustration)**. Place the negative probe on the defogger grid ground terminal.
5   Check the voltage at the center of each heating element **(see illustration)**. If the voltage is 5 or 6-volts, the element is okay (there is no break). If the voltage is zero, the element is broken between the center of the element and the positive end. If the voltage is 10 to 12-volts the element is broken between the center of the element and ground. Check each heating element.
6   Connect the negative lead to a good body ground. The reading should stay the same. If it doesn't, the ground connection is bad.
7   To find the break, place the voltmeter negative probe against the defogger ground terminal. Place the voltmeter positive probe with the foil strip against the heating element at the positive terminal end and slide it toward the negative terminal end. The point at which the voltmeter deflects from several volts to

zero is the point at which the heating element is broken **(see illustration)**.

Repair

Refer to illustration 18.13

8   Repair the break in the element using a repair kit specifically recommended for this purpose, available at most auto parts stores. Included in this kit is plastic conductive epoxy.
9   Prior to repairing a break, turn off the system and allow it to cool off for a few minutes.
10   Lightly buff the element area with fine steel wool, then clean it thoroughly with rubbing alcohol.
11   Use masking tape to mask off the area being repaired.
12   Thoroughly mix the epoxy, following the instructions provided with the repair kit.
13   Apply the epoxy material to the slit in the masking tape, overlapping the undamaged area about 3/4-inch on either end **(see illustration)**.
14   Allow the repair to cure for 24 hours before removing the tape and using the system.

18.7 To find the break, place the voltmeter negative lead against the defogger ground terminal, place the voltmeter positive lead with the foil strip against the heating element at the positive terminal end and slide it toward the negative terminal end. The point at which the voltmeter reading changes abruptly is the point at which the element is broken

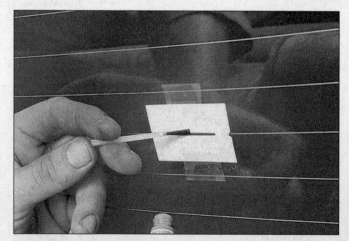

18.13 To use a defogger repair kit, apply masking tape to the inside of the window at the damaged area, then brush on the special conductive coating

19 Electric side view mirrors - general information

1   Most electric rear view mirrors use two motors to move the glass; one for up and down adjustments and one for left-right adjustments.

2   The control switch has a selector portion that sends voltage to the left or right side mirror. With the ignition ON but the engine OFF, roll down the windows and operate the mirror control switch through all functions (LEFT-RIGHT and UP-DOWN) for both the left and right side mirrors.

3   Listen carefully for the sound of the electric motors running in the mirrors.

4   If the motors can be heard but the mirror glass doesn't move, there's a problem with the drive mechanism inside the mirror.

5   If the mirrors do not operate and no sound comes from the mirrors, check the fuse (see Section 3).

6   If the fuse is OK, remove the mirror control switch. Have the switch continuity checked by a dealership service department or other qualified automobile repair facility.

7   Make sure the mirror is properly grounded.

8   If the mirror still doesn't work, remove the mirror and check the wires at the mirror for voltage.

9   If there's not voltage in each switch position, check the circuit between the mirror and control switch for opens and shorts.

10   If there's voltage, remove the mirror and test it off the vehicle with jumper wires. Replace the mirror if it fails this test.

20 Cruise control system - general information

There are no conventional cruise control system components on these vehicles. The cruise control system is an integral subsystem of the electronic throttle body, which is controlled by the Powertrain Control Module (PCM). If the cruise control system isn't functioning correctly, take the vehicle to a dealer service department or other qualified repair shop for diagnosis.

21 Power window system - general information

1   The power window system operates electric motors, mounted in the doors, which lower and raise the windows. The system consists of the control switches, the motors, regulators, glass mechanisms and associated wiring.

2   The power windows can be lowered and raised from the master control switch by the driver or by remote switches located at the individual windows. Each window has a separate motor, which is reversible. The position of the control switch determines the polarity and therefore the direction of operation.

3   The circuit is protected by a fuse and a circuit breaker. Each motor is also equipped with an internal circuit breaker; this prevents one stuck window from disabling the whole system.

4   The power window system will only operate when the ignition switch is ON. In addition, many models have a window lock-out switch at the master control switch which, when activated, disables the switches at the rear windows and, sometimes, the switch at the passenger's window also. Always check these items before troubleshooting a window problem.

5   These procedures are general in nature, so if you can't find the problem using them, take the vehicle to a dealer service department or other properly equipped repair facility.

6   If the power windows won't operate, always check the fuse and circuit breaker first.

7   If only the rear windows are inoperative, or if the windows only operate from the master control switch, check the rear window lockout switch for continuity in the unlocked position. Replace it if it doesn't have continuity.

8   Check the wiring between the switches and fuse panel for continuity. Repair the wiring, if necessary.

9   If only one window is inoperative from the master control switch, try the other control switch at the window. **Note:** *This doesn't apply to the driver's door window.*

10   If the same window works from one switch, but not the other, check the switch for continuity.

11   If the switch tests OK, check for a short or open in the circuit between the affected switch and the window motor.

12   If one window is inoperative from both switches, remove the trim panel from the affected door and check for voltage at the switch and at the motor while the switch is operated.

13   If voltage is reaching the motor, disconnect the glass from the regulator (see Chapter 11). Move the window up and down by hand while checking for binding and damage. Also check for binding and damage to the regulator. If the regulator is not damaged and the window moves up and down smoothly, replace the motor. If there's binding or damage, lubricate, repair or replace parts, as necessary.

14   If voltage isn't reaching the motor, check the wiring in the circuit for continuity between the switches and motors. You'll need to consult the wiring diagram for the vehicle. If the circuit is equipped with a relay, check that the relay is grounded properly and receiving voltage.

22 Power door lock system - general information

1   A power door lock system operates the door lock actuators mounted in each door. The system consists of the switches, actuators, a control unit and associated wiring. Diagnosis can usually be limited to simple checks of the wiring connections and actuators for minor faults that can be easily repaired.

2   Power door lock systems are operated by bi-directional solenoids located in the doors. The lock switches have two operating positions: Lock and Unlock. When activated, the switch sends a ground signal to the door lock control unit to lock or unlock the doors. Depending on which way the switch is activated, the control unit reverses polarity to the solenoids, allowing the two sides of the circuit to be used alternately as the feed (positive) and ground side.

3   Some vehicles may have an anti-theft system incorporated into the power locks. If you are unable to locate the trouble using the following general Steps, consult a dealer service department or other qualified repair shop.

4   Always check the circuit protection first. Some vehicles use a combination of circuit breakers and fuses.

5   Operate the door lock switches in both directions (Lock and Unlock) with the engine off. Listen for the click of the solenoids operating.

6   Test the switches for continuity. Remove the switches and have them checked by a dealer service department or other qualified automobile repair facility.

7   Check the wiring between the switches, control unit and solenoids for continuity. Repair the wiring if there's no continuity.

8   Check for a bad ground at the switches or at the control unit.

9   If all but one of the lock solenoids operate, remove the trim panel from the door with the problem (see Chapter 11) and check for voltage at the solenoid while the lock switch is operated. One of the wires should have voltage in the Lock position; the other should have voltage in the Unlock position.

10   If the inoperative solenoid is receiving voltage, replace the solenoid.

11   If the inoperative solenoid isn't receiving voltage, check the relay for an open or short in the wire between the lock solenoid and the control unit.

23 Daytime Running Lights (DRL) - general information

The Daytime Running Lights (DRL) system illuminates the headlights whenever the engine is running. The only exception is with the engine running and the parking brake engaged. Once the parking brake is released, the lights will remain on as long as the ignition switch is on, even if the parking brake is later applied.

The DRL system supplies reduced power to the headlights so they won't be too bright for daytime use, while prolonging headlight life.

24 Airbag system - general information and precautions

General information

1 All models are equipped with two front airbags, formally known as the Supplemental Inflatable Restraint (SIR) system. This system is designed to protect the driver and the front seat passenger from serious injury in the event of a frontal collision. It consists of an array of external and internal (inside the SDM) information sensors (decelerometers), the Inflatable Restraint Sensing and Diagnostic Module (SDM), the inflator modules (a driver's airbag in the steering wheel and a passenger airbag in the dash) and the wiring and connectors tying all these components together. An optional pair of side-impact airbags, also known as "roof rail" or "side curtain" airbags, is available for protection against side impacts. The side-impact airbags, if equipped, are located along the left and right edges of the headliner, above the doors.

Airbag/inflator modules

Driver's airbag/inflator module

2 The airbag inflator module in the steering wheel consists of a housing, the *cushion* (airbag), an initiating device and a canister of gas-generating material. The initiator is part of the inflator module deployment loop. When a collision occurs, the SDM sends current through the deployment loop to the initiator. Current passing through the initiator ignites the material in the canister, producing a rapidly expanding gas, which inflates the airbag almost instantaneously. Seconds after the airbag inflates, it deflates almost as quickly through airbag vent holes and/or the airbag fabric.

3 When the SDM sends current to the initiator, it travels through the airbag circuit to the steering column. From there, a clockspring on the steering wheel delivers the current to the module initiator. This clockspring assembly, which is the final segment of the airbag ignition circuit, functions as the bridge between the end of the airbag circuit on the (fixed) steering column and the beginning of the circuit on the (rotating) steering wheel. It's designed to maintain a closed circuit between the steering column and the steering wheel regardless of the position of the steering wheel. For this reason, removing and installing the clockspring is critical to the performance of the driver's side airbag. For information on how to remove and install the driver's side airbag, refer to *Steering wheel - removal and installation* in Chapter 10.

Passenger's airbag/inflator module

4 The passenger's airbag/inflator module is mounted above the glove compartment. It's similar in design to the driver's airbag except that it doesn't use a clockspring. When deployed by the SDM, the passenger's airbag bursts through the dashboard above the glove box. Although this area looks like it's simply part of the dashboard, it's actually a trim cover with a perforated seam that allows the cover to separate from the dash when the passenger's airbag inflates.

Side impact airbags

Impala models

5 The (optional) side-impact airbag/inflator (roof rail) modules are mounted along the outer edges of the headliner, right above the door openings. They extend from the A-pillar (front windshield pillar) to the C-pillar (rear window pillar). Each module consists of a housing, an inflatable airbag, an initiator and a canister of gas-generating material. Each roof rail module employs its own side impact sensor (SIS), which contains a sensing device that monitors changes in vehicle acceleration and velocity. This data is sent to the SDM, which compares it with its program. When the data exceeds a certain threshold, the SDM determines that the vehicle has been hit hard enough on one side or the other to warrant deployment of the roof rail on that side. The SDM doesn't deploy the roof rail airbags on both sides, just on the side being hit. Then the SDM sends current to the roof rail initiator to inflate the airbag, ripping open the headliner trim as it deploys to protect the occupant(s) on the left or right side of the vehicle. Side impact airbag/inflator modules are long enough to protect the driver and a left-side rear-seat passenger, or a front seat passenger and right-side rear-seat passenger.

Monte Carlo models

6 Some Monte Carlo models are equipped with optional side-impact airbags in the outer part of the driver and passenger rear seat backs. They are triggered the same way as the Impala roof rail airbags described in Step 5.

Inflatable Restraint Sensing and Diagnostic Module (SDM)

7 The SDM is the computer module that controls the airbag system. Besides a microprocessor, the SDM also includes an array of sensors. Some of them are inside the SDM itself. Other external sensors are located throughout the vehicle. All of the sensors, internal and external, send a continuous voltage signal to the SDM, which compares this data to values stored in its memory. When these signals exceed a threshold value, i.e. when the SDM determines that the vehicle is decelerating more quickly than the threshold value, the SDM allows current to flow through the circuit to the appropriate airbag module(s), which initiates deployment of the airbag(s).

8 For more information about the airbag system in your vehicle, refer to your owner's manual.

Disarming the system and other precautions

Warning: *Failure to follow these precautions could result in accidental deployment of the airbag and personal injury.*

9 Whenever working in the vicinity of the steering wheel, instrument panel or any of the other SIR system components, the system must be disarmed. To disarm the system:

a) *Point the wheels straight ahead and turn the key to the Lock position.*

b) *Disconnect the cable from the negative battery terminal. Refer to Chapter 5, Section 1 for the disconnecting procedure.*

c) *Wait at least two minutes for the back-up power supply to be depleted.*

10 Whenever handling an airbag module, always keep the airbag opening (the trim side) pointed away from your body. Never place the airbag module on a bench or other surface with the airbag opening facing the surface. Always place the airbag module in a safe location with the airbag opening (the upholstered side) facing up.

11 Never measure the resistance of any SIR component or use any electrical test equipment on any of the wiring or components. An ohmmeter has a built-in battery supply that could accidentally deploy the airbag.

12 Never dispose of a live airbag/inflator module. Return it to a dealer service department or other qualified repair shop for safe deployment and disposal.

13 Never use electrical welding equipment in the vicinity of any airbag components. The connectors for the system are easy to spot because they're bright yellow. Do NOT disconnect or tamper with these connectors, or you run the risk of setting a Diagnostic Trouble Code (DTC) in the SDM. Like the PCM, the SDM has a malfunction indicator light, known as the AIR BAG indicator light, on the instrument cluster. When you turn the ignition key to ON, the SDM checks out all of the SIS components and circuits. If everything is okay, the AIR BAG indicator light goes off, just like the PCM's Malfunction Indicator Light (MIL). But if there's a problem somewhere, the light stays on, and will remain on until the problem is repaired and the DTC(s) cleared from the SDM's memory.

Impact seat belt retractors

14 All models are equipped with pyrotechnic (explosive) units in the front seat belt retracting mechanisms for both the lap and shoulder belts. During an impact that would trigger the airbag system, the airbag control unit also triggers the seat belt retractors. When the pyrotechnic charges go off, they accelerate the retractors to instantly take up any slack in the seat belt system to more fully prepare the driver and front seat passenger for impact.

15 The airbag system should be disabled any time work is done to or around the seats. **Warning:** *Never strike the pillars or floorpan with a hammer or use an impact-driver tool in these areas unless the system is disabled.*

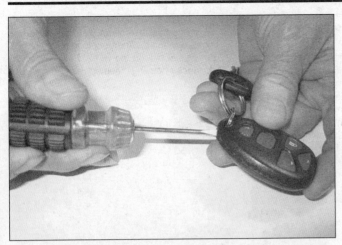

25.3 To separate the two halves of the remote keyless entry fob, insert a small screwdriver into the notch near the panic alarm/ vehicle locator button and carefully pry them apart

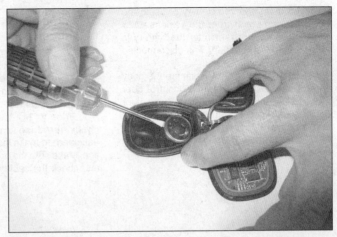

25.4 To remove the old battery from the remote keyless entry fob, carefully pry it out with a small screwdriver. When installing the new battery, be sure to use a CR2032 or equivalent

25 Remote keyless entry system - battery replacement and matching the transmitter to the vehicle

1   Here's how the transmitter inside the remote keyless entry fob should work:

• *You need to be within 65 feet of the car to unlock the doors and/or trunk lid.*
• *When you press the UNLOCK button, the driver's door unlocks. If you press the UNLOCK button a second time within five seconds, all the doors unlock.*
• *When you press the remote TRUNK RELEASE button on the transmitter for one second, it releases the trunk lid. (The remote TRUNK RELEASE button doesn't work unless the transmission shift lever is in PARK.)*
• *If a door or the trunk lid is open, you cannot lock the doors and trunk with the transmitter.*

Battery replacement

Refer to illustrations 25.3 and 25.4

2   The transmitter battery should last about four years. When the transmitter becomes weak, operation will become intermittent and require you to be closer to the vehicle for it to work. Eventually it won't work at all.

3   To replace the transmitter battery, carefully pry open the keyless entry fob by inserting a screwdriver into the notch near the panic alarm/vehicle locator button **(see illustration)** and separate the upper and lower halves of the fob.

4   Carefully pry out the old battery with a small screwdriver **(see illustration)**.

5   Installation is the reverse of removal. Make sure that the new battery is a CR2032 or equivalent. And make sure that the two halves of the cover snap together tightly to keep out dirt, dust, humidity and rain.

Matching the transmitter to the vehicle

Note: *Use the Driver Information Display (DIC) to match the transmitter to the vehicle. The DIC buttons are located to the right of the instrument cluster. The display screen is located right below the speedometer in the instrument cluster. The DIC does a lot of things, but here we're interested only in how it's used to match the transmitter to the vehicle. (For more information about what the DIC can do, and how to use it, refer to your owner's manual.)*

6   To use the DIC, turn the ignition key to ON. Press the VEHICLE INFORMATION button until PRESS TO RELEARN REMOTE KEY appears on the DIC display.

7   Press the SET/RESET button. The message REMOTE KEY LEARNING ACTIVE will appear on the DIC display.

8   Simultaneously press and hold the LOCK and UNLOCK buttons on the first transmitter for about 15 seconds. A chime will sound, indicating that the transmitter is matched to the vehicle.

9   To match other transmitters at this time, repeat Step 8. You can match up to eight transmitters to the vehicle.

10   To exit the programming mode, turn the ignition key to OFF.

26 Vehicle theft deterrent system - general information

Immobilizer system - description and operation

1   The immobilizer system is controlled by the Theft Deterrent Module (TDM) and the engine control module (ECM). When an ignition key is inserted into the ignition lock cylinder and the ignition is turned ON, the TDM

and ECM compare the signal sent from the key and lock cylinder to determine if the correct value is present. If the incorrect value is sent, the TDM will send the fuel disable password to the ECM, no fuel injector pulse will be sent to the fuel injectors and the vehicle will not start.

2   The components of the Immobilizer system are the theft deterrent module, engine control module, ignition key and the security indicator

3   Master keys have a black plastic head for full access operation of the vehicle. With a master key you can start the vehicle, lock or unlock all the doors, rear compartment and all storage compartments. Valet keys, available on some vehicles, have a gray plastic head and are for limited operation of the vehicle. With a valet key you can start the vehicle and lock or unlock all the doors only.

4   If the vehicle won't start or starts then immediately stops running and the " Security" light is illuminated, there may be a problem related to the vehicle theft deterrent system and it should be diagnosed by a dealership service department, professional repair facility or in some instances a qualified locksmith.

Content Theft Deterrent system - description and operation

5   When armed, the Content Theft Deterrent (CTD) system is designed to deter vehicle content theft by sounding the horns and flashing the exterior lamps for approximately 30 seconds when an unauthorized vehicle entry is detected. The CTD system does not affect engine starting.

6   An unauthorized entry can be any of the following when the CTD system is armed: Entry into the engine compartment if equipped with remote vehicle start, entry into the trunk, if any door is opened without first being

unlocked using the vehicle key or using the UNLOCK command from the keyless entry transmitter (key fob), or after the battery is reconnected if the battery was disconnected with the CTD system armed.

7   Components of the system are the body control module (BCM), remote control door lock receiver, the security indicator, hood, door and trunk switches, horn relay, exterior lights and the driver's door key cylinder switch.

8   Refer to the vehicle owners manual for instructions on arming and disarming the CTD system.

27 Wiring diagrams - general information

Since it isn't possible to include all wiring diagrams for every year covered by this manual, the following diagrams are those that are typical and most commonly needed.

Prior to troubleshooting any circuits, check the fuse and circuit breakers (if equipped) to make sure they're in good condition. Make sure the battery is properly charged and check the cable connections (see Chapter 1).

When checking a circuit, make sure that all connectors are clean, with no broken or loose terminals. When unplugging a connector, do not pull on the wires. Pull only on the connector housings themselves.

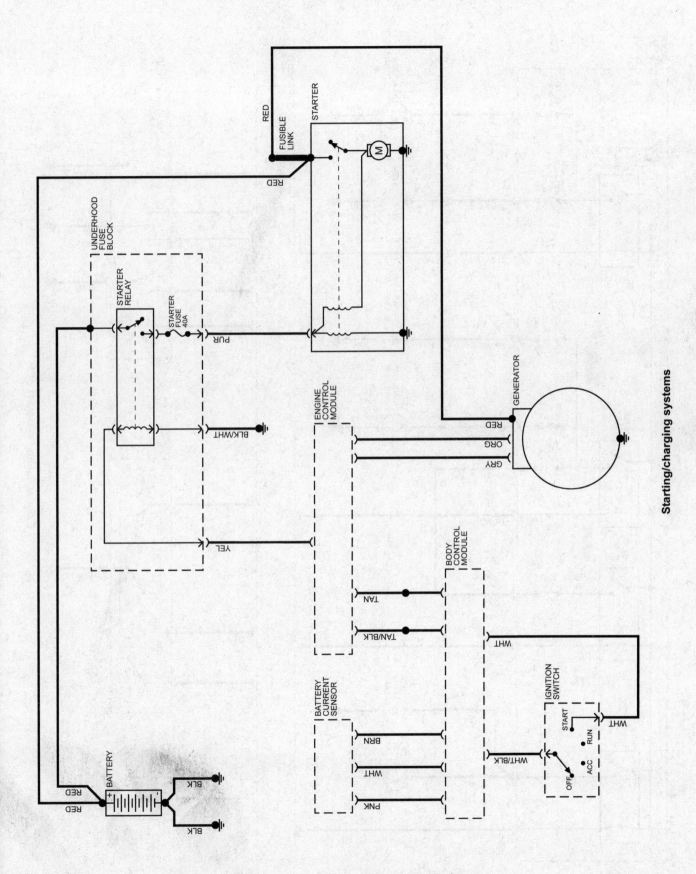

Starting/charging systems

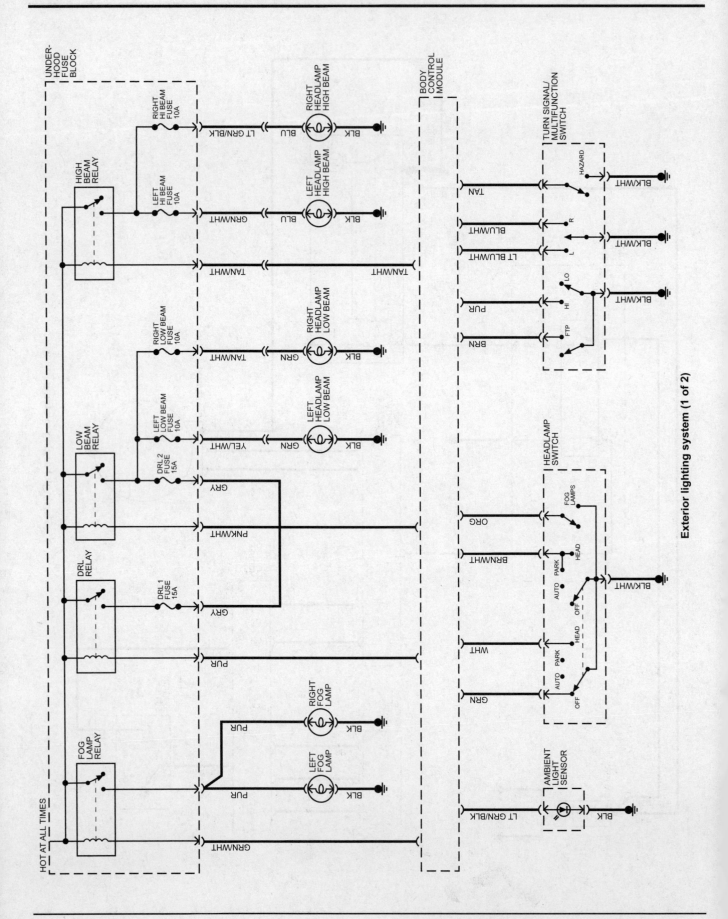

Exterior lighting system (1 of 2)

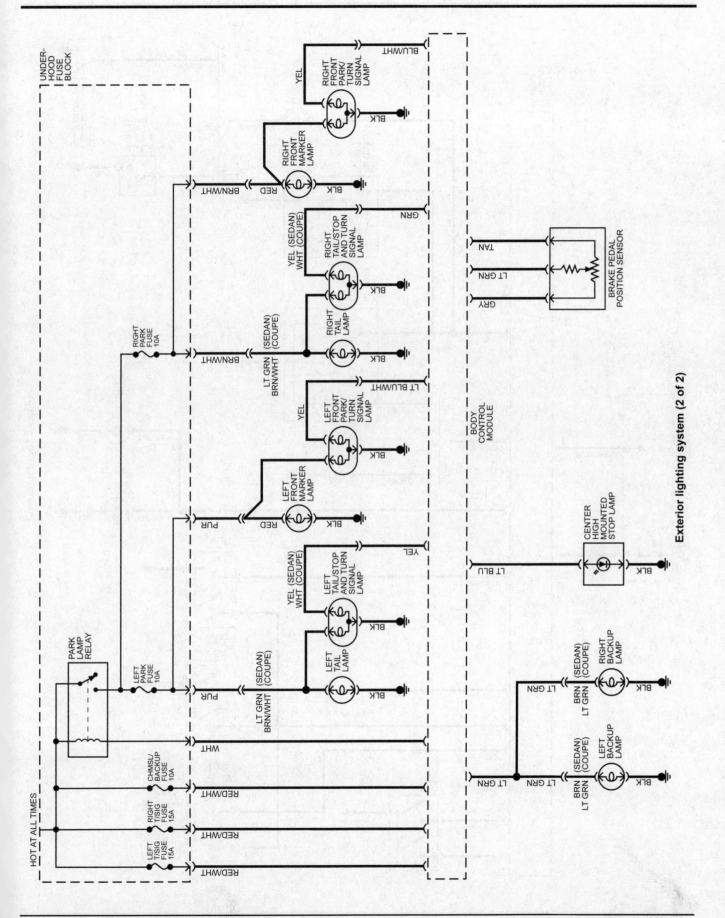

Exterior lighting system (2 of 2)

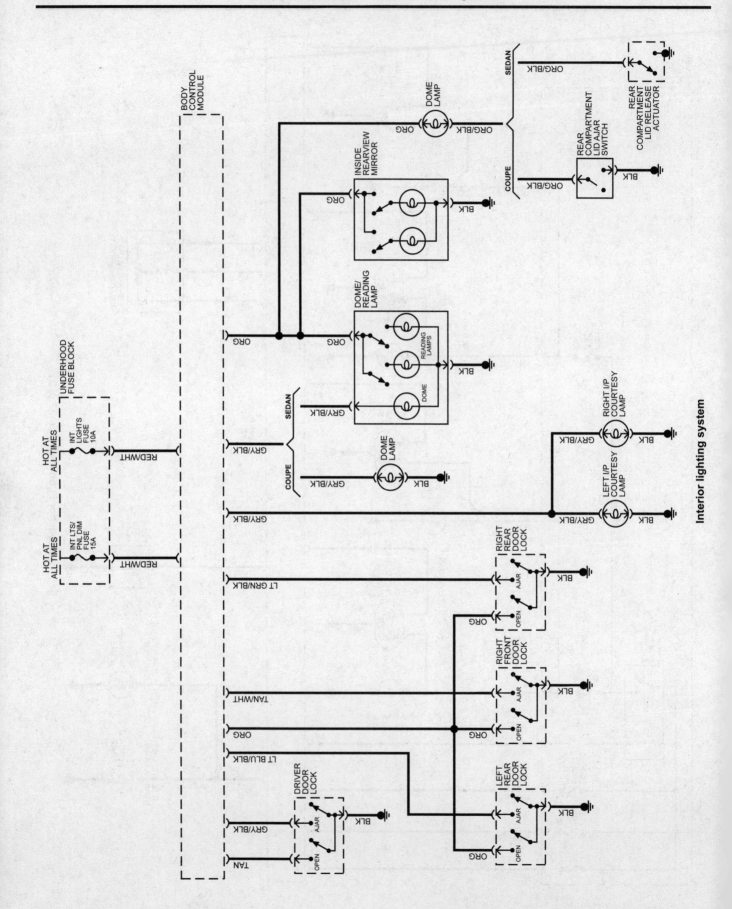

Interior lighting system

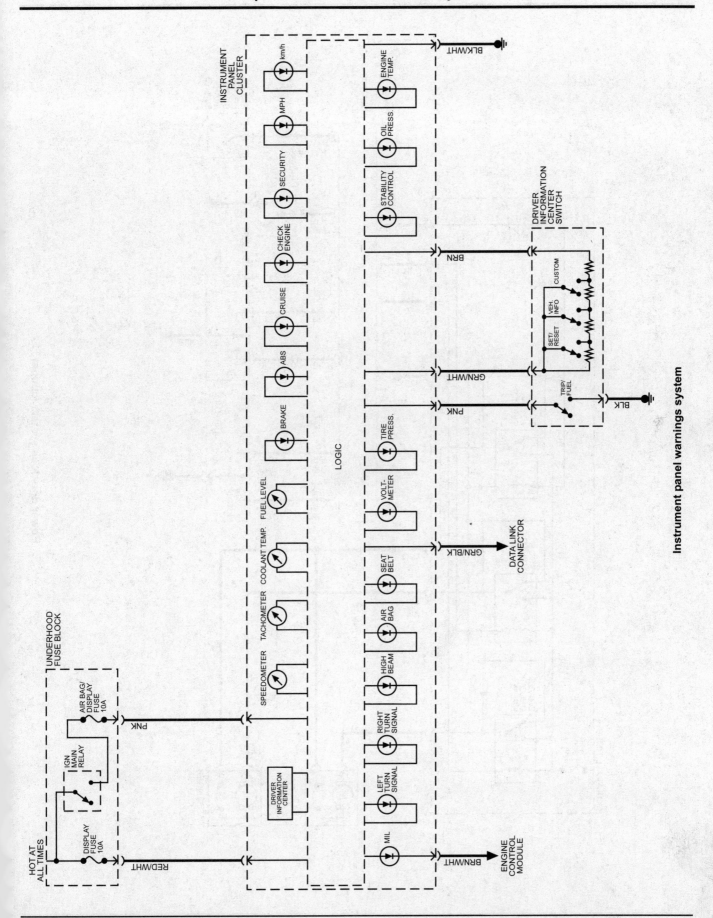

Instrument panel warnings system

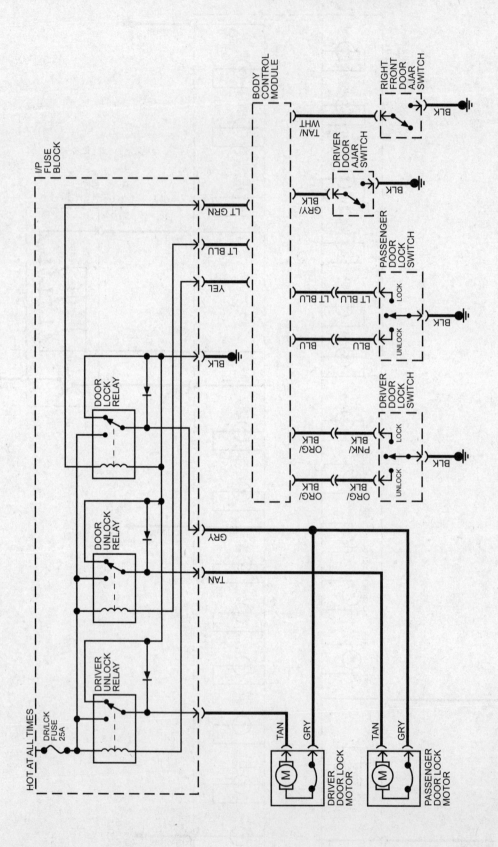

Power door lock system (coupe)

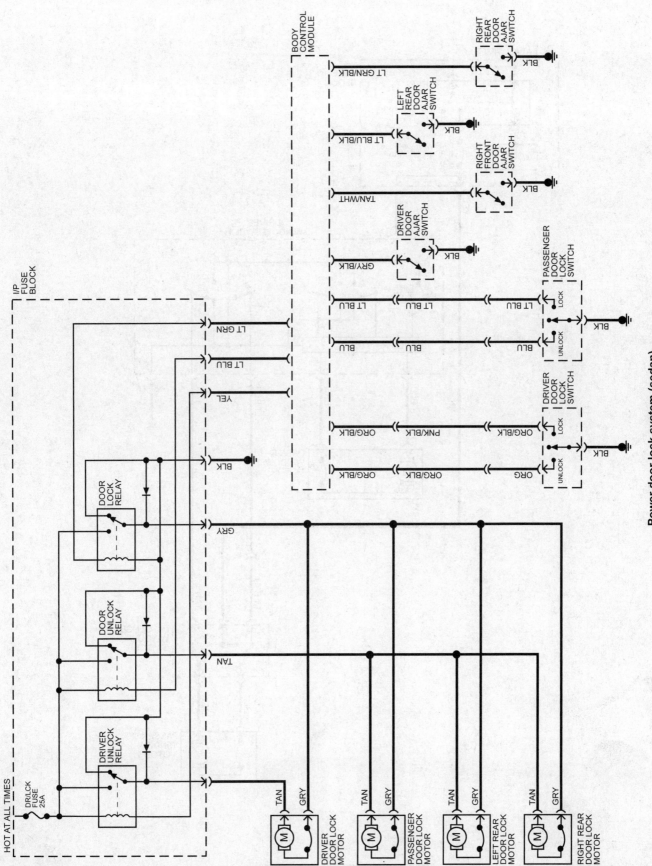

Power door lock system (sedan)

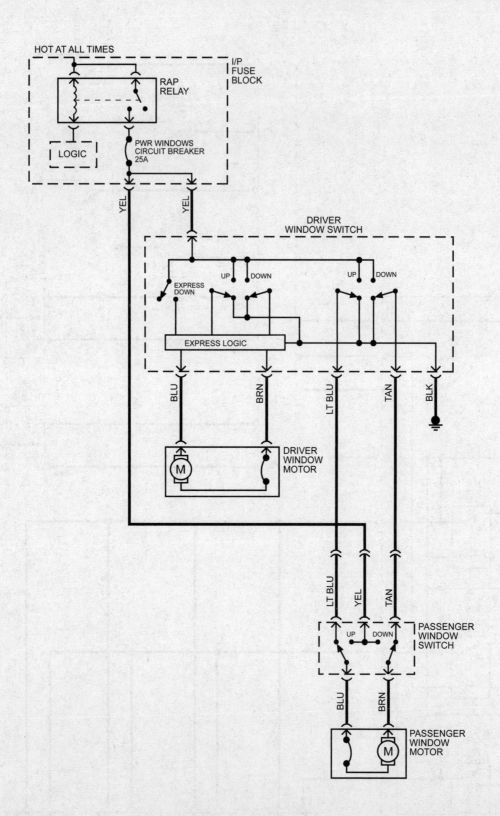

Power windows system (coupe)

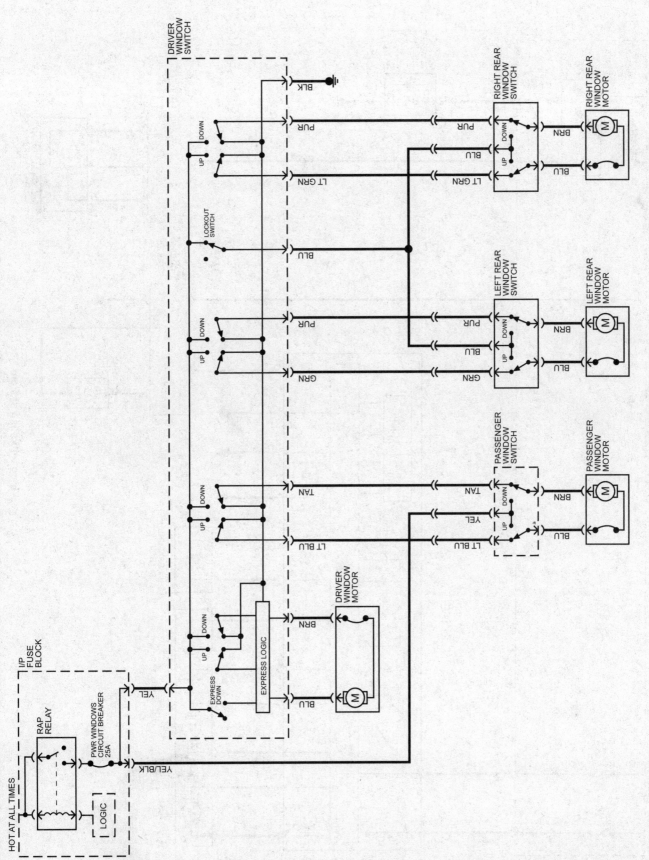

Power windows system (sedan)

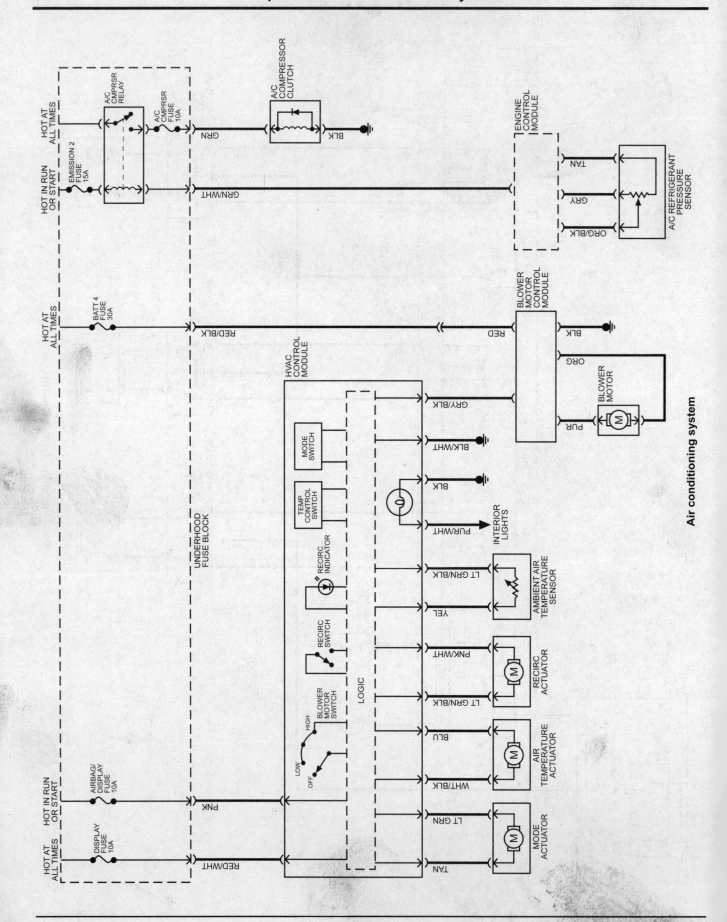

Air conditioning system

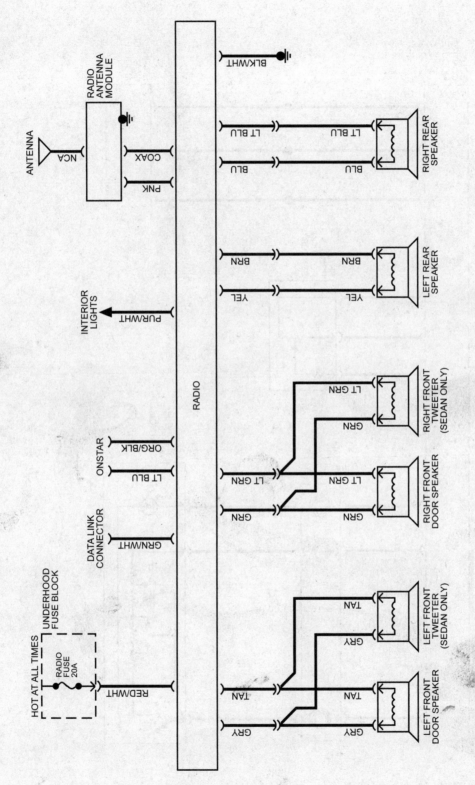

Base audio system

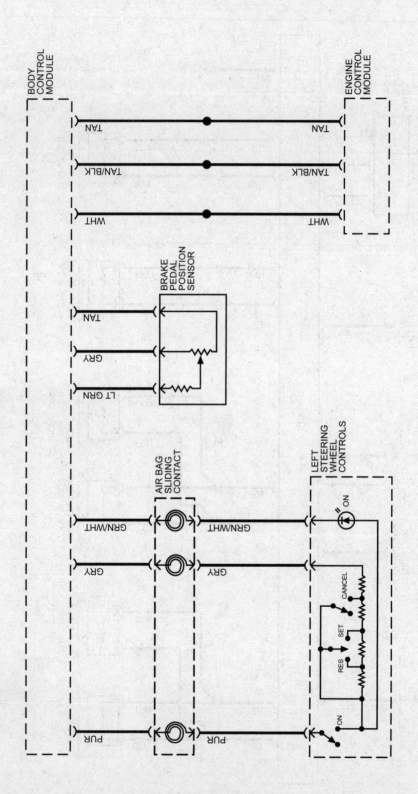

Cruise control system

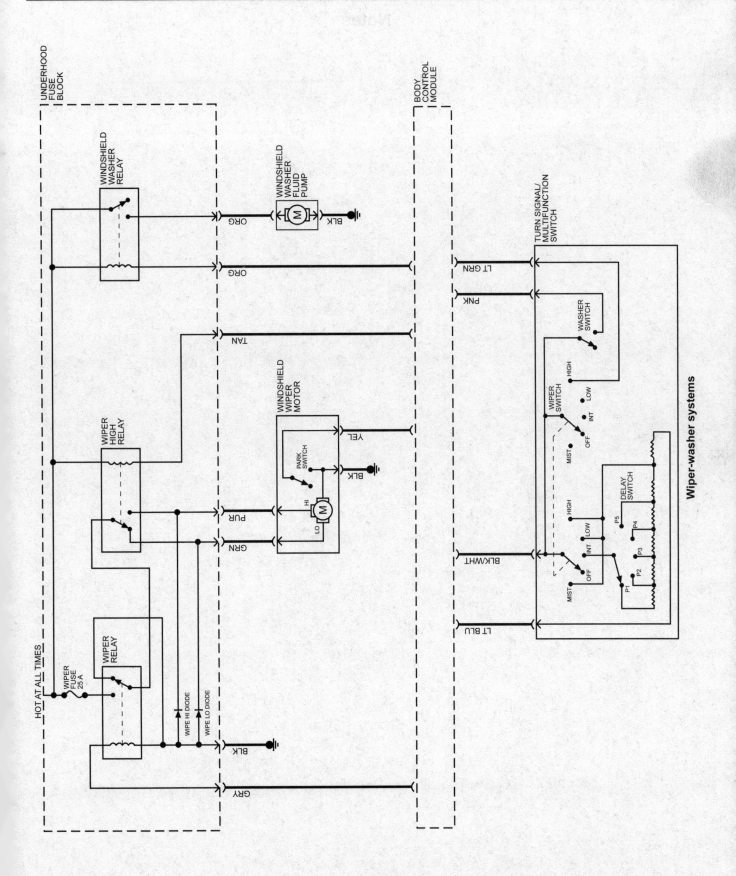

Wiper-washer systems

Notes

Index

Notes

Haynes Automotive Manuals

ACURA
12020 **Integra** '86 thru '89 & **Legend** '86 thru '90
12021 **Integra** '90 thru '93 & **Legend** '91 thru '95
    Integra '94 thru '00 - see HONDA Civic (42025)
    MDX '01 thru '07 - see HONDA Pilot (42037)
12050 **Acura TL** all models '99 thru '08

AMC
    Jeep CJ - see JEEP (50020)
14020 **Mid-size models** '70 thru '83
14025 **(Renault) Alliance & Encore** '83 thru '87

AUDI
15020 **4000** all models '80 thru '87
15025 **5000** all models '77 thru '83
15026 **5000** all models '84 thru '88
    Audi A4 '96 thru '01 - see VW Passat (96023)
15030 **Audi A4** '02 thru '08

AUSTIN-HEALEY
    Sprite - see MG Midget (66015)

BMW
18020 **3/5 Series** '82 thru '92
18021 **3-Series** incl. Z3 models '92 thru '98
18022 **3-Series** incl. Z4 models '99 thru '05
18023 **3-Series** '06 thru '10
18025 **320i** all 4 cyl models '75 thru '83
18050 **1500 thru 2002** except Turbo '59 thru '77

BUICK
19010 **Buick Century** '97 thru '05
    Century (front-wheel drive) - see GM (38005)
19020 **Buick, Oldsmobile & Pontiac Full-size (Front-wheel drive)** '85 thru '05
    Buick Electra, LeSabre and Park Avenue; **Oldsmobile** Delta 88 Royale, Ninety Eight and Regency; **Pontiac** Bonneville
19025 **Buick, Oldsmobile & Pontiac Full-size (Rear wheel drive)** '70 thru '90
    Buick Estate, Electra, LeSabre, Limited, **Oldsmobile** Custom Cruiser, Delta 88, Ninety-eight, **Pontiac** Bonneville, Catalina, Grandville, Parisienne
19030 **Mid-size Regal & Century** all rear-drive models with V6, V8 and Turbo '74 thru '87
    Regal - see GENERAL MOTORS (38010)
    Riviera - see GENERAL MOTORS (38030)
    Roadmaster - see CHEVROLET (24046)
    Skyhawk - see GENERAL MOTORS (38015)
    Skylark - see GM (38020, 38025)
    Somerset - see GENERAL MOTORS (38025)

CADILLAC
21015 **CTS & CTS-V** '03 thru '12
21030 **Cadillac Rear Wheel Drive** '70 thru '93
    Cimarron - see GENERAL MOTORS (38015)
    DeVille - see GM (38031 & 38032)
    Eldorado - see GM (38030 & 38031)
    Fleetwood - see GM (38031)
    Seville - see GM (38030, 38031 & 38032)

CHEVROLET
10305 **Chevrolet Engine Overhaul Manual**
24010 **Astro & GMC Safari Mini-vans** '85 thru '05
24015 **Camaro V8** all models '70 thru '81
24016 **Camaro** all models '82 thru '92
24017 **Camaro & Firebird** '93 thru '02
    Cavalier - see GENERAL MOTORS (38016)
    Celebrity - see GENERAL MOTORS (38005)
24020 **Chevelle, Malibu & El Camino** '69 thru '87
24024 **Chevette & Pontiac T1000** '76 thru '87
    Citation - see GENERAL MOTORS (38020)
24027 **Colorado & GMC Canyon** '04 thru '10
24032 **Corsica/Beretta** all models '87 thru '96
24040 **Corvette** all V8 models '68 thru '82
24041 **Corvette** all models '84 thru '96
24045 **Full-size Sedans** Caprice, Impala, Biscayne, Bel Air & Wagons '69 thru '90
24046 **Impala SS & Caprice and Buick Roadmaster** '91 thru '96
    Impala '00 thru '05 - see LUMINA (24048)
24047 **Impala & Monte Carlo** all models '06 thru '11
    Lumina '90 thru '94 - see GM (38010)
24048 **Lumina & Monte Carlo** '95 thru '05
    Lumina APV - see GM (38035)
24050 **Luv Pick-up** all 2WD & 4WD '72 thru '82
    Malibu '97 thru '00 - see GM (38026)
24055 **Monte Carlo** all models '70 thru '88
    Monte Carlo '95 thru '01 - see LUMINA (24048)
24059 **Nova** all V8 models '69 thru '79
24060 **Nova and Geo Prizm** '85 thru '92
24064 **Pick-ups** '67 thru '87 - Chevrolet & GMC
24065 **Pick-ups** '88 thru '98 - Chevrolet & GMC

24066 **Pick-ups** '99 thru '06 - Chevrolet & GMC
24067 **Chevrolet Silverado & GMC Sierra** '07 thru '12
24070 **S-10 & S-15 Pick-ups** '82 thru '93, **Blazer & Jimmy** '83 thru '94,
24071 **S-10 & Sonoma Pick-ups** '94 thru '04, including **Blazer, Jimmy & Hombre**
24072 **Chevrolet TrailBlazer, GMC Envoy & Oldsmobile Bravada** '02 thru '09
24075 **Sprint** '85 thru '88 & **Geo Metro** '89 thru '01
24080 **Vans - Chevrolet & GMC** '68 thru '96
24081 **Chevrolet Express & GMC Savana** Full-size Vans '96 thru '10

CHRYSLER
10310 **Chrysler Engine Overhaul Manual**
25015 **Chrysler Cirrus, Dodge Stratus, Plymouth Breeze** '95 thru '00
25020 **Full-size Front-Wheel Drive** '88 thru '93
    K-Cars - see DODGE Aries (30008)
    Laser - see DODGE Daytona (30030)
25025 **Chrysler LHS, Concorde, New Yorker, Dodge** Intrepid, **Eagle Vision**, '93 thru '97
25026 **Chrysler LHS, Concorde, 300M, Dodge** Intrepid, '98 thru '04
25027 **Chrysler 300, Dodge Charger & Magnum** '05 thru '09
25030 **Chrysler & Plymouth Mid-size** front wheel drive '82 thru '95
    Rear-wheel Drive - see Dodge (30050)
25035 **PT Cruiser** all models '01 thru '10
25040 **Chrysler Sebring** '95 thru '06, **Dodge Stratus** '01 thru '06, **Dodge Avenger** '95 thru '00

DATSUN
28005 **200SX** all models '80 thru '83
28007 **B-210** all models '73 thru '78
28009 **210** all models '79 thru '82
28012 **240Z, 260Z & 280Z** Coupe '70 thru '78
28014 **280ZX** Coupe & 2+2 '79 thru '83
    300ZX - see NISSAN (72010)
28018 **510 & PL521 Pick-up** '68 thru '73
28020 **510** all models '78 thru '81
28022 **620 Series Pick-up** all models '73 thru '79
    720 Series Pick-up - see NISSAN (72030)
28025 **810/Maxima** all gasoline models '77 thru '84

DODGE
    400 & 600 - see CHRYSLER (25030)
30008 **Aries & Plymouth Reliant** '81 thru '89
30010 **Caravan & Plymouth Voyager** '84 thru '95
30011 **Caravan & Plymouth Voyager** '96 thru '02
30012 **Challenger/Plymouth Saporro** '78 thru '83
30013 **Caravan, Chrysler Voyager, Town & Country** '03 thru '07
30016 **Colt & Plymouth Champ** '78 thru '87
30020 **Dakota Pick-ups** all models '87 thru '96
30021 **Durango** '98 & '99, **Dakota** '97 thru '99
30022 **Durango** '00 thru '03 **Dakota** '00 thru '04
30023 **Durango** '04 thru '09, **Dakota** '05 thru '11
30025 **Dart, Demon, Plymouth Barracuda, Duster & Valiant** 6 cyl models '67 thru '76
30030 **Daytona & Chrysler Laser** '84 thru '89
    Intrepid - see CHRYSLER (25025, 25026)
30034 **Neon** all models '95 thru '99
30035 **Omni & Plymouth Horizon** '78 thru '90
30036 **Dodge and Plymouth Neon** '00 thru '05
30040 **Pick-ups** all full-size models '74 thru '93
30041 **Pick-ups** all full-size models '94 thru '01
30042 **Pick-ups** full-size models '02 thru '08
30045 **Ram 50/D50 Pick-ups & Raider and Plymouth Arrow Pick-ups** '79 thru '93
30050 **Dodge/Plymouth/Chrysler** RWD '71 thru '89
30055 **Shadow & Plymouth Sundance** '87 thru '94
30060 **Spirit & Plymouth Acclaim** '89 thru '95
30065 **Vans - Dodge & Plymouth** '71 thru '03

EAGLE
    Talon - see MITSUBISHI (68030, 68031)
    Vision - see CHRYSLER (25025)

FIAT
34010 **124 Sport Coupe & Spider** '68 thru '78
34025 **X1/9** all models '74 thru '80

FORD
10320 **Ford Engine Overhaul Manual**
10355 **Ford Automatic Transmission Overhaul**
11500 **Mustang** '64-1/2 thru '70 Restoration Guide
36004 **Aerostar Mini-vans** all models '86 thru '97
36006 **Contour & Mercury Mystique** '95 thru '00
36008 **Courier Pick-up** all models '72 thru '82
36012 **Crown Victoria & Mercury Grand Marquis** '88 thru '10
36016 **Escort/Mercury Lynx** all models '81 thru '90
36020 **Escort/Mercury Tracer** '91 thru '02

36022 **Escape & Mazda Tribute** '01 thru '11
36024 **Explorer & Mazda Navajo** '91 thru '01
36025 **Explorer/Mercury Mountaineer** '02 thru '10
36028 **Fairmont & Mercury Zephyr** '78 thru '83
36030 **Festiva & Aspire** '88 thru '97
36032 **Fiesta** all models '77 thru '80
36034 **Focus** all models '00 thru '11
36036 **Ford & Mercury Full-size** '75 thru '87
36044 **Ford & Mercury Mid-size** '75 thru '86
36045 **Fusion & Mercury Milan** '06 thru '10
36048 **Mustang V8** all models '64-1/2 thru '73
36049 **Mustang II** 4 cyl, V6 & V8 models '74 thru '78
36050 **Mustang & Mercury Capri** '79 thru '93
36051 **Mustang** all models '94 thru '04
36052 **Mustang** '05 thru '10
36054 **Pick-ups & Bronco** '73 thru '79
36058 **Pick-ups & Bronco** '80 thru '96
36059 **F-150 & Expedition** '97 thru '09, **F-250** '97 thru '99 & **Lincoln Navigator** '98 thru '09
36060 **Super Duty Pick-ups, Excursion** '99 thru '10
36061 **F-150** full-size '04 thru '10
36062 **Pinto & Mercury Bobcat** '75 thru '80
36066 **Probe** all models '89 thru '92
    Probe '93 thru '97 - see MAZDA 626 (61042)
36070 **Ranger/Bronco II** gasoline models '83 thru '92
36071 **Ranger** '93 thru '10 & **Mazda Pick-ups** '94 thru '09
36074 **Taurus & Mercury Sable** '86 thru '95
36075 **Taurus & Mercury Sable** '96 thru '05
36078 **Tempo & Mercury Topaz** '84 thru '94
36082 **Thunderbird/Mercury Cougar** '83 thru '88
36086 **Thunderbird/Mercury Cougar** '89 thru '97
36090 **Vans** all V8 Econoline models '69 thru '91
36094 **Vans** full size '92 thru '10
36097 **Windstar Mini-van** '95 thru '07

GENERAL MOTORS
10360 **GM Automatic Transmission Overhaul**
38005 **Buick Century, Chevrolet Celebrity, Oldsmobile Cutlass Ciera & Pontiac 6000** all models '82 thru '96
38010 **Buick Regal, Chevrolet Lumina, Oldsmobile Cutlass Supreme & Pontiac Grand Prix** (FWD) '88 thru '07
38015 **Buick Skyhawk, Cadillac Cimarron, Chevrolet Cavalier, Oldsmobile Firenza & Pontiac J-2000 & Sunbird** '82 thru '94
38016 **Chevrolet Cavalier & Pontiac Sunfire** '95 thru '05
38017 **Chevrolet Cobalt & Pontiac G5** '05 thru '11
38020 **Buick Skylark, Chevrolet Citation, Olds Omega, Pontiac Phoenix** '80 thru '85
38025 **Buick Skylark & Somerset, Oldsmobile Achieva & Calais and Pontiac Grand Am** all models '85 thru '98
38026 **Chevrolet Malibu, Olds Alero & Cutlass, Pontiac Grand Am** '97 thru '03
38027 **Chevrolet Malibu** '04 thru '10
38030 **Cadillac Eldorado, Seville, Oldsmobile Toronado, Buick Riviera** '71 thru '85
38031 **Cadillac Eldorado & Seville, DeVille, Fleetwood & Olds Toronado, Buick Riviera** '86 thru '93
38032 **Cadillac DeVille** '94 thru '05 & **Seville** '92 thru '04 **Cadillac DTS** '06 thru '10
38035 **Chevrolet Lumina APV, Olds Silhouette & Pontiac Trans Sport** all models '90 thru '96
38036 **Chevrolet Venture, Olds Silhouette, Pontiac Trans Sport & Montana** '97 thru '05
    General Motors Full-size Rear-wheel Drive - see BUICK (19025)
38040 **Chevrolet Equinox** '05 thru '09 **Pontiac Torrent** '06 thru '09
38070 **Chevrolet HHR** '06 thru '11

GEO
    Metro - see CHEVROLET Sprint (24075)
    Prizm - '85 thru '92 see CHEVY (24060), '93 thru '02 see TOYOTA Corolla (92036)
40030 **Storm** all models '90 thru '93
    Tracker - see SUZUKI Samurai (90010)

GMC
    Vans & Pick-ups - see CHEVROLET

HONDA
42010 **Accord CVCC** all models '76 thru '83
42011 **Accord** all models '84 thru '89
42012 **Accord** all models '90 thru '93
42013 **Accord** all models '94 thru '97
42014 **Accord** all models '98 thru '02
42015 **Accord** '03 thru '07
42020 **Civic 1200** all models '73 thru '79
42021 **Civic 1300 & 1500 CVCC** '80 thru '83
42022 **Civic 1500 CVCC** all models '75 thru '79

(Continued on other side)

Haynes Automotive Manuals (continued)

NOTE: If you do not see a listing for your vehicle, consult your local Haynes dealer for the latest product information.

42023 **Civic** all models '84 thru '91
42024 **Civic & del Sol** '92 thru '95
42025 **Civic** '96 thru '00, **CR-V** '97 thru '01,
Acura Integra '94 thru '00
42026 **Civic** '01 thru '10, **CR-V** '02 thru '09
42035 **Odyssey** all models '99 thru '10
Passport - *see ISUZU Rodeo (47017)*
42037 **Honda Pilot** '03 thru '07, **Acura MDX** '01 thru '07
42040 **Prelude CVCC** all models '79 thru '89

HYUNDAI
43010 **Elantra** all models '96 thru '10
43015 **Excel & Accent** all models '86 thru '09
43050 **Santa Fe** all models '01 thru '06
43055 **Sonata** all models '99 thru '08

INFINITI
G35 '03 thru '08 - *see NISSAN 350Z (72011)*

ISUZU
Hombre - *see CHEVROLET S-10 (24071)*
47017 **Rodeo, Amigo & Honda Passport** '89 thru '02
47020 **Trooper & Pick-up** '81 thru '93

JAGUAR
49010 **XJ6** all 6 cyl models '68 thru '86
49011 **XJ6** all models '88 thru '94
49015 **XJ12 & XJS** all 12 cyl models '72 thru '85

JEEP
50010 **Cherokee, Comanche & Wagoneer Limited** all models '84 thru '01
50020 **CJ** all models '49 thru '86
50025 **Grand Cherokee** all models '93 thru '04
50026 **Grand Cherokee** '05 thru '09
50029 **Grand Wagoneer & Pick-up** '72 thru '91
Grand Wagoneer '84 thru '91, Cherokee & Wagoneer '72 thru '83, Pick-up '72 thru '88
50030 **Wrangler** all models '87 thru '11
50035 **Liberty** '02 thru '07

KIA
54050 **Optima** '01 thru '10
54070 **Sephia** '94 thru '01, **Spectra** '00 thru '09, **Sportage** '05 thru '10

LEXUS
ES 300/330 - *see TOYOTA Camry (92007) (92008)*
RX 330 - *see TOYOTA Highlander (92095)*

LINCOLN
Navigator - *see FORD Pick-up (36059)*
59010 **Rear-Wheel Drive** all models '70 thru '10

MAZDA
61010 **GLC Hatchback** (rear-wheel drive) '77 thru '83
61011 **GLC** (front-wheel drive) '81 thru '85
61012 **Mazda3** '04 thru '11
61015 **323 & Protegé** '90 thru '03
61016 **MX-5 Miata** '90 thru '09
61020 **MPV** all models '89 thru '98
Navajo - *see Ford Explorer (36024)*
61030 **Pick-ups** '72 thru '93
Pick-ups '94 thru '00 - *see Ford Ranger (36071)*
61035 **RX-7** all models '79 thru '85
61036 **RX-7** all models '86 thru '91
61040 **626** (rear-wheel drive) all models '79 thru '82
61041 **626/MX-6** (front-wheel drive) '83 thru '92
61042 **626, MX-6/Ford Probe** '93 thru '02
61043 **Mazda6** '03 thru '11

MERCEDES-BENZ
63012 **123 Series Diesel** '76 thru '85
63015 **190 Series** four-cyl gas models, '84 thru '88
63020 **230/250/280** 6 cyl sohc models '68 thru '72
63025 **280 123 Series** gasoline models '77 thru '81
63030 **350 & 450** all models '71 thru '80
63040 **C-Class:** C230/C240/C280/C320/C350 '01 thru '07

MERCURY
64200 **Villager & Nissan Quest** '93 thru '01
All other titles, see FORD Listing.

MG
66010 **MGB** Roadster & GT Coupe '62 thru '80
66015 **MG Midget, Austin Healey Sprite** '58 thru '80

MINI
67020 **Mini** '02 thru '11

MITSUBISHI
68020 **Cordia, Tredia, Galant, Precis & Mirage** '83 thru '93
68030 **Eclipse, Eagle Talon & Ply. Laser** '90 thru '94
68031 **Eclipse** '95 thru '05, **Eagle Talon** '95 thru '98
68035 **Galant** '94 thru '10
68040 **Pick-up** '83 thru '96 & **Montero** '83 thru '93

NISSAN
72010 **300ZX** all models including Turbo '84 thru '89
72011 **350Z & Infiniti G35** all models '03 thru '08
72015 **Altima** all models '93 thru '06
72016 **Altima** '07 thru '10
72020 **Maxima** all models '85 thru '92
72021 **Maxima** all models '93 thru '04
72025 **Murano** '03 thru '10
72030 **Pick-ups** '80 thru '97 **Pathfinder** '87 thru '95
72031 **Frontier Pick-up, Xterra, Pathfinder** '96 thru '04
72032 **Frontier & Xterra** '05 thru '11
72040 **Pulsar** all models '83 thru '86
Quest - *see MERCURY Villager (64200)*
72050 **Sentra** all models '82 thru '94
72051 **Sentra & 200SX** all models '95 thru '06
72060 **Stanza** all models '82 thru '90
72070 **Titan pick-ups** '04 thru '10 **Armada** '05 thru '10

OLDSMOBILE
73015 **Cutlass** V6 & V8 gas models '74 thru '88
For other OLDSMOBILE titles, see BUICK, CHEVROLET or GENERAL MOTORS listing.

PLYMOUTH
For PLYMOUTH titles, see DODGE listing.

PONTIAC
79008 **Fiero** all models '84 thru '88
79018 **Firebird** V8 models except Turbo '70 thru '81
79019 **Firebird** all models '82 thru '92
79025 **G6** all models '05 thru '09
79040 **Mid-size Rear-wheel Drive** '70 thru '87
Vibe '03 thru '11 - *see TOYOTA Matrix (92060)*
For other PONTIAC titles, see BUICK, CHEVROLET or GENERAL MOTORS listing.

PORSCHE
80020 **911** except Turbo & Carrera 4 '65 thru '89
80025 **914** all 4 cyl models '69 thru '76
80030 **924** all models including Turbo '76 thru '82
80035 **944** all models including Turbo '83 thru '89

RENAULT
Alliance & Encore - *see AMC (14020)*

SAAB
84010 **900** all models including Turbo '79 thru '88

SATURN
87010 **Saturn** all S-series models '91 thru '02
87011 **Saturn Ion** '03 thru '07
87020 **Saturn** all L-series models '00 thru '04
87040 **Saturn VUE** '02 thru '07

SUBARU
89002 **1100, 1300, 1400 & 1600** '71 thru '79
89003 **1600 & 1800** 2WD & 4WD '80 thru '94
89100 **Legacy** all models '90 thru '99
89101 **Legacy & Forester** '00 thru '06

SUZUKI
90010 **Samurai/Sidekick & Geo Tracker** '86 thru '01

TOYOTA
92005 **Camry** all models '83 thru '91
92006 **Camry** all models '92 thru '96
92007 **Camry, Avalon, Solara, Lexus ES 300** '97 thru '01
92008 **Toyota Camry, Avalon and Solara and Lexus ES 300/330** all models '02 thru '06
92009 **Camry** '07 thru '11
92015 **Celica Rear Wheel Drive** '71 thru '85
92020 **Celica Front Wheel Drive** '86 thru '99
92025 **Celica Supra** all models '79 thru '92
92030 **Corolla** all models '75 thru '79
92032 **Corolla** all rear wheel drive models '80 thru '87
92035 **Corolla** all front wheel drive models '84 thru '92
92036 **Corolla & Geo Prizm** '93 thru '02
92037 **Corolla** models '03 thru '11
92040 **Corolla Tercel** all models '80 thru '82
92045 **Corona** all models '74 thru '82
92050 **Cressida** all models '78 thru '82
92055 **Land Cruiser** FJ40, 43, 45, 55 '68 thru '82
92056 **Land Cruiser** FJ60, 62, 80, FZJ80 '80 thru '96
92060 **Matrix & Pontiac Vibe** '03 thru '11
92065 **MR2** all models '85 thru '87
92070 **Pick-up** all models '69 thru '78
92075 **Pick-up** all models '79 thru '95
92076 **Tacoma, 4Runner, & T100** '93 thru '04
92077 **Tacoma** '05 thru '09
92078 **Tundra** '00 thru '06 & **Sequoia** '01 thru '07
92079 **4Runner** all models '03 thru '09
92080 **Previa** all models '91 thru '95
92081 **Prius** all models '01 thru '08
92082 **RAV4** all models '96 thru '10
92085 **Tercel** all models '87 thru '94
92090 **Sienna** all models '98 thru '09
92095 **Highlander & Lexus RX-330** '99 thru '07

TRIUMPH
94007 **Spitfire** all models '62 thru '81
94010 **TR7** all models '75 thru '81

VW
96008 **Beetle & Karmann Ghia** '54 thru '79
96009 **New Beetle** '98 thru '11
96016 **Rabbit, Jetta, Scirocco & Pick-up** gas models '75 thru '92 & Convertible '80 thru '92
96017 **Golf, GTI & Jetta** '93 thru '98, **Cabrio** '95 thru '02
96018 **Golf, GTI, Jetta** '99 thru '05
96019 **Jetta, Rabbit, GTI & Golf** '05 thru '11
96020 **Rabbit, Jetta & Pick-up** diesel '77 thru '84
96023 **Passat** '98 thru '05, **Audi A4** '96 thru '01
96030 **Transporter 1600** all models '68 thru '79
96035 **Transporter 1700, 1800 & 2000** '72 thru '79
96040 **Type 3 1500 & 1600** '63 thru '73
96045 **Vanagon** all air-cooled models '80 thru '83

VOLVO
97010 **120, 130 Series & 1800 Sports** '61 thru '73
97015 **140 Series** all models '66 thru '74
97020 **240 Series** all models '76 thru '93
97040 **740 & 760 Series** all models '82 thru '88
97050 **850 Series** all models '93 thru '97

TECHBOOK MANUALS
10205 **Automotive Computer Codes**
10206 **OBD-II & Electronic Engine Management**
10210 **Automotive Emissions Control Manual**
10215 **Fuel Injection Manual** '78 thru '85
10220 **Fuel Injection Manual** '86 thru '99
10225 **Holley Carburetor Manual**
10230 **Rochester Carburetor Manual**
10240 **Weber/Zenith/Stromberg/SU Carburetors**
10305 **Chevrolet Engine Overhaul Manual**
10310 **Chrysler Engine Overhaul Manual**
10320 **Ford Engine Overhaul Manual**
10330 **GM and Ford Diesel Engine Repair Manual**
10333 **Engine Performance Manual**
10340 **Small Engine Repair Manual, 5 HP & Less**
10341 **Small Engine Repair Manual, 5.5 - 20 HP**
10345 **Suspension, Steering & Driveline Manual**
10355 **Ford Automatic Transmission Overhaul**
10360 **GM Automatic Transmission Overhaul**
10405 **Automotive Body Repair & Painting**
10410 **Automotive Brake Manual**
10411 **Automotive Anti-lock Brake (ABS) Systems**
10415 **Automotive Detailing Manual**
10420 **Automotive Electrical Manual**
10425 **Automotive Heating & Air Conditioning**
10430 **Automotive Reference Manual & Dictionary**
10435 **Automotive Tools Manual**
10440 **Used Car Buying Guide**
10445 **Welding Manual**
10450 **ATV Basics**
10452 **Scooters 50cc to 250cc**

SPANISH MANUALS
98903 **Reparación de Carrocería & Pintura**
98904 **Manual de Carburador Modelos Holley & Rochester**
98905 **Códigos Automotrices de la Computadora**
98906 **OBD-II & Sistemas de Control Electrónico del Motor**
98910 **Frenos Automotriz**
98913 **Electricidad Automotriz**
98915 **Inyección de Combustible** '86 al '99
99040 **Chevrolet & GMC Camionetas** '67 al '87
99041 **Chevrolet & GMC Camionetas** '88 al '98
99042 **Chevrolet & GMC Camionetas Cerradas** '68 al '95
99043 **Chevrolet/GMC Camionetas** '94 al '04
99048 **Chevrolet/GMC Camionetas** '99 al '06
99055 **Dodge Caravan & Plymouth Voyager** '84 al '95
99075 **Ford Camionetas y Bronco** '80 al '94
99076 **Ford F-150** '97 al '09
99077 **Ford Camionetas Cerradas** '69 al '91
99088 **Ford Modelos de Tamaño Mediano** '75 al '86
99089 **Ford Camionetas Ranger** '93 al '10
99091 **Ford Taurus & Mercury Sable** '86 al '95
99095 **GM Modelos de Tamaño Grande** '70 al '90
99100 **GM Modelos de Tamaño Mediano** '70 al '88
99106 **Jeep Cherokee, Wagoneer & Comanche** '84 al '00
99110 **Nissan Camioneta** '80 al '96, **Pathfinder** '87 al '95
99118 **Nissan Sentra** '82 al '94
99125 **Toyota Camionetas y 4Runner** '79 al '95

Over 100 Haynes motorcycle manuals also available

7-12